About the book;

The topics in Canada in Crisis (2) cover a broad spectrum of his large and diverse country and its governance. These topics require the knowledge, experience, and skills of many people to properly assess past policies of the government, and to propose new policies. However, any undertaking must begin with one initial step, in the nope that others will take up the challenge. The following analyses and suggested goals serve only to scratch the surface of Canada's past history and future potential. The topics are presented in a strategic perspective, in the hope of encouraging others to expand on this small beginning of an urgent endeavour to achieve a better future for Canada. Please take up the torch . . .

To appreciate this document, one must have a vision of Canada's potential, the path to attain that potential, and the future that Canada deserves to enjoy. Canada is a bountiful country blessed with an abundance of human and material resources, but burdened with excessive government. We must reduce the dead weight of government as a proportion of Canada's Gross Domestic Product and allow the people and the private sector to prosper.

About the author;

Bob and his wife Ruth both grew up in Burlington Ontario. Bob graduated from the University of Toronto in 1959 with a BASc (P Eng), married Ruth, and served eight years in the RCAF in Germany and Alberta from 1958 to 1966. He left the RCAF to earn an MBA from the University of Western Ontario in 1968. After graduation Bob joined the federal government and they moved to Ottawa, where Ruth taught Kindergarten. They have two married sons and three grand-children. Bob retired in 1992.

During his 30 years with the federal government (including the RCAF), Bob worked in 14 different agencies, bureaux, boards, commissions, departments, secretariats, and Crown corporations. These included such agencies as the Department of Industry Trade and Commerce, the Bureau of Management Consultants, the Treasury Board Secretariat, the Anti-Inflation Board, the Audit Services Bureau, the Unemployment Insurance Commission, the Canadian Saltfish Corporation (in Newfoundland), the Department of Indian Affairs, and the Export Development Corporation (as Deputy Chief of Industrial Analysis). In 1992, Bob appeared before the Finance Committees of Parliament and the Senate to advocate that all pensions and life annuities be made optional, portable, and commutable at any time by the employee.

CANADA in CRISIS (2)

An Agenda for Survival of the Nation

Order this book online at www.trafford.com
or email orders@trafford.com

Most Trafford titles are also available at major online book retailers.

Printed in Victoria, BC, Canada.

ISBN: 978-1-4269-3391-2 (sc)
ISBN: 978-1-4269-3392-9 (hc)
ISBN: 978-1-4269-3393-6 (e-book)

Library of Congress Control Number: 2010908386

Our mission is to efficiently provide the world's finest, most comprehensive book publishing service, enabling every author to experience success. To find out how to publish your book, your way, and have it available worldwide, visit us online at www.trafford.com

Trafford rev. 6/14/2010

www.trafford.com

North America & international
toll-free: 1 888 232 4444 (USA & Canada)
phone: 250 383 6864 • fax: 812 355 4082

To my family:
my wonderful wife Ruth of 50 years,
our two sons and their wives,
Kevin & Erica, and Chris & Teresa,
and our three grandchildren.
Jordan & Amanda, and Cassie

Table of Contents

Prologue

This current book "Canada in Crisis (2) . . . An Agenda for Survival of the Nation" is a sequel to its predecessor "Canada in Crisis (1) . . . An Agenda to Unify the Nation". The paramount precedence for unity was based on the well known axiom "United we stand . . . divided we fall," espoused by Aesop in the fable of the lion and the four oxen, and repeated on occasion by later distinguished leaders and politicians.

The American statesman, Patrick Henry used the phrase in his last public speech, given in March 1799, in which he denounced The Kentucky and Virginia Resolutions to nullify federal laws. Clasping his hands and waving his body back and forth, Henry declaimed, *"Let us trust God, and our better judgment to set us right hereafter. United we stand, divided we fall. Let us not split into factions which must destroy that union upon which our existence hangs."*

The current book could be read without recourse to its predecessor. While that would be possible, much would be lost in the context and proposals established in the former book. To do so would be comparable to an excellent entrée well served and delicious, but devoid of its requisite apératif. As an alternative metaphor, one might consider the comparison as "a marriage without a courtship".

Foremost in the process intended to place both books in context is a quote from Cicero, "The peoples' good is the highest law". This axiom is fundamental to making the proper choice between competing managerial or political options and choices . . . when in doubt, always opt for that action which is in the best interests of the people of Canada at large, rather than any special interest group of people or organization with conflicting interests.

A second major step in the process is the reliance on the internet for the historic backgrounds on the arcane subject matter for the convenience of the readers, and the reliance on recent articles by well known journalists in national newspapers. The latter articles are provided as a proxy for the voice of the nation's people as to what concerns them, and what they consider to be "the people's good". Statements by political parties are often unreliable proxies for "the peoples' good". History has shown repeatedly that party politics may often be at odds with "the peoples' good", resulting in the passage of contentious and disputatious legislation.

For these reasons, the author has provided bibliographies in the full and original text (or lightly edited), with proper attribution of the source of the articles, both from the internet and from articles by journalists. This has been done to provide quick and easy access to the background necessary to a full and proper understanding of the condensed and much briefer commentary. The proposals made by the author are his own personal conclusions for the topics and goals of the book. These conclusions have been influenced by other authors and books such as Atlas Shrugged, Fearful Symmetry, and Why Your World Is About To Get A Whole Lot Smaller.

Both of the recent books, "Canada in Crisis (1) . . . An Agenda to Unify the Nation", and "Canada in Crisis (2) . . . An Agenda for Survival of the Nation", continue to be works in progress. The author hopes that others will voice their opinions on the governance of Canada as well. The survival of Canada as it once was, and should be, rests in the hands of you the people. To effect change, the people must vote to elect a strong government.

Introduction

In the previous book, the unity of Canada seemed of paramount importance, or *"primus inter pares"* among all other criteria to create a better nation. However, on further reflection came the realization that unity was not enough; it was incomplete. "Canada in Crisis (1) . . . An Agenda to Unify the Nation demanded amplification by this second book, "Canada in Crisis (2) . . . An Agenda for Survival of the Nation".

The unification of Canada is the necessary first step, but unity alone is not sufficient for Canada to be a western, democratic nation striving to attain its full potential. Unification alone is not sufficient to those goals, while the future existence of the nation and the lives of its people remain at risk. What is unity worth, if there is no security? For Canada to survive and achieve its proper potential, the conditions of both unity and security must be fulfilled to meet the standards of a developed western nation. The survival of Canada and all western nations as we knew them remains at risk; Canada is not secure, nor is the nation's survival certain.

Historically, all nations are insecure when faced with change, and change has been the main constant throughout man's history. The current world is rife with change. Changes may be either good or bad, and those that are bad may be deemed threats to a nation. For a nation to survive, it must be prepared to defend itself against those threats which are present, and those which may not yet be present but are foreseeable. The threats to a nation may take many and various forms.

There are admittedly some changes that are impossible or extremely difficult to reverse. The act of apostasy, that is for a Muslim to renounce

Islam, is well nigh impossible as the apostate would instantly become the object of a death sentence sanctioned by that religion and obliging any and every other Muslim to kill him. The onset of most cancers, or necrotizing fasciitis is virtually impossible to cure unless detected and treated in early stages. While it is possible to purchase a life annuity with funds from many varied sources, it is virtually impossible in Canada to reverse the process by commutation of the annuity to retrieve any funds not yet disbursed. These situations are immutable in practice, even in a free and democratic society.

Nations may be threatened by the invasion of its lands and territories by other nations or merely by other peoples. Invasions across its borders or its coastlines may be either by openly military and political means, or by more covert means. The threats may be economic in nature, waged in the courts and financial markets of the country, or open attacks upon the political or military powers of the nation. The threats may be attacks upon the energy and power systems of the nation, its pipelines, hydro electric grids, generating stations, water systems, or other major targets. The targets may be the nation's transportation centres such as airports, seaports, landports, bridges, or major storage depots of fuel, water, and foods. Communication systems, towers, landlines, broadcast centres, financial centres and markets, and other facilities are possible targets. The political system itself may come under attack by terrorists or separatists. Even the original peoples may be overwhelmed simply by the sheer number of newer and different peoples at festivals, sporting events, and the activities of daily life. The ultimate failure of survival may occur when elections lead to a loss of democracy and the imposition of different governments and laws incompatible with the former nation.

To counter these threats, the nation should enhance its competence and effectiveness in defending the security of its people in all these locations and situations. The nation should eliminate any incapacities or impediments to protective measures already in place. Finally, the nation must adopt an attitude which will demand both lawful behaviour within the nation, and enhance the provision of (and accountability for) all its security measures.

Chapter 1 - Security of the Lands, Borders, & Coastlines

The Lands and Inland Waters

(Bibliography: Security of the Lands - The Lands and Inland Waters)

Canada has ten provinces and three territories. The total area of a province or territory is the sum of its lands and freshwater areas. The lands and waters apportioned by governance vary widely in area. The largest portion of Canada by land area is the territory of Nunavut, having some 2,093,190 square kilometres. The largest portion of Canada by inland water area is the province of Quebec, having a total of 176,928 square kilometres of lakes and rivers. The smallest portion in both lands and inland waters area is the province of Prince Edward Island, having a total area of lands and waters of only 5,660 square kilometres.

Canada is the second largest country in the world having a total area of lands and waters of 9,984,670 square kilometres, (Russia is the largest at 17,075,400 square kilometres). However, in terms of dry land area, Canada ranks fourth at 9,093,507 square kilometres. In terms of fresh waters area, Canada is the largest country with a total of 891,163 square kilometres of inland waters (including Hudson Bay whose salinity is lower than the oceans).

The majority of the population is spread along the southern border with the United States, while areas to the north are sparsely populated. The four largest cities by population are Toronto (4,753,000), Montreal (3,316,000), Vancouver (1,953,000), and Calgary (988,000), which of themselves account for 34% of the total population of 31,612,000 (2006 census).

The Borders and Coastlines

(Bibliography: Security of the Lands - The Borders and Coastlines)

Coastlines and shorelines are quite different concepts. A Coastline follows the general line of the coast, but sometimes, in the case of small inlets or bays, the coastline is measured as running directly across the bay or inlet to rejoin the coastline on the opposite side. A shoreline is the perimeter of the land along the water's edge, measured with the greatest accuracy possible, and is usually longer for a particular location than its coastline. The coastline is not measured as precisely as the shoreline, as the coastline takes shortcuts across the mouths of rivers and small bays. The total national coastline includes the coastlines of the mainland and offshore islands of the oceans, and the coastlines of the inland waters and offshore islands of the Great Lakes and the St Lawrence River within the international borders of Canada.

Canada has the longest coastline of any country in the world, having a total length of 243,042 kilometres. That total is composed of three categories: mainland coast of 57,759 km, major islands of 112,922 km, and minor islands of 72,361 km (many islands are unpopulated). The total includes the two categories of the Great Lakes and St Lawrence River shorelines: the inland coast of 5,238 km, and the inland islands of 4,676 km, for a sub-total of 9,914 km.

The Agencies of Security

The Canadian Coast Guard

(Bibliography: Security of the Lands - The Canadian Coast Guard)

The Canadian Coast Guard (CCG) is one of the guardians of Canada's coasts. It is the civilian federal agency responsible for providing maritime search and rescue (SAR), aids to navigation, marine pollution response, marine radio, and ice breaking. It was formed in 1962 under the Department of Transport (DOT). In 1994, the CCG was transferred to the Department of Fisheries and Oceans (DFO). In 2003, several functions were again transferred back to DOT under a re-organization of government ministries, although the service was still responsible to the Minister of DFO. In 2005, the CCG was designated as a Special Operating Agency still under the DFO, but serving both DFO and DOT. The creation of the Special Operating Agency operating under its own Commissioner, similar to the RCMP, gave the CCG greater autonomy in its daily operations.

The Canadian Coast Guard's responsibility encompasses Canada's 243,042 kilometre long coastline, the longest of any nation in the world. It operates over an area of ocean and inland waters covering approximately 8 million square kilometres. The service has some 4,500 employees, 114 ships, 22 helicopters (including a hovercraft), and an annual budget around $300 million. The CCG is a civilian, non-military organisation, unlike the United States Coast Guard (USCG). The CCG cooperates with other government agencies as an integrated border enforcement teams (IBET) with the RCMP and Canada Border Services Agency, and provides Search and Rescue (SAR) services and marine support to the other federal government departments. The Canadian Coast Guard is headquartered in Ottawa.

The Royal Canadian Mounted Police

(Bibliography: Security of the Lands - The Royal Canadian Mounted Police)

The RCMP force is unique in the world as a national, federal, provincial, and municipal policing body. The RCMP provides federal policing service to all of Canada, and policing services under contract to the three territories, eight provinces (except Ontario and Quebec), more than 190 municipalities, 184 Aboriginal communities, and three international airports.

As the federal police force for Canada, the Royal Canadian Mounted Police is responsible for enforcing federal laws throughout Canada, while general law and order including enforcement of the Criminal Code and applicable provincial legislation is constitutionally the responsibility of the provinces and territories. This responsibility is sometimes further delegated to municipalities which may form their own municipal police departments. This is common in the largest cities; every city with a population over 500,000 operates its own force.

The RCMP is responsible for an unusual breadth of duties. Under their federal mandate, the RCMP provides policing throughout Canada, including Ontario and Quebec. Federal operations include; enforcing federal laws including commercial crime, counterfeiting, drug trafficking, border integrity, organized crime, and other related matters; providing counterterrorism and domestic security; providing protection services for the Monarch, Governor General, Prime Minister and other ministers of the Crown, visiting dignitaries, and diplomatic missions; and participating in various international policing efforts.

The enforcement of laws in Canada's territorial seas is the responsibility of the Royal Canadian Mounted Police, as all ocean waters in Canada are under federal jurisdiction. The enforcement of saltwater fisheries is an exceptional and specific responsibility of DFO's Fisheries Officers.

In 2006, the United States Coast Guard's Ninth District and the RCMP began a program called "Shiprider," in which 12 Mounties from the RCMP detachment at Windsor and 16 Coast Guard boarding officers from stations in Michigan ride in each others' vessels. The intent is to allow for seamless enforcement of the international border.

The Provincial Police Forces of Canada

Three provinces of Canada maintain their own provincial police forces, in addition to any services provided by the federal RCMP. The Ontario Provincial Police (OPP) are staffed with 5,618 uniformed, 853 auxiliary, and 1,765 civilian personnel. The Quebec Provincial Police (La Sûreté du Québec) has a force of some 5,163 officers. The third province having its own provincial police is that of Newfoundland and Labrador, where the Royal Newfoundland Constabulary has a force of some 400 officers, and is assisted by the RCMP in rural and remote areas. All of these provincial forces may become routinely involved in protecting the nation from the threat of illegal immigrants or visitors.

The Canada Border Services Agency

(Bibliography: Security of the Lands - The Canadian Border Services Agency)

The Canada Border Services Agency (CBSA) is a federal law enforcement agency responsible for guarding the nation's borders, and providing customs services. The Agency was created on December 12, 2003 by amalgamating Canada Customs with border enforcement personnel from Citizenship and Immigration Canada (CIC) and the Canadian Food Inspection Agency (CFIA). The agency's authority derives from the Canada Border Services Agency Act of 2005. The 11 September 2001 attacks on the United States placed greater emphasis on Canada's border operations, national security, and public safety. The Canada/America Smart Border Declaration provides cooperation between Canadian and American border operations.

The CBSA oversees approximately 1,200 service locations across Canada, and 39 in other countries. It employs over 12,000 public servants, and offers round the clock service at 61 land border crossings and nine international airports, and oversee operations at three major sea ports and three mail centres. The CBSA operates detention facilities in Laval, Toronto, Kingston, and Vancouver. The CBSA operates an Inland Enforcement branch which tracks and removes inadmissible foreign nationals. Inland Enforcement Officers are plain clothes units, and are armed with the same sidearm (PX4 Storm) as port of entry Border Services Officers.

A Border Services Officer (BSO) is a federal law enforcement agent employed by the Canada Border Services Agency. BSOs are designated peace officers , and primarily enforce customs and immigration related legislation, in particular the Customs Act and the Immigration and Refugee Protection Act as well as over 90 other Acts of Parliament. Because of their peace officer designation, they also have the power to enforce other Acts of Parliament, including the Criminal Code of

Canada. Border Services Officers are equipped with Beretta PX4 Storm pistols, handcuffs, batons, and oleoresin capsicum (OC) spray.

The Department of Citizenship & Immigration

(Bibliography: Security of the Lands - Citizenship and Immigration Canada)

The Department of Citizenship and Immigration Canada (CIC) is the department of the government of Canada with responsibility for issues dealing with immigration and citizenship. The department was established in 1994 following a reorganization within the federal government.

CIC operates a large network of "Citizenship and Immigration Centres" throughout Canada and in a number of embassies, high commissions, and consulates abroad. Service Canada recently started to assume some of the domestic field operations of the department, while the Canada Border Services Agency took over the control of enforcement and entry control at borders and airports. CIC remains responsible for the establishment of policies and processing of permanent and temporary residence visa, refugee protection, and citizenship applications.

The Department of Public Safety

(Bibliography: Security of the Lands - The Department of Public Safety Canada)

Public Safety Canada (PSC), formerly known as Public Safety and Emergency Preparedness Canada, legally incorporated as the federal Department of Public Safety and Emergency Preparedness, is the department of the government of Canada with responsibility for protecting Canadians and helping to maintain a peaceful and safe society.

Legislation for the agency began in February 2001, the department was created in December 2003 during a reorganization of the federal government, and it became legally established when the Department of Public Safety and Emergency Preparedness Act came into force on

April 4, 2005. The agency Emergency Preparedness Canada was created under the auspices of the Defence department before the establishment of the department by the Emergency Preparedness Act of 1988.

The department was created to have a single entity with responsibility for ensuring public safety in Canada and is a direct result of lessons learned from the September 11 attacks on the United States in 2001. The department is in many ways similar to the U.S. Department of Homeland Security, though it does not cover the protection of maritime sovereignty.

Most of the department comprises organizations that were previously placed under the Department of the Solicitor General of Canada. However the reorganization of several federal departments and ministries added the Canada Border Services Agency to the portfolio, after the two streams of the former Canada Customs and Revenue Agency were split in 2003. In addition, the Office of Critical Infrastructure Protection and Emergency Preparedness (OCIPEP) from the Department of National Defence was also brought into the Department. The Department of Public Safety works in association with the following agencies: the Canada Border Services Agency, the Royal Canadian Mounted Police, the Canadian Security Intelligence Service, the Correctional Service Canada, and the National Parole Board.

The Canadian Military Forces

The Chief of the Defence Staff, or CDS, is General Walter Natynczyk. He is responsible for the conduct of military operations and for the readiness of the Canadian Forces to carry out the tasks that Parliament assigns through the Minister. The CDS authority extends to the Navy, the Army and the Air force. The Department of National Defence (DND) is the largest federal government department. DND and the CF together have a budget of approximately 18 billion dollars, and over 110,000 employees, including: 65,000 Regular Force members; 25,000 Reserve Force members (including 4,000 Canadian Rangers); and 28,000 civilians.

The Institute for Catastrophic Loss Reduction

The Institute for Catastrophic Loss Reduction (ICLR) is a world class centre for multi-disciplinary disaster prevention research and communications. The ICLR was established by Canada's property and casualty (p&c) insurance industry as an independent, not for profit research institute affiliated with the University of Western Ontario. Institute staff and research associates are international leaders in wind and seismic engineering, atmospheric science, risk perception, hydrology, economics, geography, health sciences, public policy and a number of other disciplines.

To help address this impending increase in natural disaster losses, the Institute for Catastrophic Loss Reduction (ICLR) has developed a long term communications strategy to enhance its messaging. Under a broad theme of "science to action, Canada's insurers building disaster resilient communities" the strategy is centred around three programs:

* RSVP cities (resilient, sustainable, vibrant and prosperous cities);
* Designed for safer living (safer design and construction of buildings); and
* Open for Business (TM) (disaster risk reduction for small business).

Working through ICLR, Canada's insurers are the only group in the country providing comprehensive disaster loss prevention advice to homeowners and home builders, as well as to owners of small businesses. Actions have been identified to help homeowners and owners of small business reduce the risk of injury, damage, and interruption of business due to severe wind, hail, earthquakes, flood, wildfire and a number of other hazards. We are also working to promote the construction of disaster resilient homes. ICLR is internationally recognized for its leadership in multi-disciplinary disaster prevention research.

There are essentially three systems utilized within Canada to manage disasters at community or municipal level. Within these systems there are variations reflecting provincial standards, organizational culture, and to a degree the preference of those who employ these systems.

The ICLR is committed to reducing disaster deaths, injuries and property damage through the development of disaster prevention knowledge, and the broad dissemination of its research findings. Moreover, the Institute is working to transfer this emerging scientific knowledge into information available to decision makers to support actions to build resilient communities. This research deals with damage from wind, snow, ice, earthquakes, mould and a range of other hazards.

Commentary

The most startling revelation from the above history and context is that there were some 200,000 illegal immigrants already in Canada in 2009, an increase from the 40,000 reported some two or three years before. It seems likely that many of these may be unqualified for residence in Canada for a variety of reasons, not the least of which might be the distinct possibility that some of these have criminal histories in their countries of origin. Prospective immigrants to Canada must be made to follow the prescribed processes for admission to the country. Those processes must be revised to provide stringent controls to determine; firstly the identity and suitability of all of those applicants for admission, and secondly the location of the successful applicants for a number of years after their acceptance.

That these illegal immigrants may have been admitted originally on the basis of false claims for refugee status derives from lax and inadequate research by immigration staff. It is also Canada's excessive generosity in granting refugee claimants full and immediate access to all of the rights, privileges, appeals, and welfare assistance of a Canadian citizen that is at fault. These privileges should not be granted to refugee claimants until their proper refugee status has been verified. The privileges for refugees should be withheld until residency conditions have been met. Since 1994, a child born in France of foreign parents does not obtain French nationality and associated privileges under "jus soli" (right of territory) until residency conditions have been met. That the current location of these illegal immigrants to Canada is unknown to the immigration authorities is a further surprise that has been revealed to the nation. Such laxity on the part of the immigration authorities is unacceptable to the people of Canada, or any other nation.

The second revelation of the lax security of the nation is the profusion and confusion of the government organizations which are responsible for the management of the potential threats to the nation from external and internal sources. These include the following dozen or more major agencies: the Canadian Coast Guard (CCG), the Canada Border Services Agency (CBSA), the Royal Canadian Mounted Police (RCMP), various Provincial Police Forces (OPP, QPP, and RNC) and Municipal Police Forces, the Department of Fisheries and Oceans (DFO), the Department of Transport (DOT), Citizenship and Immigration Canada (CIC), the new Public Safety Canada (PSC), and the Institute for Catastrophic Loss Reduction (ICLR). Last but not least are the forces of the Canadian military, the army, navy, and air force. Their duties in regard to the homeland are the constant protection and patrols of our lands, seas, and air space against harmful intrusion; and the provision of additional support to other agencies in the event of catastrophic disasters. Their other responsibilities lie in the field of control of international conflicts in conjunction with NATO or other forces.

Each of these departments or agencies has a multitude of tasks, usually derived from several different Acts of Parliament, so there are always a variety of organizational configurations which are possible for the allocation of those duties. However, there seems little doubt that those duties relating to the security of the nation must take precedence over all other duties or public administration. In this respect, and as an example of a possible organizational structure that may warrant review, the Canadian Coast Guard was originally the responsibility of the Department of Transport but is currently under the purview of Department of Fisheries and Oceans. That configuration in the past had created internal problems of administration. A more suitable reorganization might be to have the Canadian Coast Guard responsible to Transport again, or to the newer Department of Public Safety which is already associated with such similar security agencies as the Canada Border Services Agency, the Royal Canadian Mounted Police, and the Canadian Security Intelligence Service.

Government policy in this broad field derived initially from the Department of Citizenship and Immigration. The current Minister, Jason Kenney, has made several commendable and major changes to improve the performance of the immigration process, where he possessed the requisite authority. It seems likely that changes to various Acts of Parliament would be necessary to implement many of the changes that are warranted. An example of a much needed change would be the introduction of identification cards based on the latest available biometric qualities such as eye scans, facial scans, finger prints, blood type, and DNA data embedded in computer chips in biometric identification (BIDs) cards. This would vastly improve both the immediate and accurate identification of suspected persons, and enhance any subsequent law enforcement and legal processes in the courts of law. As noted under later discussions of the justice system, Canada needs a thorough review of the professional competence and conduct of law enforcement agencies at all levels.

The current rapid loss of permanent ice in the Arctic appears to be a precursor to a feasible shipping route adjacent to Canada's northern coast in the Arctic Ocean. The protection and security of these coastal shores will likely require additional personnel, ships and aircraft by at least one or more of the agencies responsible for Canadian territory and coastlines.

Finally, one must bear in mind that government organizations, and the citizens themselves must take all reasonable precautions against potential threats to the security of the nation. Such threats may arise in two ways: by the forced entry or improper admission of threatening people to Canada from outside the borders and coastal waters of the country; or by the presence of threatening people already within the lands and territory of Canada.

Suggestions and Proposals

The federal government, in consultation with provincial governments, should create and apply more appropriate criteria to determine the suitability of applicants for admission to Canada.

The use of biometric identification cards (BIDs) and location tracking for all immigrants should be mandatory for five or ten, or more years following their arrival in Canada. Access to such a database should be permitted to all appropriate agencies of the Canadian government.

Persons arriving in Canada by any means other than the normal administrative processes of entry ("jumping the queue") and applying for refugee status should be subject to intensive research of their situations to verify their claims. Such persons should be detained and denied all of the privileges, appeals, and welfare benefits of Canadian citizens, until the veracity of their refugee status has been established. Those not so entitled should be returned to their homeland with despatch, and without further application or appeal.

There should be regular review and discipline of the professional conduct of immigration and law enforcement personnel. That should include the appointment and performance of members of the Immigration Review Board, with decisions of that Board subject to Ministerial or Cabinet approval or revision without further appeal to any court.

The various agencies responsible for the nation's security at the borders and coasts should be better organized, consolidated, and coordinated to contain potential threats from immigrants arriving at the nation's borders and coasts, as well as those persons already within its borders.

The police, border service officers, and coast guards should be given the enforcement powers, vehicles, ships, aircraft, etc, and suitable training and defensive weapons necessary to the containment of any and all potential threats to Canada and its lands, borders, and coasts.

Chapter 2 - Security of Justice & Law Enforcement

The Canadian Judicial System

(Bibliography: Security of Justice - The Canadian Judicial System)

There are basically four levels of courts in Canada. First there are provincial/ territorial courts, which handle the majority of cases that come into the system. Second are the provincial/ territorial superior courts. These courts deal with more serious crimes and also take appeals from provincial/ territorial court judgments. On the same level, but responsible for different issues, is the Federal Court. At the next level are the provincial/ territorial courts of appeal and the Federal Court of Appeal, while the highest level is the Supreme Court of Canada.

Provincial/ Territorial Courts

Each province and territory, with the exception of Nunavut, has a provincial/ territorial court, and these courts hear cases involving either federal or provincial/ territorial laws. In Nunavut, there is no territorial court, matters normally heard at that level are heard by the Nunavut Court of Justice, which is a superior court. The names and divisions of these courts may vary from place to place, but their role is the same. Provincial/ territorial courts deal with most criminal offences, family law matters (except divorce), young persons in conflict with the law (12 to 17 years old), traffic violations, provincial/ territorial regulatory offences, and claims involving money, up to a certain amount. Private disputes involving limited sums of money may also be dealt with at this level in Small Claims courts. In addition, all preliminary inquiries, hearings to determine whether there is enough evidence to justify a full trial in serious criminal cases, take place before the provincial/ territorial courts.

A number of courts at this level are dedicated exclusively to particular types of offences or groups of offenders. One example is the Drug Treatment Court (DTC) program, which began in Toronto in 1998, followed over several years by Vancouver, Edmonton, Regina, Winnipeg, and Ottawa. The object of the DTCs is to address the needs of non-violent offenders who are charged with criminal offences that were motivated by their addiction. Those who qualify are offered an intensive combination of judicial supervision and treatment for their dependence, drawing on a range of community support services.

Youth courts handle cases where a young person, from 12 to 17 years old, is charged with an offence under federal youth justice laws. Procedures in youth court provide protections appropriate to the age of the accused, including privacy protections. Courts at either the provincial/ territorial or superior court level may be designated youth courts.

Some provinces and territories (Ontario, Manitoba, Alberta, and the Yukon) have established Domestic Violence Courts to improve the response of the justice system to incidents of spousal abuse by decreasing court processing time; increasing conviction rates; providing a focal point for programs and services for victims and offenders; and in some cases, allowing for the specialization of police, Crown prosecutors, and the judiciary in domestic violence matters.

Provincial/ Territorial Superior Courts

Each province and territory has superior courts. These courts are known by various names, including Superior Court of Justice, Supreme Court (not to be confused with the Supreme Court of Canada), and Court of Queen's Bench. But while the names may differ, the court system is essentially the same across the country with the exception of Nunavut, where the Nunavut Court of Justice deals with both territorial and superior court matters.

The superior courts have "inherent jurisdiction," which means that they may hear cases in any area except those that are specifically limited to another level of court. The superior courts try the most serious criminal and civil cases, including divorce, and cases that involve large amounts of money (the minimum value is set by the province or territory in question).

In most provinces and territories, the superior court has special divisions, such as the family division. Some have established specialized family courts at the superior court level to deal exclusively with certain family law matters including divorce and property claims. The superior courts also act as a court of first appeal for the underlying court system that provinces and territories maintain. Although superior courts are administered by the provinces and territories, the judges are appointed and paid by the federal government.

Courts of Appeal

Each province and territory has a court of appeal or appellate division that hears appeals from decisions of the superior courts and provincial/territorial courts. The number of judges on these courts may vary from one jurisdiction to another, but a court of appeal usually sits as a panel of three. The courts of appeal also hear constitutional questions that may be raised in appeals involving individuals, governments, or governmental agencies.

The Federal Courts

The Federal Court and the Federal Court of Appeal are essentially superior courts with civil jurisdiction. However, since the Courts were created by an Act of Parliament, they may deal only with matters specified in federal statutes (laws). In contrast, provincial and territorial superior courts have jurisdiction in all matters except those specifically excluded by a statute.

The Federal Court is the trial level court; appeals from it are heard by the Federal Court of Appeal. While based in Ottawa, the judges of both Courts conduct hearings across the country. The Courts' jurisdiction includes interprovincial and federal provincial disputes, intellectual property proceedings (e.g. copyright), citizenship appeals, Competition Act cases, and cases involving Crown corporations or departments of the Government of Canada. As well, only these Courts have jurisdiction to review decisions, orders, and other administrative actions of federal boards, commissions and tribunals; these bodies may refer any question of law, jurisdiction, or practice to one of the Courts at any stage of a proceeding.

For certain matters, such as maritime law, a case may be brought before the Federal Court or Federal Court of Appeal, or before a provincial or territorial superior court. In this respect, the Federal Court and the Federal Court of Appeal share jurisdiction with the superior courts.

Trial by Jury

Under the Canadian Charter of Rights and Freedoms, individuals accused of the most serious criminal offences generally have the right to choose to be tried either by a jury or by a judge alone. A jury is a group of people, chosen from the community. The facts and arguments of the case are presented by lawyers for the prosecution, and for the defence. After a judge explains the law to the jurors, the jurors assess the facts of the case. They then make a decision, usually of innocence or guilt, based on their assessment. Sentencing, however, is left to the judge. Trial by jury is also available in some civil litigation, but is rarely used.

The Supreme Court of Canada

The Supreme Court of Canada is the final court of appeal from all other Canadian courts. The Supreme Court has jurisdiction over disputes in all areas of the law, including constitutional law, administrative law, criminal law, and civil law.

The Court consists of a Chief Justice and eight other judges, all of whom are appointed by the federal government. The Supreme Court Act requires that at least three judges must come from Quebec. Traditionally, of the other six judges, three are from Ontario, two from western

Canada, and one from the Atlantic provinces. The Supreme Court sits in Ottawa for three sessions a year – winter, spring and fall.

Before a case may reach the Supreme Court of Canada, it must have used up all available appeals at other levels of court. Even then, the Court must grant permission or "leave" to appeal before it will hear the case. Leave applications are usually made in writing and reviewed by three members of the Court, who then grant or deny the request without providing reasons for the decision. Leave to appeal is not given routinely, it is granted only if the case involves a question of public importance; if it raises an important issue of law, or mixed law and fact; or if the matter is for any other reason significant enough to be considered by the country's Supreme Court.

In certain situations, however, the right to appeal is automatic. For instance, no leave is required in criminal cases where a judge on the panel of a court of appeal has dissented on how the law should be interpreted. Similarly, where a court of appeal has found someone guilty who had been acquitted at the original trial, that person automatically has the right to appeal to the Supreme Court.

The Supreme Court of Canada also plays a special role as adviser to the federal government. The government may ask the Court to consider questions on any important matter of law or fact, especially concerning interpretation of the Constitution. It may also be asked questions on the interpretation of federal or provincial/ territorial legislation, or the powers of Parliament or the legislatures. (Provincial and territorial courts of appeal may also be asked to hear references from their respective governments.)

The Nunavut Court of Justice - a New Approach

When the territory of Nunavut was established in 1999, a new kind of court in Canada was created as well. The Nunavut Court of Justice combines the powers of the superior trial court and the territorial court so that the same judge may hear all cases that arise in the territory. In Nunavut, most of the communities are small and isolated from the capital of Iqaluit, so the court travels to them "on circuit." The circuit court includes a judge, a clerk, a court reporter, a prosecutor, and at least one defence attorney. Court workers and Crown witness coordinators may also travel with the circuit court, depending on the cases to be heard. Interpreters are hired in the communities when possible, or travel with the circuit court when necessary. In addition to holding regular sessions in Iqaluit, the court flies to most of the communities in Nunavut at intervals that range from six weeks to two years, depending on the number of cases.

The Constitution & Division of Powers

(Bibliography: Security of Justice - The Constitution & Division of Powers)

The Constitution of Canada is the supreme law of the country, and consists of written text and unwritten conventions. The Constitution Act of 1867 (revised 1982) affirmed a governance based on parliamentary precedent similar to that of the United Kingdom, and divided powers between the federal and provincial governments. The British Statute of Westminster of 1931 granted full autonomy to Canada.

The Constitution Act of 1982 added the Canadian Charter of Rights and Freedoms, which guaranteed basic rights and freedoms usually not overridden by any level of government. The exception was a "Notwithstanding" clause allowing parliament and provincial legislatures to override certain sections of the Charter for five years, and an added constitutional amending formula. Except where provinces have exclusive powers, the federal government has the power "to make laws for the peace, order and good government of Canada".

The federal government has many exclusive powers among which are:

trade & commerce	post office
the census	national defence
citizenship	money and banking
copyrights	criminal law
employment insurance	foreign policy

Through their legislatures, the provincial governments have the power to enact or amend laws and programs related to; hospitals, social services, natural resources & environment, education, provincial property & civil rights, and the administration of justice and provincial prisons. The provinces directly fund or transfer money to institutions to ensure the delivery of these important responsibilities, as well as funding provincial highways, culture and tourism, prisons, post-secondary education, and other services. The provincial legislatures also have power over all municipal institutions in the provinces.

Criminal law is solely a federal responsibility and is applicable uniformly throughout Canada. English common law prevails everywhere in Canada except Quebec, where civil law is based on the Code Napoleon and major revisions made in the 1990s. Law enforcement including the criminal courts is a provincial responsibility, but in rural areas of all provinces except Ontario and Quebec, policing is contracted to the federal Royal Canadian Mounted Police. In Ontario, law enforcement is the responsibility of the Ontario Provincial Police, and in Quebec the Quebec Provincial Police. Many municipalities have their own police forces.

The Goals of the Justice System

The elements of the justice system most relevant to the potential threats which may face the nation are the Constitution, the responsibility of the federal government for all criminal law, and the administration of those laws by the provinces in their regions, and the investigative procedures of the federal (RCMP) and provincial law enforcement agencies. Some of the major shortfalls of the Constitution has been documented in the book "Canada in Crisis (1) - An Agenda to Unify the Nation". The suggestions and proposals offered to correct those Constitutional shortfalls will not be repeated here.

The concerns here pertain to the potential threats facing the nation which arise in the responsible and timely management and administration of the laws which are the foundation of the justice system. The suggested goals for the justice system in Canada may be simply stated as:

- being seen as a firm deterrent, but equitable and fair
- being seen as absolutely ethical and above reproach
- being delivered in a prompt and timely manner, and
- being cost effective, after attainment of the previous.

Past Cases of Egregious Justice

In general, Canadians take reasonable pride in the knowledge that they are living in a safe and peaceful country. They have taken particular pride in the courts, RCMP, and provincial police. They have faith in the judicial system; in this land, you need never fear being pulled over by a corrupt police officer, or worry that you haven't enough money to bribe your way out of a false charge. The vast majority of cases brought before the courts scrupulously follow proper legal process and are well managed, while the judges and lawyers pay meticulous attention to legal etiquette. However, as with any large bureaucracy or corporation, there are some occasional transgressions which serve to illustrate an urgent need for improvements and safeguards. The following examples highlight some of the unfortunate situations of the past. Greater detail of these examples may be found in the bibliography.

Steven Truscott Murder Case 1959

(Bibliography: Security of Justice - Steven Truscott Murder Case)

Steven Murray Truscott, born 18 January 1945 in Vancouver, British Columbia, was sentenced to death in 1959, when he was a 14 year old student, for the alleged murder of classmate Lynne Harper. His death sentence was commuted to life imprisonment, and he continued to maintain his innocence until 2007 when his conviction was declared a miscarriage of justice and he was formally acquitted of the crime.

On 29 November 2001, Truscott filed an application for a review of his 1959 murder conviction. Hearings in a review of the Truscott case were heard at the Ontario Court of Appeal. On 28 August 2007, after review of nearly 250 fresh pieces of evidence, the court declared that Truscott's conviction had been a miscarriage of justice. As he was not declared factually innocent, a new trial could have been ordered, but this was a practical impossibility given the passage of time. Accordingly, the court acquitted Truscott of the murder. On July 7, 2008, the government of Ontario awarded him $6.5 million in compensation.

David Milgaard Murder Case 1969

(Bibliography: Security of Justice - David Milgaard Murder Case)

In 1969, David Milgaard and two friends, Ron Wilson and Nichol John, decided to take a road trip across the Canadian prairies. While they were in Saskatoon, a 20 year old nursing student, Gail Miller, was found dead on a snowbank. At the time Milgaard and his friends had stopped to pick up Larry Fisher, an ex-con who would later be found guilty of the crime. The British Columbia police arrested Milgaard in May 1969 and sent him back to Saskatchewan where he was charged with Miller's murder. Milgaard was convicted of murder and sentenced to life in prison on January 31, 1970, exactly a year after Miller's murder.

He appealed his conviction several times, but was blocked both by bureaucracy and by a justice system unreceptive to those who were not willing to admit their guilt. On 18 July 1997, a DNA laboratory in the United Kingdom released a report confirming that semen samples on the victim's clothing did not originate with Milgaard . . . for all intents and purposes clearing Milgaard of the crime. The Saskatchewan government then apologized for the wrongful conviction. On 25 July 1997, Larry Fisher was arrested for the murder and rape of Ms. Miller. On 17 May 1999, the Saskatchewan government announced that a settlement had been reached with Milgaard, and that he would be paid compensation of $10 million.

Larry Fisher had lived a few doors down from where Gail Miller was raped and murdered, yet at the time was not seriously considered as a suspect. Fisher was arrested 25 July 1997 in Calgary. He was convicted 22 November 1999, and sentenced on 4 January 2000. Fisher was given a life sentence. Due to applicable laws at the time of the crime, he was eligible to apply for parole in 10 years rather than the current 25 years. On 23 September 2003, the Court of Appeal for

Saskatchewan unanimously denied Fisher's appeal of his conviction. Prior to this conviction, Fisher had served 23 years for numerous rapes in the cities of Winnipeg (Manitoba), Saskatoon and North Battleford (Saskatchewan).

Donald Marshall Murder Case 1971

(Bibliography: Security of Justice - Donald Marshall Murder Case)

HALIFAX: Donald Marshall Jr.'s fight to win his freedom captured the nation's attention and changed Nova Scotia's justice system forever. Mr. Marshall was one of 13 children of Caroline and the late Donald Marshall Sr., grand chief of the Mi'kmaq nation. He died at age 55, having spent 11 years in prison for a murder he did not commit. Marshall was eventually exonerated and his case forced changes in the way natives are treated by Nova Scotia's police and courts.

When Marshall was 17, an all white jury convicted him of murder in the 1971 stabbing death of Sandy Seale in Sydney, Cape Breton. "If you were Mi'kmaq, you were guilty and that was that." Marshall was released in 1982 after RCMP reviewed the case, and acquitted in 1983. Roy Ebsary was later convicted of manslaughter in Seale's death and spent a year in jail. In 1990, Marshall was finally exonerated in the report of a royal commission into the wrongful murder conviction. The inquiry concluded Nova Scotia's justice system had failed him. Marshall received compensation of about $250,000 cash and a monthly lifetime pension.

The seven volume report pointed the finger at police, judges, Marshall's original defence lawyers, Crown lawyers and bureaucrats. Bruce Archibald, a consultant to the royal commission, said Marshall's courage was evident. "He was not going to be bullied by the justice system, he stood firm on that," said Archibald, a law professor at Dalhousie University.

A second high profile legal case involved Marshall's 1996 conviction for catching and selling eels out of season, and without a licence. In 1999, the Supreme Court of Canada upheld a centuries old treaty between

Mi'kmaq natives and the British Crown in acquitting Marshall. The high court ruling also confirmed Mi'kmaq and Maliseet in New Brunswick and Nova Scotia have the right to earn a moderate livelihood from hunting, fishing and gathering.

The fisheries victory had an impact on thousands of people across Canada, said Bernd Christmas, Nova Scotia's first Mi'kmaq lawyer, who now works in Toronto. "It made sure aboriginal people's rights that were documented hundreds of years ago are still valid."

Robert Dziekanski Taser Incident 2007

(Bibliography: Security of Justice - Robert Dziekanski Taser Case)

Robert Dziekanski (April 15, 1967–October 14, 2007) was a Polish immigrant to Canada. He was in the process of emigrating from Gliwice, Poland to live with his mother, Zofia Cisowski, in Kamloops, British Columbia. Mr. Dziekanski died on October 14, 2007 after being tasered five times by the Royal Canadian Mounted Police (RCMP) at Vancouver International Airport. The incident was filmed by a member of the public, Paul Pritchard. The police initially took possession of the video and refused to return it to Pritchard, who later went to court to obtain it and then released the video to the press.

Dziekanski's flight was two hours late, and arrived at about 3:15 pm on October 13, 2007. According to official sources, Dziekanski required language support to complete initial customs formalities. Cisowski had been making enquiries of airport staff since the early afternoon, but could not provide information about the airline, flight number, or scheduled arrival time. Airport staff told her Dziekanski was not at the airport and she had returned to Kamloops at about 10 pm, believing her son had missed his flight.

When Dziekanski left the Customs hall, he became visibly agitated. Bystanders and airport security guards were unable to communicate with him because he did not speak English, and they did not use the airport's telephone translation service. He used chairs to prop open the one-way doors between a Customs clearing area and a public lounge and at one point threw a computer and a small table to the floor before the police arrived.

Four RCMP officers, Constables Gerry Rundel, Bill Bently, Kwesi Millington, and supervisor Corporal Benjamin Robinson, arrived and entered the Customs room. Corporal Robinson ordered the Taser to be used. Constable Millington tasered Dziekanski. He began to convulse and was tasered several more times after falling to the ground, where the four officers pinned, handcuffed and continued to taser him. One eyewitness, who recorded the incident on her cellphone, told CBC News that Dziekanski had been tasered four times. "The third and fourth ones were at the same time" delivered by the officers at Dziekanski's right and left, just before Dziekanski fell. According to B.C. Crown counsel spokesman Stan Lowe, Dziekanski was tasered a total of five times. Dziekanski did not receive CPR until paramedics arrived 15 minutes later, were unable to revive him, and pronounced him dead at the scene.

Before the video was released to the public, the RCMP repeatedly claimed that only three officers were at the scene. There were actually four officers at the scene. The RCMP also said that they did not use pepper spray because of the risk it would have posed to bystanders. The video shows the incident occurred in an area separated from bystanders by a glass wall. An RCMP spokesperson stated batons were not used, which was also contradicted by the video.

Airport security has been roundly criticized for not assisting Dziekanski during his many hours in the airport. Once he became agitated, security guards made little attempt to communicate with him or defuse the situation. In February 2009 it was reported that Canada had unilaterally suspended its mutual legal assistance treaty with Poland, thus blocking Poland's own investigation of the Dziekanski Taser incident. Both the Toronto Police and the Royal Newfoundland Constabulary, meanwhile, have put large orders of Tasers for their front-line officers on hold.

The Braidwood Inquiry was established by the Provincial Government of British Columbia to report on the use of conducted energy weapons and the death of Mr. Dziekanski.

Aqsa Parvez Honour Killing 2007

(Bibliography: Security of Justice - Aqsa Parvez Honour Killing)

Aqsa "Axa" Parvez (April 22, 1991 – December 10, 2007) was the victim of an alleged honour killing in Mississauga, Ontario, Canada. Parvez was a student of Applewood Heights Secondary School in Mississauga, Ontario, Canada. Her father, Muhammad Parvez, was a taxicab driver. He is accused of strangling his daughter, then calling police to turn himself in. His daughter died in hospital shortly after being taken there.

Growing up in a Muslim family of Pakistani origin, she was required to wear a hijab outside the house. However, her friends claimed that she refused to wear the veil and would change her clothing at school and then change back before going home. Her friends also claimed that she was drawn to Western culture, and was not getting along well with her family who adhered to a devout form of Islam. A week before her death, she had moved in with a friend to escape tension with her family.

Muhammad Parvez was charged with second degree murder and denied bail. Aqsa's older brother Waqas Parvez was ordered by his father not to communicate with police, and was charged with obstructing police and placed in custody. Aqsa Parvez's death revived the story of a similar honour killing in 1989 where Zein Isa killed his 16 year old daughter Tina. On 27 June, Waqas Parvez was charged by Peel Regional Police with first degree murder.

Some people consider her murder to be a case of an honour killing, while Islamic leaders state this is a case of domestic violence. Her death has also sparked a debate about the status of women in Islamic communities. A public funeral was to take place for Parvez at a Mississauga mosque on December 15, 2007. Hours before the funeral, her family decided instead to have a private funeral. Parvez was buried in an unmarked grave and her family refused a donation for a gravestone and a memorial.

Honour Killings in Canada 2009

(Bibliography: Security of Justice - Honour Killings in Canada)

As many as 5,000 women and girls lose their lives, most at the hands of family members in "honour killings", around the world each year according to the United Nations. Up to a dozen have died for the same reason in Canada in the last decade.

The police in Kingston, Ontario investigated honour killings as a motive in the deaths of three teenage sisters and an older female relative who were found in a car submerged in the Rideau Canal in Kingston on 30 June 2009. The girls' mother, father, and brother were arrested and charged with first degree murder. Kingston Police Chief Stephen Tanner said at a news conference that the three Canadian teenagers had all the freedom and rights of expression of all Canadians.

Honour killings may be sparked by a woman talking to an unrelated man, having a boyfriend, wearing makeup or revealing clothing, or even seeking a divorce. Immigrant children who grow up in western nations take those freedoms for granted, which may throw them into conflict with their parents' rigid standards. When people leave their country, they leave their possessions behind. But they bring their beliefs with them; their culture, their traditions, and their religion. Unfortunately, the worst and criminal part of that is controlling women.

In 2003, Amandeep Atwal, 17, died after her father stabbed her 17 times. The Kitimat, BC, teen had been secretly seeing a boyfriend. Sixteen year old Aqsa Parvez's father and brother are currently awaiting trial for her strangulation death in 2007, and friends said the Brampton, Ontario teen had been clashing with her family over her refusal to wear the hijab. In May, an Ottawa man was sentenced to life in prison for killing his sister Khatera Sadiqi and her fiancé.

Honour killing is most prevalent in nations with large Muslim populations, but there's nothing in Islam that sanctions the practice. Some perpetrators use religion as a "cloak", but honour killing is about culture and patriarchy, it is not about religion. A few women are sacrificed to terrorize all women, to push them into submission, where they cannot defend themselves or even their daughters or sisters. In Canada, we may have been overly sensitive to culture, but there are cultural components in these crimes which we cannot ignore.

Honour killings or Domestic Abuse 2000 - 2009

(Bibliography: Security of Justice - Honour Killings or Domestic Abuse)

Near the Kingston Mills locks on the Rideau Canal, three teenage sisters and their father's first wife died on June 30, 2009 in what was suggested was an honour killing. The term "honour killing" muddies the issue of domestic abuse with religious connotations. For others, it's a cultural phenomenon distinct from domestic violence. Originated as a patriarchal tribal custom, honour killings were believed to restore a family's or community's reputation. Though often associated with Muslim cultures, they also happen among Sikhs and Hindus.

A 2000 report by the United Nations estimated that as many as 5,000 women and girls are killed each year by relatives for dishonouring their family. Many cases involve the "dishonour" of having been raped. Though often linked to sexual issues such as adultery and premarital sex, the perceived "offences" that have prompted honour killings have come to include a woman's push for independence. The following are several alleged honour killings in Canada.

Farah Khan, 5: Her father beat the Toronto girl to death and dismembered her in 1999 while her stepmother watched. The father is said to have killed the little girl because he believed she wasn't biologically his own.

Jaswinder Kaur Sidhu, 25: The BC born woman was found dead in 2000 after moving to India to live with her new husband, who was also beaten a day earlier. Her mother and uncle were among nine people charged in India with conspiracy to kill Sidhu.

Amandeep Atwal, 17: Her father was convicted in her stabbing death in 2003 in BC. He apparently disapproved of her relationship with her high school sweetheart, who was from a different ethnic group.

Khatera Sadiqi, 20: Sadiqi and her fiancé were shot to death in 2006 while parked in a car outside an Ottawa shopping plaza. Her brother was found guilty of murdering them. He told the court that he wanted his sister to respect their father.

Aqsa Parvez, 16: The teen was found strangled in her family's Mississauga home in 2007. Her brother and father have been charged with first degree murder. Parvez's friends said she'd been having arguments with her father about wearing a traditional hijab.

The Shafia family: The Shafia sisters, Zainab 19, Sahar 17, and Geeti 13, were found dead in a submerged car in Kingston, Ontario, on June 30, 2009, along with their father's first wife, Rona Mohammed 50. The sisters' parents and 18 year old brother have been charged with four counts of first degree murder. Although police have not released an official motive for the killing, they have hinted at cultural undertones in the case and are investigating the possibility that the deaths were honour killings.

Debate rages over whether honour killings are simply cases of domestic abuse by another name. Many Muslim groups say the term "honour killing" is a misnomer that stigmatizes their religion and are quick to denounce the label. Writing in the spring edition of the U.S. policy journal Middle East Quarterly, American feminist writer Phyllis Chesler argues that honour killings are distinct from domestic violence. She listed several distinctions between the two forms of violence:

- Planning — Domestic abuse cases tend to be spontaneous. The perpetrator's family may repeatedly threaten the victim with death if she dishonours her family. Honour killings are planned in advance.
- Complicity — Domestic abuse cases rarely see more than one family member involved in the killing. Honour killings

can include multiple family members, even fathers, brothers, uncles, and cousins.

- Stigma — Where domestic abusers are often ostracized, perpetrators of honour killings don't face the same stigma.

Chesler says the idea of honour killing needs to be recognized by governments, police forces and Islamic organizations so society can begin to tackle the problem. Amin Muhammad, a psychiatry professor with Newfoundland's Memorial University who studies honour killings, agrees that the term needs to be acknowledged. "I think everybody is scared of this term, but I think it is important to accept that this term is there," Muhammad said.

Light Sentences for Killers 2007

(Bibliography: Security of Justice - Light Sentences for Killers)

Victoria, BC: A man convicted of murdering a Victoria area teenager has had his day parole extended for another six months. In 1999, Warren Glowatski was convicted of second degree murder in the swarming and drowning death of 14 year old Reena Virk on Nov 14, 1997. He was sentenced to life in prison with no chance of parole for seven years. Glowatski was granted day parole in June 2007. The parole board decided in late last month to grant Glowatski, now 28, another six months on day parole so long as he abstains from alcohol and drugs, has no contact with people involved in criminal activity or substance abuse, and returns to his halfway house every night. His parole will be reviewed in another six months.

Caledonia Land Dispute 2006

(Bibliography: Security of Justice - Caledonia Land Dispute)

The current Grand River land dispute came to the attention of the general public of Canada on February 28, 2006. On that date, protesters from the Six Nations of the Grand River began a demonstration to raise awareness about First Nation land claims in Ontario, Canada, and particularly about their claim to a parcel of land in Caledonia, Ontario, a community within the single-tier municipality of Haldimand

County, roughly 20 kilometres southwest of Hamilton. Soon after this demonstration, the demonstrators assumed control of the disputed land.

The land at the centre of the dispute in Caledonia covers 40 hectares which was to be developed by Henco Industries Ltd. into a residential subdivision known as the Douglas Creek Estates. It is part of a 385,000 hectare plot of land known as the "Haldimand Tract", which was granted, in 1784, by the Crown to the Six Nations of the Grand River, for their use in settlement. Henco argues that the Six Nations surrendered their rights to the land in 1841, and Henco later purchased it from the Crown. The Six Nations, however, maintain that their title to the land was never relinquished.

Since the occupation began, Caledonia residents have complained that they have been subject to threats and violence from Native protesters, and the Ontario Provincial Police (OPP) failed to take any action to protect them. David Brown who lives with his wife near the disputed area, stated in court testimony in November 2009 that he needed to carry a native issued passport, and get approval from the protesters to enter his own house. He also claimed that after arriving "after curfew" one day, he was denied entry and jailed by the OPP when he ignored the natives. Brown alleged that Native protesters threatened and harassed him repeatedly and that rocks and mud were thrown at his family and their home. Brown and his wife are seeking $7 million dollars in a civil lawsuit against the OPP on the basis that the police did nothing to protect him and his family during the occupation.

In court testimony, OPP Inspector Brian Haggith stated that the Native protesters "set up a checkpoint . . . almost like the entrance to another country," and that the community lost confidence in the OPP's ability to protect them. Haggith also testified that when natives set fire to a wooden bridge in town, the fire department withdrew from fighting the blaze when confronted by death threats from the protesters. The fire chief told the OPP he did not believe the OPP would protect him or his men if they went against the natives' wishes. In addition, an electrical substation was then destroyed, causing more than $1 million in damage and a blackout, when a truck crashed through its gates and was left ablaze. Once again, Haggith stated that there was little response from the police. Inspector Haggith also testified that he asked for a change in policy at a meeting with his superiors but that his request was denied.

Former Nazi Deportations 2002 - 2009

(Bibliography: Security of Justice - Former Nazi Deportations)

Michael Seifert

Canada's highest court refused to hear the appeal of a former Nazi guard fighting deportation to Italy where he was convicted of war crimes in World War Two. Michael Seifert was a Ukranian who has lived in Canada since 1951. He acknowledged being a guard at a prison in Bolzano Italy that held Jews and others headed to German concentration camps, but denied he murdered anyone. Seifert appealed his deportation and argued Canadian courts ignored weaknesses in the Italian trial. The Supreme Court of Canada refused to hear the case.

Seifert was born in 1924 in a town in Ukraine which was then part of the Soviet Union, and began work as a guard for the Nazi SD after the German occupation. He was transferred to Italy in 1944 and stayed there until the war ended. An Italian military court convicted him in absentia in 2000 of torturing and killing nine people, and sentenced him to life in prison. Press reports said Seifert and another guard were called "The Beasts of Bolzano."

Seifert eventually immigrated to Vancouver where he was employed as a mill worker and raised a family. He was arrested by Canada in 2002. A judge in November upheld a decision by immigration officials to strip Seifert of Canadian citizenship for hiding the fact that he had been a Nazi SD prison guard and claiming he was born in Estonia. Canada barred former members of the Nazi SS and related units such as the Nazi SD from immigrating after the war because of their involvement in concentration camps and other war crimes.

But the court ruling also said immigration officials had failed to prove

Seifert was responsible for any war crimes, raising the prospect that the Supreme Court might hear a deportation appeal. The Canadian Jewish Congress estimated between 1,000 and 3,000 people with Nazi pasts were able to get into Canada illegally between 1947 and 1956, but only two have had their Canadian citizenship revoked.

Helmut Oberlander

A federal appeal court has ordered the federal cabinet to revisit its decision to strip accused Nazi war criminal Helmut Oberlander of his Canadian citizenship. In a decision made public, the Federal Court of Appeal told cabinet to reconsider the issue of whether Oberlander was a willing member of his military unit, given that the penalty for desertion was execution.

In writing for the majority, Justice Carolyn Layden-Stevenson said Oberlander's citizenship is a matter for cabinet to determine. "However, in view of its serious consequences, it is critical that all relevant issues be considered and analyzed. The process must not only be proper and fair, it must be seen to be so."

Oberlander and his wife came to Canada in 1954. He became a Canadian citizen six years later. He did not disclose his wartime experience when he applied to enter Canada or seek citizenship. Canadian Jewish Congress president Mark Freiman said Wednesday it was frustrating that the court based its decision on a "hyper technical point of interpretation". Ultimately, the issue is not how Oberlander came to join the Nazi death squad, but rather that he lied to gain entry into Canada and to obtain Canadian citizenship.

Polygamy in British Columbia 2007

(Bibliography: Security of Justice - Polygamy in British Columbia)

Bountiful is a settlement located in the Creston Valley of southeastern British Columbia, Canada, near Cranbrook and Creston. The closest community is Lister, British Columbia. Bountiful's community is made up of members of a polygamist Mormon fundamentalist group. The polygamists live in a commune style compound outside of Lister. The settlement is named after Bountiful in the Book of Mormon. In 1998 the population was about 600 and has since grown to about 1,000, and most residents are descended from only half a dozen men. Some residents thought that the president of the church, Warren Jeffs, had exceeded his authority and become too dictatorial.

Bountiful has come under intense scrutiny for its involvement in the polygamous sect. On 28 January 2006, the Vancouver Sun released information stating that Utah's Attorney General was collaborating with British Columbia's Attorney General to deal with polygamy and the alleged abuse in these communities. On September 25, 2007 Jeffs was found guilty of being an accomplice to rape. Prosecutors said Jeffs forced a 14 year old girl into marriage and sex with her 19 year old first cousin. Jeffs faces five years to life in prison on each of two felony charges. Utah Attorney General Mark Shurtleff said, "Everyone should now know that no one is above the law, religion is not an excuse for abuse, and every victim has a right to be heard".

In Bountiful, Winston Blackmore invited the media to visit on May 16, 2006 in response to a recent visit by the Royal Canadian Mounted Police, indicating that they felt persecuted. Three of his wives may face deportation, as they are U.S. citizens and would not be considered legally married to a Canadian.

On June 6, 2007, the province of British Columbia announced the appointment of Vancouver lawyer Richard Peck as a special prosecutor to review the results of a police investigation into possible polygamous activity by members of the community. On August 1, 2007, Richard Peck concluded that there isn't enough evidence to charge the group with sexual abuse or exploitation charges as it has been extraordinarily difficult to find victims willing to testify and the defendants are likely to claim "religious freedom" as a defence.

Peck suggested that British Columbia ask the courts whether the current laws concerning polygamy are constitutional. Peck said that it's time to find out once and for all if Canada's laws against polygamy will stand. He stated that, "If the law is upheld, members of the Bountiful community will have fair notice that their practice of polygamy must cease." Lawyer Leonard Doust said the court should be asked whether Canada's laws against polygamy are constitutionally valid, and whether they could withstand a court challenge on the grounds that multiple marriages fall under the right of religious freedom. Attorney General Wally Oppal said it's no secret he favours a more aggressive approach to the issue, but he must consider the opinions given by two highly respected lawyers, Doust and the special prosecutor (Peck) who gave the same advice earlier.

IRB and Refugee Backlogs 2009

(Bibliography: Security of Justice - IRB and Refugee Backlogs)

When the Conservatives came to power in January 2006, the backlog of people waiting for their claims to be heard by members of the Immigration and Refugee Board (IRB) was slightly less than 20,000. Since then, the number of people on the waiting list has grown to 62,000.

When the Conservatives took power, the IRB had 164 members to hear cases. By March 31, 2008, that number dipped to 106. IRB members are appointed by the government, and critics say the Conservatives have politicized that appointment process in taking too long to fill vacancies while the backlog continues to grow.

When the Liberals were still in power earlier this decade, they made changes to the IRB, reducing the number of board members hearing cases from two to one and promising to create an appeal board. The aim of the appeal body would be to catch the inevitable mistakes that would happen with only one person presiding over the original hearings. Politicians from all parties vowed to take the politics out of the appointment process. But advocates are still waiting for an appeal board, and complaining about a political appointment process.

This week, Immigration Minister Jason Kenney announced that he has filled most of the vacant board positions and expects to have a full complement by Christmas. A more complete board will help reduce the backlog, which was created in part by an influx of refugee claimants from Mexico and the Czech Republic. In the summer, the government imposed visa restrictions on individuals from those countries.

The Provinces bear the brunt of backlog. As for the people who must wait and endure the backlogs, their lives can be frustrating. The Immigration Minister provided a breakdown of wait times from 2005 to the end of August 2009. In 2006 the average wait was 11.7 months, while by the end of August 2009 it was 17.7 months.

The refugee claim is only the beginning of the process of gaining refugee status. Traditionally, the board has rejected about half of all claims. If the initial claim is rejected, the applicant can ask the federal court to review the case. "Leave to appeal," as the process is called in legal jargon, is only granted in about 10 per cent of cases. If the claimant's request has failed, the individual can apply to the Department for what's called a "pre-removal" hearing. But here, too, the backlog can push the wait to two years. Finally, there is the option of appealing to the Minister to stay in Canada based on humanitarian grounds.

While refugee claimants wait for the process to unfold, they qualify for health care, education and legal aid . . . and the costs are borne by the lower levels of government, especially the provinces. There is some evidence that provincial and municipal authorities are growing weary of paying for these services.

Ontario Court Backlog 2003 - 2009

(Bibliography: Security of Justice - Ontario Court Backlog)

The Ontario justice system has fallen into a state of disrepair highlighted by punitive federal legislation and a legion of accused criminals who languish behind bars awaiting trial, according to an influential Ontario Court of Appeal judge. Mr. Justice Marc Rosenberg, regarded as the finest criminal law mind in the country, said that Canadians must take stock of the shambles that has been created through indiscriminate use of imprisonment. "Something has gone terribly wrong," Judge Rosenberg told a Toronto legal conference. "On any day in Canada, we have more people in pretrial custody than actually serving sentences. The constitutional guarantees of the presumption of innocence and reasonable bail seem illusory."

Ottawa lawyer Norm Boxall said, "as Canada's foremost authority on criminal law, a former Crown attorney and defence counsel, Justice Rosenberg is our conscience. When someone of his stature makes an impassioned plea to reverse the direction in which we are travelling, with the increased use of incarceration both pre- and post- trial, everyone should listen."

Judge Rosenberg also took a swing at the under funding of legal aid programs: "Ensuring adequate funding for legal aid has been an ongoing struggle for decades," he said. "Legal aid is a cornerstone of our system. We cannot continue to bring the most vulnerable in our society to the precipice every few years." Coming at a time when virtually all experienced defence lawyers are boycotting the legal aid plan to protest its low fee structure, Judge Rosenberg's endorsement of legal aid "cannot be ignored," said Mr. Boxall.

In Kitchener in 2009, an Ontario Superior Court judge has turned down a request from three men charged with murder to order the province to pay their lawyers at least $170 per hour, which would be 70% higher than the legal aid rate. The decision by Justice James Ramsay was issued yesterday during the seventh month of a boycott of major cases by criminal lawyers in Ontario, who are protesting against legal rates that have increased by only 15% since 1987. The lawyers that Ronald Cyr, Zdenek Zvolensky and Nashat Qahwash want to hire as defence counsel have said they will not handle the case for the fees that Legal Aid Ontario is willing to pay. Legal Aid Ontario has found two lawyers willing to represent the defendants, although one is 73 years old and the other has never handled a murder trial.

In 2005,the Ministry of the Attorney General said 36 per cent of charges took eight months or more to move through the courts last year, down slightly from 39 per cent in 2001/2002, a backlog auditor Jim McCarter called "the worst in a decade" in his 2003 report.

In 1990, the Supreme Court of Canada ruled that a typical case should go to trial within eight to 10 months in order to avoid prejudicing the rights of an accused. Following that ruling, known as the Askov decision, Ontario withdrew more than 50,000 criminal charges. Not all cases fit the Askov mould; a complex case might require more court or preparation time, or be subjected to stalling tactics by the defence, and won't get tossed out by a judge.

The province is still aiming for a more efficient paperless justice system, Bryant said. Despite that, the 2002 collapse of a project to create a province wide computerized justice network forced the provincial government to spend $63 million in 2005 to settle a related lawsuit.

> *In 2009 there was an eruption of concern over the similar spiralling costs of a paperless health record system. Documents obtained by CBC News showed the health agency doled out $4.8 million in contracts without outside bidders within the first four months of its creation in September 2008. The agency paid consultants millions of dollars for watching TV, reading the New York Times and holding a conversation on the subway.*

In the Newmarket lower court, the Ontario Court of Justice, which takes all of the charges in the York region, there were almost 30,000 criminal charges laid in 2007. It took an average of eight and a half court appearances over 195 days to conclude a single criminal charge. If you set a trial date in the lower court, you may have to wait over 11 months. The Attorney General's office is presently attempting to deal with these delays. They have an initiative and Newmarket is one of the areas at which that they are looking.

Ponzi Schemes & Earl Jones 2009

(Bibliography: Security of Justice - Ponzi Schemes & Earl Jones)

Earl Jones, a Montreal financial adviser accused by regulators of running a Ponzi scheme that defrauded clients of as much as $50 million was arrested 27 July by Quebec provincial police.

The Autorité Des Marches Financiers, the Montreal securities regulator for Quebec, announced on July 10 it would freeze Jones's bank accounts after receiving complaints from investors in Montreal and other parts of Canada and the U.S. Jones's business has "all the hallmarks of a Ponzi scheme," Sylvain Theberge, a spokesman for the regulator, said in a July 14 interview.

Neil Stein, who is representing the victims, said Wednesday there are three groups of creditors: those who are beneficiaries of wills that were being administered by Jones; those who entrusted Jones to take care of their money; and those who lent money to successors of wills, using assets listed on the will as collateral. "He was saying it was a bridge loan, that the succession needed money on a temporary basis because it can't sell off the assets quick enough and wants to provide liquidity to the beneficiaries," Stein explained.

But not one of the borrowers was ever aware that money was being lent for their alleged benefit. All the money, he said, seems to have disappeared. Stein said they aren't sure how many people were swindled by Jones, but about 100 wills were found in his office. Another 30 people, such as Peter Kent's mother, had put Jones in charge of all their finances, from paying the phone bill to paying their taxes. "In addition to that, there are people who have lent money," Stein said. Jones "appears to be hopelessly insolvent and appears to be involved in a major fraud of the nature of a Ponzi scheme, which has now collapsed due to the fact its clients all want their money back," Stein's motion reads.

Real estate agents mandated to sell a condo in Dorval, a Montreal suburb, which served as the main residence of the Jones family from 1999 until his downfall last summer, were to conduct media tours of the residence. The posh two bedroom waterfront condo, with an asking price of $925,000, offers lavish 180-degree views of Lake St. Louis, in addition to a renovated kitchen, two bathrooms and indoor parking. Trustee RSM Richter seized the home from Jones Sept 11. A relatively small proportion of the sale proceeds will apparently be going to clients Jones is alleged to have bilked of some $75 million over the years.

Ponzi Schemes & Pension Plans 1950s - 2010
(Bibliography: Security of Justice - Ponzi Schemes & Pension Plans)

Large numbers of Canadians who have spent their working lives putting money aside for their old age have suddenly discovered it was a waste of effort. The odds on a private sector employee having a decent pension are about one in five. That's the percentage of Canadians who can boast of a defined benefit plan, the kind that pays a set amount based on salary level and years of service.

Companies don't like defined benefit plans because they're expensive and force companies to play nanny to aging non workers. So a lot of them switched to "defined contribution" plans, which promise nothing except regular deductions from your pay cheque. The money goes into the markets, and if the markets tank, well . . . tough.

People with defined contribution pensions are looking at a long, bleak old age. Retirement? Forget it. The only question is whether you keep your existing job, or get forced out and find yourself bagging groceries at the Price Chopper, where your retiree friends are forced to shop.

People on defined benefit plans are a little better off, if their company didn't go bankrupt, or threaten to go bankrupt, the better to convince Ottawa to let them out of paying employees what they promised. Auto workers, Air Canada employees and Nortel retirees know how it feels to discover all those promises about a decent retirement aren't worth last year's Pontiac.

Public employees are a different matter, safe in the knowledge taxpayers will have to foot the bill to ensure they don't suffer unduly. But they're not entirely immune. Ontario Teachers' Pension Plan, one of Canada's biggest, sent a newsletter to members this week noting cheerfully that while it lost $19 billion last year, it "tied for first place in service delivery among 58 international pension plans." Teachers already pay 11% of their salary into the plan, which has nonetheless cut benefits and increased contributions to offset earlier shortfalls. When the latest losses are accounted for in 2011, according to the report, the plan has the option of further cuts, higher contributions, or both.

There's talk of pension reform in Ottawa, but it's mainly focussed on finding ways to take even more burden off companies that can't pay what they owe. The global financial crisis means even the biggest funds have multi-billion-dollar holes in their account books. They're pressing the government for "relief", which in this instance means "please don't make us pay all those employees from whom we took money."

All this might be more bearable if Ottawa didn't make it so difficult for individuals to look after themselves. Saving is discouraged by high tax rates. RRSPs have limits on contributions, and anyone in a job that theoretically includes a pension, no matter how unlikely they are ever to collect it, is blocked from contributing more than a fraction of the maximum. The new tax free savings accounts may make a small dent, but they're a bit late in the game for most boomers.

Given the mess they've been dumped into, a lot of people would have been better off if they'd been allowed to take their pension contributions, and those of their employer, and stick it in something safe, with a small but reliable return, without Ottawa taking it all back in taxes.

Wholesale changes seem inevitable. It's hard to imagine another generation of workers being subject to similar Ponzi schemes. In the United States, Bernard Madoff took billions of dollars, made lots of promises, and reneged on them all. That's OK for a crook, but not for Canada's pension industry. Now that it's been exposed, participation in pension shouldn't be enforced to continue bilking Canadians of their money and their retirement aspirations.

Corruption in Quebec Courts 2008

(Bibliography: Security of Justice - Corruption in Quebec Courts)

In a speech at Hillsdale College in 2008, Mark Steyn made these remarks when comparing the economies of Canada and the United States. If you remove health care from the equation, the differences between the two economies become relatively marginal. The Fraser Institute's "Economic Freedom of the World 2007 Annual Report" ranked the U.S. and Canada together, tied in fifth place along with Britain. The top ten most free economies in this report are Hong Kong, Singapore, New Zealand, Switzerland, United States, United Kingdom, Canada, Estonia, Ireland, and Australia: with the exception of Switzerland and Estonia, these systems are all British derived. They're what Jacques Chirac (a former French President) dismissively calls *les anglo-saxon.* And he and many other Continentals make it very clear that they regard free market capitalism as some sort of kinky Anglo-Saxon fetish.

On the other hand, Andrew Roberts, the author of *A History of the English-Speaking Peoples since 1900*, points out the two most corrupt jurisdictions in North America are Louisiana and Quebec . . . both French derived. Quebec has a civil service that employs the same number of people as California, even though California has a population nearly five times the size.

In the province of Quebec, it's taken more or less for granted by all political parties that collective rights outweigh individual rights. For example, if you own a store in Montreal, the French language signs inside the store are required by law to be at least twice the size of the English signs. And the government has a fairly large bureaucratic agency whose job it is to go around measuring signs and prosecuting offenders.

There was even a famous case a few years ago of a pet store owner who was targeted by the Office De La Langue Francaise for selling English-speaking parrots. The language commissar had gone into the store and heard a bird saying, "Who's a pretty boy, then?" and decided to take action. I keep trying to find out what happened to the parrot. Presumably it was sent to a re-education camp and emerged years later with a glassy stare saying in a monotone voice, "Qui est un joli garçon, hein?".

Report on RCMP re Dziekanski 2009 by Commission of Public Complaints

(Bibliography: Security of Justice - Report on RCMP re Dziekanski)

Paul Kennedy, chairman of the Commission for Public Complaints, found fault with the four RCMP officers and with the subsequent investigation of the death of Robert Dziekanski at Vancouver International Airport in 2007. But Mr. Kennedy went much further than expected, taking verbal shots at stagnant RCMP culture, especially its notorious, self-destructive resistance to change. It is a "massively inert" organization, he said, and must not stand. He used the opportunity to castigate RCMP Commissioner William Elliott. They have not agreed on several issues, including Mr. Kennedy's previous, bleak assessments of internal police investigations and his request for more oversight powers.

Mr. Kennedy's report described how Mr. Dziekanski died at the airport immediately after receiving five Taser shots to his body and being wrestled on the ground by the four officers. The incident was captured on video by a passerby, Paul Pritchard, and its release brought international condemnation and shame on the Mounties. A later public inquiry into the matter by retired judge Thomas Braidwood reinforced and sharpened criticism of the RCMP.

Mr. Kennedy wrote, "the decision to approach Mr. Dziekanski to deal with the complaints was not unreasonable". Unfortunately, just about everything that followed at the airport was (unreasonable). The senior Mountie in charge, Corporal Benjamin Robinson, failed to take control of the situation and the result became chaotic.

The multiple cycles of the Taser on Mr. Dziekanski were not appropriate. And the four officers "demonstrated no meaningful attempt to de-escalate the situation, nor did they approach the situation with a measured, coordinated and appropriate response." The Taser was used too quickly, he concluded. Furthermore, wrote Mr. Kennedy, the handcuffs used on Mr. Dziekanski should have been removed as soon as the officers determined that he had lost consciousness and was in distress.

He rejected the officers' credibility. "I do not accept as accurate any of the versions of events presented by the involved members because I find considerable and significant discrepancies in the detail and accuracy of the recollections of the members when compared against the otherwise incontrovertible video evidence". In all, Mr. Kennedy made 23 findings of fact, and 16 recommendations that seem to make sense. He wishes they were acted on, now.

Tarnished Justice 2009

(Bibliography: Security of Justice - Tarnished Justice)

Canadians take pride in living in a peaceful, safe country. We take particular pride in our police and courts. We have faith in the judicial system; in this land, you never need to fear being pulled over by a corrupt police officer at night, or worry that you don't have enough money to bribe your way out of a false charge. Recent events, however, are increasingly tarnishing the shining reputation of these vital civil servants.

In Ontario, an ongoing lawsuit has provided devastating testimony that shows that the Provincial Police utterly abandoned a family to lawless chaos behind native barricades in Caledonia. In Toronto, David Chen was charged with assault and forcible confinement after he tackled and tied up a man who'd just robbed his store, holding him until police could arrive.

As if that weren't bad enough, the Crown prosecutors made a deal with the thief, reducing his sentence in exchange for testifying against the man he'd robbed!

In British Columbia, the public's confidence in the RCMP has been rocked not only by the unnecessary death of Robert Dziekanski after being tasered by a quartet of officers, but by the refusal of the Crown to press charges against one of those officers following a suspicious death on the roads. After running down motorcyclist Orion Hutchinson, the officer - Corporal Benjamin Robinson - tested over the legal blood alcohol limit on a breathalyzer test. Corporal Benjamin Monty

Robinson of the RCMP was testifying at an inquiry into the death of Robert Dziekanski. Robinson was the senior officer in charge when Dziekanski was tasered. But he claimed this was because he'd begun drinking vodka immediately after hitting the victim. Incredibly, the Crown accepted that, and Robinson will not face impaired driving charges.

In Calgary, a judge has thrown out sexual assault charges against two men arrested for a gang rape of a 15 year old girl. The case languished for a full five years, and the judge ruled that the delay violated the right of the accused to receive a speedy trial. There was obviously a good case to be made as two other men involved in the same incident were brought to trial in a timely fashion, were found guilty and given sentences of 27 and 30 months, respectively. So clearly lack of evidence wasn't the problem. Somewhere along the line, the police and the prosecution simply dropped the ball. The judge said as much when throwing out the charges, noting that the long delay was "in large part unexplained and unjustified".

Most members of police forces are honourable, and most prosecutors are dedicated professionals. Even so, there are signs the system itself is overburdened and cracking under the strain. The latter example from Calgary, in particular, is the logical result of a system so clogged with cases that suspects routinely plead to lesser charges, not because it's just or promotes the public good, but because the system would collapse if forced to actually bring each person arrested to a trial.

Being tough on crime means more than just catching criminals. It means having police and courts that have the staffing and funding necessary to do their jobs. It means having the appropriate prison infrastructure to rehabilitate those who can be redeemed while locking away the rest . . . forever, if necessary. Canadians have rested too long on our reputation for having a just society. It's time to demand improvements in our fraying system, before it gets any worse.

The Unethical Forces of Justice

From these recent examples it is clear that the repute of the nation's laws, courts, and law enforcement agencies has been sadly tarnished almost beyond repair. The principal cause for much of this may lie with a lack of appropriate transparency by those agencies of the federal and provincial governments. It is almost certain that the activities described above may be apply only to a minuscule portion of the total activities of the agencies. However, upon their discovery, those failures receive massive reviews by the media, and scorn by the public who have been duped. In the meantime, the miscreants seem to slip away in the night with little of no shame, remorse, or punishment . . . more often than not with generous gratuities to avoid legal action by the agencies who are originally to blame for the lack of oversight, proper management, and due diligence. Yet the "swiftness of divine retribution" to the miscreants by the weary tax payer seems to disappear as quickly as a snowball in a hot house.

Gone are the days of Sam Steele of the North West Mounted Police (later the RCMP), who built a force that was perceived as ethical, honourable, dependable, principled, and incorruptible.

Gone are the days of Elliot Ness of the U.S. Treasury Department, an up and coming young official known for his outspoken anti-corruption views, who was recruited to clean up the illegal smuggling of liquour. Realising the problems with trying to enforce the law, he was allowed to pick his own officers to form a team and take on Al Capone, the leading gangster of the time. Going through the records to find people who were not corrupt, he had a shortlist of only fifty names. Some he rejected because they had families, others simply on gut feel, and he formed a team of just nine officers.

Yet Canada is not without such men today. There are men who have the courage to speak their mind despite the perils and punishments accorded to whistle-blowers in government, which exist despite *(ineffective)* laws for their protection passed by those same governments. The recent report by Paul Kennedy, chairman of the Commission for

Public Complaints has carefully reviewed the actions of the RCMP in the Dziekanski case and found them sadly lacking all professional rectitude. His reward for a tough job well done? His appointment will not be renewed at the end of his term in a few months in 2010. An egregious decision.

The RCMP's Adjudications Directorate in Ottawa this week released 84 internal adjudication board decisions rendered across Canada from January 2008 to December 2009. The decisions rely on witness testimonies, admissions of fact, and proof of misconduct, and include sanctions against individual Mounties. Brian Hutchinson wrote summaries in the National Post of 12 of the 84 adjudication board decisions and a summary of one decision under appeal.

Lorne Gunter of the National Post opined that the way forward for Mr. Elliott seemed clear: Discipline now and discipline forcefully. It is the only way to begin restoring public confidence in the RCMP. But the Commissioner hasn't even bothered to respond to Mr. Kennedy's conclusions and recommendations. He insisted he was waiting on the outcome of an inquiry currently being conducted by retired judge Thomas Braidwood.

It will require strong governments both federally and provincially to retain men such as Mr. Kennedy and to take proper action. That in turn is likely to require majority governments with strong mandates from the people. Only then is it likely that Canada will have the leadership to prevent such travesties of justice from tarnishing the reputation of the country and the loss of security for the people. To quote from Cicero, *"The peoples' good is the highest law"*.

Is the title "The Unethical Forces of Justice in Canada" inappropriate or too harsh?

The Uneven Equality of Justice

As often proven, the only constant to history has been change. What may have been tolerable in times gone by either by choice or necessity, may no longer be socially or legally acceptable. The standards of conduct and propriety of the nation are constantly changing with the times. Notwithstanding an acceptance of some new standards, on further reflection they may be found less tolerable than the older values and traditions as standards of behaviour.

Disparities in Sentencing

Alvin Persaud

(Bibliography: Security of Justice - Reduced Sentence - Alvin Persaud)

In July 2008, Cathleen Lavoie suffered a gunshot wound to the neck in a domestic dispute. In the hospital she could not speak, but could communicate by lip reading and hand signals. In her early 40s, Lavoie's injuries prevent her from caring for her three children, aged 15, 13 and four, who are being raised in three different homes. In her victim impact statement, she said her independence has been shattered. I've lost my home, my children and my life."

Alvin Persaud, age 29, was sentenced to 10 years in prison for the attempted murder of his girlfriend in July 2008. The judge ruled that Persaud had accepted responsibility for the crime, and will get credit for time already served in jail. Persaud told the court "I sincerely regret my actions that night and I am truly sorry," prior to receiving his sentence.

Brett Flaten

(Bibliography: Security of Justice - Reduced Sentence - Brett Flaten)

A 16 year old girl (un-named by court order) was shot with a 22 calibre rifle by her former boy friend Brett Flaten. The bullet entered her right eye socket and entered her brain. She underwent brain and reconstructive surgery, but some bullet fragments remain in her brain. Part of her right temporal lobe was removed. The girl lost her right eye, the hearing in her right ear, and suffered facial paralysis, disfigurement, and cognitive impairment. She has had to learn to walk, speak, chew and swallow; a recovery described as painful and arduous. She is still receiving treatment from a number of specialists.

Brett Flaten was tried as an adult, even though he was 16 at the time of the offence in October of 2007. He was almost 18 when he was convicted of attempted murder and sentenced to nine years. The trial judge reduced it to eight years and two months, after counting time spent on remand. After an appeal, the Court of Appeal agreed Flaten should be tried as an adult but reduced his sentence to seven years and also increased the credit for remand time, meaning his sentence is effectively five years and nine months.

Robert Latimer

(Bibliography: Security of Justice - No Reduction - Robert Latimer)

Tracy Latimer was born November 23, 1980. An interruption in Tracy's supply of oxygen during the birth caused cerebral palsy, leading to severe mental and physical disabilities including seizures that were controlled with seizure medication. She had little or no voluntary control of her muscles, wore diapers, and could not walk or talk. Her doctors described the care given by her family as excellent. The Supreme Court judgment of 1997 noted, "It is undisputed that Tracy was in constant pain." Her condition in simple terms was best described by her father Robert, who said his actions were motivated by love for Tracy and a desire to end her pain. He described the medical treatments Tracy had undergone and was scheduled to undergo as "mutilation and torture". "With the combination of a feeding tube, rods in her back, the leg cut and flopping around and bedsores, how can people say she was a happy little girl?" Latimer asked.

Robert Latimer was convicted of second degree murder in the death of his 13 year old daughter Tracy. Although the minimum sentence for second degree murder is life with no chance of parole until after 10 years, the trial jury recommended that Latimer be eligible for parole after one year. Because he believed Latimer was motivated by compassion, the trial judge Ted Noble argued that a "constitutional exemption" could apply, and sentenced him to two years, one in jail and one under house arrest. This case sparked a national controversy on the definition and ethics of euthanasia as well as the rights of people with disabilities, and two Supreme Court decisions, R. v. Latimer (1997), on section 10 of the Canadian Charter of Rights and Freedoms, and later R. v. Latimer (2001), on cruel and unusual punishments under section 12 of the Charter. Latimer was released on day parole in March 2008 and will be eligible to apply for full parole in December 2010. Before his imprisonment, Latimer lived near Wilkie, Saskatchewan on a 1,280 acres (520 ha) wheat and canola farm with his wife Laura, and their four children.

Other Disparities

There is a great disparity in the amounts of compensation for wrongful sentences. Donald Marshall received $200,000 and a pension in 1990 for wrongful imprisonment for 11 years. David Milgaard received $10 million in 1999 for wrongful imprisonment for 29 years. Steven Truscott at age 66 received $6.5 million in 2008 for wrongful imprisonment for 48 years.

The case of David Chen in Toronto demonstrates a weird reversal of justice, in terms of common sense and traditional concepts of self-defence and protection of one's property. To add salt to the wound which was already bad enough, the Crown prosecutors agreed to a reduction of the thief's sentence in exchange for testifying against the man he'd robbed! What is the value of such self-serving testimony from an indicted perpetrator?

There is also the disbelief arising from the absolute discharge given to the perpetrator in a traffic accident. Corporal Benjamin Robinson (RCMP) ran down a motorcyclist by name of Orion Hutchinson and then tested over the legal blood alcohol limit on a breathalyzer test. But he claimed this was because he'd begun drinking vodka immediately after hitting the victim. Incredibly, the Crown accepted that, and Robinson will not face impaired driving charges. One might at least wonder where he had obtained the vodka . . . an open bottle in his own vehicle?

It may be unrealistic to expect a high degree of uniformity in sentencing, as rarely would one find comparable situations. Where there are great divergences of sentences, it may result due to different jurisdictions, eg one province having different standards than another province, or simply the lack of knowledge of other cases and jurisdiction. More likely the failure is more a lack of comparability rather than uniformity, ie between murder and white collar crime.

There may be a perception that white collar crimes are not taken sufficiently seriously. For instance, Conrad Black has been in detention for about two years of his six and a half year sentence, and the charges against him are already being touted as perhaps having been improperly laid. There is also the general policy in Canada of granting release on parole after a felon has served one-sixth of his sentence. For persons having "gotten away" with other peoples' money in the multi-millions of dollars and presumably stashed away much of that in tax havens or the names of a spouse, a few years in jail may be a small price to pay. Those who successfully masterminded a ponzi scheme in Canada, may be expecting the benefits of a lenient sentence and off shore tax havens and secret bank accounts.

And what about the perception of pensions and life annuities as massive ponzi schemes . . . purported to be in the best interests of the individuals under paternalistic concern by sanctimonious governments and the pension industry. The enforced participation in such pensions and life annuities by governments is tantamount to legislative theft. And there are no penalties on the books for these schemes as yet. You and your family and other beneficiaries have "sold the farm" and lost control of the capital contributions to such schemes. With regard to those generous pensions, one should heed the warning of Thomas Jefferson, a former distinguished president of the United States,: *"A government big enough to give you everything you want, is big enough to take away everything you have."*

One should carefully consider the structure of the pension systems under Canadian law as found at Nortel, Air Canada, Bell Canada, Canada Post, CN Rail, CP Rail. Most of the employees in these companies are facing reductions of 30 - 40% of their pensions due to under funding of the plans by the companies under government legislation. Yet the shareholders and senior management look forward to the receipt of substantial dividends, bonuses and severance packages. The rampant destruction of the employees' dreams of retirement has become a nightmare for most of their employees, with the exception of course of those at the highest management levels who are protected by different individual pension plans, generous bonuses, and severance payments.

Is the title "The Uneven Equality of Justice in Canada" inappropriate or too harsh?

The Untimely Delivery of Justice

For wrongfully incarcerated murders. the corrective measures, pardons, and restitution took years, even decades to work their way through the bureaucracy and the courts. These were delays were caused in some cases from poor investigative techniques and politics. In others the corrections arrived thanks to newer techniques such as DNA testing. The deportation of former Nazi criminals took even longer . . . as much as three to five decades in some cases. The polygamy charges against a religious sect in Bountiful BC has been delayed over concern that the Constitutional guarantees of freedom of religion would override other federal of provincial laws against plural marriages.

The Supreme Court of Canada rendered its decision in 1990 (the Askov decision) to the effect that when justice is delayed beyond eight to ten months, the result is justice denied. That in turn caused some 50,000 charges in the backlog of the Ontario court system to be withdrawn. Such conflict must be resolved, even in the face of the need to overhaul the Constitution itself.

Is the title "The Untimely Delivery of Justice in Canada" inappropriate or too harsh?

The Unknown Costs & Benefits of Justice

Virtually no information was easily available from Wikipedia, Statistics Canada, or newspaper articles. Perhaps the government thought the cost and benefits of the justice system would not be of much interest to many Canadians. Other possibilities might be that such information does not exist within government sources, or if it does, the government does not deem it of interest or worth communicating to the public. Cost and benefit analyses are certainly not the liveliest of topics of study or conversation. But they are crucial to good management, and in the case of the subject of justice, to the good governance of the nation. The following overview has been gleaned by the author from the paucity of sources easily available. The cost themselves for 1994-95 are well laid out by the John Howard Society as follows, (a few other relative facts were gleaned from Wikipedia, see Bibliography):

The John Howard Society

(Bibliography: Security of Justice - Cost of Justice - John Howard Society)
(Bibliography: Security of Justice - Prison Costs & Statistics)

In 1994-95, the administration and operation costs of criminal justice services in Canada totalled almost $10 billion, broken down as follows:

Service	Total	Per Capita
Police	$ 5,783,656,000	$ 198
Courts	$ 835,404,000	$ 29
Adult Corrections	$ 1,893,530,000	$ 65
Youth Corrections	$ 525,545,000	$ 18
Legal Aid	$ 646,433,000	$ 22
Prosecutions	$ 257,855,000	$ 9
Total	$ 9,942,423,000	$ 340

Source: Canadian Centre for Justice Statistics (1997, January, p. 9)

Crime Rates

The 2007 national crime rate reached its lowest point in 30 years. Canadian police services reported a 7% decline in crime, the third consecutive annual decrease. The violent crime rate fell by 3%, marking its lowest point since 1989. Following increases in most serious violent crimes over the past two years, the 2007 rates of homicide, attempted murder, sexual assault, robbery, aggravated assault, assault with a weapon, forcible confinement and abduction declined or remained stable. The property crime rate dropped by 8% and reached its lowest point since 1969. Break and enters were at their lowest level in 40 years, dropping by 9% in 2007. Likewise, motor vehicle thefts declined by 9%. The youth crime rate dropped by 2% in 2007, following a 3% increase in 2006. Violent crimes committed by youth remained stable, while declines were seen in most non-violent offences

Incarceration rates

The incarceration rate increased from 129 per 100,000 adult population in 2004/5 to 131 per 100,000 in 2005/6. Just over 232,800 adults were admitted to some form of custody in 2005/2006 (a 4% increase from the previous year). This increase was driven by a 6% climb in the number of admissions to remand in provincial/ territorial facilities, and a 4% increase in admissions to federal custody. The number of admissions to provincial/ territorial sentenced custody remained stable. Since 1996/1997, admissions to remand have grown steadily (+22%) while admissions to provincial/ territorial sentenced custody have fallen (-28%).

The Costs of Incarceration

Correctional services expenditures totalled almost $3 billion in 2005/6, up 2% from the previous year. Custodial services (prisons) accounted for the largest proportion (71%) of the expenditures, followed by community supervision services (14%), headquarters (14%), and National Parole Board and provincial parole boards (2%). These figures do not include policing or court costs which bring the total expenditures to more than

$10 billion for the year 2004/5. The cost of incarcerating a Federal prisoner (2004/5): $259.05 per prisoner per day ($94,553 per prisoner per year). The cost of incarcerating a federal female prisoner (2004/5): $150,000 - $250,000 per prisoner per year. The cost of incarcerating a federal male prisoner (2004/5): $87,665 per prisoner per year. The cost of incarcerating a provincial prisoner (2004/5): $141.78: per prisoner per day ($51,749 per prisoner per year). The cost of alternatives such as probation, bail supervision and community supervision range from $5 - $25 per day.

Other than the crime rate statistics, there is virtually nothing relating the costs of the justice system to the benefits derived from those costs. In the absence of such analyses, the provision of security to the people of the nation by way of the justice system itself will remain seriously impaired. Is the title "The Unknown Costs of Justice in Canada" inappropriate?

Commentary

The organization of the court system in Canada provides ample recourse by the public. That system includes courts at provincial and territorial levels, superior and appeal courts in those jurisdictions, federal courts, special federal courts for the military and tax matters, and the Supreme Court of Canada. Trial by jury is usually an option for most criminal matters and some civil matters although rarely used for the latter. The Territory of Nunavut operates in a slightly different manner due to its large geographical area and sparse population. Superior and territorial courts are combined, and the court travels by circuit to the locations in question, both on a regular basis or as required by circumstance. Translators and a defense attorney may travel with the court on occasion.

Canada possesses many well qualified law enforcement agencies, from municipal forces, to provincial forces, to the federal RCMP forces, as well as the military police forces. Canada's justice system is likely one of the best in the developed western democracies, and those are likely far superior to almost all other countries of the world. The list of past egregious cases may seem rather lengthy to the reader, but is likely far less than other countries of the world. Some of those cases occurred at a time when modern technologies such as DNA testing, accessible data bases, and other techniques and facilities were not available to law enforcement agencies. The science of investigative techniques currently is far advanced from those earlier days. This would indicate that some older cases might warrant review, which has already begun in some jurisdictions, with the result that some "cold cases" have been resolved. It would appear that more emphasis on criminology would be appropriate for many of the staff involved in law enforcement. There is much room for improvement.

As for sentencing, there are obvious disparities that demand redress at all levels and in all jurisdictions. The contrasts between crimes of violence, white collar financial crimes which destroy the lives of hundreds of people, and other petty crimes and civil matters does not seem to accord with the expectations of the majority of honest and hard working members of the public. There are simply too many disparities in sentencing, with bias on one basis or another, unwarranted leniency on one hand, and excessive zeal on the other. A thorough review of national consistency in sentencing, and public expectations is needed to remove the threats of improper conviction and sentencing.

Finally, there is the almost complete absence of the costs and benefits of the legal system. This should be provided on a regular basis to the public in a clear and understandable manner. Lack of disclosure is common with government programs, but the justice system is no more immune to improvement than other activities and operations of all levels of government.

Suggestions and Proposals

The federal government should undertake a substantial review of many of its laws and court procedures to determine, the relevance, efficacy, costs, and overall benefit to the people. Simplification and uniformity of the entire system would be a desirable goal. Such a review might include consultation with appropriate organizations representative of public opinion.

A review and updating of The RCMP Act of 1985 is clearly needed to bring the investigative and enforcement powers of the federal government to current standards and expectations.

The federal government should work in conjunction with those provincial governments which do not use the services of the RCMP to review and update their policing capabilities, standards, and enforcement powers to the same or similar standards.

Chapter 3 - Security of the Economy

Banks and Financial Services

(Bibliography: Security of the Economy - Canada's Banks)

The Bank of Canada

The Bank of Canada Act received royal assent on 3 July 1934, and in March 1935 the Bank of Canada opened its doors as a privately owned institution, with shares sold to the public. The first Governor of the Bank of Canada was Graham Towers, a thirty-seven year old Canadian who had extensive experience with the Royal Bank of Canada both in Canada and abroad. He had appeared before the Macmillan Commission on behalf of the chartered banks. He would guide the Bank for twenty years.

Soon after the Bank opened, a new government introduced an amendment to the Bank of Canada Act to nationalize the institution. In 1938, the Bank became publicly owned and remains that way today. The organization of the Bank integrated new functions with functions that already existed elsewhere. Bank note operations were transferred from the Department of Finance when the Bank opened, and the offices of the Receiver General across the country became the agencies of the Bank.

A new Research Division was established to provide information and advice on financial developments and on general business conditions at home and abroad. The Foreign Exchange Division and the Securities Division became operative almost immediately, though the transfer of the Public Debt Division from the Department of Finance was delayed until suitable quarters were available. This did not occur until 1938, following completion of the present Bank of Canada building at 234 Wellington Street, Ottawa. The same building, to which new structures have been added, houses the Bank of Canada today. The Bank of Canada Act, which defines the Bank's functions, has been amended many times since 1934. But the preamble to the Act has not changed. The Bank still exists "to regulate credit and currency in the best interests of the economic life of the nation."

The Bank is not a government department and conducts its activities with considerable independence compared with most other federal institutions. For example:

- The Governor and Senior Deputy Governor are appointed by the Bank's Board of Directors (with the approval of Cabinet), not by the federal government.
- The Deputy Minister of Finance sits on the Board of Directors but has no vote.
- The Bank submits its expenditures to its Board of Directors. Federal government departments submit theirs to the Treasury Board.
- Bank employees are regulated by the Bank, not by federal public service agencies.
- The Bank's books are audited by external auditors appointed by Cabinet on the recommendation of the Minister of Finance, not by the Auditor General of Canada.

Canadian Commercial Banks

Canada has a stable and very well developed banking system and Canadian banks play an important role in Canadian economy and society. Canadian banks are amongst the top Canadian employers, employing over 200,000 people. The banks are among the top tax payers too. Canadian Banks have created a widespread financial network consisting of over 8,000 bank branches and over 18,000 ABMs (automated banking machines). Canadian banks offer many electronic services like online banking as well as credit and debit cards.

The "Big Five" Canadian banks are Royal Bank of Canada, Toronto Dominion Bank, Bank of Nova Scotia, Canadian Imperial Bank of Commerce, and Bank of Montreal. The Big Five Canadian banks, and the National Bank operating primarily in Quebec, are frequently called the "Big Six Banks" and account for 90% of the assets of the Canadian banking business. The "Big Five" Canadian Banks have significant presence outside of Canada most notably in United States, Latin America, the Caribbean region and Asia. The Big Five banks are full service banks providing brokerage, trust, and insurance services in addition to banking. In addition to the above large banks, there are some 21 domestic bank (schedule I banks) some 25 subsidiaries of foreign banks (schedule II banks), some 23 foreign banks with branches in Canada (schedule III banks), as well as numerous credit unions, and caisses populaires.

Under the Investment Canada Act, the acquisition of any financial service, bank, brokerage, trust, etc in Canada is prohibited. During the recent recession of 2008-2009, the Canadian banking system survived the difficulties of that period with little effort. The Canadian banks, their subsidiaries, and branches were acknowledged by the G7 and the whole world as having the strength and capacity to be the best banking system in the world.

Canadian Brokerages & Stock Exchanges

Canada has 13 different jurisdictions for the issue and trading of corporate shares. The federal government is attempting to consolidate and oversee the management of a single stock exchange in Canada, but has encountered resistance from provincial governments to date. The issue should be resolved in the near future. Until then, Canadians are more vulnerable than necessary to a variety of scams and Ponzi schemes. The large banks and brokerages are reliable, but there is inadequate oversight of smaller businesses in the financial industry.

Corporations and Industries

(Bibliography: Security of the Economy - Corporations & Investment Canada)

Corporate Acquisitions by Foreign Parties

The government recognized the benefits that flow from international direct investment and introduced the Investment Canada Act in 1985. The legislation reflects Canada's policy of welcoming international investment, and indeed of attracting quality investment to all regions of Canada. For assurance that benefits accrue to Canada at the individual transaction level, the Act contains provisions for the notification and review of acquisitions of the control of significant Canadian businesses by international investors. The Act also authorizes the notification and review of new business enterprises in the cultural industries.

Literally thousands of foreign acquisitions had been approved since 1985, when Prime Minister Brian Mulroney declared Canada "open for business." Among the lost companies were such Canadian icons as Falconbridge, Inco, Domtar, Algoma Steel, Hudson's Bay Company, Stelco, Fairmont Hotels, Four Seasons Hotels, Molson's, Labatt's, and the Montreal Canadiens.

Canada is blessed with some of the best corporations and industries in the world, many of which are world leaders in their fields. Examples of these are Bombardier, Cameco, Potash of Saskatchewan, Encana, SNC Lavalin, Bell Canada Enterprises, CN Rail, Research in Motion, and many others. The Canadian corporations are all traded on various stock exchanges in Canada, and often on a few foreign exchanges as well. Mergers and acquisitions of other Canadian corporations is as common as one would expect in a free market economy, often by other Canadian corporations, and occasionally by foreign corporations as well.

In 2007, Prime Minister Steven Harper convened a Competition Policy Review Panel composed of prominent business leaders to review both the Competition Act and the Investment Canada Act. It was hoped that the panel would recommend conditions to better protect companies and industries from unwanted and opportunistic attacks by foreign corporations. To the regret of many people, the panel's report at the end of June 2008 called for the government of Canada to make it even easier for Canadian companies to be taken over. The report also advocated that Canadian banks be allowed to merge, and be made available for takeover by foreign banks, The Minister of Industry received it without comment, and the likelihood of the minority Harper government taking it seriously appears slight.

The report seemed badly behind the times to advocate an intensification of globalization and foreign ownership as practised by the multinational corporation at a time of global financial chaos. The panel admitted that Canadian business generally is insufficiently innovative. Canada has learned over the years that foreign ownership in this country is not without its costs. Historically, Canada has often been an inefficient branch plant economy protected by the tariffs. Under the last conservative government, many tariffs were eliminated in the expectation that Canadian firms would become efficient. That hasn't happened, which raises the possibility that foreign ownership itself is the problem.

Today, foreign ownership has been accused of hollowing out the corporations of Canada, with the concomitant loss of head offices and employment. However, it must be noted that Canadian investment abroad has risen significantly in past decades. Canada seems committed in the long run to free markets and trade to serve the country best, albeit with some concerns for the protection of some industries.

Corporate Acquisitions Excluded from Foreign Parties

(Bibliography: Security of the Economy - Corporations & Investment Canada)

An investment is subject to review if there is an acquisition of a Canadian business and the asset value of the Canadian business being acquired equals or exceeds the following thresholds (the following is abridged):

a. For non-WTO (World Trade Organization) investors, the threshold varies from $5 - 50 million depending primarily on whether the investment is direct or indirect.

b. Except as specified in paragraph c. below, a threshold is calculated annually for direct acquisitions subject to review. The threshold for 2009 is $312 million.

c. The limits set out in paragraph a. apply to all investors for acquisitions of a Canadian business that:
   i. produces or owns an interest in a producing uranium property in Canada;
   ii. provides any financial service;
   iii. provides any transportation service; or
   iv. is a cultural business.

2. Notwithstanding the above, any investment may be reviewed if an Order in Council directing a review is made and a notice is sent to the Investor.

The direct acquisition of a Canadian business which provides transportation services is subject to review where the value of the business acquired is $5 million or more; and the indirect acquisition of such a business is subject to review where the value is $50 million or more. Transportation services are defined in section 2.2 of the Regulations to include a Canadian business directly or indirectly engaged in the carriage of passengers or goods from one place to another by any means including air, rail, water, land, and pipeline.

The oil and gas industry makes extensive use of pipelines which are a form of transportation service. Where the transportation service provided by a pipeline is an incidental portion of a business other than a transportation service, the Investment Review Division may deem the business not to be a transportation service.

Investment Canada Act & Amendments

(Bibliography: Security of the Economy - Corporations & Investment Canada)

On March 13, 2009, Bill C-10 introduced significant changes to the Investment Canada Act, summarized as follows. The threshold for review of direct acquisitions of Canadian businesses was changed to levels determined by the federal Cabinet. These transactions were now subject to review if the value of the Canadian business exceeded $312 million, but will be subject to review only if the "enterprise value" exceeds limits from $600 million to $1 billion. This threshold will be adjusted annually. In addition, the lower threshold of $5 million formerly applicable to the transportation, financial services, and the uranium sectors was repealed. There is a new review process for investments that could be *"injurious to national security"*. The federal Cabinet is authorized to take any measures it considers advisable to protect national security, including the outright prohibition of a foreign investment in Canada.

Government Spending & Regulatory Excesses

Corporate and Regional Subsidies - Taxes & Grants

(Bibliography: Security of the Economy - Corporate & Regional Subsidies)

In the above references in the Bibliography, Terence Corcoran has compiled an excellent review, named The Chopping Block, to suggest possible reductions in government spending (waste). As Mr. Corcoran states, *" There are hundreds of corporate welfare items in Ottawa, too many to list or even count. Programs are buried within programs with grants and loans vying with tax credits and direct subsidies to relieve Canada's capitalists of risk and transfer it over to taxpayers. Many of these could be cut without the least disturbance to Canada's economic performance. More likely, Canadians would benefit if the distortions caused by these tax and spending programs were removed from the market."*

Over the past 50 years, federal and provincial governments have grown as inevitably as any common cancer. Jointly, these levels of government consume some 40%+ of the tax payers hard earned income. Canada has lost its way from those early days when governments took only some 20% of our earning, to the socialist state under which we are now burdened.

The nation must return to its early traditions of greater independence and self-reliance, and cease its incessant demands for the government to wipe its nose every time it sneezes. Free markets well regulated, competition, and personal initiative in all walks of life will make for a better, stronger nation when the need arises. Better to teach a man to fish, than to give him a fish. There are those few who are challenged by nature in one way or another, and care must be provided to those people. But the majority of the nation's people are quite able to make their own way in life, and should not be so burdened with government taxes and wasteful spending that they become unable to create a satisfactory lifestyle for themselves.

The following table from the National Post series by Terence Corcoran is reproduced here, as an excellent example of possible reductions in government spending. The series of article was published under the title of "The Chopping Block".

The Chopping Block

This table is the final tabulation of federal spending cuts proposed by *FP Comments* four week feature article, "The Chopping Block". The objective was to find $20 billion in federal spending to balance the budget by 2013 or sooner. Terence Corcoran

On the Chopping Block	Savings 2010-11	Savings 2011-12	Savings 2012-13	Savings 2013-14	Four Year Total
Southern Ontario Development Agency	$300M	$200M	$200M	$200M	$900M
Agriculture Canada	$1B	$1B	$1B	$1B	$4B
Fed Transfers to Provinces	$2.6B	$5.3B	$8.9B	$8.9B	$25.7B
Public Transit Tax Credit	$130M	$140M	$140M	$150M	$560M
First Time Home Tax Credit	$200M	$200M	$200M	$200M	$800M
Fed Carbon Capture Program	$250M	$250M	$250M	$250M	$1B
Labour Venture Capital Funds	$120M	$120M	$120M	$120M	$480M
Flow-Through Shares	$255M	$255M	$255M	$255M	$1.02M
Film/Video etc Tax Credit Production & Services	$300M	$300M	$300M	$300M	$1.2B
Scientific Research & Experimental Development Investment Tax Credit	$1.6B	$1.6B	$1.6B	$1.6B	$6.4B
Atlantic Investment Tax Credit Atlantic Opportunities Agency Western Eco Diversification	$850M	$850M	$850M	$850M	$3.4B
Canada Health Infoway	$500M		$500M	$500M	$1.5B
Federal Civil Service Employment & Wages	$1B	$2.2B	$2.8B	$3.4B	$9.4B
Equalization & Cost Sharing of Public Service Pension Plans 50% Employer/50% Employee	$177M	$363M	$555M	$850M	$1.95B
Military Spending	$500M	$966M	$1.4B	$1.5B	$4.33N
Chopping Block Initial Total	$9.8B	$13.74B	$19.03B	$20.1B	$62.64B
Fed Deficit Projection Sept 09	-$45.3B	-$27.4B	-$19.4B	-$11.2B	-$103.3B
Chopping Block Revision	-$35.3B	-$13.59B	-$322M	-$8.85B	-$40.54B

Venture Capital Regulatory Excess

(Bibliography: Security of the Economy - Venture Capital Regulatory Excess)

The article, written by Stephen A. Hurwitz in the National Post, is but one example of the heavy hand of a former government imposed upon the economy. Fortunately it is a short story of one instance where the current minority government can offer relief. This is a success story which involves a few common sense concepts: reduce the intrusion of government in the economy, encourage foreign investment in the nation, reduce the number of employees and the size of the government, spend very little money to accomplish the project, and provide relief and benefit to business and the people. To quote Cicero again, "The peoples' good is the highest law." If doctors follow the Hippocratic Oath for moral guidance, perhaps politicians should follow an "Oath of Cicero".

In a tax "master stroke", the Canadian government has just announced proposed legislation in its 2010 budget that would remove the "Section 116" barrier to the flow of international investment capital to Canadian technology companies. The new legislation will remove formidable administrative and economic burdens that have hampered the flow of potentially hundreds of millions of dollars in capital that is critically needed by Canadian technology companies. This change could alter the future of Canadian innovation and productivity.

In the past, Section 116 had required international investors, the vast majority of whom were already exempt from federal taxes on the sale of Canadian investments under Canada's broad network of tax treaties, to go through burdensome administrative hurdles before funds could freely flow to them. Documentation was required for every investor in a foreign venture capital fund, and many funds have hundreds of investors. A single sale could involve preparing and filing hundreds of pages of documents and signatures, including tax returns, even though invariably no taxes were due. This process often translated into months of delay, significant costs, and sometimes major financial loss for the international investor.

It's important to remember that the Section 116 problem was not one of the Harper government's making. It was inherited from previous governments. The current Canadian government deserves high praise for taking this unprecedented action to fix it.

The Federal Debt & GDP 2009

(Bibliography: Security of the Economy - The Federal Debt & GDP)

As pointed out by Livio Di Matteo in the reference above, Canada enjoyed splendid growth from 1961 to 1973. However the period after 1973 was a time of deficits which eventually amounted to a total debt of $563 billion by 1996. Canada is on the brink of repeating the deficit turmoil of 1973 - 1996 unless the government takes steps to avoid repetitive deficits. The speech from the throne has promised there will be no tax increases. That leaves two other deficit avoidance measures: the reduction of spending or the sale of Crown assets. There are many programs of government that may be curtailed or even cancelled entirely, which would slowly lead to a reduction of the deficit and the debt. Terence Corcoran provides an excellent list in The Chopping Block (with the possible exception of the military) of federal programs that warrant reduction or cancellation. There are also many Crown corporations, commissions, and agencies that the government might privatize or disband, a practice which has been done quite successfully in the past. The latter would be a much quicker approach to reduction of the deficit, and also the overall size and scope of the federal government.

Security of Public & Private Infrastructure

The bridges, buildings, subways, generating stations especially nuclear, transmission grids, pipelines, water reservoirs and supply systems, and sea and air ports in or near our major cities are some of the core elements of the nation's economy (some of the others are natural resources, cities, business corporations, educational institutions, churches, and the people). As such, these facilities are crucial to the people in their every day activities of living and working in the country, the cities and the towns. These facilities are vulnerable to the forces of nature, and are the potential sites of natural disasters such as earthquakes, sink holes, floods, ice storms, fires, gas leaks and other disasters. These same facilities are also potential targets for terrorist attacks to disrupt the economy. To ensure the smooth and continued operation of the economy and avoid natural or man made disasters, the security of these facilities by disaster response organizations and mechanisms is of paramount importance.

Retirement Savings of Canadians

(Bibliography: Security of the Economy - Pension Security)
(Bibliography: Security of the Economy - Retirement Lost)

Generally speaking, Canadians have access to an excellent financial services industry to administer investments for their retirement. The Registered Retirement Savings Plan (RRSP) and Registered Retirement Income Fund (RRIF) were introduced in 1978 as a better vehicle than surrendering legal title to the capital of one's savings to an insurance company for an annuity, and have proven useful to virtually all Canadians. Monies invested in such plans were not taxable while growing within the plan, but were taxable as income only on the amounts withdrawn each year, usually after retirement. Pensions were made portable to a Life Income Fund (LIF or RLIF) some 20 years ago, although strict limits were placed on the maximum amount that could be withdrawn each year. All monies which were withdrawn annually were taxable. Many people took advantage of the transfer arrangements to acquire legal title to the capital contributed to their former pension systems, despite the maximum withdrawal limit imposed by the governments. This may have been suggested by the pension industry to prevent persons from withdrawing excessive amounts, squandering the monies foolishly, and then becoming a ward of the state.

However after the major recession in the markets caused by the failure of the world's banking system that occurred in 2008, many peoples' investment assets in their LIFs were reduced to such low values that they needed the maximum withdrawal simply for living expenses in their retirement. They were then in the ridiculous position of not being permitted to withdraw additional monies to pay the taxes on the maximum withdrawals. The arbitrary limits were the problem, and the government was forced to quickly change the laws on the LIFs to permit a once in a lifetime transfer of 50% of the assets to ordinary RRIFs which had no maximum limits. This was done simply to allow the retired persons to access more of their wealth to pay the taxes due on the annual withdrawal for their living expenses in the first place.

Even people with RRIFs found that they were forced to withdraw many more shares of their investment stocks than they normally would have, due to the very low valuations of the shares under the recession. The additional monies withdrawn to pay the taxes on the normal annual RRIF withdrawals for living expenses usually placed the person in higher tax brackets. More taxable monies were then withdrawn just to pay the taxes on the withdrawals in a vicious circle. It was said that the monies in RRIFs were only 50 cent dollars due to the high taxes.

Existing pension plans were found greatly lacking during the recession of 2008. Under pension regulations, companies were not allowed to "stash" excessive amounts of money into their pension plans to avoid taxation. The result was that in hard times and lowered values of the assets in those pension plans, the plans were technically incapable of meeting their liabilities to pay full pensions as required under the pension contracts. The result was that many pensions in pay suffered devastating reductions (eg 30%+) for the retired employees.

In 2009, the federal government introduced Tax Free Savings Accounts (TFSAs) whereby contributions to the accounts received no rebate. However, the investment gains were not taxable while in the account, nor were the monies taxable when withdrawn from the account. Thus, the later withdrawals for retirement would be 100 cent dollars. The TFSAs were thus the most beneficial retirement investment vehicles for Canadians, *(and followed Cicero's maxim that, "The peoples' good is the highest law")*.

Disaster Response Services

(Bibliography: Security of the Economy - The Department of Public Safety Canada)

(Bibliography: Security of the Economy - Institute for Catastrophic Loss Reduction)

Since the inception of emergency preparedness training in Canada in the 1950s within the context of civil defence, the training has evolved with changing world conditions, modified government priorities and shifting strategic directions. Consultation and cooperation between federal, provincial and territorial governments has formed the establishment and direction of training programs. As with the previous embodiments of the College, the programs of the Canadian Emergency Management College continue to evolve to address the emergency management needs in Canada.

The history of the federal response to the emergency management of crises started in the 1950s, and has progressed through many different names and organizations.

1951-1954: Federal Civil Defence Staff College / Ottawa.
1954-1972: Canadian Civil Defence College / Arnprior.
1972-1985: Canadian Emergency Measures College / Arnprior.
1985-2003: Canadian Emergency Preparedness College / Arnprior.
2003-2006: Canadian Emergency Preparedness College / Ottawa.
2006: renamed the Canadian Emergency Management College / Ottawa.

Emergency services personnel respond and react to emergencies on a daily basis. While the emergency may be a crisis to those involved, responders are trained to deal with these situations as part of their "normal" daily functions. When emergencies escalate to disaster level, however, the response effort and the systems that guide them are also affected. Disasters are situations which are anything but normal: floods, tsunamis, forest fires, avalanches, mud slides, earthquakes, tornados, blizzards, train or traffic crashes, or even shipping collisions, aircraft crashes, terrorist attacks, or other situations. Regardless of their level of emergency preparedness, response agencies are likely to be caught off guard by the occurrence of the event or its consequences. Their response to these disasters is different from their daily operations. It demands unique roles, rarely applied procedures, specialized skills, rare and unusual resources, or additional powers.

By their definition, disasters are events of such magnitude that the response to them is often beyond the realm of a single organization. Disaster response therefore, often involves a multi-organizational and multi-jurisdictional effort. At the municipal level, it nearly always involves a broad range of response agencies including other orders of government, industry resources, and community based organizations.

Disaster response in Canada is the responsibility of elected officials at municipal level. They are mandated by law (Emergency Preparedness Canada Act, 1992) to prepare for and respond to disasters, which might affect their public. Within that broad jurisdiction are elements of various other jurisdictions: fire, police, emergency medical services, health officials, dangerous materials specialists, members of local industry and public officials from provincial and federal government departments. However, the ultimate responsibility for disaster response lies with elected officials, not the Fire Chief, emergency services personnel (EMS) or the Police Chief as many assume. The rare exceptions to the rule are disasters with broad geographical impact, or those events which affect areas under provincial or federal jurisdiction.

The multi-organizational and jurisdictional nature of disaster response demands cooperation among its response agencies and the coordination of their activities at the scene. Failure to achieve these two key requirements typically results in breakdown of communications, failure to effectively allocate scarce resources, disjointed operational tasking, and the inability by any single organization to effectively meet its response objective.

Hospitals and Health Services

There has been much debate and heated argument about health care in Canada, and in other countries as well. The subject is an all consuming passion with many people, and a major expense for governments. There are those who argue that a single government system such as that in Canada is the sole answer. Yet there are those (including Danny Williams, Premier of Newfoundland and Labrador) who contend that the individual must have free choice between government services and private services. Free choice should be the correct answer to that question. Quoting Cicero . . . *"The peoples' good is the highest law."* And that *"good"* is freedom of choice. All else is the self interest of other third parties, (other than the patient), who are presuming to making decisions better made by the patient.

The competition between public and private health care is certain to bring about overdue change. And change is something that unsettles the mind of politicians and civil servants. But the people would benefit from medical innovation in procedures, wait times, and the efficacy of the service provided, be it either from the public or private systems.

The adoption of the Twin TFSA savings system advocated in "Canada in Crisis (1) - An Agenda to Unify the Nation" could do much to reduce the patient load in hospitals, especially those in emergency wards caused by people with insignificant health problems. The choice of individuals to use their own monies from their personal restricted TFSA (restricted to health and unemployment insurance, and retirement income) for future income rather than for minor or spurious health claims should cause a reduction in nuisance cases and patient load.

A novel innovation under study in a very few hospitals in Canada has been brought about by a change in the budget process. Now, this may seem strange, but it is amazing the changes that can be introduced by a change in the incentives of payment. Hospitals currently are financed through annual budgets presented by hospital staff, and given approval and funding by an agency of government. The hospital then expends those funds over the next year as its administrators see fit to allocate. There is little incentive for change in medical processes or procedures, creating a rather stagnant environment.

The alternative under study first establishes the unit costs, (based on both quantitative and qualitative measures of performance), of a range of services provided by a particular hospital. That hospital is then paid those prices according to the number of those services which it renders during the next year. In effect, the hospital is weaned from the fixed budget and fixed salary process, to the variable process of piece work. Very much like the teenager picking strawberries on his first job, who was paid a fixed price for each box, and the more boxes he picked, the more he was paid . . . he was not paid a guaranteed salary regardless of how many, or how few boxes of strawberries he picked. Over a few years, the hospital will find ways to reduce the time and cost so as to increase the volume of cases that it can handle. The initial findings appear to favour the piece work system, as wait times were markedly reduced. Much more needs to be done to ensure the quality of care and other factors. It is a good beginning.

As for the patient, the longer he lives, the more complicated becomes the issue of his past medical history. Attempts have been made to convert to electronic records, with rather dismal success to date. But if financial companies can do it, so too can medical facilities. Perhaps they need to empower more business management staff at top levels, rather than doctors.

Commentary

The banks and banking system in Canada have proven their merit, and are perhaps the best in the world for financial prudence, strength, and stability against economic challenges. Furthermore, the acquisition of any financial institutions by foreign persons or corporations is prohibited, so there appear to be no foreign threats either real or potential for the banking system. However, the continued domestic threats of Ponzi schemes and similar criminal financial activity affecting the lives of hundreds or thousands of people is devastating and intolerable in a country such as Canada, and warrant heightened surveillance and more severe punishment by justice and law enforcement agencies for the security of the nation's people.

Almost all corporations in Canada may be acquired by competitive and open market processes under corporate law. There are exceptions however. It is doubtful any level of government in Canada would permit the acquisition of a government corporation by a foreign person or power. Examples of such corporations might be the federal Export Development Corporation, the Ontario Lottery and Gaming Corporation, or the municipal Ottawa Hydro Corporation.

Beyond those government corporations, there are entire sectors of the economy that are also excluded on grounds of national security. These industrial sectors are financial services, transportation (including certain types of pipelines), communications, cultural activities, and the mining and processing of uranium. Wise and prudent proposals have also been made from time to time for the general exclusion of resources, energy, and power from foreign acquisition. With the exception of these latter categories, Canadian corporations which are crucial to the economy appear to be reasonably protected from any potential threats of foreign acquisition. The exclusions of energy, power, and some resources do seem to be reasonable and prudent additions to the list of sectors crucial to national security.

The familiar financial savings systems of pensions and annuities were found inadequate for many Canadians during the recession of 2008. Because pensions and annuities deprive the people of legal title to the capital and leave them with inadequate incomes, they are a mugs' game. RRSPs and RRIFs are better because they provide legal title to the monies. However, the modest tax deductions for initial contributions, followed by higher taxation on the much greater assets and annual withdrawals in retirement are an excessively heavy burden. The new TFSAs have removed the onerous taxation of the RRSP and RRIF savings schemes. As the TFSA retirement accounts were introduced in 2009, they are of benefit mainly to younger people who will not retire for another 20 - 30 years or more.

The Twin TFSAs savings and retirement accounts proposed in "Canada in Crisis (1) - An Agenda to Unify the Nation" would serve Canadians much better, as clearly demonstrated in the book. The book contains two mathematical models, in which John Galt and his wife were both assumed to have died shortly after his retirement, (to simplify the models and include estate taxes). Both retirement savings systems (Twin TFSAs and pensions) assumed they had identical income streams during John's 30 year working career. Under the proposed Twin TFSA system, they left estates (and legal title to that capital of $907,517) 3.9 times larger, and potential income from that capital ($113,400) 2.99 times larger, than under a pension regime ($231,403 capital, $37.940 income). This was a "best case scenario" where John had been in good health and fully employed during his career, and had not needed to draw health or employment income from his primary TFSA, leaving more funds for his retirement. Clearly, a Twin TFSA retirement system reduces the financial threats to them and their beneficiaries.

The difference in taxation between the RRIFs for older people who are already retired, and the TFSAs for younger people who are not yet retired has created a monstrous generational disparity in wealth. The older generation is still being unjustly penalized due to the tax consequences of the very faulty and avaricious old RRIF programs. The continuation of this disparity creates a very real financial threat to the peaceful enjoyment of the retirement plans of the older generations of Canadians. A reduction of 50% on the taxes of withdrawals from RRIFs would be appropriate as a solution. As examples of other favourable tax treatments granted by government, the taxes on capital gains receive a 50% reduction relative to taxes on general income, and there is a 100% exemption for beneficiaries of life insurance policies.

The provision of disaster response services appears to be well founded in Canada in the federal government and most provinces and municipalities. A possible weakness in such situations might arise where assistance is needed across larger regions of the country, such as forest fires or floods raging across provincial boundaries. Fortunately the forest fire protection industry has practised full cooperation in such instances for many years, even across national borders in cooperation and support between the USA and Canada. Within Canada itself, the legislated adoption of a single mandatory information, control, and management system would be prudent for security in the event of truly national emergencies such as natural disasters or terrorist attacks against the nation.

Suggestions and Proposals

Given the devastating impact of frauds and Ponzi schemes upon the lives of hundreds and thousands of people, the federal and provincial governments should take stronger and more severe measures to deter all forms of white collar crimes.

The federal and provincial governments should cooperate to expand the list of economic sectors, such as energy and power and especially the transmission of the latter (eg electrical grids), where foreign acquisitions are prohibited on the grounds of national security.

The excessive growth and intrusion of politics and the government, and the excessive spending which those cause, have combined to constitute a serious threat to the peaceful existence of the people of Canada. The governments at all levels should strive to reduce their portion of the economy as a percentage of GDP from 40%+ to 20% over the next decade.

The federal government should introduce legislation to remove the inequities of the tax consequences of RRIFs compared to TFSAs by reducing the taxes on RRIF withdrawals to 50% of current rates for earned income.

As soon as possible, a single disaster response system should be selected (or created) and implemented by federal and provincial governments across the nation.

Chapter 4 - Security of Transportation

Transportation in Canada

(Bibliography: Security of Transportation - Transportation in Canada)

Canada has a transportation system which includes more than 1,400,000 kilometres (870,000 miles) of roads, 10 major international airports and 300 smaller airports, 72,093 km (44,797 mi) of functioning railway track, and more than 300 commercial ports and harbours that provide access to the Pacific, Atlantic and Arctic oceans as well as the Great Lakes and the Saint Lawrence Seaway. In 2005, the transportation sector of the economy made up 4.2% of Canada's GDP, compared to 3.7% for the mining, oil, and gas extraction industries.

The federal department of Transport Canada oversees and regulates most aspects of transportation within Canadian jurisdiction. Transport Canada is under the direction of the federal government's Minister of Transport. The Transportation Safety Board of Canada is responsible for maintaining transportation safety in Canada by investigating accidents and making safety recommendations. The acquisition by foreign corporations of any component of the transportation sector, including certain types of pipelines, is prohibited by legislation.

The roads and rail lines, the terminals, airports, seaports, and harbours are rarely the cause of natural disasters or the likely target of terrorist attacks as they are considered "hard" targets. Such targets are difficult to damage, and generally can be returned to service in short order. An exception to this was the accidental explosion of a large heavily laden munitions ship in Halifax harbour. The explosion occurred on 6 December 1917 when the city of Halifax, Nova Scotia was devastated by the monstrous detonation of the SS Mont Blanc, a French cargo ship fully laden with wartime explosives. The Mont Blanc accidentally collided with the Norwegian SS Imo in "The Narrows" section of the Halifax Harbour. About 2,000 people were killed by debris, fires, or collapsed buildings and it is estimated that over 9,000 people were injured. This is still the world's largest man made accidental explosion.

The vehicles of transportation themselves and their passengers and cargos are the potential victims of natural or man made disasters. Aircraft explosions or crashes, train crashes, ships collisions with other ships, ice bergs, or rocky shores are far more likely to be the focus of disasters. The prevention or containment of any threats of this nature are essential to the security of the people of Canada.

Transportation by Air

Air Canada is the world's 8th largest passenger airline by fleet size (2008). Air Canada had 34 million customers in 2006 and operated 368 aircraft, including Air Canada Jazz. With the advent of larger aircraft in 2009, the fleet was reduced to 202 aircraft, plus 37 Boeing 787 Dreamliners on order for 2013. WestJet is a low cost carrier formed in 1996 and is the second largest airline with 85 aircraft, plus another 50 on order. It is a rarity in the airline industry as it is a non-union, profit sharing operation. WestJet has made significant gains in domestic market share against Air Canada. In 2000 WestJet held only 7% to Air Canada's 77%, though by 2009 it had risen to 36% against Air Canada's 57%. WestJet plans to be one of the world's top five most profitable international airlines by 2016. CHC Helicopter is the world's largest commercial helicopter operators with 320 aircraft in 2008.

Transportation by Rail

In 2007, Canada had a total of 72,212 km (44,870 mi) of freight and passenger railway. Total revenues of rail services in 2006 were $10.4 billion, of which only 2.8% was from passenger services. The Canadian National and Canadian Pacific Railway are Canada's two major freight railway companies, each having operations throughout North America. In 2007, there were 357 billion tonne-kilometres of freight transported by rail, and 4.3 million passengers travelled 1.44 billion passenger-kilometres, a negligible amount compared to the 491 billion passenger-kilometres by road vehicles.

Transportation by Ship

In 2005, 139.2 million tonnes of cargo were loaded and unloaded at Canadian ports. The Port of Vancouver is the busiest port in Canada, moving 68 million tonnes or 15% of Canada's total in domestic and international shipping in 2003. Transport Canada oversees most of the regulatory functions related to marine registration, safety of large vessel, and port pilotage duties. Many of Canada's port facilities are in the process of being divested from federal responsibility to other agencies or municipalities. The inland waterways comprise 3,000 km (1,900 mi), including the Saint Lawrence Seaway. Transport Canada enforces acts and regulations governing water transportation and safety.

Transportation by Road

There are a total of 1,042,300 kilometres (647,700 miles) of road in Canada, of which 413,600 kms (257,000 mi) are paved, including 17,000 kms (11,000 mi) of expressways. As of 2006, 626,700 kms (389,400 mi) were unpaved. Roads and highways were managed by provincial and municipal authorities until construction of the Alaska Highway, and the Trans-Canada Highway. The Alaska Highway was constructed in 1942 for military purposes during World War II to connect Fort St. John, British Columbia with Fairbanks, Alaska. The transcontinental highway, a joint national and provincial expenditure, was begun in 1949 under the Trans Canada Highway Act in December 10, 1949. The 7,821 km (4,860 mi) two lane highway was completed in 1962 at a total expenditure of $1.4 billion.

According to Wendell Cox in his study "A Canadian Autobahn . . . Creating a World-Class Highway System for the Nation", Canada does not have a comprehensive national freeway system and is the largest developed nation in the world without an intercity system. The United States, Europe and Japan have freeway systems that reach virtually all of their major urban areas. China is developing a freeway system that will eventually equal the length of the world's most extensive existing system which currently is in the United States. Mexico and Brazil have developed substantial freeway systems. In addition, some nations have built some of their roads to freeway standards, which provide superior capacity, speed, and safety compared to conventional roadways.

Freeways have a significant positive impact on national and local economies, principally because saving time improves productivity. Moreover, freeways are safer than conventional roads, because there are no grade crossings. Canada is largely unconnected by freeways or autoroutes. On average, the metropolitan areas are connected to less than a quarter of other metropolitan areas. Two of the nation's six metropolitan areas with more than 1,000,000 people (Calgary and Edmonton) are not connected to any other metropolitan area by freeway, and Vancouver is connected only to Abbotsford. Calgary and Edmonton are also the only major metropolitan areas not connected to the freeway systems of the United States and Mexico. As a result, much of Canada, one of the three North American Free Trade Agreement partners, is not connected to the freeway systems of the United States and Mexico.

The shabby construction of Canadian road and highway networks is a further disgrace. New roads and highways develop cracks and potholes within 2-3 years, with subsequent collateral damage to the tires and suspension systems of all vehicles using those roads. One presumes that Canadian engineers have the capacity to design and construct excellent roads (a few are occasionally found) which will endure even under heavy loads and severe weather conditions. The fault presumably lies with short sighted government bureaucrats and politicians who scrimp on the cost of original and maintenance construction, leaving the extraordinarily high and continual maintenance costs to future politicians, and the long suffering taxpayers. The province of Ontario is an excellent example of such deplorable practice, almost defying tourists from the USA and Europe to dare to drive on its pathetic highways, despite having great scenery and potential for a thriving tourist industry.

Commentary

The personnel of the transportation industries, the airlines, railways, shipping, and trucking are themselves very highly trained to contend with the technical difficulties of natural or man made incidents in their respective industries. These threats may take the form of fires, smoke, collisions, explosions, hazardous materials, and similar related problems. Canada's disaster response agencies are well trained and able to provide additional support to the industry involved in containment of the incidents and avoidance of consequential and corollary damages. The disaster response teams are also well coordinated and capable of providing emergency medical treatment and the safe removal and treatment of the injured victims. There are likely still some refinements which could make their work less arduous. The well managed coordination of these services is essential to minimize the loss of lives.

Rather than the current hodge podge of response standards, surely a single common standard for disaster containment and management would be better across all provinces and territories within the nation. Even better than that would be the adoption of a single common standard by both Canada and the USA. In that way, disaster response teams from either country could move in all directions on either side of the land border between Canada and the USA, rather than merely eastward/ westward within the southern border of Canada, or the northern border of the USA. Disasters do not occur conveniently next to air or sea ports, so that travel by roads to the site is essential and the shortest route should be taken in emergencies whether in Canada or the USA.

There is also a need for good intelligence of potential terrorist attacks, for advance warning where such intelligence is available. The recent incident involving a Northwest Airline aircraft departing Schiphol bound for Detroit and a Yemeni terrorist demonstrated the need for the timely sharing of intelligence information regarding potential terrorist threats with all relevant agencies on both sides of the border. At least man made disasters should be avoided or contained in this manner. Regrettably, advance notice is usually not an option for disasters arising from natural causes, although in some cases that is possible.

The screening of employment applicants should be enhanced to ensure that employees have no prior or subsequent criminal records or connections. Modern high technology biometric identity cards (BIDs) should be used to confirm that all of the staff working at these ports and terminals are legitimate employees. Such procedures would help avoid potential threats and disasters at the airports, sea ports, and rail terminals by persons claiming to be the port or terminal staff working at those sites.

The biometric identity cards (BIDs) should be required and carried at all times for all legal residents in Canada, as proposed in "Canada in Crisis (1) - An Agenda to Unify the Nation". If this were done, the processing of passengers on all modes of transportation would be made much faster and simpler. All Canadians could be easily and quickly checked to confirm that they are who they claim to be. Foreign visitors should be required to show passport and other identification as the situation warrants. Again, with proper intelligence, state of the art "full body scanners", and the use of "no fly" or "no travel" lists, many of the potential threats of man made disasters or terrorist attacks should be avoided. The reduced potential for these threats should provide greater security for most travel and transportation in Canada.

All cargos to be loaded on outward bound aircraft, ships, and trains should be more carefully examined using the latest state of the art equipment (e.g. scanners for radio frequency identification chips contained in products, RFIDs) where the situation is warranted. Inward bound cargos could be checked in a similar manner if there were any suspicion of potential threats by the arrival of these cargos from troubled regions of the world.

Finally, the disaster response teams need easy and quick access to disaster sites. In essence, the existence of modern divided freeways, such as the U.S. interstate highways, the German Autobahn, the French autoroutes, the Italian autostrada, are essential to reduce the consequences of natural or man made disasters and their containment by trained disaster response teams. Such freeways are essential to the security of the people of the nation.

Profiling Travellers & Immigrants

(Bibliography: Security of the People - Profiling Acceptable in Canada & USA)

Authorities don't need to search every passenger for 100 millilitres of hand lotion just because a group of Islamic extremists in Britain planned to use sports drinks and toothpaste to blow up as many as 10 jetliners simultaneously in 2006. They don't need to have every elderly lady take off her shoes to be X-rayed, or to have every rotund Caucasian male remove his belt and hobble through the metal detector with one hand on his waistband. Screening efforts must focus on the groups that contain the most dangerous radicals.

What is needed is profiling of passengers, their behaviour, travel history, sex, ethnicity, travel companion status and outward religious appearance. Men are more likely to be terrorists than women, so men should receive greater scrutiny. Young adults are more likely to be terrorists than the aged. Religious Muslims who've travelled frequently to Yemen, Nigeria, Pakistan, or other places of concern are statistically more likely to be terrorists than nuns and Quakers.

Men travelling alone are more likely to be terrorists than men travelling with their children. No one should be treated as a presumptive terrorist. But only the wilfully blind can ignore the fact that most of the terrorist threat originates with a small subset of the travelling population. The federal government's announcement that it will step up security for flights going from Canada to the United States was a mixed effort. It again focuses on interdicting dangerous objects, which is a hit and miss tactic at best. But for the first time, it does acknowledge that more profiling is necessary.

The federal government will spend $11 million installing full body scanners at airports in Vancouver, Calgary, Edmonton, Winnipeg, Toronto, Montreal, Ottawa and Halifax, the cities from which most U.S. bound Canadian flights originate. To what end, though? U.S. security experts have told several American newspapers that even these naked scanners would not have detected the explosives in Umar Farouk Abdul Mutallab's shorts when he boarded a Detroit bound flight in Amsterdam on Christmas Day. Only thermal imaging scanners could have done that. So once again, federal officials are reacting to terror threats by causing unnecessary inconvenience to the travelling public in a way that does little to heighten security.

On the other hand, transportation Minister John Baird has instructed Canadian airport security screeners to use "passenger behaviour observation" techniques (i.e. profiling). This is not much different from what screeners are doing now, but it is one of the clearest indications yet that Ottawa recognizes that not all passengers are an equal threat to air safety. The federal government needs to go several steps further though. It needs to look beyond mere behaviour and link its screening efforts to the groups in society that contain the most dangerous radicals. Right now, that principle leads us to profiling young Muslim males since nearly all the recent attacks carried out against airliners have come from this group.

One accepts that 99.999% of Muslim males are not a threat to hijack or blow up a plane. But security isn't about the 99.999%. It's about the other 0.001%. There can be no indulgence of political correctness when protecting our airspace. The profiling must match the threat.

Profiling & Targeting Threats

(Bibliography: Security of the People - Muslim Male Extremists Age 17-40)

Since terrorists select only specific targets, governments must select only specific threats. Governments must inspect only those persons or systems which pose threats.

The profiling of persons of concern who might be deemed to pose potential threats (including those with criminal records) may be accomplished in numerous ways, from simple to extreme measures. The following pertain primarily to air transportation and are largely hypothetical methods by which threats might be reduced through focussing on persons or systems of concern. Similar processes could likely be established for other modes of transportation. In the United States, the government has recently published a list of 14 countries, and all airline passengers travelling from or to those countries will be subject to complete inspection of baggage, and personal "pat-downs" (physical body searches) on entry to or exit from America.

Passengers & Aircrews of Concern

All passengers and aircrews of concern could be obliged to pass through rigorous pre-flight inspections with the highest possible levels of identification technology (BIDs). Passengers from Schiphol or Frankfurt landing in Labrador destined for other cities in Canada would then be obliged to take shuttle flights to more central airports such as Halifax or Montreal. The shuttle aircraft would not normally travel to any other destinations. This might take some time and be considered a great nuisance by the passengers. In addition, limits could be imposed on the number of trips per annum by passengers or aircrews of concern.

Baggage & Ground Crews of Concern

The baggage of passengers of concern could be given the most thorough inspection possible, including the opening of that baggage if deemed advisable. Also, the ground crews for baggage handling and maintenance of the airport and airlines (i.e. all those who work in secured areas) could be checked randomly and frequently to identify persons of concern.

Airlines & Flights of Concern

The airlines permitted to fly into Canada from countries and/ or regions of concern could be limited to only a few specific airlines and specific flight crews. These same airlines and flight crews of concern could also be excluded from making any onward flights to other parts of Canada, or between Canada and its neighbour the USA.

Airports & Maintenance Locations of Concern

The number of arrival airports where foreign flights by approved airlines may land could be restricted for example to one on the east coast and one on the west coast of Canada. These airports might be located in remote locations such as Labrador or Vancouver Island. Transportation onwards for the passengers of concern to more central locations such as Halifax and Vancouver might also be restricted, after more detailed inspections, and by certain Canadian shuttle airlines operating solely and specifically as connecting flights. Repeat inspections on arrival at the central airports could also be required.

Similarly, the number of departure ports for airlines and passengers of concern and travelling to Canada might be limited for example to Schiphol and Frankfurt in Europe, and Singapore and Kuala Lumpur in Asia. Of course, this would be quite time consuming and annoying to the passengers and airlines of concern, and would likely lead to a diminution of travel by those persons. This in turn would reduce the overall level of potential threats.

Suggestions and Proposals

The federal and provincial governments should cooperate to create a single, common disaster response procedure. If possible, this should be done in conjunction with the Americans.

Modern biometric identity cards (BIDs) should be mandatory for all employees of corporations in the transportation industries. A similar national biometric identity card should be required of all legal residents of Canada, in addition to other paper documentation. Law enforcement staff should be authorized to demand presentation of the BIDs at random times.

All passengers who are residents of Canada and are boarding outbound aircraft, ships, and trains should be required to produce biometric identity cards BIDs, and to permit confirmation by the transportation staff at entry gates that the passengers themselves are the person represented by the proffered identity cards. Foreign visitors should be required to produce similar identification documentation, and submit to confirmation that they are not on a "no fly" lists of potential miscreants or terrorist suspects.

All passengers arriving from foreign lands should be required to produce biometric identity cards (BIDs) or other suitable identification, and to permit confirmation by transportation staff at entry gates that the passengers are the person represented by the identity cards.

The government should apply strategic security restrictions to limit certain profiled persons, airlines, aircrew, and airports. Passengers of concern for potential threats, or the airlines, their aircrews, and their ports of origin of concern for potential threats may need to be received and treated with special procedures and care at remote locations in Canada.

The cargos of all modes of transportation, both outbound and inbound, should be subject to more stringent identification by state of the art equipment (e.g. RFIDs) where the situation is warranted.

All major cities in the provinces and territories should be linked by divided freeways similar to the German Autobahn, the French autoroutes, and the Italian autostrada to provide rapid access to disaster sites by the disaster response teams.

Chapter 5 - Security of Communications

Communications in Canada

(Bibliography: Security of Communications - Spectrum Policy of Canada)
(Bibliography: Security of Communications - Canada's Wireless Oligopoly)

The Minister of Communications of Canada is a now-defunct cabinet post which existed from 1969 to 1996. Its telecommunication policy functions were transferred to Industry Canada and its cultural role was assumed by the Minister of Canadian Heritage. The post had been established by the Department of Communications Act, and was abolished by the repeal of that Act in 1995. During its existence, the department was authorized to oversee radio, television, and telephone communications, and to supervise the Canadian Radio-television and Telecommunications Commission (CRTC).

Communication Spectrum & Government

The department of Industry Canada oversees several agencies involved in communications.

- Canadian Radio-television and Telecommunications Commission (CRTC)
- Spectrum Management and Telecommunications
- The Communications Research Centre (CRC) Canada
- National broadband plans from around the world

The communication spectrum (also known as radio frequency spectrum) is a unique natural resource (like sunlight) from which all aspects of society benefit. It provides access for Canadians to a range of private, commercial, consumer, defence, national security, scientific and public safety applications. The radio frequency spectrum is a technically finite resource divided into different bands used and leased under auction from the federal government by a variety of communications services including; broadcasting, cellular phones, satellite communications, public safety, and two way radio. It is the only natural resource that can support practical wireless communications in every day situations. The Department recognizes that there are a number of factors; rapidly evolving technology, changing market demands, globalization, and an increased focus on public safety and security, which need to be taken into account in an effective spectrum management program.

The wireless telecommunications sector plays an important role in the Canadian economy, accounting for some 25,000 jobs, $4.1 billion invested in infrastructure, and over $9.5 billion in revenue. In recent years the number of wireless subscribers has increased at a compound annual growth rate exceeding 17% to reach 14.9 million, while revenue has grown at a rate of 14% to reach $9.5 billion.

Over the past 15 years, the federal department of Industry Canada has licensed (under auction) the communication spectrum for Canadian use. The use of this spectrum by the wireless telecommunications industry has had a significant impact on companies that manufacture cell phones and other devices designed to operate on wireless networks. Its use has created many opportunities for innovation by Canadian industry and the public as well.

Effective management of the radio frequency spectrum by the federal government is essential to the future growth of communications in Canada. From phones, to broadcasting, to satellite services, to air traffic control, and to reaching out to remote communities, Canadians expect these services to be available, free of interference, and properly allocated and managed.

The Minister of Industry has the statutory responsibility for Canada's management of the radio frequency spectrum. The spectrum is managed on the Minister's behalf by staff who obtain, plan, and authorize its use.

The staff then use sophisticated equipment and automated systems to ensure that harmful radio signals do not hamper or impede that use by licensed and essential communications services. Without clear channels of the radio spectrum, all communications services would experience difficulty in carrying out their operations. For safety services, the inability to communicate may lead to serious injury including loss of life.

The management program has been crucial to the orderly development of Canada's wireless and broadcasting services. By establishing the proper policy and regulatory environment, the government has assisted a very vibrant wireless sector that is growing at twice the rate of the Canadian economy and significantly contributing to Canadian employment and prosperity.

The management program supports the effective use of the radio frequency spectrum including: securing Canada's access to it; the use of auctions to assign it; the development and implementation of Mutual Recognition Agreements for the approval of radio equipment; the determination of client needs and improved services; and addressing emerging priorities for new applications of technology, client expectations, and government objectives.

The pace of global economic growth in wireless technologies and services imposes increased pressure on the government's management resources and the finite spectrum available to the program. Each year more and more demand for radio frequency spectrum is placed on the program by an expanding client base. In this context, managing the radio frequency spectrum is becoming more complex, driven by continuous improvements in technology that foster the marketing of new communications products and services for industrial and consumer applications that are increasingly dependant on that finite spectrum.

The past decade has witnessed the arrival of a variety of communication services that were unavailable a generation ago. Perhaps the most widely used services for individuals are: telephones, televisions, and computers; cell phones and emails communication. There are many applications for GPS information; location information for lost travellers or hikers, equipment tracking for maintenance, customer service such as taxis, and stolen equipment recovery. Services for such communication are provided by companies in Canada such as Rogers, Bell, Telus, Globalive, Amazon, Cyberus, Hotmail, and Garmin. The difficulty with these services to date has been the lack of signal strength in rural or remote areas of Canada. Although satellites are available in some areas, they can be very expensive for individual use.

Communications Provided by Industry

(Bibliography: Security of Communications - Broadband Internet Access)

Rural Broadband

One of the great challenges of broadband is to provide service to potential customers in areas of low population density, such as farmers, ranchers, and small towns. In cities where the population density is high, it is easier for a service provider to recover equipment costs, but each rural customer may require expensive equipment to get connected. Several rural broadband solutions exist, though each has its own pitfalls and limitations. Some choices are better than others, but are dependent on how proactive the local phone company is about upgrading their rural technology.

Wireless Internet Service Providers (WISPs) are rapidly becoming a popular broadband option for rural areas, although the technology's line of sight requirements hamper connectivity in areas with hilly and heavily forested terrain. In addition, compared to hard wired connectivity, there are security risks (unless robust security protocols are enabled); speeds are significantly slower (2–50 times slower); and the network can be less stable, due to interference from other wireless devices, weather, and line of sight problems.

Cellular Broadband

Cellular phone towers are widespread, and as cellular networks move to third generation (3G) networks they can support fast data. The towers can provide broadband access to the Internet with a cell phone, or with cellular broadband routers the towers can permit several computers to be connected to the Internet using one cellular connection.

Satellite Internet

Satellites in geostationary orbits are able to relay broadband data from the satellite company to each customer. Satellite Internet is usually among the most expensive ways of gaining broadband Internet access, but in rural areas it's only competition may be cellular broadband. However, the costs have been coming down in recent years to the point that satellite service is becoming more competitive with other broadband options.

Broadband satellite Internet also has a high latency (delay) problem due to the signal having to travel to an altitude of 35,786 km (22,236 mi) above sea level (at the equator) out into space to a satellite in geostationary orbit and back to earth again. The signal delay can be as much as 500 to 900 milliseconds, which makes this service unsuitable for many applications requiring real time user input such as multi-player Internet games and first person shooters played over the connection. The functionality of live interactive access to a distant computer may also be subject to the problems caused by high latency. These problems are more than tolerable for basic email access and web browsing and in most cases are barely noticeable. For geostationary satellites in high altitude orbits, there is no technical way to eliminate the latency problem.

Medium Earth Orbit (MEO) and Low Earth Orbit (LEO) satellites however do not have such great delays. The current LEO constellations of Globalstar and Iridium satellites have delays of less than 40 ms round trip. The Globalstar constellation orbits 1,420 km above the earth and Iridium orbits at 670 km altitude. The proposed O3b Networks MEO constellation scheduled for deployment in 2010 will orbit at 8,062 km. The proposed new network is also designed for much higher throughput with links well in excess of 1 Giga bits per second.

Most satellite Internet providers also have a FAP (Fair Access Policy).

Perhaps one of the largest disadvantages of satellite Internet, these FAPs usually throttle a user's throughput to dial up data rates after a certain "invisible wall" is hit (usually around 200 MB a day). This FAP usually lasts for 24 hours after the wall is hit, and a user's throughput is restored to whatever tier they paid for. This makes bandwidth intensive activities nearly impossible to complete in a reasonable amount of time (examples include P2P and newsgroup binary downloading).

Powerline Internet

This is a new service still in its infancy that may eventually permit broadband Internet data to travel on standard high voltage power lines. The system has a number of complex issues, the primary one being that power lines are inherently a very noisy environment. Every time a device turns on or off, it introduces a pop or click into the line. Energy saving devices often introduce noisy harmonics into the line. The system must be designed to deal with these natural signal disruptions and work around them.

Broadband over power lines (BPL), also known as power line communication, has developed faster in Europe than in North America due to a historical difference in power system design philosophies. Nearly all large power grids transmit power over long distance at high voltages to reduce transmission losses, then nearer the customer step down transformers are used to reduce the voltage. Since BPL signals cannot readily pass through transformers, repeaters must be attached to the transformers. It is common practice for small transformers hung from a utility pole to serve a single house. In Europe, it is more common for somewhat larger transformers to serve 10 or 100 houses. For delivering power to customers, this difference in design makes little difference, but it means delivering BPL over the power grid of a typical North American city will require more repeaters than a comparable European city.

The second major issue is signal strength and operating frequency. The system is expected to use frequencies in the 10 to 30 MHz range, which have been used for decades by licensed amateur radio operators, as well as international shortwave broadcasters, and a variety of communications systems (military, aeronautical, etc). Power lines are unshielded and will act as transmitters for the signals they carry, and have the potential to completely wipe out the usefulness of the 10 to 30 MHz range for shortwave communications purposes, as well as compromising the security of its users.

Wireless Internet Service Providers (ISP)

This typically employs the current low cost 802.11 Wi-Fi radio systems to link remote locations over great distances, but can use other higher power radio communications systems as well. Traditionally 802.11 was licensed for omnidirectional service spanning only 100-150 metres (300–500 ft). By focussing the signal to a narrow beam with a Yagi antenna it can operate reliably over a distance of many miles, although the line-of-sight requirements hamper connectivity in areas with hilly and heavily forested terrain. In addition, compared to hard wired connectivity, there are security risks; and the network can be less stable, due to interference from other wireless devices, weather, and line-of-sight problems.

Rural Wireless ISP installations are typically not commercial in nature and are instead a patchwork of systems built up by hobbyists mounting antennas on radio masts and towers, agricultural storage silos, very tall trees, or whatever other tall objects are available. There are currently a number of companies that provide this service.

Foreign Acquisition Prohibition

As noted previously, the acquisition by a foreign person or corporation of any Canadian corporation involved in the communications industry is prohibited by legislation. Thus there are no potential threats to the security of the industry from corporate sources. The potential threats to security arise from criminal activity attempting to interfere with the daily operational transmission of information, or to retrieve information and intelligence stored within the users' database systems. Such interference may be caused by natural means such as weather storms, sun spots etc, or by man made causes of sabotage or other terrorist activities.

Commentary

The finite communication spectrum and the communications industry are well regulated by the federal government in Canada. Despite many rapid changes in technology over the last few decades, there is no doubt that communication facilities in Canada have kept pace with those changes. The point has not yet been reached however, where rapid high speed services are available to all of the people in rural and remote northern regions. With the foreseeable demand for such service in the far north as the Arctic warms and trade routes appear possible, the provision of reliable high speed service will be urgently needed.

There will likely be complications due to interference in polar regions due to the Aurora Borealis or Northern Lights, but these must be overcome. Even in areas south of the Arctic, the need for high speed communications is overdue for commercial demand and essential to provide security services to the people in those regions. The introduction of some level of foreign competition is the industry is commendable, and may well provide the stimulus needed to broaden the geographic availability of better service.

Suggestions and Proposals

The federal government should make every effort possible to rapidly advance the provision of reliable high speed communications in all urban, rural, remote, and Arctic regions of Canada to facilitate commercial and industrial growth, and to ensure the security of the people.

Recent statements in the throne speech permitting increased foreign investment and competition in communication services is a commendable policy by the current government.

Chapter 6 - Security of Energy and Power

Sources of Energy and Power

(Bibliography: Security of Energy and Power - Sources of Energy and Power)

In 2006, the largest source of energy consumption in Canada was oil (32%), followed by hydroelectricity (25%) and natural gas (24%). Both coal (10%) and nuclear (7%) constitute a smaller share of the country's overall energy mix. From 1986-2006, Canada's overall energy mix has remained relatively stable, though hydroelectricity has decreased from 31% to 25%. Recently, there have been much concern or interest in diminishing oil resources, discoveries of vast resources of gas accessible with new technologies, environmental damage from mining energy resources and the generation of power, and other sources of energy from water, wind, solar, and geothermal resources. Fuels are often used to fire boilers and steam turbines.

Fossil Fuels: Coal, Oil, Gas

Energy from Coal

(Bibliography: Security of Energy & Power - Coal Energy in Canada)

Reserves of coal in Canada rank fifth largest in the world (following the former Soviet Union, the US, China and Australia) at approximately 10 billion tonnes, 4% of the world total. This represents more energy than all of the oil and gas in the country combined. The coal industry generates CDN $5 billion annually. Most of Canada's coal mining occurs in the West of the country. British Columbia operates 10 coal mines, Alberta 9, Saskatchewan 3 and New Brunswick one. Nova

Scotia operates several small scale mines. In 2005, Canada produced 67.3 million tonnes of coal and total consumption was 60 million tonnes. Of this 56 million tonnes were used for electricity generation. The remaining 4 million tonnes were used in the steel, concrete and other industries. The largest consumers of coal in Canada are Alberta and Ontario. In 1997, Alberta accounted for 47% of Canada's coal consumption at 26.2 million tonnes, and Ontario accounted for 25% at 13.8 million tonnes. Saskatchewan, Manitoba, Nova Scotia and New Brunswick also use coal to generate electricity to some extent.

Energy from Oil (Bibliography: Security of Energy & Power - Oil Energy & New Discoveries)

The latest estimates put Canada ahead of war torn Iraq, which the EIA estimates holds 112.5 billion barrels and is constrained from raising production for entirely different reasons. The U.S. agency estimates Saudi Arabia's recoverable oil reserves at 264 billion barrels. The EIA projects Canadian oil sands could produce 2.2 million barrels a day by 2025 compared with the current level of about 700,000 barrels a day, which already represents more than a fourth of total Canadian output of 3.1 million barrels a day.

The Canadian Association of Petroleum Producers (CAPP) estimates current projects will raise Alberta oil sands production to 1 million barrels a day this year, and continuing development will raise it further to 1.8 million barrels a day by 2010. Current oil sands projects are economically viable at crude oil prices of $18 - $20 a barrel, though the quality of oil produced can vary if production comes from "in situ" reserves that require drilling assisted by steam injection pressure or from simple mining. CAPP's own estimate of Canada's recoverable oil from oil sands is 315 billion barrels: 20% from mining and 80% from steam assisted drilling.

The U.S. government has said Canada holds the world's second largest oil reserves, taking into account Alberta oil sands previously considered too expensive to develop. The Energy Information Administration (EIA), the statistical wing of the U.S. Department of Energy, has included recent private sector estimates that an additional 175 billion barrels of oil could be recovered from resources known to exist in Western Canada, thanks to inclusion of the oil sands, also known as tar sands, now considered recoverable with existing technology and market conditions. Canada will be producing a lot of oil from the development of these heavy tar sands, but the quality of those reserves differs substantially from the Saudi light oil reserves in terms of cost and ability to bring that oil into production.

Energy from Natural Gas

(Bibliography: Security of Energy & Power - Natural Gas Energy in Canada)

Oil and gas is formed from the remains of tiny marine animals and plants that lived 50 million years ago. Over long periods of time and under immense pressure and temperature, these once living tissues turned into crude oil and natural gas. In Canada, natural gas is now the leading source of heat for homes and businesses. It continues to be adopted by more homebuilders and enterprises each year. High efficiency furnaces, water heaters, clothes dryers, stoves, fireplaces and barbecues also operate on natural gas. Its use (to fire a boiler and steam turbine) to generate electricity is a fast growing application of this fuel.

As the demand for natural gas increases, new supplies will be developed in the Yukon, Northwest Territories and Nunavut. Exploration has already established that large supplies exist in these regions. Large volume production from these frontiers will not be feasible until new pipelines are constructed to move natural gas to southern markets. At 17.1 billion cubic feet (480,000,000 cubic metres) per day in 2006, Canada is the third largest producer of natural gas in the world. Its proven reserves were 58.2 trillion cubic feet (1,650 thousand cubic metres) at the close of that year. A large portion of Canada's gas is exported to the United States; 9.9 billion cubic feet in 2006, (280,000,000 cubic metres) per day.

Energy Sources excluding Fossil Fuels

Water (Bibliography: Security of Energy & Power - Hydro Electric Energy in Canada)

Canada is the world's second largest producer of hydroelectricity in the world (after China), and one of few countries to generate the majority of its electricity from hydroelectricity (59% in 2006). In 2007, Canada produced 368 terawatt-hours (1,000,000,000,000 watt-hours) of electricity using hydroelectric dams, 11% of all the hydroelectricity generated in the world. Some provinces and territories, such as Quebec, Manitoba, Newfoundland & Labrador, and the Yukon, produce over 90% of their electricity in this manner.

Hydro Québec's extensive network of 59 hydroelectric dams have a combined capacity of 34,118 MW (1,000,000 watts), accounting for nearly half of the Canadian total. Hydro power accounts for 92% of the electricity sold by the Quebec utility. Five of Hydro Québec's hydro electric facilities are rated above 2,000 MW: the Manic 5, La Grande 4, La Grande 3, La Grande 2A and Robert Bourassa stations: while 7 others have a capacity over 1,000 MW.

Hudson & James Bay Waters

(Bibliography: Security of Energy & Power - Hudson & James Bay Waters)

The rivers flowing into Hudson Bay and James Bay carry 30 per cent of the total flow of Canada's river systems, or roughly 30,000 cubic metres per second. These two "bays" are the largest bodies of water in the world that seasonally freeze over each winter and become ice free each summer. In the past, many engineers and politicians have regarded these north flowing rivers as "wasting their way to the sea". It is not surprising, therefore, that a prodigious array of hydroelectric projects are in operation, or are planned, to divert or impound this source of renewable energy.

In the late 1960s and 1970s, large scale hydroelectric projects were announced and constructed in northern Quebec (La Grande Phase I) and northern Manitoba (Churchill - Nelson) with smaller projects in northern Ontario (Moose River basin). In the 1980s and early 1990s, other projects were completed (La Grande Phase II) and Limestone (northern Manitoba), and new megaprojects were proposed in Manitoba (Conawapa), Quebec (Great Whale, Nottaway - Rupert - Broadback) and Ontario (Moose, Abitibi, Mattagami).

Neither the utilities (all are provincial Crown corporations) nor the provincial governments have addressed the impacts that hydro electric developments within their jurisdiction may have outside provincial borders. Indeed, the utilities may have no mandate or authority to do so, and certainly provincial governments have little or no authority to apply legislation beyond their borders. The need for new means of co-operation seems obvious.

The waters of Hudson Bay and James Bay fall within exclusive federal jurisdiction and thus are not part of the territory of adjacent provinces or the Northwest territories. All of the islands of Hudson Bay and James Bay are part of the Northwest Territories and are therefore subject to federal jurisdiction as well (in co-operation with the territorial government in Yellowknife and subject to aboriginal claims). There is a federal responsibility to protect the integrity of marine and fresh water ecosystems of the region and to account for the downstream cumulative impacts of provincial projects. Authority to do so exists (e.g., Canada Water Act and the Fisheries Act). The Department of Fisheries and Oceans (DFO) has developed the Arctic Marine Conservation Strategy, although its implementation is in doubt. The federal Department of Environment has recognized the need for a study of cumulative environmental impacts and has consulted with federal departments, provincial, and territorial governments. At present the initiative is clouded by uncertainty

Nuclear Energy - Uranium

(Bibliography: Security of Energy & Power - Nuclear Energy in Canada)
(Bibliography: Security of Energy & Power - Nuclear Energy Demand)
(Bibliography: Security of Energy & Power - Nuclear Energy Supply)
(Bibliography: Security of Energy & Power - Uranium & Investment Canada)

The Investment Canada Act prohibits the acquisition by any foreign person or corporation of any Canadian corporation or business which, "engages in the production of uranium and owns an interest in a producing uranium property in Canada."

Uranium is a relatively common metal, found in rocks and even in seawater. Economic concentrations of it are not uncommon. Its availability to supply world energy needs is great both geologically and because of the technology for its use. Quantities of mineral resources are greater than commonly perceived. The world's known uranium resources increased 15% in two years to 2007 due to increased mineral exploration. Uranium is ubiquitous on the planet Earth. It is a metal approximately as common as tin or zinc, and it is a constituent of most rocks and is found even in granite and the sea. An ore body is, by definition, an occurrence of mineralisation from which the metal is economically recoverable. It is relative to both costs of extraction and market prices. At present neither the oceans nor any granites are ore bodies, but conceivably either could become so if prices were to rise sufficiently.

Measured resources of uranium, the amount known to be economically recoverable from ore bodies, are thus also relative to costs and prices. They are also dependent on the intensity of past exploration effort, and are basically a statement about what is known rather than what is there in the Earth's crust. Changes in costs or prices, or further exploration, may alter measured resource figures markedly. At ten times the current price, seawater might become a potential source of vast amounts of uranium. Thus, any predictions of the future availability of any mineral, including uranium, which are based on current cost and price data and current geological knowledge, are likely to be extremely conservative.

From time to time concerns are raised that the known resources might be insufficient when judged as a multiple of present rate of use. But this is the Limits to Growth fallacy, a major intellectual blunder recycled from the 1970s, which takes no account of the very limited nature of the knowledge we have at any time of what is actually in the Earth's crust. Our knowledge of geology is such that we can be confident that identified resources of metal minerals are a small fraction of what is there.

With those major qualifications the following gives some idea of our present knowledge of uranium resources. The countries of the world having major deposits of low cost uranium are: Australia (23%), Kazakhstan (15%), Russia (10%), South Africa (8%), Canada (8%), and the USA (6%), and Brazil (5%). Current usage is about 65,000 tonnes Uranium per year. Thus the world's present measured resources of uranium are enough to last for over 80 years. This represents a higher level of resources than is normal for most minerals. Further exploration and higher prices will certainly yield further resources as present resources are consumed.

Energy from Wind, Solar, Earth, & Space

(Bibliography: Security of Energy & Power - Wind Energy in Canada)
(Bibliography: Security of Energy & Power - Solar Energy in Canada)
(Bibliography: Security of Energy & Power - Geothermal Energy in Canada)
(Bibliography: Security of Energy & Power - Space Based Solar Power)

As found in every other country, Canada has potential energy from the wind and the sun. These are dependent on the seasons and the weather, but are preferred as they are excellent alternatives to the extraction, transportation, and consumption of fossil or nuclear fuels.

Geothermal power is used in countries along the "Ring of Fire" bordering the Pacific Ocean and its coastlines, such as Hawaii and Japan. Iceland is another excellent example. The heat from the earth's central core of magma may be available as a source of energy in certain locations under which the earth's crust is either thin or broken, as in thermal hot springs or near volcanic activity. While there are difficulties of great variability in the source, some of these sources have been successfully harvested for the "free" energy they can provide. Again, these sources are seen as excellent alternatives to fossil and nuclear fuels.

The Conversion of Energy to Power

Power, Parliament, & the BNA

(Bibliography: Security of Energy & Power - Power, Parliament & the BNA)

Section 91 (2) gives Parliament the power to pass laws related to the "regulation of trade and commerce." In comparison with the U.S. Constitution's approach to trade and commerce, the power given to Parliament is more broadly worded than that given to the U.S. government, but in Canada since Citizen's Insurance Co. v. Parsons in the 1880s it has nevertheless been typically read more narrowly, as some judges have felt that it overlaps with the provincial authority over property and civil rights. Parliament's authority over trade and commerce is said to include its "general" aspects, although this was an ambiguous definition until the 1980s when in General Motors of Canada Ltd. v. City National Leasing, it was ruled that Parliament could regulate trade and commerce if its object was to achieve something a provincial government alone could not achieve.

Power Generation & the BNA

(Bibliography: Security of Energy & Power - Power Generation & the BNA)

Under Section 92 of the BNA, provinces may exclusively make laws respecting electrical energy, and the development, conservation, and management of sites and facilities in the province for the generation and production of electrical energy. The provinces may also make laws in relation to the export from the province to another part of Canada of the production from facilities in the province for the generation of electrical energy. However, such laws may not authorize or provide for discrimination in prices or in supplies exported to another part of Canada. Nothing derogates from the authority of Parliament to enact laws regarding export of the production, prices, or supplies from those facilities and, where such a law of Parliament and a law of a province conflict, the law of Parliament prevails to the extent of the conflict.

Power and its Generation

Almost all conversions of energy to power are accomplished by the use of boilers, (excluding wind and water) and turbines, (excluding solar from both), of which one may describe the latter simply as a form of enclosed fan. Many of the turbine systems are powered by steam which is created and provided from the energy source by means of a boiler. There are however, significant differences among the actual generation and production processes.

The fossil fuels of coal, oil, and natural gas constitute about 76% of the energy sources consumed in Canada in 2006. That energy is transformed into power by the combustion of the source fuel to heat a water boiler to produce steam. The steam in turn is the passed through a turbine to turn a generator to create the electrical power sent to a transmission grid. Methane gases from biomass may also be used to power boilers and turbines.

The energy of water is also transformed to power by a turbine, but in a different manner. First, a suitable watershed and valley must be located in which a dam may be constructed to create a reservoir of the rainfall from the watershed. These are very large structures such as the La Grande Dam above James Bay in Quebec, or the Hoover Dam in the United States. The stored water behind the high dam has enormous static energy which is then transformed into kinetic energy by dropping a great height through penstocks (pipes). That kinetic water energy feeds water turbines below the dam to create electrical power to feed a transmission grid. The water then passes to the outlet of the valley, such as James Bay. The energy of water may also be obtained from turbines installed in low head (small drops of ~eight metres) dams, and more rarely from turbines powered by rivers, tidal waters, or ocean waves.

The energy of uranium or other nuclear fuels (eg thorium) is transformed into power by the heat from a nuclear reactor to create steam in a boiler. The steam is then passed through a steam turbine to turn an generator to supply electric power to a transmission grid or network.

Wind energy is transformed into electrical power by wind turbines mounted on very high towers upwards of 50 metres high. The locations of the wind turbines is very critical to ensure a reasonably steady flow of wind. The electrical power created by the turbines is then transferred to an electrical transmission grid for the region or province.

Solar energy is transformed into electrical power in an entirely different manner. Massive arrays of solar panels are arranged to capture the sunlight, and transform that light into electrical current by using silicon chips, somewhat similar to computer chips. The solar panels may be arranged in rows, usually not over ten feet in height, over large acreages. The fields containing these massive arrays may be hidden from sight by rows of trees on the perimeter. The electrical current created by the solar panels feeds an electrical transmission grid.

Geothermal energy sources are accessed by deep wells sunk into the earth's crust to obtain hot water for boilers. The boilers raise the temperature to provide steam to the steam turbines to generate electrical power to feed a transmission grid.

The heat generally involved in the power generation may also be used for heating buildings and other uses. However, the provision of power from central generating stations is almost invariably accomplished by an electrical transmission grid.

The Transmission of Power to Markets

Power Transmission & the BNA

(Bibliography: Security of Energy & Power - Power Transmission & the BNA)

Like many other powers, transportation and communication have overlapping powers between the two jurisdictions. Section 92 (10) gives the provinces power over "local work and undertakings". However, the section also excludes the provinces from undertakings related to "ships, railways, canals, telegraphs, and other works and undertakings connecting the province with any other or others of the provinces", as well as ship lines, and such works "declared by the Parliament of Canada to be for the general advantage of Canada or for the advantage of two or more provinces".

The Act is quite clear concerning the generation and production of electrical energy, and even the potential for export of that electrical energy. The Act is strangely silent on the means of transmission of that power from the site of its generation and production to any consumer either domestic to the same province, or exported to another province or country.

The point of this reference to energy and power is that the national electrical transmission grids, and the frequent power sharing among provinces, would seem to be in the same category as the exclusions of provincial authority for the various means of transfer of products and services such as ships, railways, canals, and telegraphs. Thus, the federal government may presume to have authority over the management and use of electrical transmission grids, by the generating stations who supply the power to the grids, for the shipment of that electrical power to consumers in other provinces or nations. This would clearly be for the general advantage of Canada or for the advantage of two or more provinces, as well as for national security. And as stated above under Power Generation & the BNA, section 92, "Nothing derogates from the authority of Parliament to enact laws regarding export of the production, prices, or supplies from those facilities and, where such a law of Parliament and a law of a province conflict, the law of Parliament prevails to the extent of the conflict".

Electric Power Transmission Grids

(Bibliography: Security of Energy & Power - Electrical Power Transmission)

Most of Canada's provinces and the territories are part of interconnected electric power plants, transformer substations, and electric transmission grids that cross provincial, territorial, and international borders. These networks provide electric utilities with alternative paths to sources of power in emergencies, or simply to buy and sell power from each other during construction, maintenance or other situations.

Canada's bulk transmission network consists of more than 160,000 kilometres of high voltage lines. This is enough to cross the entire country roughly 27 times. These lines carry electricity at voltages above 50 kilovolts to move electricity in bulk over long distances. Because of Canada's vast geographic size, its electricity systems require different types of high voltage lines (typically at 115 kilovolt, 230 kilovolt and 500 kilovolt levels) to deliver electricity safely, reliably and economically to customers.

Canada has three power grids: the Western grid, the Eastern grid, and the Quebec grid, which includes Atlantic Canada. The border between the Eastern and Western grids is the Alberta Saskatchewan border. Canadian grids are also tied into the U.S. grids (the Western Interconnection, the Eastern Interconnection and the Texas Interconnection). For example, the electricity grid in Alberta and British Columbia is part of the Western Interconnection in the United States.

North - South Grid Pattern

There is a predominantly north-south pattern to Canada's transmission high voltage lines. This has emerged over time as utilities develop generation sites in northern areas of the country to produce and transmit electricity to urban markets in the south. Hydro-Québec's system, for example, extends more than 1,100 kilometres from Churchill Falls in Labrador to Montreal, and from James Bay to southern load centres, which include U.S. markets. In Manitoba, a large 500 kilovolt DC system brings hydro power from the Nelson River to customers in the Winnipeg area. In Ontario and British Columbia, major 500 kilovolt systems bring electric power from northern generating sites to markets in the south.

Restructuring the Grid

Transmission lines in a given area may be owned by a single company or by a number of different companies. Similarly, the generation and the distribution facilities the transmission lines connect can be owned by the same company, or by different companies. In most provinces and territories, vertically integrated, government owned utilities look after the planning, building and operation of transmission as part of their bundled services. Some provinces are undergoing fundamental changes that have restructured their markets and unbundled generation, transmission and distribution services. The pace of change is occurring at different rates across the country. The extent of restructuring varies because regulation of the electricity industry is generally the responsibility of the provinces and territories.

In provinces such as Ontario and Alberta, vertically integrated utilities have been divided into separate generation, transmission and distribution companies. In 1999, Ontario Hydro was split into a number of successor organizations, including Ontario Power Generation and Hydro One. The former manages generation plants, and the latter owns and operates the province's transmission system. This change is most advanced in Alberta, where restructuring started in the mid-1990s, unbundling vertically integrated utilities, opening up transmission access and creating a competitive wholesale electricity market. Today Alberta's transmission facilities have become the properties of separate companies or continue to be owned by the utilities and operated by an independent system operator (ISO). Transmission facilities continue to be regulated by a commission or board in most jurisdictions.

Because of industry restructuring, "open access" has emerged as a way to ensure that owners of transmission lines allow non-discriminatory access to their lines. This is essential to enabling buyers to purchase electricity from the most competitive generation sources. Alberta, Ontario, British Columbia, Saskatchewan, Manitoba and Quebec all offer open access to transmission.

The Canadian Transmission Grids & Power Sharing

Canada, the world's second largest exporter of electricity, is an active participant in North American electricity trade. Most provinces are connected with their nearest U.S. neighbours. This cross-border trade allows generators to operate more efficiently, as they can continue to generate electricity, even when local demand is low. With open markets and shared transmission lines, power can be sold across hundreds of kilometres.

Canada typically exports between six and 10 per cent of its production to the United States. In 2002, Canada exported 36 terawatt-hours of electricity (worth $1.8 billion) to the United States. Exports are sold primarily to the New England states, New York State, the Midwest, and the Pacific Northwest and California. In 2002, Canada imported about 17 terawatt-hours of electricity from U.S. suppliers.

Hydro power systems, which can store water during off peak systems and then release the water for power production during peak periods, are well suited for the export of electricity. As a result, provinces with large hydro systems, such as Quebec, Manitoba and British Columbia, have been the largest exporters of electricity to the United States. The Quebec Hydro Corporation has made a bid for New Brunswick hydro in an effort to find a shorter route to the U.S. for power sales. That sale was initially accepted by the Premier of New Brunswick, but has been rebuffed by the taxpayers before becoming a "fait accompli". The ownership of New Brunswick Power is crucial to the four Atlantic provinces (excluding Quebec), as it acts as a portal from Quebec, the upper and proposed lower Churchhill Falls generating stations in Newfoundland & Labrador, and the three Maritime provinces of New

Brunswick, Nova Scotia, and Prince Edward Island, to the markets of the north eastern United States.

The American Transmission Grids

In the United States, the Federal Energy Regulatory Commission (FERC) has mandated that regional transmission organizations (RTOs) oversee the administration of transmission systems in competitive electricity markets. Given the international nature of the transmission grid, FERC has encouraged Canadian participation and, in some cases, has directed the RTOs to indicate how Canadian transmission entities would be represented.

All provinces are interconnected with neighbouring provinces, allowing them to import and export power. East-west transmission is less common than north-south transmission. To date, most of the inter-provincial exchange of power has occurred in Eastern Canada, with the largest transfers between Quebec and Labrador. Canadian utilities and government leaders are exploring ways to increase east-west electricity flow, especially between Ontario and Manitoba and Ontario and Quebec. The territories are neither interconnected, nor do they have connections with the provinces or the United States.

Churchill Falls Hydro Electricity Generation

(Bibliography: Security of Energy & Power - Churchhill Falls Hydro)

Newfoundland and Labrador has formally requested a new deal with Hydro Quebec to replace the controversial 1969 Churchill Falls power contract. Newfoundland is using provisions of Quebec's unique Civil Code to buttress its long held argument that Quebec has short changed the economically stressed province of Newfoundland and Labrador on the power agreement and intends to persist in the punitive arrangement.

"The gross inequity of this agreement cannot be denied", Premier Danny Williams said in a statement yesterday to the province's House of Assembly. "For example, last year we have estimated that Hydro

Quebec reaped profits from the Upper Churchill Falls contract of approximately $1.7 billion, while Newfoundland and Labrador received a mere $63 million." Mr. Williams said. "Power which is bought from our province for a quarter of a cent per kilowatt hour is then resold by Hydro Quebec for up to 36 times the price they pay for it."

The development of a new Lower Churchhill Falls generating station has been dependent on the prospect of transmitting that power by underwater cable to grid of the New Brunswick Power Corporation, and onward to the markets in the north eastern United States. A proposed sale of the New Brunswick Power Corporation to the Quebec Power Corporation has created a potential nightmare for the prospects of Newfoundland and Labrador.

Commentary

(Bibliography: Security of Energy & Power - New Brunswick Power Sale)

Canada is blessed with bountiful energy resources, and faces no threat for the lack of them. However, the extraction process does entail some damage to the environment and must be considered in any benefit analysis. That is not to say that the provision of energy resources should suffer for some relatively insignificant environmental issue: access to energy must be accorded a much higher priority than a slight degradations of habitat or loss of specie. Excessive reliance on fossil fuels places the environment in double jeopardy arising from both their extraction and their combustion, and conversion to water or other non-fossil energy sources should be a major initiative of all governments.

In general, the decentralization of the generation of power alleviates some aspects of environmental damage caused by transmission grids and towers, as well as an extra margin of safety by not having too many eggs in the same basket. In general, the transition from centralized fossil fuel generation to decentralized generation by water, solar, and geothermal would seem beneficial in the reduction of potential threats by natural or man made causes.

With the exception of the nuclear power, there are few potential threats from natural causes arising from the generation of power. Any potential threats would arise from sabotage or terrorist activities, largely against large centralized facilities such as hydro dams, nuclear generating stations, or other large generating facilities.

The potential threats to transmission facilities, either grids or pipelines, would also be limited to man made activities. Decentralized generation would of course obviate the vulnerability inherent in any transmission system.

Proposed Sale of New Brunswick Power Corp
(Bibliography: Security of Energy & Power - New Brunswick Power Sale)

The last potential threat to consider is that posed by the governance of the energy and power facilities of the nation. It is said that nature abhors a vacuum, and corporations involved in the business of energy and power have every justification for their abhorrence of a vacuum in the legislation and laws regarding their field of endeavour . . . a silent vacuum provides no guidance to business. There currently exist such vacuums in governance within the divisions between federal and provincial legislative authorities for energy and electrical power.

The mining or harnessing of primary resources of energy is clearly a provincial prerogative under the BNA. The generation of power from those energy resources is also clearly a provincial prerogative, with the exception of federal concurrence for nuclear power plants. The silence and vacuum in legislative authorities arises over the transfer of electrical power over the transmission grids to consumers. The provinces appear to have assumed, in good faith, that they may locate and construct transmission grids within their own province. The provinces also appear to have assumed that they may also transfer power to other provinces or countries over these transmission grids. The transfer of electrical power to the grids of other provinces or countries seems to have arisen from an policy of "open access", with the unwritten mutual consent of the federal and provincial governments.

If there is no legislative sanction for this arrangement, then a vacuum exists which transcends mere informal or bipartite neighbourly agreements by provinces. There are international implications due to the sharing of electrical power among the transmission grids of Canada and those of the United States. A focal point for legislative authority for the transmission of electric power within Canada is long overdue, much as a the authority of a national securities regulator is also overdue, both caused by the conflicted jurisdiction of legislative authorities between the federal and provincial governments.

Concerns over the lack of legislative clarity had recently been raised by the proposed sale, by the newly formed provincial government of New Brunswick, of the New Brunswick Power Corporation to the Quebec Power Corporation for the purpose of reducing the provincial debt. The other Atlantic provinces (Nova Scotia, Prince Edward Island, Newfoundland & Labrador) were concerned that such a sale could be seriously detrimental or totally impede the future sales of electrical power from their power corporations to the North American markets. Quebec's attempt to gain control over the transmission grids in both Quebec and New Brunswick would effectively block the other Atlantic power corporations from U.S. markets by virtue of the geography. The issue is the control of the electrical power transmission grids in the provinces and the nation, a control which is currently silent under the BNA.

The proposal for the sale failed in March of 2010, with concerns by both parties. But the issue has been raised, and deserves resolution now to avoid such situations and disputes in future. The control of electrical power transfers by transmission grids among the provinces or to other countries should be a matter for the federal government on the grounds of national security.

To resolve this issue, a brief review of relevant legislation is warranted under three sections of the British North America Act (BNA) and all its amendments, namely trade and commerce 91(2), property and civil rights 92(13), and transportation and communications 92(10).

The BNA Act Section 92(13) gives the provinces the exclusive authority to make law related to "property and civil rights in the province". But property and civil rights in the BNA is a term that predates the Constitution Act 1867, and does not have its current meaning. Property and civil rights in the time of the BNA referred to interactions between private persons.

The BNA Act of Section 92(10) gives the provinces authority over "local works and undertakings". As with many others, transportation and communications have conflicted and overlapping authority between the two jurisdictions. However, the section also excludes the provinces from such specific undertakings related to "ships, railways, canals, telegraphs, and other works and undertakings connecting the province with any other or others of the provinces", as well as ship lines, and "such works declared by the Parliament of Canada to be for the general advantage of Canada or for the advantage of two or more provinces."

The BNA Act under Section 91(2) gives Parliament the authority to make laws related to the "regulation of trade and commerce." In comparison with the U.S. Constitution's approach to trade and commerce, Parliament's authority is more broadly worded than that given to the U.S. government. Parliament's authority over trade and commerce included its "general" aspects until the 1980s when, in the case of General Motors of Canada Ltd. v. City National Leasing, the Supreme Court ruled that Parliament could regulate trade and commerce if its object was to achieve something a provincial government alone could not achieve.

The BNA Act says that the provinces may export power but at the same prices as charged within its own jurisdiction. The Act says nothing about the effects across jurisdictions of the generation of power, not the actual physical transmission of power from one province to another province. An example of the former is the situation around Hudson Bay where the watershed for hydro electric developments is within provincial borders, yet the effluent has environmental effects in the waters of Hudson and James Bays which are under federal jurisdiction. There are as well international sales of power through the transmission grids to the United States, wherein the federal government should be involved. President Barack Obama has stated it is the intention of his administration to refurbish and strengthen the electrical grid system in the United States to avoid future disaster situations as those that occurred in 2004. Such negotiations and agreements should be the prerogative of the U.S. administration and the Parliament of Canada. Unless ruled unconstitutional, the federal government could assert its authority over the location and construction of transmission grids, and the transfer of electrical power among the provinces and the nation.

The following is worthy of note as a summary:

1 Under the BNA Act Section 91(2), the courts ruled that Parliament may regulate trade and commerce if its object was to achieve something a provincial government alone could not achieve;

2 The BNA Act Section 92(13) is silent on transmission grids; it does not give the provinces exclusive authority to make laws related to electrical transmission grids;

3 The BNA Act of Section 92(10) excludes the provinces from such undertakings as railways, canals, and telegraphs, and other works and undertakings connecting any province with any other provinces.

There seem to be both physical and technical similarities between telegraph transmission lines, other forms of communication (telephones, radio, television), and electrical transmission lines in the modern context. Unless ruled unconstitutional, the federal government should therefore assert its authority over the both the location and transfer of electrical power over the transmission grids in and among all provinces of Canada under section 91(2). Thus, the agreements concerning the location of transmission grids, pricing policies, and power transfers should be negotiated between the federal government and the provincial governments for inter-provincial matters, and the federal government and U.S. administration for international matters. The ownership, construction, and physical maintenance of the transmission grids and all electrical power generating facilities should be left with the provinces.

Suggestions and Proposals

The federal government, after consultation with all provincial governments, should assume authority over the manner in which electrical transmission lines are located and operated. This will provide legislated power to ensure open access to the transmission grid for all producers, and provide one agency for policy and planning the national network.

The provision of electrical power to the nation must be viewed as a matter of national security, and having primacy over environmental matters but protecting them where possible.

In general, the federal and provincial governments should reduce the use of fossil fuels and replace them with energy derived from water, solar panels, and geothermal sources where these are practical.

Chapter 7 - Security of the People

(Bibliography: Security of the People - Wahabbi Muslim Culture & Beliefs)

The culture of Canadians has been analysed and discussed at considerable length in the author's previous book "Canada in Crisis (1) - An Agenda to Unify the Nation". Parts of the following short history are from that reference.

Canadians & Their Culture

During the period 1700 to 1900, the commonality found among the new Canadians lay in their origin from western industrialized countries of Europe, their predominantly Caucasian origin and Christian religion, their education, their worldly knowledge from past explorations and conquests, and most importantly their dreams for their new country. Until the early 1800s, they had witnessed the bestiality of religious extremism under the Spanish Inquisition, and wanted no intervention of the Church in state affairs. During the period from 1900 to 1950, these new Canadians had fought in two civil wars in South Africa and Spain, and in two world wars in Europe and the Pacific. All of these hardships had brought a great sense of identity and pride to the people who had come from such disparate lands and languages, and were now united as Canadians. The time just after World War II was an intensely proud moment for Canada, and perhaps the finest hour in its brief history. The culture of the nation and its people was now well defined.

At the end of World War II, Canadians were self reliant and industrious, well educated and ethical, moderately religious, respectful of human rights and the equality of women with men, strongly democratic and proud of their young nation. They enjoyed life . . . their churches, music, arts, theatres, sports, travel, dining out, parties and various other entertainments. The government was nominally Christian, as were national holidays etc, but the Church played no part in the administration of the nation: the state had been separated from the church for more than a century. These were the people who had nurtured and developed Canada into one of the finest countries in the world as a place to live and raise their families. These people, their culture, customs, and traditions deserved protection and preservation from any and all threats to their life styles, security and safety. The most dangerous threats which they would face in the next 50 years would originate with the assimilation of other people, the immigrants, travellers, and visitors from other lands where the cultures, customs, and traditions were quite different, and often quite incompatible with those of Canadians.

Canadian Immigration Criteria - The Guidebook

(Bibliography: Security of the People - Immigration Guidebook & Farzana Hassan)

The new guidebook issued in 2010 by Citizenship and Immigration Canada, *Discover Canada: The Rights and Responsibilities of Citizenship* has quite rightly made it clear that the extreme customs and traditions of recent immigrants are unacceptable to the Canadian government. One passage on the equality of women and men (note the word order) states:

> *"Canada's openness and generosity do not extend to barbaric cultural practices that tolerate spousal abuse, 'honour killings', female genital mutilation, or other gender based violence."*

Canada may have arrived at a watershed moment in its history. It may be said that the policy of multiculturalism had begun to threaten the established culture and customs of Canadians, and was failing the people and the government.

Farzana Hassan, a spokeswoman for the Muslim Canadian Congress, said there is nothing controversial about the statement in the new guide, adding that it is a long overdue step toward tackling a cultural practice that does not accord with Canadian values. "We cannot ignore this in the name of multiculturalism," she said. "But it's not enough to make statements about what people should or shouldn't do, because that approach doesn't register with people who are influenced by this very irrational and religious zeal."

Many of the newer immigrants had entered Canada in the belief that the Canadian government should respond to their demands for care and protection, and accept their traditions and customs. They believed that a country so blessed as Canada could afford to maintain them under a generous welfare regime. They looked to the government for all their needs and shortfalls. Such attitudes were in stark contrast to the attitudes of older generations of Canadians, those who had been crucial to the development of Canada throughout its difficult pioneering days. Such attitudes by immigrants were not welcomed by the older Canadians, who were rightfully disappointed and concerned for the future of the nation.

Some of the western European nations have also suffered disappointments with newer immigrants. Germany has had difficulties with *Gastarbeiter* (guest workers) from Turkey with their high birth rates which threatened German culture and language. France has had trouble with its colonial immigrants from Algeria with similar attitudes to the Turks. The Dutch, who are normally a very hospitable and open minded people, have been enraged at the murders of parliamentarian Pim Fortuyn and filmmaker Theo van Gogh. Both of these men were highly regarded and distinguished native Dutch citizens, who were murdered simply because their quite proper and acceptable public activities offended the recent immigrants. The common cause of all these concerns was the fundamental difference in culture between the host Christian Europeans and the recent Muslim immigrants.

The Dutch parliament recently passed legislation requiring all applicants for citizenship to pass an extensive language test at their own personal cost of €350 prior to their immigration to the Netherlands. The Dutch government was also considering a proposal to place young unemployed immigrants in empty military barracks under military discipline as an introduction to job training programs and the realities of the working world in the Netherlands. Both the French and the Dutch have restricted the dress and deportment of immigrants to encourage greater assimilation with the national traditions and customs. In the United States, the government has recently published a black list of 14 countries, and all airline passengers travelling from or to those countries will be subject to complete inspections of baggage, and personal "pat-downs" (physical body searches) on entry to or exit from America. Other western countries may soon be obliged to follow that practice as well.

The people of Canada, and those of western European countries, have a paramount right to preserve their values, customs, and traditions. The granting of citizenship to immigrants in Canada must be recognized as a privilege under which the immigrants must accept and adopt Canadian values. Immigrants should not bring old wounds, complaints, quarrels, wars and other baggage from their former lands into Canada. The immigrants must accommodate themselves to the Canadian culture, or the Canadian culture will not survive.

Different Immigrants & Cultures

During the last 40 years, liberal governments introduced major social changes and legislation to support multiculturism and bilingualism in Canada, with an expansion of the peoples eligible for immigration. Those years brought many people to Canada from the Mid-east, the Far-east, Asia, and Africa. Most of these peoples were from countries with distinctly different cultures, and religions; and governments which were neither democratic nor peaceful. Many were from countries which were quite backward culturally when compared to the more democratic, modern, and enlightened societies of western Europe and North America.

Some of these mid-eastern Muslim countries were still strongly feudal and patriarchal by custom and tradition. Women were considered as being under the strict domination of male members of their large and extended families. In many cases, the more extreme countries forbade unmarried men and women to mix in public, and forbade women from gaining an education. Shariah law was becoming more widely practised, with the strict imposition of very harsh punishments, including heavy lashings or even stoning for adultery, the amputation of hands or feet for theft, and public beheadings in extreme cases, especially where the Taliban governed. These practices were based solely on cultural traditions and customs; these practices were not based on the religious teachings of Islam.

In some of the Indo-eastern countries there were similar traditions and customs under which women were subjugated to male members of their large families. Some women who married with insufficient dowries were known to have died from accidental cooking fires. Some religious customs (practised by both Sikhs and Muslims and known as suttee) condoned the immolation of a widow, either on the husband's funeral pyre or before his anticipated death in battle.

Muslims' Incompatible Cultures

Honour Killings in Canada

(Bibliography: Security of the People - Honour Killings in Canada)

Aqsa Parvez age 16, was allegedly murdered by her father in Mississauga, Ontario in an honour killing for not wearing a hijab. The Canadian Islamic Congress brushed off the tragedy with the stunningly cynical remark that it was a teenager issue rather than a religious issue. Amandeep Atwal, age 17, of British Columbia was stabbed 11 times by her father, Rajinder Singh Atwal, for refusing to end a relationship with a non-Sikh boy friend. Silva Kashif, age 16, was a Sudanese Christian who was sentenced to 50 lashes and immediately flogged for wearing what a judge considered an "indecent" knee length skirt. Hindus and even Christians coming from some South Asian cultures occasionally kill girls and women for reasons of family or community honour. Honour killings have nothing to do with religion; they are strictly a cultural tradition by a patriarchal society.

Honour Killings and Domestic Abuse

(Bibliography: Security of the People - Honour Killings & Domestic Abuse)

Islamists insist that honour killings have nothing to do with Islam. They say that it is a "cultural" rather than an "Islamic" crime. They are wrong. Islamists also say that honour murders are the same as domestic violence. All men, all religions engage in it. Wrong. Most honour killings are committed by Muslims who believe that what they are doing is a sacred, religious act. They may misunderstand the Qu'ran but as yet, no mullah or imam has stood up in the global, public square to condemn such murders as dishonourable and anti-Islamic. No fatwa has ever been issued against a Muslim honour killer.

Muslims Raping Daughters-in-Law

(Bibliography: Security of the People - Muslims Raping Daughters-in-law)

In the far East (eg Bangladesh), it is not an uncommon occurrence for fathers-in-law to rape the wives of their sons (their daughters-in-law). The culture and traditions there usually cause people, even the sons of the father, to turn a blind eye to these offences, with little support for the daughters-in-law. On occasion, such daughters-in-law may be punished or even killed for the honour of the family or the community.

Canada's Immigration Guide & Barbaric Cultures

(Bibliography: Security of the People - Canada's Immigration Guide & Honour Killings)

The journalist, Barbara Kay, in reference to the new book from Citizen and Immigration Canada, "*Discover Canada: The Rights and Responsibilities of Citizenship*", stated that she would still say exactly what she has always said. The difference is that now that the government's official position is the same as hers, she won't have to feel defensive anymore. She was referring specifically to the passage in the section "The Equality of Women and Men" where the guidebook says: "Canada's openness and generosity do not extend to barbaric cultural practices that tolerate spousal abuse, 'honour killings', or other gender based violence." She then said, "Barbaric? Barbaric? That's a negative judgment of other people's cultural practices. We may have arrived at a watershed moment in the history of multiculturalism. Indeed, this may be our official policy of multiculturalism's 'tear down this wall' moment. It may soon be possible to say that multiculturalism has failed as a national policy without being labelled a racist."

Muslim Populations in Europe
(Bibliography: Security of the People - Muslim Populations in Europe)

Islam may still be a faraway religion for millions of Americans. But for Europeans it is the subject of local politics. The 15 million Muslims of the European Union are becoming a more powerful political force than their Arab brethren, as growing numbers of Europe's Muslims may vote in elections. This political ascendance threatens to exacerbate existing strains within the trans-Atlantic relationship. The presence of nearly 10,000,000 Muslims versus 700,000 Jews in France and Germany alone helps explain why continental Europe might look at the Middle East from a different angle than the United States. Indeed, French and German concerns about a unilateral U.S. attack on Iraq, or Washington's blind support for Israel, are at least partly related to nervousness about the Muslim street at home. Whether Brussels, Berlin, Paris, or Washington like it or not, Europe's Muslim constituencies are likely to become an even more vocal foreign policy lobby. Two trends are empowering Europe's Muslim street: demographics, and opportunities for full citizenship.

If current trends (2010) continue, the Muslim population of Europe will nearly double by 2015, while the non-Muslim population will shrink by 3.5 percent. Accompanying this population surge is a parallel process of Muslim enfranchisement. Nearly half of the 5 million to 7 million Muslims in France are already French citizens who may vote. The situation is similar for most of the 2 million Muslims in Great Britain. The overwhelming majority of Muslims living in Europe or the United States are peaceful and law abiding. However, European governments worry about the role of European Muslims in past and future terrorist attacks. This concern was stoked by the recent discovery of al Qaeda cells in Germany, France, Italy, and Britain. Given these suspicions and prejudices, Europe's budding multiculturalism will likely be a casualty of the Islamic terrorist attacks on European soil.

Europe's War against Islam

(Bibliography: Security of the People - Europe's War against Islam)

Nicolas Sarkozy, the President of France, urged French Muslims, who make up four per cent of France's population and are more numerous than in any other country in Europe, not to challenge France's Christian heritage and republican values. Sarkozy is a populist politician, and was simply reflecting widespread popular discomfort about Islam in Europe. Sarkozy has voiced his support for such a ban on burqas. "The burqa," he said, "is not a sign of religion. It is a sign of subservience. It will not be welcome on the territory of the French republic."

A 2008 survey found that more than 50 per cent of respondents in Germany, Italy, Holland, and France believe that "the Western and Muslim ways of life are irreconcilable." Islam's presence isn't very visible in Swiss architecture. In the entire country, there are a grand total of only four minarets, the steeple like spires that often adorn mosques where Muslims pray. But those were four minarets too many for the Swiss. More than 57 per cent of participating voters approved the proposed ban, with majorities in 22 out of 26 cantons supporting the constitutional amendment. One in four Swedes is in favour of banning the construction of more minarets.

In Italy, a member of the Northern League, which is a junior partner in Prime Minister Silvio Berlusconi's coalition government, called for a vote to ban minarets modelled after the Swiss referendum. Opposition to visible signs of Islam in Germany is rarely explicit. Josef Joffe, editor of the German news weekly Die Zeit, said "We do this more subtly." People are unlikely to complain about the mosque itself, but rather the resulting noise or lack of parking.

In Holland, Geert Wilders, the leader of the Party for Freedom, has seen his popularity soar on the strength of an unequivocal stand against Islam. Never mind the minarets which annoy the Swiss. He wants to ban the whole Quran.

The British National Party today focuses its vitriol almost exclusively against Muslims. "To incite racial hatred is unfair because no one can change their birth, said BNP chairman Nick Griffin. "On the other hand, to criticize a religion is entirely justifiable, because everybody has the choice to change a religion if it's bad." Griffin describes Islam as "a wicked, vicious faith" and "a cancer eating away at our freedoms, our democracy, and rights for our women."

At issue is a question of national identity, what it means to be English, Dutch, French, German, or Italian. Europeans have not had to enunciate their national identities in a formal or bureaucratic manner, as historically they have not relied on immigration for much of their growth. In contrast, the United States, Canada, Australia and New Zealand have found it necessary to define themselves, as those newly found countries have had to rely on immigrants from quite different customs and cultures to populate and build their nations.

Tariq Ramadan, a Muslim Swiss author and academic, blamed the minaret ban partly on his compatriots' fear of Islam. He has said integration won't be easy. But it's difficult to imagine a stable and harmonious continent unless this occurs. Those who want to ban minarets might not want to acknowledge it, but Islam is now a European religion.

Islamization of Catholic Europe

(Bibliography: Security of the People - Islamization of Catholic Europe)

Europeans are allowing Islam to conquer the continent, according to a leading Roman Catholic cardinal. Miloslav Vlk, the Archbishop of Prague, said Muslims were well placed to fill the spiritual void, "created as Europeans systematically empty the Christian content of their lives . . . Europe will pay dearly for having left its spiritual foundations". This was the last chance to do something about it and the opportunity would not last for decades, he said in comments posted on his web site.

"Today our continent *(Europe)* does not have firm spiritual and moral foundations," said Archbishop Vlk, 77. His remarks were made in an interview to mark his retirement as leader of the Czech church.

"Europe has denied its Christian roots from which it has risen and which could give it the strength to fend off the danger that it will be conquered by Muslims", he said. "At the end of the Middle Ages and in the early modern age, Islam failed to conquer Europe with arms. The Christians beat them then. Today, when the fighting is being done with spiritual weapons, which Europe lacks while the Muslims are perfectly armed, the fall of Europe is looming." Archbishop Vlk called on Christians to respond by living their faith more observantly.

Sharia Laws & Courts in Britain

(Bibliography: Security of the People - Sharia Courts in Britain)

In the United Kingdom there exist officially sanctioned Sharia Courts which pass legally binding Sharia judgements. While legal Muslim tribunal courts had been started in August 2007, the first official Sharia court was opened in September 2008. By June 2009 the existence of at least 85 official Sharia courts was revealed. A report stated that Sharia courts "operate behind doors that are closed to independent observers and their decisions are likely to be unfair to women and backed by intimidation". Past rulings of those courts included the following:

- "that Muslim woman may not marry a non-Muslim unless he converts to Islam, and the children of a woman who does should be taken from her until she marries a Muslim".
- "the courts granted approval of polygamous marriage and enforcement of a woman's duty to have sex with her husband at his demand".
- "a male child belongs to the father after age seven, regardless of circumstances".

Theocracy Trumps Democracy in Ontario

(Bibliography: Security of the People - Theocracy Trumps Democracy)

Brampton, Ontario: Weeks before police rounded up the "Toronto 18," Shareef Abdelhaleem obtained a fatwa from his father confirming that a terrorist attack on Canadian soil would be justifiable, a Brampton Superior Court judge heard. "He told me his father told him there is nothing wrong with it; in other words, it's acceptable," witness and police agent Shaher Elsohemy testified during the trial of Mr. Abdelhaleem, who stands accused of playing a key role in the foiled 2006 plot to attack targets in Ottawa and Toronto.

The fatwa, or religious ruling, from Mr. Abdelhaleem's father held significance because the elder Mr. Abdelhaleem operated an Islamic education school in Mississauga. For Shareef Abdelhaleem, who had been somewhat sceptical, the fatwa affirmed that the plot to detonate truck bombs in Ontario was Islamically sound, Mr. Elsohemy testified. He (Abdelhaleem) has no doubt of the plot's Islamic correctness, Mr. Elsohemy told the judge.

Muslim Confiscation of Schools in Ontario

(Bibliography: Security of the People - Muslim Confiscation of Schools)

This story involves a Jewish teacher in an Ontario French high school whose name cannot be revealed because she fears physical retaliation. "Miriam" had taught in French language schools in the 1970s and 1980s in schools with large Lebanese Christian populations without incurring any anti-Semitism. In her current employment, she works with Muslims. A child of Holocaust survivors, Miriam is demonstrably neither racist nor anti-Muslim.

In 2001 Miriam started teaching at a school largely populated by children of refugees, mainly from Djibouti and Eritrea, countries where there are no Jews but where the hatred of Jews is deeply entrenched in the culture. During the academic year of 2002-2003 Miriam started to encounter anti-Semitic taunts from students, such as "Does someone see a Jew here, someone smell a Jew? It stinks here". When she reported this and similar insults to the principal, the principal did not follow up.

During the invasion of Iraq, moments of silence were held in the classroom. Cultural presentations involved only Muslim culture and no Canadian content. Students were allowed to leave assembly during the playing of the Canadian national anthem. The crisis of this story occurred when Miriam admonished a student in class. The student screamed: "I don't have to listen to you; you are not a person, you are nothing, you do not exist as a person." When Miriam demanded he accompany her to the principal's office, the student followed her yelling, "Don't speak to me, don't look at me, you are not human, you are a Jew".

In 2004, the year Miriam left, a full 60 out of 75 francophone teachers asked for a transfer, not because of anti-Semitism but because of anti-Western sentiment. French Canadian children had already stopped enrolling and the school is now virtually all Muslim, including the teachers and principal. If preventative measures are not taken, hatred of Jews will metastasize exponentially in those cultural communities that consider it normal.

In the Ottawa Citizen (newspaper) dated 7 March 2010, the reporter Matthew Pearson described the high academic achievements of the private Islamic elementary Abraar school in the west end of the city. He went on to say; "In 2005, the school made headlines after an essay glorifying martyrdom and violence against Jews was made public. Two investigators from the province's Ministry of Education said the essay, and the approving comments from two teachers, did not represent a systemic problem at the school". The majority of Canadians might disagree with that determination by the Ontario Ministry.

Recruiting Jihadis in North America

(Bibliography: Security of the People - Recruiting Jihadis in North America)

Beginning in late 2007, dozens of young men of Somali descent started disappearing from communities in the West. It turned out they were returning to Somalia to train in Shabab camps or to take up arms against Shabab's enemies within the country. Islamists of non-Somali descent were also travelling there to join Shabab.

This phenomenon has been repeating itself in a number of countries. Canadian government sources claim that 20 to 30 Canadians have joined Shabab, a development that public safety minister Peter Van Loan has said alarmed him. In the U.S. the disappearances have primarily clustered around Minneapolis and St. Paul, but there are credible reports of disappearances in other U.S. cities with large Somali populations as well.

Shabab recruiting is a security concern for both Somalia and the rest of the world. Within Somalia, Shabab's implementation of a strict version of shariah raises human rights worries. For example, according to Amnesty International, Shabab jurists sentenced a 13 year old rape victim in Kismayo to be stoned to death last year for alleged adultery. But authorities' biggest concern is what happens when they return to the countries from which they came. There are fears that these men could end up involved in a terrorist plot - fears bolstered by the fact that Shabab's training is both military and ideological.

A Fatwa against Terrorism & Al Qaeda

(Bibliography: Security of the People - A Fatwa Against Terrorism & Al Qaeda)

Dr. Tahir ul-Qadri, an influential Muslim scholar from Pakistan, has issued a 600 page global ruling against terrorism and suicide bombing. Dr. Qadri says his fatwa completely dismantles al-Qaeda's violent ideology. The scholar describes al-Qaeda as an "old evil with a new name" that has not been sufficiently challenged. The scholar's movement is growing in the UK and has attracted the interest of policymakers and security chiefs.

In his religious ruling delivered in London, Dr. Qadri says that Islam forbids the massacre of innocent citizens and suicide bombings. Although many scholars have made similar rulings in the past, Dr.

Qadri argued that his massive document goes much further by omitting the "ifs and buts" added by other thinkers. He said that his ruling and the fatwa set out a point by point theological rebuttal of every argument used by al-Qaeda inspired recruiters. The populist scholar developed his document last year as a response to the increase in bombings across Pakistan by the militants. The terrorists can't claim that their suicide bombings are martyrdom operations. There is no place for any martyrdom and their acts are never, ever to be considered jihad.

The European Court of Human Rights

(Bibliography: Security of the People - European Court of Human Rights)

The European Court of Human Rights (ECHR) upheld the Turkish Constitutional Court's dissolution of The Welfare Party (Refah Partisi v Turkey 2003) for violating Turkey's principle of secularism by calling for the re-introduction of religious law. The ECHR then held "that sharia is incompatible with the fundamental principles of democracy."

Muslim Populations in Canada

(Bibliography: Security of the People - Muslim Populations in Canada)

It has been said that the devil's in the detail . . . but one might say that the devil's also in the demographics of Canada's population. Once considered a predominantly Christian country, Canada will experience a dramatic shift in the religious composition of its population when it reaches its 150th birthday. Statistics Canada forecasts major changes to the religious landscape of the country by 2017. Projections of the size of religious groups suggest potentially important challenges for the future as governments across the country examine issues associated with the place of religion in schools and in public institutions.

Canada's Limits to Tolerance

(Bibliography: Security of the People - Canada's Limits to Tolerance)

Canadians are generally well known around the world as well meaning and friendly people, tolerant of other peoples' customs when travelling in foreign lands. They are equally easy going in their own country when they encounter visitors from other lands and nations. But that tolerance does have limits on certain matters, such as the equality of women with men, and all human rights in general. While the Charter of Rights and Freedoms guarantees many rights, it does so in general, without any ranking or preference of one right over another. In practice, this deserves greater distinction, as most people would likely prefer some sort of hierarchy of rights. In particular, many people would likely rank human rights above religious rights. They would do so on the basis that the former were likely based on the beliefs of many people, while religious rights might be based solely on the intangible and ethereal beliefs of a very small group of persons, or even a single individual. For example, one person's human rights should never be subordinate to another persons's religious rights or beliefs. To put it succinctly, most people would likely judge that, "human rights trump religious rights".

Canadians Against Terrorism

(Bibliography: Security of the People - Canadians Against Terrorism)

Canada is not immune to the violence engendered by religion and culture, and by religious extremists who feel free to ignore the laws of their adopted country. Such actions cannot be tolerated by the peace loving people of Canada, and the firmest of measures must be accepted to forestall any continuation of such threats to the people of Canada. The Canadian government must not let the obvious elude them in enforcing the security of the nation.

A Salute to Denmark

(Bibliography: Security of the People - A Salute to Denmark)

The Danes should remember Piet Hein, a scientist, mathematician, inventor, and poet who lived during World War II and wrote thousands of short little poems called "gruks" as symbols of their resistance against the Nazis. The plight of the Danish people faced with a large and growing population of ardent Muslims has forced a significant change to their former policy of openness in immigration. As with

Holland, the Danes introduced very restrictive regulations in 2007 for all applicants seeking to immigrate to their country.

If you wish to become Danish, you must attend three years of language classes. You must pass a test on Denmark's history, culture, and language. You must live in Denmark for seven years before applying for citizenship. You must demonstrate an intent to work, and have a job waiting. If you wish to bring a spouse into Denmark, you must both be over 24 years of age, and it won't be easy to bring friends and family to Denmark with you. You will not be allowed to build a mosque in Copenhagen. Although your children have a choice of some 30 Arabic culture and language schools in Denmark, they will be strongly encouraged to assimilate to Danish society in ways that past immigrants were not.

Commentary

It has been said that one of the constants in life is that of change. Perhaps the innumerable wars and conflicts among mankind, most of which are caused by differing religious beliefs, are another and more regrettable constant in life. Changes are arriving almost daily in many countries of western Europe: in England, France, Germany, the Netherlands, Denmark, Spain. and Switzerland.

In the last decade, the first in the new millennium of 2000, the world has seen the ruthless conquest of Tibet and continued suffering of the Tibetan people under the ruling Han Chinese. The people of Burma continue to suffer under their own military dictatorship, despite the distinguished leader of the previous democratic government, Aung San Suu Kyi, having been awarded the Nobel Peace Prize in 1991. Further west in Sri Lanka, the indigenous Sinalese have finally repulsed the extremist Tamil Tigers who have fled back to their native lands in the state of Tamil Nadu in India. North west of India in the Punjab regions, disputes still fester among the Hindus, Sikhs, and Muslims living in Pakistan, India, and Kashmir.

In the mid-east, fierce wars have broken out among many of the Islamic countries in that region, as different factions (Ismaili, Sufi, Shiite, Sunni, Wahabbis) of the Muslim faith have fought each other for supremacy in Iran, Iraq, Afghanistan, Pakistan and other "... stans" (eg Waziristan). Interventions by western powers in Iraq and Afghanistan to assist moderate Muslims to combat al Qaeda, the Taliban, and other local warlords and develop modern democracies has had of dubious success at great cost of life to all involved. The Israelis continue to fiercely protect their homeland against the surrounding Muslims, some of whom have called for the Jewish people to be wiped off the face of the earth. Further west, the Muslims of the southern Balkans have succeeded in establishing themselves in Kosovo where they outnumber the Serbs who had ruled there for 400 years. In western Europe, the Muslim population continues to grow due to immigration and higher birth rates than the Christians who historically were the dominant people of western Europe. Some projections for countries like the Netherlands, France, Germany and England suggest that the majority of those populations may become Muslim within one generation, or two at the most.

According to the Canadian Census in 2001, there were 578,000 Muslims in Canada (~254,000 Toronto), in 2006 there were 783,000, and the projection for 2017 is 1,421,000. The fertility rate in both Canada and the United States is currently 1.6 children per family. To maintain a population at its current levels, a fertility rate of 2.11 is needed. Historically, Muslim birth rates in some countries have been as high as 8.1, possibly due to polygamy and the lack of birth control practice by Muslims. If higher birth rates and the current immigration policies continue, the Muslim populations in Canada may be expected to rise at faster rates than the current predominantly Christian population. The majority of Canadians and Americans could soon be Muslim, and their politics and government would surely follow shortly thereafter.

There is ample evidence that the culture, customs, and traditions of the Muslim people are quite different from those of the Christian people of western Europe and North America. The Christian people in western societies have risen above the barbaric acts which they had perpetrated long ago. During their struggles from feudal fiefdoms to modern democracies, the Christians recognized the rights of people, the equality of women and men, and the rule of law with charters of rights and constitutions. In this 21st century, there is no place in western society for Muslims who condone and perpetuate honour killings, rape and sodomy, spousal abuse, polygamy, deaths by stoning, the severing of limbs or heads, lashings for petty crimes, the mutilation of female genitals, suicide bombings of civilians by Muslim men, women, and children, the issue of fatwas decreeing death, or calls for jihad and the genocide of entire populations of other peoples on the basis of their race, religion, or politics.

Many Muslims will argue that their behaviour is based on the doctrines of holy Islam, and demand that the western world accept that religion. To the people of the western world, the truth behind the incompatible customs and behaviour of Muslims is based not on religious doctrine, but almost entirely on the culture and traditions of a feudal, patriarchal society that has evolved unchanged from the seventh century AD over 1300 years ago. As the European Commission for Human Rights stated in 2003, the Muslim religion is incompatible with the principles of western democracies.

There are other collateral changes to Canadian culture and society that would certainly ensue after a change to a Muslim government. After a short time in power, one might well expect the conversion from English common law to Sharia law, and even the introduction of some combination of Taliban and Wahabbi justice. One may certainly expect the prohibition of the Christian, Jewish, and other religions, music, art and sculptures, theatres and opera, most sports, travel, education for females, most forms of literature, dancing and dining out, various foods such as pork and alcohol, and other entertainments. In short, Canadians may expect the rapid and rigid curtailment of the traditional freedoms inherent in a western democracy.

There are people whom we admit to Canada, and there are those to whom we may deny admission. The latter include those who would harm the people or threaten the security of Canada. If Islam and its people are incompatible with western democracy . . . should the Islamic religion and Muslims be welcomed in Canada? Perhaps Canada should eliminate any potential conflict of interest in its people by the rescission of dual citizenships for those people of incompatible cultures (and persons of concern).

The first question facing the western world is how to react to the growing presence and immediate dangers of the Muslim extremists. The second question is how to react to the moderate Muslims who are indistinguishable from the extremists. The third question is why have the moderate Muslims not brought the extremists under their control, or otherwise assisted the western world in constraining and countering the ravaging attacks of the extremists. The fatwa against terrorism and suicide bombing issued by the eminent Islamic scholar Dr. Qadri is certainly welcome beginning, but it begs the question as to whether the extremists will heed its message to cease their goal of world conquest, and the obliteration of most other societies. These threats to the security of the western world must be repulsed.

The first category of human threats facing Canada and the western world must be recognized as those posed by the extremists of the Muslim population. The provision of military assistance to some of the major Muslim host countries to control the extremists and assist with the transition to modern democratic societies is well intended, but costly and of dubious permanence and value. The permanence of that military assistance is dubious based on the experience of the British in India, the French in Indo-China, the Americans in Vietnam, and the Russians in Afghanistan. Western values are no more compatible in Asian lands than are Asian values in western lands. The best solution may be first to dissociate the two societies as much as possible, second to establish good intelligence systems to warn of any overt or covert actions against the west, and third to maintain police and military forces prepared to counter the launch of any potential extremist initiatives against any western democracy.

The second category of human threats facing Canada and the western world are those posed by the moderate Muslims themselves. That threat is quite simple: that given a generation or more with high birth rates and current immigration policies, the majority of the population of western societies will have become adherents to the Muslim religion. At that time, there would be demands for the adoption of sharia law for all Canadians despite their religion, even if the Christian and other religions still existed in western society. The people of Canada and other western nations would be required to assimilate themselves into a Muslim world; not by bullets and the force of arms, but through sustained high birth rates, the initial perversion of the democratic process to replace the incumbent government, followed by the imposition of an Islamic government by the new and Muslim majority of the population.

Countering the threats from moderate Muslims could be approached by first identifying those Muslims who are already either citizens or residents of Canada both permanent of temporary. This could be done as part of a national program to require all residents of Canada to acquire state of the art biometric identification cards (BIDs). These BIDs could be used as alternate passports, although they would offer even better identification that traditional passports. As the profiling of people has now become acceptable and necessary to the security of the nation, the data in the BID cards must include the religion of the person. During World War II, Canadian military "dog tags" provided the name, rank, serial number, blood type, and religion, so that adding religion to the new BID cards should not be a problem. After all, such a provision for national security must be accepted, as the situation is tantamount to a state of undeclared war. Patriotic and law abiding Canadians would have nothing to fear; the new BIDs would be little different than a credit card which is required as identification to withdraw money from a bank or ATM. Surely the requirement for identification for purposes of national security is more crucial than identification for a mere financial transaction. The requirement to carry the BID card at all times would also assist law enforcement and border control officers to perform their routine duties more quickly and with greater cost effectiveness.

In a process similar to the above, all immigrants and travellers to Canada could be issued temporary BID cards on their arrival, with the injunction that the cards must be carried at all times by the person.

They should also be advised that Canadian law enforcement officers may demand to see the BID at any time. On their departure from Canada, the travellers would be required to return the BID as proof that they have left the country. Immigrants applying for residence should be advised that the temporary BID card would be exchanged for a permanent BID if their application for residence were approved.

Suggestions and Proposals

In cooperation with other western democracies, the federal government should continue to maintain and strengthen its intelligence facilities, law enforcement and border control agencies, and military forces to prevent any initiatives by terrorists or Muslim extremists against Canada or other western countries.

The government should also quickly establish state of the art biometric identification cards (BIDs) which include such things as name, date of birth, address, DNA, religion, and other biometric identification data. All citizens and residents of Canada should be required to carry these cards at all times. Temporary versions of the BIDs should be issued to immigrants and travellers, to be carried at all times and to be returned when leaving the country or gaining residence. Very strong penalties, including heavy fines and possible immediate detention, should be legislated to ensure that the new policy is followed to the letter of the law.

The government should consider the recission of dual citizenship for people of incompatible cultures and persons of concern as a means of ensuring that the patriotism of Canadian citizens and residents is not placed in any conflict of interest.

The government should amend the Constitution to ensure that the rights of society prevail over the rights of the individual where security of the people and the nation are concerned.

The government should amend the Constitution to subordinate the rights and freedoms of all religious practices when such beliefs, practices, customs, or behaviour are in contravention of, or conflict with, any other rights and freedoms guaranteed under the Charter.

The government should rescind its policies and previous emphasis on multiculturalism, place greater emphasis on the enhancement of the Canadian culture and democracy, and drastically reduce and restrict the immigration of incompatible cultures and persons of concern to protect and preserve the Canadian culture and democracy.

Chapter 8 - Summary of Suggestions & Proposals

Chapter 1 - Security of the Lands, Borders & Coastlines

Suggestions and Proposals

The federal government, in consultation with provincial governments, should create and apply more appropriate criteria to determine the suitability of applicants for admission to Canada.

The use of biometric identification cards (BIDs) and location tracking for all immigrants should be mandatory for five or ten, or more years following their arrival in Canada. Access to such a database should be permitted to all appropriate agencies of the Canadian government.

Persons arriving in Canada by any means other than the normal administrative processes of entry ("jumping the queue") and applying for refugee status should be subject to intensive research of their situations to verify their claims. Such persons should be detained and denied all of the privileges, appeals, and welfare benefits of Canadian citizens, until the veracity of their refugee status has been established. Those not so entitled should be returned to their homeland with despatch, and without further application or appeal.

There should be regular review and discipline of the professional conduct of immigration and law enforcement personnel. That should include the appointment and performance of members of the Immigration

Review Board, with decisions of that Board subject to Ministerial or Cabinet approval or revision without further appeal to any court.

The various agencies responsible for the nation's security at the borders and coasts should be better organized, consolidated, and coordinated to contain potential threats from immigrants arriving at the nation's borders and coasts, as well as those persons already within its borders.

The police, border service officers, and coast guards should be given the enforcement powers, vehicles, ships, aircraft, etc, and suitable training and defensive weapons necessary to the containment of any and all potential threats to Canada and its lands, borders, and coasts.

Chapter 2 - Security of Justice & Law Enforcement

Suggestions and Proposals

The federal government should undertake a substantial review of many of its laws and court procedures to determine, the relevance, efficacy, costs, and overall benefit to the people. Simplification and uniformity of the entire system would be a desirable goal. Such a review might include consultation with appropriate organizations representative of public opinion.

A review and updating of The RCMP Act of 1985 is clearly needed to bring the investigative and enforcement powers of the federal government to current standards and expectations.

The federal government should work in conjunction with those provincial governments which do not use the services of the RCMP to review and update their policing capabilities, standards, and enforcement powers to the same or similar standards.

Chapter 3 - Security of the Economy

Suggestions and Proposals

Given the devastating impact of frauds and Ponzi schemes upon the lives of hundreds and thousands of people, the federal and provincial governments should take stronger and more severe measures to deter all forms of white collar crimes.

The federal and provincial governments should cooperate to expand the list of economic sectors, such as energy and power and especially the transmission of the latter (eg electrical grids), where foreign acquisitions are prohibited on the grounds of national security.

The excessive growth and intrusion of politics and the government, and the excessive spending which those cause, have combined to constitute a serious threat to the peaceful existence of the people of Canada. The governments at all levels should strive to reduce their portion of the economy as a percentage of GDP from 40%+ to 20% over the next decade.

The federal government should introduce legislation to remove the inequities of the tax consequences of RRIFs compared to TFSAs by reducing the taxes on RRIF withdrawals to 50% of current rates for earned income.

Chapter 4 - Security of Transportation

Suggestions and Proposals

The federal and provincial governments should cooperate to create a single, common disaster response procedure. If possible, this should be done in conjunction with the Americans.

Modern biometric identity cards (BIDs) should be mandatory for all employees of corporations in the transportation industries. A similar national biometric identity card should be required of all legal residents of Canada, in addition to other paper documentation. Law enforcement staff should be authorized to demand presentation of the BIDs at random times.

All passengers who are residents of Canada and are boarding outbound aircraft, ships, and trains should be required to produce biometric identity cards BIDs, and to permit confirmation by the transportation staff at entry gates that the passengers themselves are the person represented by the proffered identity cards. Foreign visitors should be required to produce similar identification documentation, and submit to confirmation that they are not on a "no fly" lists of potential miscreants or terrorist suspects.

All passengers arriving from foreign lands should be required to produce biometric identity cards (BIDs) or other suitable identification, and to permit confirmation by transportation staff at entry gates that the passengers are the person represented by the identity cards.

The government should apply strategic security restrictions to limit certain profiled persons, airlines, aircrew, and airports. Passengers of concern for potential threats, or the airlines, their aircrews, and their ports of origin of concern for potential threats may need to be received and treated with special procedures and care at remote locations in Canada.

The cargos of all modes of transportation, both outbound and inbound, should be subject to more stringent identification by state of the art equipment (e.g. RFIDs) where the situation is warranted.

All major cities in the provinces and territories should be linked by divided freeways similar to the German Autobahn, the French autoroutes, and the Italian autostrada to provide rapid access to disaster sites by the disaster response teams.

Chapter 5 - Security of Communication

Suggestions and Proposals

The federal government should make every effort possible to rapidly advance the provision of reliable high speed communications in all urban, rural, remote, and Arctic regions of Canada to facilitate commercial and industrial growth, and to ensure the security of the people.

Recent statements in the throne speech permitting increased foreign investment and competition in communication services is a commendable policy by the current government.

Chapter 6 - Security of Energy & Power

Suggestions and Proposals

The federal government, after consultation with all provincial governments, should assume authority over the manner in which electrical transmission lines are located and operated. This will provide legislated power to ensure open access to the transmission grid for all producers, and provide one agency for policy and planning the national network.

The provision of electrical power to the nation must be viewed as a matter of national security, and having primacy over environmental matters but protecting them where possible.

In general, the federal and provincial governments should reduce the use of fossil fuels and replace them with energy derived from water, solar panels, and geothermal sources where these are practical.

Chapter 7 - Security of the People

Suggestions and Proposals

In cooperation with other western democracies, the federal government should continue to maintain and strengthen its intelligence facilities, law enforcement and border control agencies, and military forces to prevent any initiatives by terrorists or Muslim extremists against Canada or other western countries.

The government should also quickly establish state of the art biometric identification cards (BIDs) which include such things as name, date of birth, address, DNA, religion, and other biometric identification data. All citizens and residents of Canada should be required to carry these cards at all times. Temporary versions of the BIDs should be issued to immigrants and travellers, to be carried at all times and to be returned when leaving the country or gaining residence. Very strong penalties, including heavy fines and possible immediate detention, should be legislated to ensure that the new policy is followed to the letter of the law.

The government should consider the recission of dual citizenship for people of incompatible cultures and persons of concern as a means of ensuring that the patriotism of Canadian citizens and residents is not placed in any conflict of interest.

The government should amend the Constitution to ensure that the rights of society prevail over the rights of the individual where security of the people and the nation are concerned.

The government should amend the Constitution to subordinate the rights and freedoms of all religious practices when such beliefs, practices, customs, or behaviour are in contravention of, or conflict with, any other rights and freedoms guaranteed under the Charter.

The government should rescind its policies and previous emphasis on multiculturalism, place greater emphasis on the enhancement of the Canadian culture and democracy, and drastically reduce and restrict the immigration of incompatible cultures and persons of concern to protect and preserve the Canadian culture and democracy.

Chapter 9 - A Generation Later: 2012 - 2030

Preface - A Composite Future Scenario

This book concerns the survival of the nation, and is a sequel to the previous book "Canada in Crisis (1) - An Agenda to Unify the Nation". In that first book, the last chapter was a futuristic scenario from 2008 to 2030, which portrayed the acceptance and implementation of all the proposals to unify the nation by various governments over that future time period.

The last chapter of this sequel "Canada in Crisis (2) - An Agenda for Survival of the Nation" is therefore a composite scenario, which combines the presumed implementation of the proposals from the first book and the presumed implementation of the proposals made in this second book, the sequel. So that the reader may distinguish the difference, the scenarios of the first book (unification) are shown in the form, *"The Period 2008 - 2012 From Canada in Crisis (1)"*. Scenarios from the sequel (survival) are shown in the form, *"The Period 2008 - 2012 From Canada in Crisis (2)"*. Events from the sequel appear in the middle of the two earliest periods, as issues of survival necessitated more urgent implementation than issues of unity. Please note that some proposals may have affected both unification and survival.

The Period 2008 - 2012 From Canada in Crisis (1)

In 2008, Canada was suffering from the collapse of the American and world financial systems, as were all countries. Many Canadians had suffered losses to their life savings and investments, but Canada was more fortunate than most countries in having a conservative and prudent banking system. The International Monetary Fund had recently praised the Canadian banks as the best of the G8 group of developed countries. The minority government was determined to pursue its plans to strengthen and unify the country further, to ensure that such catastrophes as the current crisis did not threaten its people in future.

The federal government chose to implement changes in the financial system, in particular the stock exchanges, to bring those entities within the same unified structure as the Canadian banks. Even from its position as a minority, the government was able to introduce and secure passage of several changes, as they were clearly moving to a simpler and more effective structure. First was the introduction of one National Stock Exchange, supported by various divisions representing sub-exchanges for Commodities, Venture capital, Savings, and Bonds etc. Each of these in turn had regional offices in the five important regions of Canada, the Western provinces, the Northern Territories, Ontario, Quebec, and the Atlantic provinces.

In 2010, the Savings Exchange had been established for the investment of retirement savings and income securities with minimal volatility and trading, and with restrictions to ensure steady and reliable growth. Married couples had been encouraged to consolidate their accounts voluntarily for simplified administration by themselves and by the insurance companies, brokerages, and banks. Former savings and income vehicles such as RRSPs, RRIFs, LIFs, etc were permitted to gradually rollover to the Tax Free Savings Accounts (TFSAs) which had been introduced in 2009 and were the best savings vehicle. Best of all, the government passed portability legislation to ensure that pensions and life annuities were optional, commutable, and portable to RRSPs, RRIFs, and LIFs, at any time at the direction of the individual employee or former employee. So many Members of Parliament and federal civil servants immediately chose to transfer their pension plans to their privately administered plans, that considerable cost savings were achieved in the administration of the few remaining pension plans until they expired. Eventually, all of the pension plans administered by the government would cease to exist.

All of these changes had been supported by the opposition parties as proper and sensible. The effect of these changes was to reduce the overhead costs and remove restrictions to freedom of choice that had previously been imposed by excessive regulation of monies that were morally the property of the individual Canadian. Needless to say, the people of Canada were very pleased with these changes, as were all political parties who gave their non-partisan support.

In a similar vein, the federal government, with the consent of the opposition, passed legislation to permit the filing of income taxes on a flat rate basis. There are currently 22 countries in eastern Europe that have a flat tax system already in place, even Russia since 2001, and Great Britain, Germany, France, Spain, Poland, Hungary, and Greece are contemplating its adoption. Business and individuals were immensely relieved that the non-partisan cooperation in Parliament facilitated passage of the legislation. The effectiveness of both government and business will be enhanced by the reduction of previously wasted money, time, and effort.

In a welcome display of cooperation, the provinces agreed with the government's proposed legislation to remove virtually all remaining impediments to the free and open mobility of products, professionals, and tradesmen within Canada. All of the Premiers have enacted similar provincial legislation to accord with the federal initiative. These cooperative initiatives have reduced unemployment rates in virtually all provinces and territories, and as well as the costs of the federal employment insurance program.

The government continued to review both quantitative and qualitative measures of performance in its daily operations based on economic cost and benefit analysis at the highest levels, to ensure that the conduct of those departments was in the best interests of Canadians.

In late 2010 the federal government, with the consent of the opposition, passed legislation to recognize Christianity as the official religion of Canada. The government was careful to stress that all peaceful religions in Canada would be welcome to practise in their traditional manner as they had in the past. The legislation was intended merely to clarify that Christmas, Easter and other national holidays were to be accorded traditional terminology and respect.

The Period 2008 - 2012 From Canada in Crisis (2)

With the consent of the provinces, the federal government legislated its paramount role in the location and management of all electrical transmissions grids, excluding urban centres, within Canada and all transfers of power between Canada and the United States. The construction, routine operation, and ownership of the transmission grids and generating facilities continued to belong to the provinces, under negotiated agreements with the federal government. That legislation also prohibited the ownership of all power generating and transmission facilities by foreign persons. The provision of electrical power to the nation was viewed as a national priority, and given primacy over environmental matters where there is no reasonable alternative. At the same time, the federal government opened the communication industry to foreign ownership to stimulate the provision of high speed communications to all urban, rural, remote, and Arctic regions of Canada.

At the same time, the federal government introduced tax relief legislation to permit annual withdrawals from RRIF accounts to be taxed at half the rate of income which would otherwise apply. This taxation relief was well received by seniors disadvantaged by the recent recession, and by comparisons with tax free insurance benefits and TFSAs which provided tax free withdrawals for future generations.

With regard to immigration, continued improvements were introduced by the federal government, in consultation with the provinces. Biometric identification cards (BIDs) were to be introduced as mandatory for all Canadian citizens and residents over the next two years. All travellers entering Canada would be issued temporary BIDs, which were to be returned on leaving the country. The travellers were advised that the BIDs must be carried at all times, in addition to their passports. Refugees in particular were detained in close custody until investigations by the department of Citizenship and Immigration could determine the legitimacy of their claims. During that time, the refugees were denied any entitlement to the rights and privileges accorded to Canadians until their refugee claims were proven. The number of Muslim immigrants to Canada was reduced to minimum levels, and the issue of dual citizenships was under continual consideration, but was as yet unresolved. The number of flights from Muslim countries was reduced to a minimum, as were the airports of origin and entry to Canada, in the interests of greater efficiency and convenience for those travellers.

Further review was undertaken by the department to ensure the proper professional conduct of all employees and law enforcement officers involved in the immigration process. The border staff of all affected agencies of the federal government were reorganized to coordinate and consolidate their activities. All border staff having front line contact with immigrants and travellers were given enforcement powers and training in the use of appropriate defensive weapons necessary to their activities.

The government began a lengthy program of reductions in their overall operations to reduce its excessive intrusion in the economy of the country. Over an extended time frame, the government sought to reduce the impact of all levels of government operations from 40% to 20% of GDP. The public would be expected to become more self reliant and independent of governments' assistance, as had been the tradition of the founding people of the nation.

The Period 2008 - 2012 From Canada in Crisis (1)

In a rare occurrence in 2011, the federal government rescinded its official recognition of Quebec as a nation within Canada, and passed legislation that no group of people would be recognized as a nation within Canada. The term was simply misleading and causing confusion. The government also passed legislation to rescind the formation of unions within the federal civil service on grounds that all of its services were essential to the economy of Canada. Provincial and municipal governments began to follow this policy.

Albeit with some lively dissension, the government finally succeeded in securing an amendment to the Constitution to deny eligibility for election to the federal Parliament of any person who has a criminal record in Canada or abroad, or advocates the dissolution of Canada or the secession of any part of Canada.

By the end of 2012, the goals for one nation, one official religion, and a major portion of one economy had been achieved. The changes to the financial and investment environment alone had greatly improved the lifestyle and retirement security for all Canadians. People were more confident and content about their own futures, and that of their families.

The Period 2012 - 2016 From Canada in Crisis (1)

In the previous four years the federal government, with the provinces collaborating on occasion, introduced major changes to legislation to improve the operations of their many departments and Crown corporations. Many agencies, boards, and Crown corporations had been privatized of simply abolished. The voting public was impressed, and the government received a comfortable majority in the election of 2012. Canadians in general had had their faith restored, as well as their financial fortunes, as unemployment shrank and stock markets swelled with activity. The recent creation of tax free savings plans (TFSAs) had caused a quantum increase in the savings rate of Canadians, the gradual transfer of monies from older LIFs, RRSPs, and RRIFs had begun, resulting in a stronger economy for the nation.

The consolidation and privatization of employer pensions, the CPP, and health and employment insurance to individual employees with private Twin TFSAs was warmly received by the employees, banks and other financial corporations. Business had become less burdened with taxes and had come to live comfortably with the higher dollar, albeit with the usual concerns from exporters. The Canadian dollar had risen to parity with most other major currencies, and governments now played a much smaller role in the economy.

The Period 2012 - 2016 From Canada in Crisis (2)

Changes were made to strengthen the intelligence facilities, law enforcement agencies, and military forces to deter initiatives by terrorists against Canada in cooperation with other western democracies. Under active consideration was the recission of dual citizenship for all Canadians to reduce the potential for conflict of interest among the people. Along the same vein, the federal government introduced stringent controls on all passengers, flights, air crews, ground crews, and foreign departure and domestic arrival airports for greater efficiency and convenience of those travellers, and to reduce the potential threats from persons or organizations of concern anywhere in the world. The BIDs (Biometric ID cards) were an key part of these new policies which involved the surveillance and targeting of passengers of concern for enhanced security.

Additional changes were begun to review the justice system, the many laws, court procedures, sentencing protocols to improve the relevance and overall cost and benefit to the people. In particular, past cases of egregious justice were to be re-examined in the light of contemporary investigative procedures and facilities. The federal government continued to review the enforcement powers and conduct of the RCMP, and encouraged the provinces to undertake similar review of their forces. Of especial concern by the federal government was a review of white collar financial crimes (Ponzi schemes and other scams) which were so devastating to the retirement plans of all Canadians.

Finally, the federal government in conjunction with the provinces, agreed to place greater emphasis on the completion of a much larger network of major highways connecting all major cities and regions of the country. The goal was to develop a system of highways comparable to those of the United States, Germany, Holland and other western democracies within the next ten years. This would provide benefits in the way of security, industry, and tourism.

The Period 2012 - 2016 From Canada in Crisis (1)

On the basis of the recent success at the polls, the federal government introduced legislation to rescind the Official Languages (Bilingual) Act of 1969, as amended in 1988. There were strong objections from some quarters, but as the Bloc Quebecois party no longer existed in Parliament, the resistance was far more muted than it would have been when the Bloc constituted one sixth of the Members of Parliament. As the French language had steadily fallen from its former position among the many languages spoken by Canadians, and as the Province of Quebec persisted in being unilingually French, the federal government could no longer justify any obligation to operate under the administrative burden of more than one language.

As the issue of bilingualism was so divisive and of national importance, the government decided to hold a referendum. It introduced the newer, faster, and far less expensive means of internet voting with ample security measures to sanction abolition of the country's bilingualism policy. The result was participation by 76% of the population, agreement by 67% of Canadians and even 21% of francophones. The legislation was then introduced and passed in the summer of 2012 to amend the Official Languages Act to declare English to be the only official language of the federal government, to the relief of the majority of Canadians.

During the next winter, the government again introduced new legislation to rescind the Indian Act, and to abrogate all treaties and trusts with the Indian bands of Canada. This had been proposed some 40 years ago by Jean Chrétien as Minister of Indian Affairs. The Indian Act was an anachronism, and a form of "Apartheid" that was no longer tolerable in Canadian society. Again, because of its importance, the government held a referendum by internet voting, and the results were positive with approval by 83% of adult Canadians, and 63% of Indians.

The "Notwithstanding" clause of the Constitution was invoked to abrogate restrictions imposed under the Constitution on the government's treatment of Indians. The process of assimilation was to be gradual, with the return of all lands and trust monies (or equivalent compensation) to individual Indians on a per capita basis. In addition, program monies were to be provided over one generation for education and interim income assistance until full assimilation was achieved. Canadians were pleased that the aboriginal people were finally to be treated as equals with all other Canadians.

Although financial support for the aboriginal people was to endure for another 20 years, Canadians appreciated the government program with annual expenditures of $8 -10 billion for the Indian people would finally end. Such costs were bearable until that time as a result of foreseeable longer term savings by the eventual cancellation of the Indian and other programs.

Without passage of official legislation, the government gave tacit recognition to the evolving culture of Canadians. In public announcements, various publications, and political events, the government stressed the country's pioneering qualities of hard work, self-reliance and independence, integrity and ethical behaviour, and especially respect for the equality of women with men.

Changes had been made as well in the immigration process. New candidates for Canadian residence and citizenship were cautioned that such status was a privilege to be earned by proper behaviour; it was not a right acquired simply by arriving on the shores of the country. Eligibility to immigrate was based on the ability of a candidate to speak reasonably fluent English, to contribute to the Canadian way of life, to respect the equality of women with men, and to find gainful employment in the economy.

The former practice of permitting related family members to follow in the footsteps of the youngest and brightest was quietly abandoned in favour of requiring positive contributions to the economy and social fabric of the country from all immigrants. Citizenship was granted on a probationary level for ten years, and immigrants were expected to quickly assimilate themselves to the English language, culture, dress and behaviour of the Canadian population. They were also assured of tolerance of their private and peaceful religious activities, customs, and traditions in Canada. The introduction of high technology identification cards to all Canadians had facilitated the location of 87% of the 40,000 recent immigrants under deportation orders, and the subsequent execution of those orders.

By the end of 2015, the goals of one official language, one culture, and essentially one people were well underway or had already been achieved. Canadians from all regions and walks of life were becoming more confident in their government and its achievements, more comfortable with the majority government, and much prouder of their newly revitalized country. Visitors to the country such as tourists, business people, and government officials from other countries had also begun to take note of Canada's achievements, and spoke highly of the changes.

The Period 2016 - 2030 From Canada in Crisis (1)

Based on its performance over the previous eight years, the people gave the government an overwhelming majority in the election of early 2016. Over those years, a much greater rapport had been developed between the federal, provincial, and major municipal levels of government. Following on those achievements, the government bent itself to the task of reforming the Constitution and the governance of the country.

As the government had done before, it now held meetings with the provincial premiers, other political parties, the mayors of major cities, businesses, and the people, to set the stage for wide-ranging amendments to the Constitution. For the most part, the proposed amendments were not contentious, especially with regard to the first three of the five major constitutional issues.

- First, to enshrine the distinctions between rights, privileges, duties and obligations.
- Second, to enshrine the rights of society over the rights of the individual, particularly in matters of culture and national security.

- Third, to enshrine rights to the peaceful enjoyment of individual and business property, in accordance to recent Supreme Court rulings.

The fourth major issue was the abolition of the Senate, about which there was much "Sturm und Drang", or more heat than light. Following on the previous successes with internet referenda, the government proposed the abolition of the Senate to the people. The response was again a resounding success, with 83% in favour of abolition of the Senate, and a response by 79% of the voting population. Referenda for major issues were proving popular.

- The government was prepared to abolish the Senate among proposed amendments to the Constitution. The government of Canada would then become a simple unicameral structure, and more representative of the people of the nation.

The remaining fifth major issue to be amended in the Constitution was the sharing of control and revenues from Canada's copious natural resources. What was needed was a simple and uniform solution applicable to all regions of the country. Past experience on this issue by various Prime Ministers since 2000 was the key to the successful resolution of this. Almost every conceivable formula had been tried before, but not always consistently in every region, which had created considerable discord. Eventually, mutual agreement on the sharing of these resources was established, with a simple and uniform formula for all provinces and the federal government.

- The federal and provincial governments reached an accord on sharing the control and revenue of natural resources by a single, simple formula for all regions of Canada.

In April of 2016, federal and provincial agreement was achieved for the introduction and passage of amendments to the Constitution of Canada, containing clauses for all of the above, and the amended Constitution was officially ratified in June of 2016.

A Consensual Parliament in 2020

In 2017, the federal government sought to change the very structure of Parliament by the introduction of a consensual parliament. Ontario had flirted in 2008 with discussions of a consensual legislature with greater cooperation among the political parties. Well argued support had been offered for such a change by Vaughan Lyon, Professor of political studies at Trent University in Peterborough. But the government wished to go further, to remove the last vestige of adversarial confrontation from the federal Parliament by the abolition of all federal political parties. Such a consensual Parliament would be modelled not on the English Parliament, but rather on the legislature of Nunavut. Eighteen years ago in April 1999, legislation had been passed by the federal government to establish the northern Canadian Territory of Nunavut.

Nunavut comprised one fifth of the area of Canada, and had a population of fewer than 30,000 persons. The first election in Nunavut was held in 1999, and 19 members were elected to the Nunavut Legislative Assembly. Unlike provincial legislatures, the Nunavut Legislative Assembly did not operate on the basis of political parties, but instead operated on a consensus basis. With a party system, the leader of the party which won the most seats in an election became premier. In Nunavut, the elected members chose the premier and cabinet ministers. The premier then assigned portfolios to the ministers.

On reflection, one must realize that political parties are a redundant intercession between the citizens and their government. The parties are an artifice for control designed by members of the parties themselves for financing and winning elections, based on the axiom "united we stand, divided we fall". Unfortunately, the goals and political ambitions of the parties may often supercede the best interests of the people and the nation. For example, there is a compulsion based on sheer ego for any political party to be continually in power, regardless of its lack of competence or loss of confidence of the House of Commons. Under a consensual parliament there would be no "trained seals" clapping in the back rows, forced to follow party lines even though those party lines were against the members' own principles and beliefs.

There have been many egregious activities by parties or politicians, such as the sponsorship scandal (1993 to 2006) involving the Liberal party, or the strange consulting fees of former Prime Minister Brian Mulroney. Another shameful party activity was the cancellation of the Sea King helicopter contract. On his first day in office in 1993 with a liberal majority, Jean Chrétien cancelled a signed contract to purchase 28 navy helicopters and 15 search and rescue versions. Chrétien said the country could not afford "Cadillac" helicopters when the national deficit was so high. The cancellation of the project triggered more than $1 billion in penalties, write offs, and extra maintenance costs for the existing fleet of Sea King helicopters.

In 1959 in a similarly repugnant activity, Prime Minister John Diefenbaker ordered the destruction by cutting torches of five prototype Avro Arrow CF-105 fighter aircraft. The result was the virtual dismemberment of Canada's highly respected and innovative aerospace industry, which sadly left for better employment opportunities in the United States. During the Liberal reign of the 1990s, the government oversaw the inexcusable obsolescence and decay of Canada's military equipment in its army, navy and air force. At the same time, dangerous military commitments had been and continued to be made to position Canadian forces in harm's way in the former Yugoslavia, Afghanistan and other hot spots. And finally in the midst of these egregious activities, were the continued but unwarranted entitlements to excessive pensions for Members of Parliament.

Such activities as these would have been inconceivable without the power and protection of "the party". Such activities as these would have been equally inconceivable under a consensual government. Any political party is an anachronism from the past which no longer serves a useful purpose in a western democracy such as Canada in the 21st century.

There was strong opposition by the politicians and initially by some of the public to the government's proposal to abolish all federal political parties. The Bill to enact the required legislation failed to pass in the existing Parliament in 2017. Following the defeat of the bill to abolish all federal political parties, the government launched an information campaign to bolster its proposal for a consensual parliament over the following years. In 2019, and still with a strong majority, the government held another referendum on the proposed abolition of federal political parties to construct a consensual parliament. The referendum succeeded this time, with a vote of 84% in favour of the change and a voter participation rate of 73%. The legislation was passed officially in 2020.

After ten years of working within a consensual parliament, the improvement in decorum and effectiveness was astounding. The principal reasons were the absence of delays and filibustering (and plain blustering) either by an opposition party, or by a recalcitrant Senate. In addition to those factors, all 212 (a reduction from the former 308) of the members were now working to a common purpose. Draft bills prepared by sub-committees were more quickly and effectively reviewed, and subsequently placed before the full parliament for debate and then passed. All appointments to government office were based on competence, not party patronage.

The success of the change to a consensual parliament by the federal government was noticed by the Atlantic provinces, who were burdened historically with excessive bureaucracies and badly in need of reforms themselves. After much negotiation, the four provinces agreed to amalgamate into a single entity called the Atlantic Province, with a consensual legislature having one third the number of members as the total of the previous legislatures. Amendments to the Constitution and to federal and provincial legislation to achieve this were passed in 2023.

With another election coming within a year, the government decided to provide an overview of its achievements over the past dozen years in office. In addition to simplifications and qualitative improvements, there were substantial financial savings from reductions in program costs or outright cancellation of some programs, as follows:

From Canada in Crisis (1);

- greatly reduced costs by conversion from income tax to a value added tax (VAT)
- reduced costs by conversion of pensions to TFSAs for Members of Parliament
- greatly reduced costs by conversion of pensions & employment insurance to TFSAs
- greatly reduced costs by cancellation of the bilingual program
- reduced costs by abolition of employee unions in the federal service
- reduced costs by privatization or abolition of some agencies, boards, corporations
- greatly reduced costs (and imminent cancellation) of the Indian program
- reduced costs under more selective and restrictive immigration policies
- reduced costs in immigration and law enforcement by use of biometric BID cards
- reduced costs and time delays by expulsion of separatist MPs (Bloc Quebecois)
- reduced costs and time delays by abolition of the Senate
- reduced time and cost by conversion from confrontational to consensual parliament
- government appointments were based on competence (no parties, no patronage)
- reduced federal government portion of GDP from 43% (2007) to 27% in 2028

From Canada in Crisis (2);

- immediate 50% reduction of income tax on retirement withdrawals from RRIFs
- greater security by BIDs for all Canadians and travellers (& persons of concern)
- greater security provided by targeting of persons of concern in transit

- greater security by strengthened enforcement powers for border & coastal staff
- greater security by federal management of electrical power transmission grids
- greater security from improved justice, courts, law enforcement, & sentencing
- greatly improved highways and communications in all regions of the nation
- reduced immigration of incompatible cultures to protect western culture & democracy
- greater security by rescission of dual citizenship for incompatible cultures

The public was so pleased with the new structures of parliament that the election of 2024 was held without any negative campaigning, and at greatly reduced cost. The candidates who were standing for office did so based on their professional competence and proven experience to fairly represent their ridings. The professional competence of successful candidates provided greater choice from a larger field of elected members for the prime minister to form a strong cabinet.

Canada in 2030 - a Nation United and Secure

From Canada in Crisis (1) & (2)

By 2030, all of the goals for Canada to become a united country had finally been accomplished; One Country, One Nation, One Governance, One Justice, One Economy, One Religion, One Language, One Culture, and One People. Canada and the Canadian people had regained their identity. By 2030, the security of the nation had been greatly strengthened, and the survival of the nation was more assured than before.

By the year 2030, Canada was a more united and secure nation than it had ever been before.

Epilogue

Canada is one of the most admired countries in the world for many reasons: its democratic government, its rule of law, employment opportunities, open spaces, fresh water, vibrant economy, religious, educational, and political freedoms, and many more. That said, there remains a lack of national unity, and there continue to be issues of personal and national security which should be resolved to create an even better nation. There may well be other important criteria for a better lifestyle as well. There is always room for improvement.

A century ago, the newly created nation had only a rudimentary government which dared not burden its struggling pioneers with a high level of taxes. Over the next century, more and more social services were demanded by the people, or as was more often the case, were offered by the government as a means of securing re-election. The people have lost their resilience, independence, and self-reliance, and have come to expect assistance from government for a host of issues. These range from pensions, employment guarantees, health benefits, paid parental leave for fathers, bilingual services for minorities, university attendance for everyone, and many, many other social services.

The result of these benefits bestowed by the governments to the people, has simply resulted in high taxation levels and intrusion by governments into the economy and society of the nation at twice the historic levels. The government now attempts to do many activities which are best left to business and individuals to do. But the government now fails to do well those activities which a government should do . . . to provide an environment in which the people may safely and securely prosper and enjoy the fruits of their own labours.

The unity of the nation and the security of the people must be the prime concerns of the government. The threats posed to Canada's lands, justice system, law enforcement, and economy by inadequate or ineffective legislation should be corrected by a government with a mandate for improvement. The security of the nation's transportation, energy and power infrastructure, and telecommunications should be protected from ineffective legislation, natural disasters, and terrorist threats. The most serious of all threats may be the loss of our values, customs, traditions, and even our treasured democracy itself. To do so, the government must be more proactive in its policies to safeguard the people and the nation.

The proposals in this book are intended to enhance and ensure the security of the nation, its customs, and its life styles. The proposals are feasible and should create a better nation and a true democracy; as Cicero clearly proclaimed, "The peoples' good is the highest law".

Few of the above changes will succeed unless the voters demand the proposed changes from their candidates for government before the next election.

Few of the above changes will succeed unless the voters provide that government with a sufficiently strong majority to implement extensive changes at the highest levels.

The Bibliography for Canada in Crisis (2)

An Agenda for Survival of the Nation

Preface

The author's goal is to create a book that every Canadian may read and appreciate the process of governance in our nation. Part of that goal was to make such reading easy, without recourse to a computer or a library to learn more about a subject. Traditionally, many books provide their research material only by a numerically annotated reference and attribution of the source. People today generally do not have the time, interest, energy, or facilities to locate the reference and conduct such research themselves. Hence the author's attempt to provide full-text information, either in the beginning of each chapter for the proper background and context, or in the Bibliography for more additional and extensive reading on an subject. Thus the book may be easily read in the shade or in the sun, on the patio or on the dock at a cottage or resort.

The backgrounds for historic events in each chapter provide extensive information on complex matters which would generally be unfamiliar to most people. Those backgrounds are meant to provide reasonably reliable information of historic events. The backgrounds are attributed to such sources as Wikipedia which in turn were often from academic sources, the Canadian federal Department of Finance, and other government organizations.

The backgrounds for current events in each chapter express the concerns of the Canadian people in their daily lives. These backgrounds are usually attributed to newspaper articles or opinions written by well known journalists. The references show that the readers may not be alone in forming similar opinions on the subject matter. These current event citations should also assure the governments at federal, provincial, and municipal levels as to which issues concern the people of Canada, as well as the opinions of the people on those issues.

The governance of our nation is forever changing, hopefully for the better, but not always. Where the change is neither understood, nor found acceptable, the governments should be aware of the sentiments of the people, especially before the election of new governments.

And lastly, the author trusts that his suggestions and proposals have been made on the basis of reliable information, observation, simple truths and common sense. Given proper knowledge of history and events, one might say, "Don't let the obvious (solutions) elude you."

Security of the Lands

From Wikipedia: (Lightly edited and formatted):
http://en.wikipedia.org/wiki/List_of_Canadian_provinces_and_territories_by_area

The Lands & Inland Waters

As a country, Canada has ten provinces and three territories. These portions vary widely in both land and inland water area. The largest portion by land area is the territory of Nunavut. The largest portion by inland water area is the province of Quebec. The smallest portion in both land and inland water area is the province of Prince Edward Island. Canada is the second largest country in the world: however, in terms of dry land area, Canada ranks fourth; in terms of freshwater area, Canada is the largest country.

The total area of a province or territory is the sum of its land and freshwater areas. Areas are rounded to the nearest square kilometre or square mile. Percentages are given to the nearest tenth of a percent.

Total Areas of Lands and Inland Fresh Waters (including Hudson Bay)

Rank	Name	Total Area (sq km)	Total Area (sq m)	Percentages
1	Nunavut	2,093,190	808,199	21.0
2	Quebec	1,542,056	595,402	15.4
3	Northwest Territories	1,346,106	519,744	13.5
4	Ontario	1,076,395	415,606	10.8
5	British Columbia	944,735	364,771	9.5
6	Alberta	661,848	255,545	6.6

Rank	Name	Total Area (sq km)	Total Area (sq m)	Percentages
7	Saskatchewan	651,036	251,371	6.5
8	Manitoba	647,797	250,120	6.5
9	Yukon	482,443	186,276	4.8
10	Newfoundland and Labrador	405,212	156,456	4.1
11	New Brunswick	72,908	28,150	0.7
12	Nova Scotia	55,284	21,346	0.6
13	Prince Edward Island	5,660	2,185	0.1
	Canada Total	9,984,670	3,855,171	100

Fresh Water Areas (including Hudson Bay)

Fresh water areas consist of lakes, rivers, and reservoirs. These exclude territorial waters claimed by Canada in the Atlantic, Pacific, and Arctic oceans. Canada has no significant inland areas of salt water. Hudson Bay is slightly salty, but the salinity levels are lower than the oceans. Hudson Bay is connected to the Atlantic by some narrow straits, this keeps circulation down. Hudson Bay is fed by many rivers . . . a lot of freshwater flows into it. And finally, the bay is covered with ice for about six months per year. This keeps the evaporation rate down. Evaporation is mainly what causes the Great Salt Lake and the Dead Sea to be so salty.

Rank	Name	Fresh Water Area (sq kms)	Fresh Water Area (sq miles)	Fresh Water Area as % of Total Water	Fresh Water Area as % of Total Canada
1	Quebec	176,928	68,313	19.9	11.5
2	Northwest Territories	163,021	62,944	18.3	12.1
3	Ontario	158,654	61,258	17.8	14.7
4	Nunavut	157,077	60,649	17.6	7.5
5	Manitoba	94,241	36,387	10.6	14.5
6	Saskatchewan	59,366	22,922	6.7	9.1
7	Newfoundland & Labrador	31,340	12,101	3.5	7.7
8	British Columbia	19,549	7,548	2.2	2.1
9	Alberta	19,531	7,541	2.2	3.0
10	Yukon	8,052	3,109	0.9	1.7
11	Nova Scotia	1,946	751	0.2	3.5
12	New Brunswick	1,458	563	0.2	2.0
13	Prince Edward Is	0	0	0	0
	Canada Totals	891,163	344,086	100 %	8.9 %

Land Areas

Land areas consist of dry land, excluding areas of freshwater. Areas are rounded to the nearest whole unit. Percentages are given to the nearest tenth of a percent.

Rank	Name	Land Area (sq km)	Land Area (sq mi)	Percentages
1	Nunavut	1,936,113	747,551	21.3
2	Quebec	1,365,128	527,088	15.0
3	Northwest Territories	1,183,085	456,800	13.0
4	British Columbia	925,186	357,216	10.4
5	Ontario	917,741	354,348	10.1
6	Alberta	642,317	275,000	7.1
7	Saskatchewan	591,670	228,449	6.5
8	Manitoba	553,556	213,733	6.1
9	Yukon	474,391	183,167	5.2
10	Newfoundland & Labrador	373,872	144,355	4.1
11	New Brunswick	71,450	27,587	0.8
12	Nova Scotia	53,338	20,594	0.6
13	Prince Edward Is	5,660	2,185	0.1
	Canada Total	9,093,507	3,511,085	100 %

The Borders and Coastlines

From The Atlas of Canada; (lightly edited and formatted):
http://atlas.nrcan.gc.ca/site/english/learningresources/facts/coastline.html

Coastlines and Shorelines are different concepts

A Coastline follows the general line of the coast, but sometimes, in the case of small inlets or bays, the coastline is measured as running directly across the bay or inlet to rejoin the coastline on the opposite side. The coastline is not measured as precisely as is shoreline. The coastline includes the mainland coast and also the coasts of offshore islands. Canada has the longest coastline of any country in the world. The total length of Canada's coastline is 243,042 kilometres. A Shoreline is the perimeter of the land along the water's edge, measured to the closest exactness possible. Shoreline is, therefore, usually longer for a particular location than is its coastline.

Criteria Employed in Measuring the Coastline

The Canadian Hydrographic Service has measured the coastlines and islands of Canada, using National Topographic System maps at the scale of 1:250 000. To differentiate between the coastline and the shoreline at the mouths of rivers and streams, the mouths were closed off with arbitrary closing lines. These closing lines were not included in coastline measurements. For rivers such as the Mackenzie River and Fraser River having deltas at their mouths, closing lines joined the seaward points of the outermost islands of the delta. Bodies of water contained by bays, fiords, inlets, sounds or straits were considered part of the open sea, and the adjacent coastlines were included in the total length of coastline. In northern regions, glacier edges, as depicted on the maps, were assumed to be coincidental with the mean sea level contour and the seaward edges of glaciers were included in coastline measurements.

Coastline of Coastal Waters by Province and Territory (in kilometres)

Provinces & Territories	Mainland Coast	Major Islands Perimeter	Minor Islands Perimeter	Total
Newfoundland & Labrador	8,172	11,548*	9,236	28,956
Prince Edward Island	na	1,107*	153	1,260
Nova Scotia	4,051	1,883**	1,645	7,579
New Brunswick	1,524	177	568	2,269
Quebec	10,389	554	2,380	13,323
Ontario	1,210	na	na	1,210
Manitoba	917	na	na	917
Saskatchewan	na	na	na	na
Alberta	na	na	na	na
British Columbia	7,022	10,835	7,868	25,725
Yukon	343	na	na	343
Northwest Territories & Nunavut	24,131	86,818	50,511	161,460
Total	57,759	112,922	72,361	243,042

* Mainland only

Source: L. M. Sebert and M. R. Monroe 1972 - Dimensions and Areas of maps of the National Topographic System of Canada. Technical Report 72-1. Ottawa Department of Energy, Mines, and Resources, Surveys and Mapping Branch

Coastline of Inland Waters by Body of Water (in kilometres)

Body of Water	Canada Mainland	Canada Islands	United States Mainland	United States Islands
Lake Superior	1,394	990	1,389	615
St Marys River	106	101	47	143
Lake Michigan	0	0	2,253	383
Lake Huron	2,044	2,768	933	414
St Clair River	48	8	45	0
Lake St Clair	114	69	95	135
Detroit River	48	53	48	63
Lake Erie	592	47	693	69
Niagara River	48	5	58	55
Lake Ontario	537	80	483	45
St Lawrence 01	166	253	171	175
St Lawrence 02	241	302	243	264

St Lawrence 01 Lake Ontario to Iroquois Dam
St Lawrence 02 Iroquois Dam to Moses-Saunders Dam
Source: Coordinated Great Lakes Physical Data, Cornwall Ontario 1977 Coordinating Committee on Great Lakes Basic Hydraulic and Hydrological Data

---

The Canadian Coast Guard

From Wikipedia; (lightly edited and formatted)
http://en.wikipedia.org/wiki/Canadian_Coast_Guard

The Canadian Coast Guard (CCG) (French: Garde côtière canadienne - GCC) is the coast guard of Canada. It is the civilian federal agency responsible for providing maritime search and rescue (SAR), aids to navigation, marine pollution response, marine radio, and ice breaking. The Canadian Coast Guard is headquartered in Ottawa, Ontario and is a Special Operating Agency within the Department of Fisheries and Oceans.

Geographic area of responsibility

CCG's responsibility encompasses Canada's 202,080 km (109,110 nmi) long coastline, the longest of any nation in the world.(2) It operates over an area of ocean and inland waters covering approximately 8 million km2 (2.3 million nm2).

History - Predecessor agencies and formation (1867–1962)

Originally a variety of federal departments and even the navy performed the work which CCG does today. Following Confederation in 1867, the federal government placed many of the responsibilities for maintaining aids to navigation (primarily lighthouses at the time), marine safety, and search and rescue under the Marine Service of the Department of Marine and Fisheries, with some responsibility for waterways resting with the Canal Branch of the Department of Railways and Canals. Lifeboat stations had been established on the east and west coasts as part of the Canadian Lifesaving Service, and the Dominion Lifesaving Trail (now called the West Coast Trail) provided a rural communications route for survivors of shipwrecks on the treacherous Pacific Ocean coast off Vancouver Island.

After the Department of Marine and Fisheries was split into separate departments, the Department of Marine continued to take responsibility for the federal government's coastal protection services. During the inter-war period, the Royal Canadian Navy also performed similar duties at a time when the navy was wavering on the point of becoming a civilian organization. Laws related to customs and revenue were enforced by the marine division of the Royal Canadian Mounted Police. A government reorganization in 1936 saw the Department of Marine and its Marine Service, along with several other government departments and agencies, folded into the new Department of Transport.

Following the Second World War, Canada experienced a major expansion in ocean commerce, culminating with the opening of the St. Lawrence Seaway in 1958. The shipping industry was changing throughout eastern Canada and required an expanded federal government role in the Great

Lakes and the Atlantic coast, as well as an increased presence in the Arctic and Pacific coasts for sovereignty purposes. The government of Prime Minister John Diefenbaker decided to consolidate the duties of the Marine Service of the Department of Transport and on January 28, 1962, the Canadian Coast Guard was formed as a subsidiary of DOT. One of the more notable inheritances was the icebreaker Labrador, transferred from the Royal Canadian Navy.

Expansion years (1962–1990)

A period of expansion followed the creation of CCG between the 1960s and the 1980s. The outdated ships CCG inherited from the Marine Service were scheduled for replacement, along with dozens of new ships for the expanding role of the organization. Built under a complementary national shipbuilding policy which saw the CCG contracts go to Canadian shipyards, the new ships were delivered throughout this "Golden Age" of the organization.

In addition to expanded geographic responsibilities in the Great Lakes, the rise in coastal and ocean shipping ranged from new mining shipments such as Labrador iron ore, to increased cargo handling at the nation's major ports, and Arctic development and sovereignty patrols; all requiring additional ships and aircraft. The federal government also began to develop a series of CCG bases near major ports and shipping routes throughout southern Canada, for example Victoria, BC, Dartmouth, NS, and Parry Sound, ON.

The expansion of the CCG fleet required new navigation and engineering officers, as well as crew members. To meet the former requirement, in 1965 the Canadian Coast Guard College (CCGC) opened on the former navy base HMCS Protector at Point Edward, Nova Scotia on Sydney Harbour, Cape Breton Island. By the late 1970s the college had outgrown the temporary navy facilities and a new campus was opened in Westmount in 1981.

During the mid-1980s, the long standing disagreement between the U.S. and Canada over the legal status of the Northwest Passage came to a head after the USCGC Polar Sea transited the passage in what were asserted by Canada to be Canadian waters and by the U.S. to be international waters. During the period of increased nationalism that followed this event, the Conservative administration of Brian Mulroney announced plans to build several enormous icebreakers, the Polar 8-class which would be used primarily for sovereignty patrols.

However the proposed Polar 8 class was abandoned during the late 1980s as part of general government budget cuts; in its place a program of vessel modernizations was instituted. Additional budget cuts to CCG in the mid-1990s following a change in government saw many of CCG's older vessels built during the 1960s and 1970s retired.

From its formation in 1962 until 1995, CCG was the responsibility of the Department of Transport. Both the department and CCG shared complementary responsibilities related to marine safety, whereby DOT had responsibility for implementing transportation policy, regulations and safety inspections, and CCG was operationally responsible for navigation safety and SAR, among others.

Budget cuts and bureaucratic oversight (1994–2005)

Following the 1994 budget, the federal government announced that it was transferring responsibility for CCG from the Department of Transport to the Department of Fisheries and Oceans. The reason for placing CCG under DFO was ostensibly to achieve cost savings by amalgamating the two largest civilian vessel fleets within the federal government under a single department. Pundits at the time wryly referred to this arranged shotgun wedding as the 'Department of Fish and Ships'.

Arising from this arrangement, CCG became ultimately responsible for crewing, operating, and maintaining a larger fleet, both the original CCG fleet before 1995 of dedicated SAR vessels, NAVAID tenders, and multi-purpose icebreakers along with DFO's smaller fleet of scientific research and fisheries enforcement vessels, all without any increase in budget, in fact the overall budget for CCG was decreased after absorbing the DFO patrol and scientific vessels.

There were serious stumbling blocks arising out of this reorganization, namely in the different management practices and differences in organizational culture at DFO versus DOT. DFO is dedicated to conservation and protection of fish through enforcement whereas CCG's primary focus is marine safety and SAR. There were valid concerns raised within CCG about reluctance on the part of the marine community to ask for assistance from CCG vessels, since CCG was being viewed as aligned with an enforcement department. In the early 2000s, the federal government began to investigate the possibility of making CCG a separate agency, thereby not falling under a specific functional department and allowing more operational independence.

Special Operating Agency (2005)

In one of several reorganization moves of the federal ministries following the swearing in of Prime Minister Paul Martin's cabinet on December 12, 2003, several policy/ regulatory responsibilities (including boating safety and navigable waters protection) were transferred from CCG back to Transport Canada to provide a single point of contact for issues related to marine safety regulation and security, although CCG maintained an operational role for some of these tasks.

On April 4, 2005, it was announced by the Minister of Fisheries and Oceans that CCG was being designated a "Special Operating Agency", the largest one in the federal government. Although CCG still falls under the ministerial responsibility of the Minister of Fisheries and Oceans, it has more autonomy as it is not as tightly integrated within the department.

An example is that now all CCG bases, aids to navigation, vessels, aircraft, and personnel are wholly the responsibility of the Commissioner of the Canadian Coast Guard. The commissioner is supported by the CCG headquarters which develop a budget for the organization. The arrangement is not unlike the relationship of the Royal Canadian Mounted Police toward that organization's parent department, the Department of Public Safety.

The Special Operating Agency reorganization is different from the past under both DOT and DFO where regional directors general for these departments were responsible for CCG operations within their respective regions (where there were problems under DFO that did not occur under DOT). Now all operations of CCG are directed by the commissioner, who reports directly to the deputy minister and the CCG's assistant commissioners in each region. This management and financial flexibility is being enhanced by an increased budget for CCG to acquire new vessels and other assets to assist in its growing role of helping to ensure maritime (i.e. non-naval, non-military) security.

CCG continues to provide vessels and crew for supporting DFO's fisheries science, enforcement, conservation, and protection requirements. The changes resulting in CCG becoming a Special Operating Agency under DFO did not address some of the key concerns raised by a Parliamentary committee investigating low morale among CCG employees following the transfer from DOT to DFO, and budget cuts since 1995. This committee had recommended that CCG become a separate agency under DOT and that its role be changed to a paramilitary organization involved in maritime security by arming its vessels with deck guns, similar to the United States Coast Guard, and that employees be given peace officer status for enforcing federal laws on the Oceans and Great Lakes. As a compromise, the CCG now partners with the Royal Canadian Mounted Police (RCMP) and Canada Border Services Agency (CBSA) to create what are known as integrated border enforcement teams (IBETs), which patrol Canadian waters along the International Boundary.

Fleet modernization (1990–present)

In the 1990s–2000s, CCG modernized part of its SAR fleet after ordering British Royal National Lifeboat Institution (RNLI) designed ARUN class high-endurance lifeboat cutters for open coastal areas, and the USCG designed 47 foot Motor Lifeboat (designated by CCG as the Cape class) as medium endurance lifeboat cutters for the Great Lakes and more sheltered coastal areas. The CCG ordered five 14.6 metres (48 ft) motor lifeboats in September 2009, to add to the 31 existing boats. New vessels delivered to the CCG in 2009 included the hovercraft ACV Mamilossa and the near shore fisheries research vessel CCGS Kelso. Several major vessels have undergone extensive refits in recent decades, most notably CCGS Louis S. St Laurent in place of procuring the Polar 8 class of icebreakers.

In the first decade of the 21st century, CCG announced plans for the Mid-Shore Patrol Vessel Project (a class of 9 vessels) as well as a "Polar" class icebreaker project, in addition to inshore and offshore fisheries science vessels and a new oceanographic research vessel as part of efforts to modernize the fleet.

Non-military

Unlike the United States Coast Guard (USCG), CCG is a civilian, non-paramilitary organisation. The enforcement of laws in Canada's territorial sea is the responsibility of Canada's federal police force, the Royal Canadian Mounted Police (RCMP) as all ocean waters in Canada are under federal (not provincial) jurisdiction. Saltwater fisheries enforcement is a specific responsibility of DFO's Fisheries Officers.

Also, unlike the USCG, CCG does not have a "reserve" element. There is a Canadian Coast Guard Auxiliary (CCGA) which is a separate non-profit organization composed of some 5,000 civilian volunteers across Canada who support search and rescue activities. CCG does not have a military style rank structure; instead, its rank structure roughly approximates that of the civilian merchant marine.

The Royal Canadian Mounted Police

From Wikipedia: (Greatly abridged, and lightly edited)
http://en.wikipedia.org/wiki/Royal_Canadian_Mounted_Police

The Royal Canadian Mounted Police (RCMP) colloquially known as Mounties, and internally as 'The Force' is the national police force of Canada, and one of the most recognized of its kind in the world. It is unique in the world as a national, federal, provincial and municipal policing body. The RCMP provides federal policing service to all of

Canada, and policing services under contract to the three territories, eight provinces (except Ontario and Quebec), more than 190 municipalities, 184 Aboriginal communities, and three international airports.

As the federal police force of Canada, the Royal Canadian Mounted Police is primarily responsible for enforcing federal laws throughout Canada, while general law and order including the enforcement of the Criminal Code and applicable provincial legislation is constitutionally the responsibility of the provinces and territories. This responsibility is sometimes further delegated to municipalities which may form their own municipal police departments. This is common in the largest cities; every city with a population over 500,000 operates its own force.

The two most populous provinces, Ontario and Quebec, maintain their own provincial forces; the Ontario Provincial Police and Sûreté du Québec. The other eight provinces, however, have chosen to contract most or all of their provincial policing responsibilities to the RCMP. Under these contracts the RCMP provides front-line policing in those provinces under the direction of the provincial governments in regard to provincial and municipal law enforcement. When Newfoundland joined confederation in 1949 the RCMP entered the province and absorbed the then Newfoundland Rangers and took over that area. Today the Royal Newfoundland Constabulary has reclaimed some of that province to their jurisdiction. In the three territories, the RCMP serves as the sole territorial police force.

The RCMP is responsible for an unusually large breadth of duties. Under their federal mandate, the RCMP provides policing throughout Canada, including Ontario and Quebec. Federal operations include; enforcing federal laws, including commercial crime, counterfeiting, drug trafficking, border integrity, organized crime and other related matters; providing counterterrorism and domestic security; providing protection services for the Monarch, Governor General, Prime Minister and other ministers of the Crown, visiting dignitaries, and diplomatic missions; and participating in various international policing efforts.

Under provincial and municipal contracts the RCMP provides front line policing in all areas outside of Ontario and Quebec that do not have an established local police force. There are detachments located in small villages in the far north, remote First Nations reserves, and rural towns, but also larger cities such as Surrey, BC (population 394,976). In these provinces the RCMP maintains units that provide investigational support to their own detachments, as well as smaller municipal police forces, including the investigation of major crimes such as homicides, forensic identification services, police dog services, emergency response teams, explosives disposal, undercover operations, and others.

Under its National Police Services branch the RCMP provides support to all police forces in Canada through the operation of support services such as the Canadian Police Information Centre, the Criminal Intelligence Service Canada, Forensic Science and Identification Services, the Canada Firearms Centre and the Canadian Police College.

The RCMP Security Service was a specialized political intelligence and counterintelligence branch with national security responsibilities, but was replaced with the Canadian Security Intelligence Service (CSIS) in 1984, following revelations of illegal covert operations relating to the Quebec separatist movement. CSIS is not part of the RCMP, but is its own entity.

In 2006, the United States Coast Guard's Ninth District and the RCMP began a program called "Shiprider," in which 12 Mounties from the RCMP detachment at Windsor and 16 Coast Guard boarding officers from stations in Michigan ride in each other's vessels. The intent is to allow for seamless enforcement of the international border.

The Quebec Provincial Police Force (Sûreté du Québec)

From Wikipedia; lightly edited and formatted:
http://en.wikipedia.org/wiki/S%C3%BBret%C3%A9_du_Qu%C3%A9bec

The Sûreté du Québec or SQ (or "Quebec Provincial Police" QPP) is the provincial police force for the Canadian province of Québec. The headquarters of the Sûreté du Québec are located on Parthenais street in Montreal and the force employs roughly 5,163 officers.

The primary function of the Sûreté du Québec is to enforce provincial laws, some municipal bylaws, the criminal code, and many other laws throughout Quebec and to assist municipal police forces when needed. Members of the force can also act by law as forest conservation agents for example. The Sûreté du Québec is also responsible for providing municipal police services to municipalities in the province that do not otherwise have municipal or regional police services. By law, that includes municipalities with under 50,000 people. As such, the force is mainly present in small rural and suburban areas. The force also patrols provincial highways. In addition, the Sûreté du Québec may investigate any incident that involves wrong doing by a municipal police force or a case where a police intervention caused death.

The Ontario Provincial Police Force

From Wikipedia; lightly edited and formatted:
http://en.wikipedia.org/wiki/Ontario_Provincial_Police

The Ontario Provincial Police (OPP) is the largest deployed police force in Ontario and the second largest in Canada. The service is responsible for providing policing services throughout the province in areas lacking local police forces. It also provides specialized support to smaller municipal police forces, investigates province wide and cross jurisdictional crimes, patrols provincial highways (including Ontario's 400 Series Highways) and is responsible for many of the waterways in the province. The OPP also works with other provincial agencies, including the Ministry of Transportation and Ministry of Natural Resources to enforce highway safety and conservation regulations, respectively. The OPP officers provide security at the Ontario Legislature at Queen's Park in Toronto.

The Ontario Provincial Police is responsible for providing policing services over one million square kilometres of land and 174 000 km² of water to a population of 2.3 million people (3.6 million in the summer months). Currently (2009), the OPP has over 5,618 uniformed, 853 auxiliary and 1,765 civilian personnel. The vehicle fleet consists of 2,290 vehicles, 114 marine vessels, 286 snow and all terrain vehicles, 2 helicopters and 2 fixed wing aircraft. Field and operational services are provided from 163 police stations and satellite locations throughout Ontario. OPP stations are called "detachments."

The OPP General Headquarters are located in Orillia. Until 1995, the administration and headquarters divisions operated out of a number of buildings in Toronto. From 1973 to 1995 the headquarters were based out of the old Workmen's Compensation Board Building at 90 Harbour Street. Operations were moved to Orillia as part of a government move to decentralize ministries and operations to other parts of Ontario.

The Royal Newfoundland Constabulary

From Wikipedia; lightly edited and formatted:
http://en.wikipedia.org/wiki/Royal_Newfoundland_Constabulary

The Royal Newfoundland Constabulary (RNC) is a police force in the Canadian province of Newfoundland and Labrador. The RNC provides policing to the communities of St. John's and the Northeast Avalon Peninsula, Corner Brook, Churchill Falls, and Labrador City.

The RNC dates back to 1729 with the appointment of the first police constables. In the 19th century, the RNC was modelled after the Royal Irish Constabulary with secondment in 1844 of Timothy Mitchell of the Royal Irish Constabulary to be Inspector General, making it the oldest civil police force in North America. Mitchell served as inspector and superintendent of police until 1871, when the Newfoundland Constabulary was reorganized with a new Police Act. Other officers recruited from the Royal Irish Constabulary to take command of the Newfoundland force included Thomas J. Foley who served from 1871 to 1873, Paul Carty, who headed the RNC from 1873 to1895, and John Roche McGowen, who served as constabulary inspector general from 1895 to1908.

During World War II, the RNC pursued not only spies but also criminal elements within the foreign military stationed at St. John's. Their investigation into the 1942 Knights of Colombus hostel fire has become popular knowledge. In 1979, Her Majesty Queen Elizabeth II conferred the insignia 'Royal' on the Newfoundland Constabulary in recognition of its long history of service to Newfoundland and Labrador. On May 3, 2005, the RNC made a formal exchange of colours with Garda Síochána na hÉireann to mark the historic links between the two forces.

The Royal Newfoundland Constabulary serves alongside the Royal Canadian Mounted Police, which is contracted by the provincial government to provide provincial and community policing services. The Royal Newfoundland Constabulary serves mainly major metropolitan areas while the RCMP serves smaller and remote rural areas. The RNC has a force of some 400 officers, and started regularly carrying weapons in 1998; the Sig Sauer P226 handgun, and rifles, shotguns and tasers, although the latter have been under suspension since 2007.

The Canada Border Services Agency

From Wikipedia: (Lightly edited and formatted):
http://en.wikipedia.org/wiki/Canada_Border_Services_Agency

The Canada Border Services Agency is a federal law enforcement agency responsible for guarding the nation's borders and providing customs services. The Agency was created on December 12, 2003 by amalgamating Canada Customs with border and enforcement personnel from the Department of Citizenship and Immigration Canada (CIC) and the Canadian Food Inspection Agency (CFIA). The agency's creation was formalized by the Canada Border Services Agency Act which received Royal Assent on November 3, 2005. Since the September 11, 2001 attacks against the United States, Canada's border operations have placed a dramatic new emphasis on national security and public safety. The Canada / United States Smart Border Declaration created by John Manley and Tom Ridge has provided objectives for cooperation between Canadian and American border operations.

The CBSA oversees approximately 1,200 service locations across Canada, and 39 in other countries. It employs over 12,000 public servants, and offers round the clock service at 61 land border crossings and nine international airports, and oversee operations at three major sea ports, and three mail centres. CBSA operates detention facilities in Laval, Toronto, Kingston and Vancouver. The CBSA operates an Inland Enforcement branch, which tracks and removes inadmissible foreign nationals. Inland Enforcement Officers are plain clothes units, and are armed with the same sidearm (PX4 Storm) as port of entry Border Services Officers.

Border Services Officer

A Border Services Officer (BSO) is a federal law enforcement agent employed by the Canada Border Services Agency. BSOs are designated peace officers , and primarily enforce customs and immigration related legislation, in particular the Customs Act and the Immigration and Refugee Protection Act as well as over 90 other Acts of Parliament. Because of their peace officer designation, they also have the power to enforce other Acts of Parliament, including the Criminal Code of Canada. Border Services Officers are equipped with Beretta PX4 Storm pistols, with handcuffs, batons, and oleoresin capsicum (OC) spray.

Border Services Officers are trained at the CBSA Learning Centre, located in Rigaud, Quebec. The training begins with 4 weeks done online called Pre-POERT and then a 10-week program called Port of Entry Recruit Training (POERT), which covers a range of topics from criminal law to customs legislation. Followed by four weeks on the job "Field Coaching" and another three weeks of training called "In Service Post POERT".

Changes to the CBSA

Since the creation of the Agency in 2003, the CBSA has undergone significant changes to its overall structure as services previously offered by different agencies are now housed under a single banner. Not only has the structure of the organization changed, but the range of duties and the institutional priorities have changed. Where the prior coupling of Canada Customs with the Canada Revenue Agency lent itself to a focus on tax collection, the new Agency was created to address heightened security concerns post-9/11, and to respond to criticisms, mostly from the United States, that Canada was not doing enough to ensure the security of North America.

Substantial changes began before the 2001 terrorist attacks in the US. In May 1998, the Government of Canada passed Bill C-18, which changed agency policy to allow the officers to arrest and detain individuals at the border for non-customs related violations of Canadian law. These new responsibilities led to the implementation of use of force policies. Border Services Officers across Canada started to carry collapsible batons, OC spray and handcuffs. The 2006 Canadian federal budget introduced $101 million to equip CBSA officers with side arms and to eliminate single-person border crossings to help officers perform their duties. The decision to arm BSOs has been a subject of some controversy in Canada for several years, but the idea has had the support of other law enforcement agencies as well as the union that represents the affected officers.

In August 2006, Prime Minister Stephen Harper announced that arming BSOs would begin in early 2007 and would continue over the next 10 years. Some of the first officers to be armed will be those working at the Windsor, Ontario port of entry, the busiest highway port of entry in Canada. Arming at the other Ports of Entry across Canada is being conducted systematically with those Ports considered the busiest and/or most dangerous to be completed first. At this time it has not been decided whether officers at airports will be armed. It has been officially confirmed that CBSA officers will be armed with the 9mm Beretta Px4 Storm.

Immigration to Canada

The CBSA plays a key role in the immigration of people to Canada, as it has assumed the port of entry and enforcement mandates formerly held by the Department of Citizenship and Immigration Canada. CBSA officers work on the front lines, screening persons entering the country and removing those who are unlawfully in Canada.

As of the end of 2003 there were up to 200,000 illegal immigrants in Canada (most residing in Ontario). Most were refugee claimants whose refugee applications were rejected by the Immigration and Refugee Board of Canada. There are very few illegal immigrants who enter the country without first being admitted by the CBSA. The reason for this is that Canada is physically very difficult to get to, with the exception of crossing the Canada / U.S. border. As the U.S. is itself a prime destination for illegal immigrants, not many illegal immigrants attempt to cross the border into Canada in the wild. This differs significantly from the illegal immigration patterns in the US, which stem from illegal border crossings.

Examinations, searches and seizures

All persons and goods entering Canada are subject to examination by CBSA officers. An examination can be as simple as a few questions, but can also include an examination of the subject's vehicle and/or luggage, more intensive questioning, or personal searches. The intensity of an examination depends on the reasonable grounds that the officer has to escalate the intensiveness of a search.

Examinations are performed to ensure compliance with Customs and Immigration legislation. CBSA officers are given their authority by the Customs Act and the Immigration and Refugee Protection Act. In addition, BSOs are also able to enforce other Acts of Parliament as they are designated as Peace Officers under the Criminal Code of Canada.

The agency will also seize items it labels obscene, as it did in February 2009 when it detained and banned two films by the adult film director Michael Lucas. The CBSA's Policy On The Classification Of Obscene Material states that the "ingestion of someone else's urine... with a sexual purpose" makes a film obscene.

Intelligence and Enforcement

The Canada Border Services Agency maintains a robust and comprehensive Intelligence program, which is mandated to provide timely, accurate and relevant intelligence support to operational decision makers at all levels within the Agency. Information is lawfully collected from a variety of sources, including open and closed source materials, domestic and international intelligence partners, joint operations with other law enforcement agencies, sophisticated technical means, covert surveillance, and informants/human intelligence. Intelligence officers and analysts are deployed within Canada - along the borders and throughout the country - as well as overseas.

The CBSA turns the information it collects into intelligence by using automated risk analysis, analytical tools, and risk management. This allows it to work toward its objective of balancing security concerns with the need to facilitate the flow of people and goods. The Agency seeks to manage risks through a number of means, including the collection and analysis of intelligence information, the use of detection tools, the analysis of indicators and judgment of front-line officers, and random checks.

Threat and risk assessments are widely recognized as valuable decision-making tools when setting examination priorities. The Agency's intelligence directorate conducts a border risk assessment of its border operations every 2-3 years. Under this process, the Agency assesses the risks of smuggling contraband, such as drugs, firearms, proceeds of crime, child pornography, illicit tobacco etc. The information is assessed and ranked by commodity and by mode of transport. The Agency will include the risks of irregular or illegal migration of people, and the movement of food, plants, and animals, now under the Agency's broader mandate, in the next version of its border risk assessment.

The Agency also prepares a national port risk assessment every two years. The Agency assessed the relative risk to 168 ports of entry in 2006 and 220 in 2004. Regional intelligence analysts, in consultation with other sources and port operational staff, complete a questionnaire detailing port demographics, traffic volume, enforcement, and intelligence information. The 2006 risk assessment ranked 23 ports as high-risk and included information on suspected criminal and national security risks, as well as the risk of irregular or illegal migration of people.

In addition to the border and port risk assessment processes, the intelligence directorate provides daily, weekly and monthly updates on specific threats and trends in unlawful activities. Intelligence officers and analysts frequently participate in tactical and operational law enforcement activities such as search warrants, arrests, surveillance, the recruitment and retention of confidential informers, interviews of detainees and the analysis of seized goods and evidence.

Border Watch

The CBSA Border Watch toll free info line offers citizens the opportunity to report suspicious cross border activity directly to the Agency in a direct and confidential manner. The Border Watch line differs from other phone lines for the public, such as Crime Stoppers or the Royal Canadian Mounted Police info line in that it is designed to focus directly on border related intelligence. The toll free number is 1-888-502-9060.

Smart Border Declaration and Action Plan

The Smart Border Declaration and Action Plan, also known as the Smart Border Accord, was signed in 2001 and is an initiative of the Government of Canada, specifically the CBSA, RCMP and the Department of Foreign Affairs and International Development, and the Government of the United States, specifically the Department of Homeland Security, U.S. Customs and Border Protection and the United States Coast Guard. The two major signatories to the Declaration were Canadian Deputy Prime Minister John Manley and then-US Director of Homeland Security Tom Ridge.

The Accord was set up in order to facilitate the cross-border flow of travellers and goods, while co-ordinating enforcement efforts in the two countries. The Accord consists of 30 points of common interest to improve both security and trade between the two countries. Included in the plan are initiatives to improve the biometric features of Permanent Resident Cards in both countries, sharing Advanced Passenger Information, and creating compatible immigration databases.

Canada-United States Integrated Border Enforcement Teams

Integrated Border Enforcement Teams (IBETs) were created as a part of the Accord to consolidate the law-enforcement and intelligence gathering expertise of different agencies in both countries. The key Canadian contributors to the IBETs are the CBSA, RCMP, U.S. Customs and Border Protection, U.S. Coast Guard, and U.S. ICE Teams. However, IBETs also enlist the help of other municipal, state/provincial and federal agencies on certain projects.

In Canada, IBETs operate in 15 regions across the Canada-US Border in air, sea and land modes. They are based on a model started along the British Columbia-Washington State border in 1996. Since their inception, IBETs have helped disrupt smuggling rings involved in the drug trade, alcohol, tobacco and vehicle smuggling, and human trafficking.

The Department of Citizenship & Immigration

From Wikipedia: (Lightly edited and formatted):
http://en.wikipedia.org/wiki/Citizenship_and_Immigration_Canada

The Department of Citizenship and Immigration Canada (CIC) is the department of the government with responsibility for issues dealing with immigration and citizenship. The department was established in 1994 following a reorganization within the federal government.

CIC operates a large network of "Citizenship and Immigration Centres" throughout Canada and in a number of embassies, high commissions, and consulates abroad. Service Canada recently started to take over some of the domestic field operations of the department, while the Canada Border Services Agency took over the control of enforcement and entry control at borders and airports. CIC remains responsible for the establishment of policies and processing of permanent and temporary residence visa, refugee protection and citizenship applications.

The Immigration and Refugee Protection Act (IRPA)

Immigration and Refugee Protection Act (IRPA) is an Act of the Parliament of Canada, passed in 2001 as Bill C-11, which replaced the Immigration Act of 1976 as the primary federal legislation regulating Immigration to Canada. The IRPA, for the most part, came into force on June 28, 2002. Controversially, the Government failed to implement a component of the legislation that would have implemented a Refugee Appeal Division as part of Canada's immigration system.

IRPA creates a high level framework detailing the goals and guidelines the Canadian government has set with regards to immigration into Canada by foreign residents. The Immigration and Refugee Protection Regulations (IRPR) contain the laws created to fit within the IRPA in order to specify how the IRPA is to be applied.

Constitutionality

In the 2007 case of Charkaoui v. Canada (Citizenship and Immigration) (2007), Chief Justice McLachlin of the Supreme Court of Canada held that certain aspects of the scheme contained within the IRPA for the detention of permanent residents and foreign nationals on the grounds of national security violates s7 of the Canadian Charter of Rights and Freedoms by "allowing the issuance of a certificate of inadmissibility based on secret material without providing for an independent agent at the stage of judicial review to better protect the named person's interests." She also concluded that "some of the time limits in the provisions for continuing detention of a foreign national violate ss. 9 and 10© (of the Charter) because they are arbitrary." The Government of Canada responded by introducing a revised security certificate regime in the IRPA that includes the use of special advocates to review a summary of the evidence without being able to share this information with the accused. The bill to amend the IRPA was passed by Parliament with support from the Conservative and Liberal caucuses and received royal assent in 2008.

Canadian immigration and refugee law

Canadian immigration and refugee law concerns the area of law related to the admission of foreign nationals into Canada, their rights and responsibilities once admitted, and the conditions of their removal. The primary law on these matters is in the Immigration and Refugee Protection Act, which goals include economic growth, family reunification, and compliance with humanitarian treaties.

Enabling law

The primary statute is the Immigration and Refugee Protection Act (IRPA) which was introduced in 2002 to replace the former Immigration Act of 1976. The many changes included broader discretion for immigrations officers when evaluating applications. The IRPA is accompanied by the Immigration and Refugee Protection Regulations. Other relevant legislation include the Citizenship Act, and certain immigration and refugee-related provisions of the Criminal Code of Canada.

Admission classes

Canadian immigration policy allows several classes of people to enter. The Family Class allows permanent residents or citizens to sponsor a family member's entrance into the country. The Economic Class provides admission to applicants (and their immediate families) who are supposed to be likely to find employment and contribute to the Canadian economy. This is determined by the weighing of factors such as education, language skills, and work experience.

Claims and appeals

Claims for refugee status and for admissibility as well as appeals of the decisions of the immigration officers are direct to the Immigration and Refugee Board of Canada. The Board is the largest tribunal in Canada and hears over 25,000 claims a year. Decision of the Board can be appealed to the Federal Court, which hears about 2,500 appeals on immigration and refugee matters a year.

The Department of Public Safety Canada

From Wikipedia: (Lightly edited and formatted)
http://en.wikipedia.org/wiki/Public_Safety_Canada

Public Safety Canada, formerly known as Public Safety and Emergency Preparedness Canada, legally incorporated as the federal Department of Public Safety and Emergency Preparedness, is the department of the government of Canada with responsibility for protecting Canadians and helping to maintain a peaceful and safe society.

Legislation for the agency began in February 2001 and the department was created in December 2003 during a reorganization of the federal government, and it became legally established when the Department of Public Safety and Emergency Preparedness Act came into force on April 4, 2005. The agency Emergency Preparedness Canada was created under the auspices of the Defence department before the establishment of the department by the Emergency Preparedness Act of 1988.

The department was created to have a single entity with responsibility for ensuring public safety in Canada and is a direct result of lessons learned from the September 11 attacks on the United States in 2001. The department is in many ways similar to the U.S. Department of Homeland Security, though it does not cover the protection of maritime sovereignty.

Most of the department comprises organizations that were previously placed under the Department of the Solicitor General of Canada. However the reorganization of several federal departments and ministries added the Canada Border Services Agency to the portfolio, after the two streams of the former Canada Customs and Revenue Agency were split in 2003. In addition, the Office of Critical Infrastructure Protection and Emergency Preparedness (OCIPEP) from the Department of National Defence was also brought into the Department.

The first Public Safety and Emergency Preparedness minister was Anne McLellan, who also served as Deputy Prime Minister. On October 30, 2008, Peter Van Loan was appointed Minister of Public Safety by Prime Minister Stephen Harper.

In addition to the department, there are five agencies and three review bodies within the Public Safety portfolio headed by the Minister of Public Safety.

Associated Agencies

Canada Border Services Agency
Royal Canadian Mounted Police
Canadian Security Intelligence Service
Correctional Service Canada
National Parole Board

Review Bodies

Commission for Public Complaints Against the RCMP
RCMP External Review Committee
Office of the Correctional Investigator

Also reporting to the Deputy Minister and Minister of Public Safety is the Inspector General of CSIS, one of two review bodies for the agency.

Senior officials of Public Safety include:

Parliamentary Secretary to the Public Safety minister
Deputy Minister Public Safety.
Senior Assistant Deputy Minister, Emergency Management and National Security
Assistant Deputy Minister, Policing, Law Enforcement and Inter-operability
Assistant Deputy Minister, Strategic Policy
Assistant Deputy Minister, Community Safety and Partnerships
Assistant Deputy Minister, Corporate Management
Inspector General of CSIS

The Canadian Military Forces

From Wikipedia; lightly edited and formatted:
http://www.forces.gc.ca/site/acf-apfc/index-eng.asp

The Canadian Forces

The Chief of the Defence Staff, or CDS, is General Walter Natynczyk. He is responsible for the conduct of military operations and for the readiness of the Canadian Forces to carry out the tasks that Parliament assigns through the Minister. The CDS authority extends to the Navy, the Army and the Air force as well as to the four commands.

The Department of National Defence (DND) is the largest federal government department. DND and the CF together have a budget of approximately 18 billion dollars, and over 110,000 employees, including:

* 65,000 Regular Force members;
* 25,000 Reserve Force members (including 4,000 Canadian Rangers); and
* 28,000 civilians.

The Navy

Canada's Navy is a highly adaptable and flexible force. While being Canada's outer line of defense against an armed aggressor, it conducts sovereignty patrols, search and rescue operations, and assists other government departments in everything from disaster relief to law enforcement, such as conducting fishery or drug patrols. The Navy also supports Canadian foreign policy by remaining engaged internationally in everything from humanitarian assistance, to peace support operations, to maritime security operations.

The Army

The Canadian Army's mission is to provide trained, combat-ready, agile and quickly responsive troops to meet Canada's defense objectives. The Canadian Army is ready to respond to conflicts across the globe. With an international reputation for excellence, the well-equipped Canadian soldier is instrumental in the fight for freedom, stability and human rights around the world. Through the Disaster Assistance Response Team (DART), the Army is also prepared to send soldiers and equipment to assist international and national authorities with natural disasters, such as earthquakes, floods, storms, and forest fires.

The Air Force

Canada's Air Force protects Canadians, Canadian sovereignty and Canadian interests at home and abroad. The Air Force defends Canadian airspace and, working with the Navy, Army and other government departments, conducts maritime and northern patrols, search and rescue missions, and intercepts of vessels carrying illegal drugs. The Air Force also airlifts military personnel and supplies at home and abroad, and moves disaster relief supplies to stricken regions. Abroad, combat-ready forces take an active role in multinational missions, representing Canada's interests and helping maintain global stability.

The Four Commands

Four operational structures, called "commands", are in place for a responsive and efficient Canadian Forces creating a synergy among the Navy, Army and Air Force. The four commands are: the Canada Command, the Canadian Expeditionary Force Command, the Canadian Special Forces Command, and the Canadian Operational Support Command.

The mandate of Canadian Forces is three-fold:

1. Protecting Canada and defending our sovereignty.
2. Working with Canada's closest ally, the United States, to defend North America.
3. Contributing to international peace and security through operations around the world, most often in partnership with allies from other countries.

1. Protecting Canada

Because Canada is the number one priority, every day, over 9,000 members of the Canadian Forces look out for our peace and security on the home front. They patrol Canada's coasts and monitor its skies, lead search and rescue missions, assist civilian rescue authorities with disaster relief, and protect Canada's sovereignty.

The Canadian Forces deliver effective disaster relief to Canadians in distress with unique capabilities to provide support to civilian rescue authorities during forest fires, floods, avalanches, hurricanes or whenever disasters strike. Search and rescue crews respond rapidly to distress calls anywhere in our vast country and its surrounding seas. Every year, daring rescues, often conducted under hazardous conditions, save more than 1,000 lives and assist thousands more people in distress.

The Canadian Forces engage in operations, patrol and train in the Arctic to assert Canadian sovereignty and to improve surveillance and

reconnaissance. More than 4,000 dedicated Canadian Rangers provide local expertise and guidance in the North.
Rangers

2. Defending North America

Canada and the United States work together at North American Aerospace Defense Command (NORAD) to monitor and defend our continental airspace and ocean areas. Canadian Forces ships and aircrafts patrol our skies and seas.

The Canadian Forces play a leading role in enforcing our sovereignty and providing security throughout Canada's ocean areas. In addition to monitoring Canada's coastline, the longest of any nation in the world, the department of National Defence and the Canadian Forces support other federal partners such as the RCMP and the Canadian Coast Guard in tracking and intercepting vessels violating Canadian law.

3. Contributing to International Peace and Security

The Canadian Forces contribute to international peace and security through operations around the world. Currently, more than 3,000 Canadian soldiers, sailors and Air Force personnel are deployed overseas on operational missions. On any given day, about 8,000 Canadian Forces members – one third of the deployable force – are preparing for, engaged in, or returning from an overseas mission.

The Institute for Catastrophic Loss Reduction

From the Institute for Catastrophic Loss Reduction; lightly edited and formatted: http://www.iclr.org/aboutus.html

The Institute for Catastrophic Loss Reduction (ICLR) is a world class centre for multi- disciplinary disaster prevention research and communications. The ICLR was established by Canada's property and casualty (p&c) insurance industry as an independent, not for profit research institute affiliated with the University of Western Ontario. Institute staff and research associates are international leaders in wind and seismic engineering, atmospheric science, risk perception, hydrology, economics, geography, health sciences, public policy and a number of other disciplines.

To address this impending increase in natural disaster losses, the Institute for Catastrophic Loss Reduction (ICLR) has developed a long term communications strategy to enhance its messaging. Under a broad theme of "science to action, Canada's insurers building disaster resilient communities" the strategy is centred around three programs:

* RSVP cities (resilient, sustainable, vibrant and prosperous cities);
* Designed for safer living (safer design and construction of buildings); and
* Open for Business (TM) (disaster risk reduction for small business).

Working through ICLR, Canada's insurers are the only group in the country providing comprehensive disaster loss prevention advice to homeowners and home builders, as well as to owners of small businesses. Actions have been identified to help homeowners and owners of small business reduce the risk of injury, damage, and interruption of business due to severe wind, hail, earthquakes, flood, wildfire and a number of other hazards. We are also working to promote the construction of disaster resilient homes. ICLR is internationally recognized for its leadership in multi- disciplinary disaster prevention research.

There are essentially three systems utilized within Canada to manage disasters at community or municipal level. Within these systems there are variations reflecting provincial standards, organizational culture, and to a degree the preference of those who employ these systems.

The ICLR is committed to reducing disaster deaths, injuries and property damage through the development of disaster prevention knowledge, and the broad dissemination of its research findings. Moreover, the

Institute is working to transfer this emerging scientific knowledge into information available to decision makers to support actions to build resilient communities. This research deals with damage from wind, snow, ice, earthquakes, mould and a range of other hazards.

From the Institute for Catastrophic Loss Reduction: (lightly edited and formatted)

http://www.iclr.org/images/Disaster_response_in_Canada.pdf

Disaster Response Systems in Canada

By Kuban R., MacKenzie-Carey H., and Gagnon A.

Emergency services personnel respond and react to emergencies on a daily basis. While the emergency may be a crisis to those involved, responders are trained to deal with these situations as part of their "normal" daily functions. When emergencies escalate to disaster level, however, the response effort and the systems that guide them are also affected. Disasters are situations, which are anything but normal. Regardless of their level of emergency preparedness, response agencies are likely to be caught off guard by the occurrence of the event or its consequences. Their response to these disasters is also "abnormal" and different from their daily operations. It demands unique roles, rarely applied procedures, specialized skills, rare and unavailable resources, or additional powers.

By their definition, disasters are events of such magnitude that the response to them is often beyond the realm of a single organization. Disaster response, therefore, often involves a multi-organizational and multi-jurisdictional effort. At the municipal level, it nearly always involves a broad range of response agencies including other orders of government, industry resources, and community-based organizations.

Disaster response in Canada is the responsibility of elected officials at municipal level. They are mandated by law to prepare for and respond to disasters, which might affect their public (EPC, 1992). Within that broad jurisdiction are elements of various other jurisdictions:

fire, police, emergency medical services, health officials, dangerous good specialists, members of local industry and public officials from provincial and federal government departments. However, the ultimate responsibility for disaster response lies with elected officials, not of the Fire Chief, EMS personnel or Police Chief as many assume. The rare exceptions to the rule are disasters with broad geographical impact (i.e. those affecting a number of communities), or those events, which affect areas under provincial or federal jurisdiction.

The multi-organizational and jurisdictional nature of disaster response demands cooperation among its response agencies and the coordination of their activities at the scene. Failure to achieve these two key requirements typically results in breakdown of communications, failure to effectively allocate scarce resources, disjointed operational tasking, and the inability by any single organization to effectively meet its response objective.

The multi-agency nature of municipal response necessitates an emergency management system, which is unlike that designed to meet the needs of single organizations or jurisdictions. Furthermore, because of the unique context of disasters all emergency management systems must be designed to meet an additional number of principles. These include:

- Appropriate response to unique situations
- Flexibility and adaptability
- Cooperation across organizations and jurisdictions
- Traditional supremacy of elected officials maintained
- Provincial and federal governments "in support"
- Coordination of planning and response efforts
- Enhancement of the flow and distribution of information
- An Emergency Operation Center (EOC) must be functional and
- Disaster site management through team effort

An effective emergency management system must permit a team effort from those used to responding to emergencies on the one hand, and integrate the jurisdictional needs of the municipality's elected officials on the other. The system must factor-in the involvement of elected officials, who most likely have little experience with emergency response, and must ultimately lay the responsibility for response on their shoulders.

Within Canada three basic systems could be used to manage disasters. These systems include the Incident Command System (ICS), British Columbia Emergency Response Management System (BCERMS) and Emergency Site Management System (ESM). These systems have some common elements, and some unique features.

The Incident Command System (ICS)

The ICS was conceived following a set of wild land fires, which devastated southern California in 1970. Kramer and Bahme (1992) reported the tremendous devastation of these fires. They also noted that what was even more devastating was the organizational chaos which ensured during the response efforts. This prompted the U.S. Federal Emergency Management Agency (FEMA) to fund a special project titled "Firescope" which led to the creation of the Incident Command System. In time it was rightly promoted as a way to better manage the operation at the site.

The ICS structure and application is focussed on the disaster scene and generally speaking, the Fire Services. It is designed with the expectation that all of those who take part within it would become 'integrated'. That integration assumes that everyone would understand or comply with the ICS terminology, organizational structure, roles and responsibilities. The ICS system contains five basic components or "cells" of operation:

- Command (i.e., conduct the overall operation)
- Operations (i.e., perform the tactical tasks)
- Logistics (i.e., secure necessary services and support)
- Planning (i.e., map out upcoming activities)
- Finance/administration

Each function is represented by an organizational cell, and is further sub-divided into a number of other roles or functions. These are filled or performed as necessary by those who arrive at the scene as the situation escalates. Consequently, the overall organizational structure enlarges to accommodate the necessary tasking as well as the added resources that are available to the disaster response effort. Conversely, as the situation stabilizes and resources begin to shift away from the disaster scene to other duties, the organizational structure begins to constrict and eventually 'disintegrate' with everyone returning to other duties.

British Columbia Emergency Response Management System (BCERMS)

This British Columbia Emergency Response Management System (BCERMS) identifies the standardized approach to emergency response management to be utilized and practised by provincial government ministries, agencies and crown corporations." BCERMS is based upon the Incident Command System as developed and practised throughout the United States. Since the fall of 1992, the B.C. provincial government endorsed this emergency management response system mandated its application for all its ministries. BCERMS defines a process for organizing and managing a response to emergencies and disasters based on a framework of five components: operations and control, qualifications, technology, training, and publications. The BCERMS is modular with four levels of operation including site, site support, Provincial Regional Coordination and Provincial Central Coordination. These four levels allow elements to be activated or deactivated as the needs of the incident/emergency change over time. The system also provides for expansion, as additional resources are required.

Site Level

At the site level, resources are utilized to manage problems presented by an emergency incident. The BC Incident Command System (ICS) is used to manage the response using responders from all levels of government and the private sector. A single command or unified command from an on site incident command post structure is utilized.

Site Support Level

When the site level response requires off site support, an Emergency Operations Center (EOC) may be activated at this second level of response. The EOC supports the site by providing communication with the site level, establishing policy guidance, managing the local multiple agency support to the site, as well as acquiring and deploying additional resources as required at the site.

Provincial Regional Coordination Level

This third level of activation provides further support to the site level support or EOC if required by an escalation in the magnitude of emergency. The provincial regional coordination level manages the assignment of multiple-ministry and agency support to individual site support locations or multiple site support level locations. It acquires and deploys requests of the site support level, and provides emergency response services where incidents cross local authority boundaries or where local authorities are not organized to fulfill their role. This regional level does not normally communicate directly with the site level but rather communicates through the EOC or site support level.

Provincial Centre Coordination Level

The fourth level exists to expand support into an overall provincial government response. Persons within this level would have the responsibility for the provision of support for the regional levels. It is within this level of activation that authority of the minister for a declaration of a provincial emergency is obtained, direction of senior elected officials is sought, and provincial policy and priority guidance is provided. This group is responsible for managing the provincial emergency public information activities as well as the acquisition and deployment of provincial, federal, inter-provincial and international resources. If required, this group would provide coordination and support services to provincial Ministry Operation Centres (MOCs) and Crown Corporation's centres as well as Federal emergency response agencies.

The system is used not only in emergency situations but in private sector emergency response and management programs as well as for planned events such as celebrations, parades, and concerts. It thus allows more practice and familiarity with the system should it be needed in an emergency. The "all hazard" approach in B.C. includes: fires, HAZMAT (HAZardous MATerials), and multi-casualty incidents, search and rescue missions, oil spill response and recovery incidents, air, rain water or ground transportation accidents. It is an integral part of its earthquake preparedness and response plans.

Emergency Site Management

Canadian emergency services tend to receive training manuals and reading material from the United States where the pool of resources is significantly larger. Therefore, most services practise some form of the ICS system. Although not as widely used or known as the ICS system, another approach called Emergency Site Management (ESM) has been documented for Canadian communities as a guide during community wide disasters or emergencies.

Emergency Preparedness Canada (EPC)

Emergency Preparedness Canada initially formulated the Emergency Site Management (ESM) system in the early 1980's. The ESM system started by being a replica of the ICS approach, yet another permutation. However, over time it developed its own structure, mandate, roles and responsibilities to the point that it is now an independent and unique approach to the management of disasters both at the scene as well as at the local Emergency Operations Centre, away from the site.

The ESM unique approach is based on the Canadian system of emergency management. More often than not that approach places the focus of emergency planning and disaster response squarely on the shoulders of municipal elected officials. They, and NOT their representatives at the various agencies, are ultimately responsible for the effectiveness of their municipal plans and response effort.

The ESM approach considers and addresses two areas of operation: the Site, and the Municipal EOC. The EOC is intended to contain all key decision makers whose input may be of significance to the operation as a whole. Their role is to support the operational effort at the scene, as well as to carry on the day to day business of the rest of the community. While removed from the scene (or Site), the members of the EOC are nevertheless of great value because they are the formal link between the Site and the rest of the world.

Disaster situations involve many organizations from diverse jurisdictions. By the time that a community realizes that it is confronting a disaster, rather than a day to day emergency that is manageable by emergency services alone, a number of things have happened. Various agencies have begun their individual response to the incident. Those at the site have tried to work together. Someone assumed the role of a Site Manager coordinating efforts at the scene, and a call may have gone out to activate the EOC.

Once activated, the EOC personnel formally appoint a Site Manager and advise all responding agencies of his/her identity. (This person is typically recruited or appointed from the ranks of the local fire, police or EMS services, depending on the nature of the disaster.) From that point on, all key functions at the site are typically coordinated through the Site Manager. This appointment allows incoming resource agencies to have a contact person.

The Site Manager has a challenging role. He or she must accept that every key agency at the Site will maintain its own chain of command, mandate, and roles. But, at the same time, the Site Manager must create the operational structure at the scene that would provide an effective process to manage information, delegate responsibilities or resources, and coordinate action among the diverse agencies on site. Additionally, the Site Manager must maintain a link between the scene and the municipal EOC. This allows communication to flow from those involved in tasks at the scene to their lead officer, from that lead officer to the overall site manager, and from the site manager to the municipal EOC. The flow of communication also works in reverse when being initiated from the EOC to the site.

In essence, everything within the perimeter boundary of the Site is the responsibility of the Site Manager and the Site Team. This 'team' includes the senior representatives of the key agencies as well as the Incident Commander, who commands the Fire Services resources at the scene. This group, under the guidance and coordination of the Site Manager, manage the response to the disaster event at the site.

The EOC team is responsible for everything outside the outer boundary of the Site. The EOC team must also be available to support the operation within that Site boundary, if and when requested. Roles and responsibilities for the EOC team include media contacts, resource allocation, integration and communication with other communities and government, and public information access. Such responsibilities are not far from the daily responsibilities of these elected officials and allow for a smooth transition from daily operational to disaster mode.

The ESM system allows each organization to employ the process, which best fits its needs, while still maintaining operational coordination and communication both at the site as well as between the site and the EOC. For example, Fire personnel could continue to use the Incident Command System, without detracting from the ESM process. Similarly, Municipal officials are encouraged to employ their own operational system and to make strategic decisions away from the chaos of the site. The EOC and the site team are disbanded when their respective services are no longer required.

While it varies from situation to situation, this action typically signals the end of the disaster response operation. However, recovery operations may continue for a much longer period. Like any other management system, the ESM (disaster management) system requires senior management commitment. It also requires broad multi-organizational involvement and on going planning effort.

Two key elements exist in effective disaster response: the presence of response networks and planning. Disaster networks, which are based on contact between individuals from different agencies, have a number of important benefits. They help bridge organizational boundaries, enhance cooperation, and facilitate resource acquisition These networks need time to be developed and should be part of the disaster planning process (Kuban, 1993).

The planning process is also critically important (Auf der Heide, 1989; Drabek and Hoetmer, 1991; Dynes, 1979). Each municipality should have its own 'Municipal Emergency Plan' (MEP). This plan, and the planning process leading to it, should naturally include representatives from all key potential response organizations.

Summary

There are essentially three systems utilized within Canada to manage disasters at community or municipal level. Within these systems there are variations reflecting provincial standards, organizational culture, and to a degree the preference of those who employ these systems.

The ICS system (Incident Command System) is well known by most first responders in Canada, particularly those from the fire services. Responders at site level who wish to manage emergencies and follow an existing chain of command, frequently use the ICS system. Because of their prior knowledge of this system and its application, ICS often becomes the preferred or default system for large scale emergencies. Unfortunately, many municipal officials may not have experience with the ICS system or be aware of the terminology, intricate command structure, or reporting procedures. Their lack of understanding combined with their overall responsibility for an effective disaster management could lead to confusion, awkward shifts of command and control, and ultimately an uncoordinated response.

The ESM model was designed to address this concern and clearly indicates the roles and responsibilities of municipal officials. The problem with this system however, is the lack of regular exposure to the process. Many communities and their diverse agencies do not regularly plan or train for disasters. Their three key response agencies (i.e. Fire, EMS, and Police) plan and regularly train their personnel. They also have regular exposure to emergencies and typically use the structure (i.e. ICS), which suits their respective professional needs during 'normal' emergencies. When these emergencies expand to require more agencies to work together, the three response agencies may be reluctant to switch to the ESM model. This reluctance may occur because the ESM system has not been properly practised, or due to an initial commitment at the site to the ICS approach.

In times of stress, and most disasters are stressful, people revert to what they know or are comfortable with rather than try new methods. Consequently, the ESM system, which otherwise would assist in coordination and communication, is left untried. This may be particularly confusing and frustrating for municipal officials who are not familiar with any of the existing roles and responsibilities.

British Columbia may have developed a solution to the problem by customizing the ICS system to incorporate municipal leaders and government officials with the intention of providing harmony. Although the system should provide effective emergency management practices within the province in which is was designed, it may cause significant conflicts in cross border disaster situations when other provinces or states respond by using other systems. The BCERMS system (BC Emergency Response Management System) also requires fairly extensive training by all those who would perform a role in the various levels of activation.

In the final analysis, any system will work if there is an agreed plan among all responding agencies and officials to use it. If everyone agrees before a disaster occurs on which process will be used, and is trained in its application, the system is very likely to work. Conversely, no system, no matter how well designed will work during a disaster if those who are responsible for overall management are unaware or unwilling to use the system.

Education and practice involving all those who would respond to disaster is essential. Effective models exist but are not useful if they are not practised and understood by responders and municipal leaders. Training in disaster response at the community level is essential to ensure smooth transition from 'normal' emergencies to disaster response with its multi-agency effort.

Security of Justice

The Canadian Judicial System

From the federal Department of Justice: (lightly edited and formatted)
http://www.justice.gc.ca/eng/dept-min/pub/ccs-ajc/page3.html

There are basically four levels of court in Canada. First there are provincial/territorial courts, which handle the great majority of cases that come into the system. Second are the provincial/territorial superior courts. These courts deal with more serious crimes and also take appeals from provincial/territorial court judgments. On the same level, but responsible for different issues, is the Federal Court. At the next level are the provincial/territorial courts of appeal and the Federal Court of Appeal, while the highest level is occupied by the Supreme Court of Canada.

Provincial/ Territorial Courts

Each province and territory, with the exception of Nunavut, has a provincial/territorial court, and these courts hear cases involving either federal or provincial/territorial laws. (In Nunavut, there is no territorial court – matters that would normally be heard at that level are heard by the Nunavut Court of Justice, which is a superior court.) The names and divisions of these courts may vary from place to place, but their role is the same. Provincial/territorial courts deal with most criminal offences, family law matters (except divorce), young persons in conflict with the law (from 12 to 17 years old), traffic violations, provincial/territorial regulatory offences, and claims involving money, up to a certain amount (set by the jurisdiction in question). Private disputes involving limited sums of money may also be dealt with at this level in

Small Claims courts. In addition, all preliminary inquiries – hearings to determine whether there is enough evidence to justify a full trial in serious criminal cases – take place before the provincial/territorial courts.

A number of courts at this level are dedicated exclusively to particular types of offences or groups of offenders. One example is the Drug Treatment Court (DTC) program, which began in Toronto in 1998, followed over several years by Vancouver, Edmonton, Regina, Winnipeg, and Ottawa. The object of the DTCs is to address the needs of non-violent offenders who are charged with criminal offences that were motivated by their addiction. Those who qualify are offered an intensive combination of judicial supervision and treatment for their dependence, drawing on a range of community support services.

Youth courts handle cases where a young person, from 12 to 17 years old, is charged with an offence under federal youth justice laws. Procedures in youth court provide protections appropriate to the age of the accused, including privacy protections. Courts at either the provincial/territorial or superior court level can be designated youth courts.

Some provinces and territories (such as Ontario, Manitoba, Alberta and the Yukon) have established Domestic Violence Courts in order to improve the response of the justice system to incidents of spousal abuse by decreasing court processing time; increasing conviction rates; providing a focal point for programs and services for victims and offenders; and, in some cases, allowing for the specialization of police, Crown prosecutors and the judiciary in domestic violence matters.

Provincial/ Territorial Superior Courts

Each province and territory has superior courts. These courts are known by various names, including Superior Court of Justice, Supreme Court (not to be confused with the Supreme Court of Canada), and Court of Queen's Bench. But while the names may differ, the court system is essentially the same across the country, with the exception, again, of Nunavut, where the Nunavut Court of Justice deals with both territorial and superior court matters.

The superior courts have "inherent jurisdiction," which means that they can hear cases in any area except those that are specifically limited to another level of court. The superior courts try the most serious criminal and civil cases, including divorce cases and cases that involve large amounts of money (the minimum is set by the province or territory in question).

In most provinces and territories, the superior court has special divisions, such as the family division. Some have established specialized family courts at the superior court level to deal exclusively with certain family law matters, including divorce and property claims. The superior courts also act as a court of first appeal for the underlying court system that provinces and territories maintain.

Although superior courts are administered by the provinces and territories, the judges are appointed and paid by the federal government.

Courts of Appeal

Each province and territory has a court of appeal or appellate division that hears appeals from decisions of the superior courts and provincial/territorial courts. The number of judges on these courts may vary from one jurisdiction to another, but a court of appeal usually sits as a panel of three. The courts of appeal also hear constitutional questions that may be raised in appeals involving individuals, governments, or governmental agencies.

The Federal Courts

The Federal Court and Federal Court of Appeal are essentially superior courts with civil jurisdiction. However, since the Courts were created by an Act of Parliament, they can only deal with matters specified in federal statutes (laws). In contrast, provincial and territorial superior courts have jurisdiction in all matters except those specifically excluded by a statute.

The Federal Court is the trial-level court; appeals from it are heard by the Federal Court of Appeal. While based in Ottawa, the judges of both Courts conduct hearings across the country. The Courts' jurisdiction includes interprovincial and federal-provincial disputes, intellectual property proceedings (e.g. copyright), citizenship appeals, Competition Act cases, and cases involving Crown corporations or departments of the Government of Canada. As well, only these Courts have jurisdiction to review decisions, orders and other administrative actions of federal boards, commissions and tribunals; these bodies may refer any question of law, jurisdiction or practice to one of the Courts at any stage of a proceeding.

For certain matters, such as maritime law, a case may be brought either before the Federal Court or Federal Court of Appeal, or before a provincial or territorial superior court. In this respect, the Federal Court and the Federal Court of Appeal share jurisdiction with the superior courts.

Specialized Federal Courts

In order to deal more effectively with certain areas of the law, the federal government has created specialized courts, notably the Tax Court of Canada and courts that serve the Military Justice System. These courts have been created by statute and can only decide matters that fall within the jurisdiction given to them by statute.

The Tax Court of Canada

The Tax Court of Canada gives individuals and companies an opportunity to settle disagreements with the federal government on matters arising under federal tax and revenue legislation. The Tax Court of Canada primarily hears disputes between the federal government and taxpayers after the taxpayer has gone through all other options provided for by the Income Tax Act. The Tax Court is independent of the Canada Revenue Agency and all other government departments.

Its headquarters are in Ottawa , and it has regional offices in Montreal, Toronto and Vancouver .

Military Courts

Military courts, or courts martial, were established under the National Defence Act to hear cases involving the Code of Service Discipline. The Code applies to all members of the Canadian Forces as well as civilians who accompany the Forces on active service. It lays out a system of disciplinary offences designed to further the good order and proper functioning of the Canadian Forces.

The Court Martial Appeal Court hears appeals from military courts. Its function is comparable to that of a provincial/territorial appeal court, and it has the same powers as a superior court. Judges in the Court Martial Appeal Court are selected from the Federal Courts and other superior courts throughout the country. Like other courts of appeal, the Court Martial Appeal Court hears cases as a panel of three.

Trial by Jury

Under the Canadian Charter of Rights and Freedoms, individuals accused of the most serious criminal offences generally have the right to choose to be tried by a jury or by a judge alone. A jury is a group of people, chosen from the community, who assess the facts of a case after a judge explains the law to them. They then make a decision based on their assessment. Sentencing, however, is left to the judge. Trial by jury is also available in some civil litigation, but is rarely used.

The Supreme Court of Canada

The Supreme Court of Canada is the final court of appeal from all other Canadian courts. The Supreme Court has jurisdiction over disputes in all areas of the law, including constitutional law, administrative law, criminal law and civil law.

The Court consists of a Chief Justice and eight other judges, all appointed by the federal government. The Supreme Court Act requires that at least three judges must come from Quebec. Traditionally, of the other six judges, three come from Ontario, two from western Canada, and one from the Atlantic provinces. The Supreme Court sits in Ottawa for three sessions a year – winter, spring and fall.

Before a case can reach the Supreme Court of Canada, it must have used up all available appeals at other levels of court. Even then, the Court must grant permission or "leave" to appeal before it will hear the case. Leave applications are usually made in writing and reviewed by three members of the Court, who then grant or deny the request without providing reasons for the decision. Leave to appeal is not given routinely – it is granted only if the case involves a question of public importance; if it raises an important issue of law or mixed law and fact; or if the matter is, for any other reason, significant enough to be considered by the country's Supreme Court.

In certain situations, however, the right to appeal is automatic. For instance, no leave is required in criminal cases where a judge on the panel of a court of appeal has dissented on how the law should be interpreted. Similarly, where a court of appeal has found someone guilty who had been acquitted at the original trial, that person automatically has the right to appeal to the Supreme Court.

The Supreme Court of Canada also plays a special role as adviser to the federal government. The government may ask the Court to consider questions on any important matter of law or fact, especially concerning interpretation of the Constitution. It may also be asked questions on the interpretation of federal or provincial/territorial legislation or the powers of Parliament or the legislatures. (Provincial and territorial courts of appeal may also be asked to hear references from their respective governments.)

The Nunavut Court of Justice

When the territory of Nunavut was established in 1999, a new kind of court in Canada was created as well. The Nunavut Court of Justice combines the power of the superior trial court and the territorial court so that the same judge can hear all cases that arise in the territory. In Nunavut, most of the communities are small and isolated from the capital of Iqaluit, so the court travels to them "on circuit." The circuit court includes a judge, a clerk, a court reporter, a prosecutor, and at least one defence attorney. Court workers and Crown witness coordinators might also travel with the circuit court, depending on the cases to be heard. Interpreters are hired in the communities when possible, or travel with the circuit court when necessary. In addition to holding regular sessions in Iqaluit, the court flies to most communities in Nunavut at intervals that range from six weeks to two years, depending on the number of cases.

Unified Family Courts

Unified family courts, found in several provinces, permit all aspects of family law to be dealt with in a single court with specialized judges and services. The unified family courts consist of superior court judges, who hear matters of both provincial/territorial and federal jurisdiction. These courts encourage the use of constructive, non-adversarial techniques to resolve issues, and provide access to a range of support services, often through community organizations. These services differ from province to province but typically include such programs as parent-education sessions, mediation, and counselling.

Sentencing Circles

Sentencing circles, pioneered in the Yukon Territorial Court in the early 1990s, are now used in much of the country, mostly at the provincial/territorial court level and in cases involving Aboriginal offenders and victims. Sentencing circles are part of the court process, though not courts in themselves, and they can be a valuable means of getting input and advice from the community to help the judge set an appropriate and effective sentence.

Sentencing circles generally operate as follows: After a finding or admission of guilt, the court invites interested members of the community to join the judge, prosecutor, defence counsel, police, social service providers, community elders, along with the offender, the victim and their families and supporters, and meet in a circle to discuss the offence, factors that may have contributed to it, sentencing options, and ways of reintegrating the offender into the community. Everyone is given the chance to speak. Often the circle will suggest a restorative community sentence involving some form of restitution to the victim, community service, and/or treatment or counselling. Sometimes members of the circle will offer to help ensure that the offender lives up to the obligations of the community sentence, while others may offer to provide support to the victim.

It is important to note, though, that sentencing circles do sometimes recommend a period of custody. Moreover, the judge is not bound to accept the circle's recommendations.

Justice for Nunavut http://carleton.ca/Capital_News/26031999/f4.htm

New structure for unique territory By Trisha Buchanan

OTTAWA – March 11, 1999 may not go down in Canadian history books as an important date, but it should. This was the day Bill C-57 was given Royal Assent in the Senate, and the people of Nunavut got a justice system unlike any other in the country. Introduced in the House of Commons on Oct. 22, 1998, the bill creates the Nunavut Court of Justice. It sets out the formation of a single-level trial court for Canada's newest territory. This court replaces both the Supreme Court of the Northwest Territories and the Territorial Court, which used to preside over the area.

Nunavut will be the only one of Canada's provinces and territories to have this single-court structure. All of the other provinces' and territories' justice systems have more than one level of courts, with each level hearing specialized types of cases.

In the Nunavut Court of Justice, this hierarchy will be eliminated. Superior Court judges will be able to hear any type of case, including civil, family and criminal disputes in both adult and youth courts. There will also be a court of appeal to reconsider decisions by the judges of the new court system. The new territory's system is special because Nunavut is not like any of Canada's other provinces or territories.

Under the system being replaced, it is not uncommon for people to wait months for a trial, or between a guilty verdict and a sentencing hearing. The victims of crimes sometimes have to live in the same communities as offenders before the convicts are sent to jail. Nancy Karetak-Lindell, Liberal MP for Nunavut, described the situation during House of Commons debates over Bill C-57. "There are also suicides directly related to people waiting for the dates of their court cases," said Karetak-Lindell. "I personally know of a young family where the husband took his life, leaving a wife and two children, because of the stress involved with waiting for a court case to come around."

This bill, and the subsequent creation of the Nunavut Court of Justice, shows that the federal government is conscious and open to the unique needs and culture of Nunavut and its people. The fact that the Nunavut people were asked by Ottawa to be involved in the creation of the system is almost as important as the legislation itself. "It really is an encouraging story," said Andy Watt, co-ordinator of northern issues for the justice department. "The people of Nunavut stated this is the kind of system that they wanted and we went from there."

Nunavut is a place where about 26,000 people live in a geographic area covering almost 2 million square kilometres. Court members such as judges and lawyers must be flown into isolated communities to hear cases. "I personally know of a young family where the husband took his life, leaving a wife and two children, because of the stress involved with waiting for a court case to come around"

Because of the distance, court officials may only make three or four trips to any given community each year. Under the old system, even when the judges did arrive, they weren't able to handle all the cases on the waiting lists. Criminal court judges heard charges laid by police. Civil courts dealt with property and family law disputes. In late March, judges for the new court system were appointed by the federal government, just like judges for the other provinces and territories.

The new single tier system means any of the judges of the Nunavut Court of Justice may hear any type of case. There will no longer be a need to transport judges with different specialties into and out of the communities. This should mean shorter waits for the Nunavut people for trials and hearings.

As well, the new system hopes to make better use of justices of the peace. There are currently about 80 justices of the peace and they live in the Nunavut communities, rather than having to be flown in. "There is a high expectation for the justices of the peace," said Watt. "The hope is that some of the old roles of the judges can be taken over by these people who are right in the community." These roles include such things as conducting preliminary hearings and maybe even trials for less serious offences. First, however, the justices of the peace will have to take training courses. The hope is that all of these changes will help make the justice system in Nunavut more efficient and accessible.

The Constitution

From Wikipedia: (lightly edited and formatted)
http://en.wikipedia.org/wiki/Constitution_of_Canada

The Constitution

The Constitution of Canada (La Constitution du Canada in French) is the supreme law in Canada; the country's constitution is an amalgamation of codified acts and uncodified traditions and conventions. It outlines Canada's system of government, as well as the civil rights of all Canadian citizens. Interpretation of the Constitution is called Canadian constitutional law.

The composition of the Constitution of Canada is defined in subsection

52(2) of the Constitution Act, 1982 as consisting of the Canada Act 1982 (including the Constitution Act, 1982), all acts and orders referred to in the schedule (including the Constitution Act, 1867, formerly the British North America Act), and any amendments to these documents. The Supreme Court of Canada held that the list is not exhaustive and includes unwritten components as well.

Newfoundland never ratified the Statute, so that it was still subject to imperial authority when its entire system of government and economy collapsed utterly in the mid-1930's. Canada did ratify the Statute, but had requested an exception be made under which it did "not" acquire full independence because the Canadian federal and provincial governments could not agree on an amending formula for the Canadian Constitution. It would be another 50 years before this was achieved. In the interim, the British Parliament periodically passed enabling acts and other legislation to retroactively legitimate the actions of the Canadian Parliament and government. This was never anything but a rubber stamp, but it did mean Canada was still legally a colony instead of a fully fledged member of the sisterhood of nation states.

The patriation of the Canadian Constitution was achieved in 1982 when the British and Canadian parliaments passed parallel acts – the Canada Act, 1982 ((UK) 1982, c.11) in London, and the Constitution Act 1982 in Ottawa. Thereafter, the United Kingdom was formally absolved of any remaining responsibility for, or jurisdiction over, Canada; and Canada became responsible for her own destiny. In a formal ceremony on Parliament Hill in Ottawa, the Queen signed both acts into law on April 17, 1982.

The Canada Act/ Constitution Act included the Canadian Charter of Rights and Freedoms. Prior to the Charter, there were various statutes which protected an assortment of civil rights and obligations, but nothing was enshrined in the Constitution until 1982. The Charter has thus placed a strong focus upon individual and collective rights of the people of Canada.

Enactment of the Charter of Rights and Freedoms has also fundamentally changed much of Canadian constitutional law. Before the Charter, civil rights and liberties had no solid constitutional protection in Canada. Whenever one level of government passed a law that seemed oppressive to civil rights and liberties, Canadian constitutional lawyers had to argue creatively, such as by saying that the oppressive law violates division of federal and provincial powers or by citing some other technical flaw that had little to do with the concept of civil rights and liberties. Even the Magna Carta, which does have constitutional status in Canada, was occasionally called into service in legal argument. Since 1982, however, the arguments have been easier to make, because lawyers have been able to cite the relevant sections of the constitution rather than rely upon legal abstraction.

The Act also codified many previously oral constitutional conventions, and has made amendment of the Constitution significantly more difficult. Previously, the Canadian federal constitution could be amended by solitary act of the Canadian or British parliaments, by formal or informal agreement between the federal and provincial governments, or even simply by adoption as ordinary custom of an oral convention or unwritten tradition that was perceived to be the best way to do something — or just the way things had always worked. For example, Canada has had a Prime Minister since 1867, but there is no mention of the office in the Constitution until as late as 1982. Yet, there remains no legal definition as to what a Prime Minister specifically is. Since the Act, amendments must now conform to certain specified provisions in the written portion of the Canadian Constitution (see amendment formula).

Constitution Act, 1867

This was an Act of the British Parliament, originally called the British North America Act 1867, that created the Dominion of Canada out of three separate provinces in British North America (Province of Canada, New Brunswick, and Nova Scotia) and allowed for subsequent provinces and colonies to join this union in the future. It outlined Canada's system of government, which combines Britain's Westminster model of parliamentary government with division of sovereignty (federalism). Although it is the first of twenty British North America Acts, it is still the most famous of these and is understood to be the document of Canadian Confederation (i.e. union of provinces and colonies in British North America). With the patriation of the Constitution in 1982, this Act was renamed Constitution Act, 1867. In recent years, the Constitution Act, 1867 has mainly served as the basis on which the division of powers between the provinces and federal government have been analyzed.

Constitution Act, 1982

Endorsed by all the provincial governments except Quebec's, this was an Act by the Canadian Parliament requesting full political independence from Britain. Part V of this Act created a constitution-amending formula that did not require an Act by the British Parliament. Further, Part I of this Act is the Canadian Charter of Rights and Freedoms which outlines the civil rights and liberties of every citizen in Canada, such as freedom of expression, of religion, and of mobility. Part II deals with the rights of Canada's Aboriginal people.

Canadian Charter of Rights and Freedoms

As noted above, this is Part I of the Constitution Act, 1982. The Charter is the constitutional guarantee of collective and individual rights. It is a relatively short document and written in plain language in order to ensure accessibility to the average citizen. It is said that it is the part of the constitution that has the greatest impact on Canadians' day-to-day lives, and has been the fastest developing area of constitutional law for many years.

Amending formula

With the Constitution Act, 1982, amendments to the constitution must be done in accordance with Part V of the Constitution Act, 1982 which provides for five different amending formulas. Amendments can be brought forward under section 46(1) by any province or either level of the federal government. The general formula is set out in section

38(1), known as the "7/50 formula", requires: (a) assent from both the House of Commons and the Senate; (b) the approval of two-thirds of the provincial legislatures (at least seven provinces), representing at least 50% of the population (effectively, this would include at least Quebec or Ontario, as they are the most populous provinces). This formula specifically applies to amendments related to the proportionate representation in Parliament, powers, selection, and composition of the Senate, the Supreme Court and the addition of provinces or territories. The other amendment formulas are for exceptional cases as provided by in the Act:

- In the case of an amendment related to the Office of the Queen, the number of senators, the use of either official language (subject to section 43), the amending formula, or the composition of the Supreme Court, the amendment must be adopted by unanimous consent of all the provinces in accordance with section 41.
- However, in the case of an amendment related to provincial boundaries or the use of an official language within a province alone, the amendment must be passed by the legislatures affected by the amendment (section 43).
- In the case of an amendment that affects the federal government alone, the amendment does not need approval of the provinces (section 44). The same applies to amendments affecting the provincial government alone (section 45).

The Division of Powers

From Wikipedia: (lightly edited and formatted)
http://en.wikipedia.org/wiki/Canadian_federalism#Distribution_of_Legislative_Powers_in_the_Constitution_Act.2C_1867

Canadian federalism

Canadian federalism is one of the three pillars of the constitutional order, along with responsible government and the Canadian Charter of Rights and Freedoms. It means that Canada has two distinct jurisdictions of political authority: on the one hand, the central Canadian parliament and, on the other hand, legislative assemblies in the ten provinces. Linked together by the Canadian Crown, from which all derive their sovereignty and authority, the federal parliament and the legislative assemblies of the provinces are independent with respect to certain areas of legislative authority. A few subjects are shared (agriculture and immigration).The three territories are creations of the Federal Parliament and exercise delegated power and not sovereign power. The United Kingdom did not follow this model when Confederation was realized, making Canada different from its mother country (and similar to its southern neighbour, the United States) in this respect.

The federal nature of Canadian constitution was a reaction to the colonial diversities in the Maritimes and the Province of Canada, in particular the strong distinction between the French speaking inhabitants of Lower Canada (Quebec) and the English speaking inhabitants in Upper Canada (Ontario) and the Maritimes. Federalism was considered essential to the co-existence of the French and English communities. John A. Macdonald, who became the first Prime Minister of Canada, had at first opposed a federalist system of government, favouring a unitary system of government. Macdonald later supported the federalist system after seeing the carnage of the American Civil War. He sought to avoid the same violent conflicts by maintaining a fusion of powers rather than a separation of powers south of the border.

The division of powers between the federal and provincial governments was initially outlined in the British North America Act, 1867 (now the Constitution Act, 1867), which, with amendments (in the British North America Acts and the Constitution Act, 1982), form the Constitution of Canada.

The Crown

As a federal monarchy, the Canadian Crown is unitary throughout all jurisdictions in the country, with the headship of state being a part of all equally. As such, the sovereignty of the each is passed on not by the Governor General or federal parliament, but through the overreaching

Crown itself as a part of the executive, legislative, and judicial operations. Though singular, linking the federal and provincial governments into a federal state, the Crown is thus "divided" into eleven legal jurisdictions, or eleven "crowns" – one federal and ten provincial. The Fathers of Confederation viewed the system of constitutional monarchy as a bulwark against any potential fracturing of the Canadian federation.

Distribution of Legislative Powers in the Constitution Act, 1867

The federal-provincial distribution of legislative powers (also known as the division of powers) defines the scope of the power of the federal parliament of Canada and the powers of each individual provincial legislature or assembly. These are contained in sections 91, 92, 92A, 93, 94, 94A and 95 of the Constitution Act, 1867. Much of the distribution, however, has been ambiguous, leading to disputes that have been decided by the Judicial Committee of the Privy Council and, after 1949, the Supreme Court of Canada. Doctrines of judicial interpretation of federalism include pith and substance, double aspect, paramountcy and inter-jurisdictional immunity

The Canadian constitution has created an overarching federal jurisdiction based upon the power known as peace, order and good government (section 91). However, the Canadian constitution also recognizes certain powers that are exclusive to the provinces and outside federal jurisdiction (section 92). The preamble of section 91 makes this clear: "It shall be lawful for the Queen, (...) to make laws for the Peace, Order, and good Government of Canada, in relation to all Matters not coming within the Classes of Subjects by this Act assigned exclusively to the Legislatures of the Provinces;" Thus, the federal government of Canada is partly limited by the powers assigned exclusively to the provincial legislatures. For example, the Canadian constitution created a very broad provincial jurisdiction over direct taxation, property, and civil rights. Many disputes between the two levels of government revolve around conflicting interpretations of the meaning of these two powers.

A quick perusal of these powers shows that while the federal government has exclusive jurisdiction over criminal law (defined in the Margarine Reference) and procedure (section 91(27)) the provinces have jurisdiction over the administration of justice, including criminal matters (section 92(14)) and penal matters (section 92(15)) regarding any laws made within provincial jurisdiction. Thus Canada has a single Criminal Code but many provincial laws that can result in incarceration or penalty. The courts have recognized that the provinces and the federal government have the right to create corporations; only the federal government has the right to incorporate banks, though provinces may incorporate credit unions which offer similar services as the federally chartered banks.

In relation to marriage and divorce, the federal government's exclusive authority over these subjects (section 91(26)) has given Canada uniform legislation on them, yet the provinces can pass laws regulating the solemnization of marriage (section 92(12)) and wide variety of subjects pertaining to civil and political rights (section 92(13)) and have created institutions such as common-law marriage and civil union.

Nowhere in the division of powers of the Constitution Act, 1867 is there a mention of a treaty power, reserved to the British Empire. Power for external relations was granted to Canada only after the passage of the Statute of Westminster in 1931. The domestic implementation of treaties, however, remains divided between the two levels of government.

Trade and commerce

Section 91(2) gives Parliament the power to make law related to the "regulation of trade and commerce." In comparison with the U.S. Constitution's approach to trade and commerce, the power given to Parliament is more broadly worded than that given to the U.S. government, but in Canada since Citizen's Insurance Co. v. Parsons in the 1880s it has nevertheless been typically read more narrowly, as some judges have felt that it overlaps with the provincial authority over property and civil rights. Parliament's authority over trade and commerce is said to include its "general" aspects, although this was an ambiguous definition until the 1980s when in General Motors of Canada Ltd. v. City National Leasing it was ruled Parliament could regulate trade and commerce if its object was to achieve something a provincial government alone could not achieve.

Property and civil rights

Section 92(13) gives the provinces the exclusive power to make law related to "property and civil rights in the province". In practice, this power has been read broadly giving the provinces authority over numerous matters such as professional trades, labour relations, family law and consumer protection. Property and civil rights is a term that predates the Constitution Act, 1867, and does not mean what it means today. It primarily refers to interactions between private persons. This would include the great majority of what any government would regulate, which means Parliament would be powerless if it were not for its enumerated powers in section 91 and for peace, order and good government.

Transportation and communication

Like many other powers, transportation and communication have overlapping powers between the two jurisdictions. Section 92(10) gives the provinces power over "local work and undertakings". However, the section also excludes the provinces from undertakings related to "ships, railways, canals, telegraphs, and other works and undertakings connecting the province with any other or others of the provinces", as well as ship lines, and such works "declared by the Parliament of Canada to be for the general advantage of Canada or for the advantage of two or more provinces." Further divisions of responsibilities by jurisdiction are as follows:

Federal

* defence
* criminal law
* employment insurance
* postal service
* census

* copyrights
* trade regulation
* external relations
* money and banking
* transportation
* citizenship
* Indian affairs

Provincial

* property and civil rights
* administration of justice
* natural resources and the environment
* education
* health
* welfare

Municipal

* water
* sewage
* waste collection
* public transit
* land use planning
* libraries
* emergency services
* animal control
* economic development

Federalism and the Charter

In 1982 the Canadian Charter of Rights and Freedoms was brought into effect. This was not meant to affect the workings of federalism, though some content was moved from section 91 to section 4 of the Charter. Mainly, the Charter is meant to decrease powers of both levels of government by ensuring both federal and provincial laws respect Charter rights, under section 32. The relationship between federalism and the Charter is directly dealt with in section 31, in which it is made clear neither the federal nor provincial governments gain powers under the Charter. In R. v. Big M Drug Mart Ltd. (1985) it was found that if laws violate Charter rights, they cannot be justified under section 1 of the Charter if their purpose was inconsistent with the proper division of powers.

History

The relationship between Canada and the provinces has changed throughout time, with an increasing amount of decentralization taking place as years passed. Throughout the Macdonald era (1867-1873, 1878-1891), the Confederation was such that it has been described by political scientist K. C. Where as "Quasi-Federalism". This meant that the political and judicial elites of the 19th century read the Constitution of Canada in a way that gave the federal Parliament extensive powers that essentially made the provinces "subordinate to Ottawa." The Macdonald government's use of disallowance and reservation also reinforced the supremacy of the federal government at that time.

With the election of Sir Wilfrid Laurier came a new phase of Confederation that Dyck refers to as "Classical Federalism". This was marked by a more equal relationship between the federal government and the provinces, as the Judicial Committee of the Privy Council settled several disputes in favour of the latter. The federal government also allowed its disallowance and reservation powers to fall into disuse. This style of governance continued throughout the early years of the leadership of Prime Minister William Lyon Mackenzie King (although legislation from Alberta was disallowed in the 1930s).

During the two world wars, Ottawa expanded its powers greatly. This was done through the War Measures Act and constitutionally justified by the peace, order and good government clause. During the First World War, Parliament increased its taxation powers by establishing income taxes. Finally, during the Second World War, the federal government convinced the provinces to transfer jurisdiction over unemployment insurance to Ottawa.

Canada emerged from the Second World War with more association or cooperation between federal and provincial levels of government. This owed to the rise of the welfare state and the health care system (as the Canadian government acted to ensure that Canadians as a people had some common quality of service), to the fact that many of the jurisdictions of the two levels of government were closely related, and to the fact that this allowed the federal government to retain a great deal of control that they had enjoyed during World War II. Keynesian economics were also introduced by the federal government through this system. The period was also marked by a number of First Ministers meetings (ie., meetings between the prime minister and the provincial premiers).

After 1960 and Quebec's Quiet Revolution, Canada moved toward a greater degree of administrative decentralization, with Quebec often opting out of important federal initiatives, such as the Canada Pension Plan (Quebec created its own pension plan). As the federal government became more centralist in ideology. Under the leadership of Prime Minister Pierre Trudeau, Canada entered a stage of "conflictual federalism" that could be said to have lasted from 1970 to 1984. The National Energy Program sparked a great deal of bitterness against the federal government in Alberta; indeed, the federal government was also involved in disputes over oil with Newfoundland and Saskatchewan at this time. (These culminated in the addition of section 92A to the Constitution Act, 1867, by the Constitution Act, 1982; the new section gave the provinces more power with regard to these resources).

The Progressive Conservative Party of Canada under Joe Clark and Brian Mulroney favoured devolution of powers to the provinces, culminating in the failed Meech Lake and Charlottetown accords. After a merger with the heavily devolutionist Canadian Alliance, the new Conservative Party of Canada under Stephen Harper has continued the same stance.

After the 1995 Quebec referendum on Quebec sovereignty, one of several actions by then Prime Minister Jean Chrétien was to put some limits on the ability of the federal government to spend money in areas of provincial jurisdiction. Thus, in 1999, the federal government and all provincial governments except Quebec's agreed to the Social Union Framework Agreement, which promoted common standards for social programs across Canada. Former Prime Minister Paul Martin has used the term asymmetrical federalism to describe this arrangement.

Steven Truscott Murder Case

From the Guelph Mercury 2009/10/31 by Judith McKenzie

With the assistance of the Association in Defence of the Wrongfully Convicted, Steven Truscott's conviction was overturned on Aug 28 2007, after he had been charged and convicted in the murder of Lynn Harper in June 1959. In total, his original trial lasted 10 days and resulted in a conviction and a sentence that this 14 year old boy be " . . . hanged by the neck until dead." Eventually, the sentence was commuted to life by the federal cabinet. This case was an important and controversial one that pressured the federal government to abandon capital punishment.

From the time he was charged, Truscott maintained his innocence. For a small town boy from Clinton, it's difficult to have any understanding what this event must have meant to his family. Truscott's mother stayed in a trailer across from the jail in Goderich where he was originally detained. Although she has since died, she lived to hear that his conviction was overturned.

Truscott has always said that without the love and support of his family, he would have never survived the trauma of having spent 10 years in prison for a crime he did not commit. At the age of 15, Steven began his sentence at the Guelph jail. At 18, he was sent to the Collin's Bay Prison in Kingston to serve the remainder of his sentence. He was released in October 1969.

In 1970, he was invited to Guelph by Isabel LeBourdais, the writer of The Trial of Steven Truscott, who knew that the Withers family locally had a longtime continuing interest in his case. Ultimately, he met and eventually married the love of his life, Marlene, and together they had three children. Marlene has always stated that after she read the LeBourdais book, she was outraged about how the case was handled. Forced to live in the community using his mother's maiden name (as a condition of his parole), he lived in Guelph as a stellar citizen, and worked as a millwright at Owens Corning. He is now retired and is a doting grandfather to his four grandchildren.

The Truscott case has become symbolic of the dangers of what may occur when the justice system fails. It also highlights the need for co-ordinated policy responses in order to ensure such miscarriages become a thing of the past. To this end, the University of Guelph is launching the Truscott Initiative in Justice Studies designed to expand knowledge and raise awareness among students at the University of Guelph, as well as the residents of Guelph.

Since meetings began with the Truscott family around this initiative, it has been made clear by Truscott that the initiative be named the Truscott Initiative in Justice Studies reflecting that this is very much about the challenges his family experienced over the years. Truscott's older son Ryan has represented the family at strategic planning meetings held in the past year.

Judith McKenzie is an associate professor in the department of political science and coordinator of the criminal justice and public policy program at the University of Guelph.

From Wikipedia; (lightly edited and formatted):
http://en.wikipedia.org/wiki/Steven_Truscot

Steven Truscott

Steven Murray Truscott, born 18 January 1945 in Vancouver, British Columbia, is a Canadian who was sentenced to death in 1959, when he was a 14 year old student, for the alleged murder of classmate Lynne

Harper. His death sentence was commuted to life imprisonment, and he continued to maintain his innocence until 2007, when his conviction was declared a miscarriage of justice and he was formally acquitted of the crime.

Truscott was scheduled to be hanged on 8 December 1959; however, a temporary reprieve on 20 November 1959 postponed his execution to 16 February 1960 to allow for an appeal. On 22 January 1960, his death sentence was commuted to life imprisonment. Truscott was the youngest person to be sentenced to death in Canada, and his case gave major impetus toward the abolition of the death penalty in Canada.

On 29 November 2001, Truscott filed a section 690 Criminal Code application for a review of his 1959 murder conviction. Hearings in a review of the Truscott case were heard at the Ontario Court of Appeal. On 28 August 2007, after review of nearly 250 fresh pieces of evidence, the court declared that Truscott's conviction had been a miscarriage of justice. As he was not declared factually innocent, a new trial could have been ordered, but this was a practical impossibility given the passage of time. Accordingly, the court acquitted Truscott of the murder.

On July 7, 2008, the government of Ontario awarded him $6.50 million in compensation.

David Milgaard Murder Case

From Wikipedia; (lightly edited and formatted)
http://en.wikipedia.org/wiki/David_Milgaard

Arrest and Trial

In 1969, Milgaard, along with two friends, Ron Wilson and Nichol John, decided on a whim to take a road trip across the Canadian prairies, a trip which involved some drug use and petty theft. Ron Wilson would later testify against Milgaard, claiming, among other things, that Milgaard had stolen a flashlight from a grain elevator outside Aylesbury, Saskatchewan.

While the friends were in Saskatoon, a 20 year old nursing student, Gail Miller, was found dead on a snowbank. At the time Milgaard and his friends were stopping to pick up a casual friend Albert Cadrain, whose family was renting out their basement to Larry Fisher, an ex-con who would later be found guilty of the crime.

Tipped off by Cadrain, who admitted he was mostly interested in the CAD $2,000 reward for information, British Columbia police arrested Milgaard in May 1969 and sent him back to Saskatchewan where he was charged with Miller's murder. Cadrain testified that he had seen Milgaard return the night of Miller's murder in blood stained clothing, his grip on reality however was less than secure, and he was admitted to a psychiatric hospital several months later after claiming he was the Son of God.

Both Ron and Nichol were also called to testify against him. They had originally told police that they had been with Milgaard the entire day and that they believed him to be innocent, but they changed their stories for the court. Ron later recanted his testimony claiming that he had been told he was personally under suspicion and wanted to alleviate the pressure on himself.

Milgaard was convicted of murder and sentenced to life in prison on January 31, 1970, exactly a year after Miller's murder.

Review and release

He appealed his conviction several times, but was blocked both by bureaucracy and by a justice system unreceptive to those who were not willing to admit their guilt. His formal application was completed in 1988, but was not considered until 1991 after a Liberal MP, Lloyd Axworthy addressed the Parliament: ". . . I wish to speak of a travesty of justice. I speak of the plight of David Milgaard who has spent the last twenty-one years of his life in prison for a crime he did not commit. Yet for the last two years, the Department of Justice has been sitting on an application to reopen his case. But rather than review these conclusive reports, rather than appreciate the agony and trauma of the Milgaard family, the Minister of Justice refuses to act."

Parliament acted, and rejected Milgaard's application for a Conviction Review. In her 1996 autobiography Time and Chance, former Prime Minister and then Justice Minister Kim Campbell devotes an entire chapter to Milgaard. In this she claims that one of the main reasons for the delay in acting on the request to reopen his case was due to the fact that Milgaard's lawyers continually added new documentation to the file, which slowed the process in regard to when she could begin the review proceedings.

Supreme Court of Canada reference and subsequent events

The federal government submitted a reference question to the Supreme Court of Canada, which recommended that Milgaard's conviction be set aside. Kim Campbell, then the federal Minister of Justice ordered, pursuant to section 690 of the Criminal Code, that a new trial be held on the murder charge against Milgaard. However, the Government of Saskatchewan announced that it would not hold a new trial, instead entering a stay of proceedings in the case against Milgaard, on 16 April 1992. On 18 July 1997, a DNA laboratory in the United Kingdom released a report confirming that semen samples on the victim's clothing did not originate with Milgaard . . . for all intents and purposes clearing Milgaard of the crime. The Saskatchewan government then apologized for the wrongful conviction. On 25 July 1997, Larry Fisher was arrested for the murder and rape of Ms. Miller. On 17 May 1999, the Saskatchewan government announced that a settlement had been reached with Milgaard, and that he would be paid compensation of $10 million.

On September 30, 2003, the Saskatchewan government announced that a Royal Commission would investigate Milgaard's wrongful conviction, and on 20 February 2004, Justice Edward P. MacCallum was announced as the Commissioner. Douglas Hodson was later appointed as commission counsel.

Milgaard Inquiry Results

On 26 September 2008, Justice Minister Don Morgan released the findings of the Milgaard inquiry. Among its recommendations it includes a call for the federal government to create an independent body to review allegations of wrongful conviction. The report noted that if such a body already existed, Milgaard might have been released from jail years before he actually was.

Linda Fisher, ex-wife of Gail's murderer Larry Fisher, visited the Saskatoon police department in 1980. Linda told the police that she believed Larry had likely killed Gail. The Saskatoon Police Department did not follow up on Linda's statement. The inquiry report released by Justice MacCallum states that "while MacCallum noted that Milgaard's family members mounted a formidable public awareness campaign, their efforts also created tension and resentment within the police and the Crown's office." This is seen by some as an excuse for the failure of the Saskatoon police to investigate Larry Fisher.

Larry Fisher: The Real Killer

Larry Fisher lived a few doors down from where Gail Miller was raped and murdered, yet at the time was not seriously considered as a suspect. Fisher was arrested 25 July 1997 in Calgary. He was convicted 22 November 1999, and sentenced on 4 January 2000,

Fisher was given a life sentence however due to applicable laws at the time of the crime, he will be eligible to apply for parole in 10 years rather than the current 25, after the sentence. On 23 September 2003, the Court of Appeal for Saskatchewan unanimously denied Fisher's appeal of his conviction. Prior to this conviction, Fisher had served 23 years for numerous rapes in the cities of Winnipeg (Manitoba), Saskatoon and North Battleford (Saskatchewan).

Donald Marshall Murder Case

From The Canadian Encyclopaedia; (lightly edited and formatted) http://www.thecanadianencyclopedia.com/index.cfm?PgNm=TCE&Params=A1ARTA0005123

Donald Marshall Jr. (born at Sydney, NS 13 Sept 1953; died there 6 Aug 2009).

The case of Donald Marshall became one of the most controversial in the history of the Canadian criminal justice system. Accused of the 28 May 1971 stabbing death of a black youth, Sandy Seale, in Sydney, Nova Scotia, Marshall, a 16-year old Micmac, was convicted of murder and sentenced to life imprisonment.

After he had served 11 years in a penitentiary, a re-examination of the case found him innocent of the murder, as he had maintained. Roy Ebsary was charged and convicted of manslaughter, and Marshall was acquitted in May 1983. Marshall's long incarceration for a crime he did not commit, and his subsequent struggle with provincial and federal governments for compensation, drew great interest from the general public, prison reform groups and organizations opposed to the reinstatement of capital punishment. The alleged mishandling of his case has brought the police and judicial systems under severe criticism.

In September 1987 a royal commission of inquiry began to investigate the Marshall case. In 1989, the commission headed by Chief Justice Alexander Hickman completed its investigation. It concluded that "the criminal justice system failed Donald Marshall, Jr. at virtually every turn," that the police and judiciary had acted unprofessionally and incompetently, and that racism was a factor in the wrongful conviction. The commission recommended that an independent review mechanism be instituted to handle allegations of wrongful conviction and that no limit be set on the compensation amount. Donald Marshall was awarded a lifetime pension of $1.5 million in compensation.

Robert Dziekanski Taser Incident

From Wikipedia: (lightly edited and formatted):
http://en.wikipedia.org/wiki/Robert_Dzieka%C5%84ski_Taser_incident

Robert Dziekanski (April 15, 1967– October 14, 2007; was a Polish immigrant to Canada who died on October 14, 2007 after being tasered five times by the Royal Canadian Mounted Police (RCMP) at Vancouver International Airport. Full details of the incident came to light because it was filmed by a member of the public, Paul Pritchard. The police initially took possession of the video, refusing to return it to Pritchard. Pritchard went to court to obtain it, then released it to the press. As of May 2009, the Braidwood Inquiry is underway, with public questioning and testimony of individuals involved in the incident.

On June 20, 2009, the proceedings were suspended until September, after it was discovered that an e-mail contained information indicating that the RCMP officers had already determined that they would use tasers even before encountering Dziekanski. This contradicts the officers' testimony that they only decided upon the use of tasers at the last minute.

Robert Dziekanski was a construction worker by trade, but had also worked as a miner. He was in the process of emigrating from Gliwice, Poland to live with his mother, Zofia Cisowski, in Kamloops, British Columbia.

Dziekanski's flight was two hours late, and arrived at about 3:15 pm on October 13, 2007. According to official sources, Dziekanski required language support to complete initial customs formalities. After he completed initial immigration processing, his whereabouts between 4:00 p.m. and about 10:45 p.m. remain unclear, though at various points he was seen around the baggage carrousels. Dziekanski's mother, Zofia Cisowski, had told him to wait for her at the baggage claim area but it was a secured area where she was not allowed to enter. At 10:45 p.m., when he attempted to leave the Customs hall, he was directed again to secondary immigration as his visa had not yet been processed. Dziekanski's immigration procedures were completed at about 12:15 a.m. on October 14th. After 30 minutes in an immigration waiting area, he was taken to the international arrivals reception area. Cisowski had been making enquiries of airport staff since the early afternoon, but could not provide information about the airline, flight number or scheduled arrival time. Airport staff told her Dziekanski was not at the airport and she had returned to Kamloops at about 10 p.m., believing her son had missed his flight.

When Dziekanski left the Customs hall, he became visibly agitated. Bystanders and airport security guards were unable to communicate with him because he did not speak English and they did not use the airport's telephone translation service.(citation needed) He used chairs to prop open the one-way doors between a Customs clearing area and a public lounge and at one point threw a computer and a small table to the floor before the police arrived.

Four RCMP officers, Constables Gerry Rundel, Bill Bently, Kwesi Millington, and supervisor Corporal Benjamin Robinson, arrived and entered the Customs room where Dziekanski was pacing about. They apparently directed him to stand near a counter, to which Dziekanski complied but picked up a stapler sometime after being told to place his hands on a counter. Shortly thereafter, about 25 seconds after arriving at the scene, Corporal Robinson ordered the Taser to be used. Constable Millington tasered Dziekanski. He began to convulse and was tasered several more times after falling to the ground, where the four officers pinned, handcuffed and continued to taser him.

One eyewitness, who recorded the incident on her cellphone, told CBC News that Dziekanski had been tasered four times. "The third and fourth ones were at the same time" delivered by the officers at Dziekanski's right and left, just before Dziekanski fell. According to B.C. Crown counsel spokesman Stan Lowe, Dziekanski was tasered a total of five times. Constable Millington testified that he deployed the Taser four times, but he believed that in some of those instances the probes may not have contacted Dziekanski's body. Dziekanski writhed and screamed before he stopped moving. Cpl. Benjamin Monty Robinson stated he then checked for a pulse, but his heart had stopped. Testimony from the other RCMP officers state they never saw anyone including Robinson check for a pulse. Dziekanski did not receive CPR until paramedics arrived on the scene approximately 15 minutes later. They were unable to revive him and pronounced him dead at the scene.

Controversy

The entire event was recorded by Paul Pritchard, another traveller who was at the airport. Pritchard handed his camera and the video to police who told him that they would return the video within 48 hours. Instead, they returned the camera with a new memory card and kept the original with the video, saying they needed it to preserve the integrity of the investigation. They claimed witness statements would be tainted if they viewed the video before being interviewed by police. Pritchard went to court to obtain the video, which he then released to the media on November 14, 2007; three television outlets paid fees to Pritchard for the right to broadcast the video. After the video was made available, an RCMP spokesperson cautioned the public to reserve judgment against the police because the video represents "just one small piece of evidence, one person's view."

Before the video was released to the public, the RCMP repeatedly claimed that only three officers were at the scene. There were actually four officers at the scene. The RCMP also said that they did not use pepper spray because of the risk it would have posed to bystanders. The video, however, suggests the incident occurred in an area separated from bystanders by a glass wall. An RCMP spokesperson also stated that batons were not used, which was also contradicted by the video.

Criticism of the officers and the RCMP

The RCMP officers involved in the Dziekanski death have been widely criticized for their handling of the incident. A retired Vancouver Police superintendent commented after viewing the video that Dziekanski did not appear to be making "any threatening gestures" towards the police and he did not see why it became a police incident. Particularly contentious is that the RCMP officers made no attempt to defuse or gain control of the situation before resorting to the Taser. It is noteworthy that in August 2007, before Dziekanski's death, RCMP changed its protocol on Taser use, suggesting that multiple Taser shocks may be recommendable under certain circumstances.

The RCMP's handling of the incident led to charges that they misrepresented the facts to portray the RCMP in a favourable light. The BC Civil Liberties Association has filed a complaint arguing that the evidence shows that the Taser was not used as a last resort and condemning the RCMP for its attempt to suppress the video and for casting aspersions on the character of Dziekanski. An RCMP spokesman, Sgt. Pierre Lemaitre, was heavily criticized for providing a false version of events prior to the public release of the video. He stated that Dziekanski "continued to throw things around and yell and scream", after the arrival of the police officers, which was later revealed by the video to be false.

On December 12, 2008, the Criminal Justice Branch of British Columbia issued a statement, finding that although the RCMP officers' efforts to restrain Dziekanski were a contributing cause of his death, the force they used to subdue and restrain him was reasonable and necessary in all the circumstances; thus there would not be a substantial likelihood of conviction of the officers in connection with the incident and accordingly criminal charges were not approved. Three of the officers remain on duty elsewhere in Canada, while the supervisor, Corporal Benjamin Monty Robinson, is suspended with pay awaiting trial on charges of impaired driving causing death, stemming from the death of a 21-year old Vancouver man.

The officers have been subject to public criticism, both in the media and in formal proceedings before the Braidwood Commission of Inquiry. The officers were served notices of misconduct by the commission forewarning them the commissioner may include a finding of misconduct its final report) The warnings allege specific but overlapping grounds for each of the four. The collective allegations are that they failed to properly assess and respond to the circumstances in which they found Mr. Dziekanski. They repeatedly deployed the taser without justification and separately failed to adequately reassess the situation before further deploying it. The notices allege that afterwards they misrepresented facts in notes and statements, furthered the misrepresenting before the commission and provided further misleading information about other evidence before the commission. The four officers each sought judicial review to prevent the commission from making findings based on the notices. The petitions were dismissed but at least two officers are appealing.

Taser Debate

The incident has revived debate concerning police use of Tasers. This was the 16th death following the police use of Tasers in Canada since 2003 and civil liberties groups have called for a moratorium on Tasers until training and procedures can be developed and implemented to minimize the risks. The human rights group Amnesty International repeated its call for Taser use to be suspended until an independent investigation into the medical and other effects has taken place. Meanwhile, Canada's seventeenth Taser-related death occurred less than a week later when Quilem Registre died after being tasered by police in Montreal.

The police and the manufacturer have claimed that such deaths are the result of pre-existing medical conditions, not the electrical shock of the Taser. In the Vancouver case, police have suggested that Dziekanski died from a condition described by RCMP informally as "excited delirium." A statement from TASER International, the company that makes the weapon, asserts that Dziekanski's death "appears to follow the pattern of many in-custody deaths following a confrontation with the police. Historically, medical science and forensic analysis has shown that these deaths are attributable to other factors and not the low-energy electrical discharge of the Taser."

Critics, however, point out that "excited delirium" is not recognized in the Diagnostic and Statistical Manual of Mental Disorders and claim that police overuse such so-called conditions as a matter of convenience. While some psychologists argue that excited delirium is indeed a bona fide but rare condition that can cause sudden death, experts say that delirium (without the "excited" modifier) is a well known condition, but that it is usually triggered by factors such as drugs or a pronounced mental or physical illness and that it is extremely rare for those afflicted to suddenly die. Toxicology tests found no drugs or alcohol in Dziekanski's system. An autopsy for the British Columbia Coroner's Service did not determine the cause of death, citing no trauma or disease, nor pre-existing medical conditions. The report by forensic pathologist Charles Lee, of Vancouver General Hospital, listed the principal cause of death as "sudden death during restraint", with a contributory factor of "chronic alcoholism".

Criticism of Airport

The airport has also been criticized over the incident, particularly regarding security cameras that were not functioning, no translation services available for communicating with non-English speakers, the airport supervisor's failure to call the airport's own paramedics resulting in a twelve-minute wait for city paramedics to arrive, and for staff not helping Dziekanski's mother locate her son. Airport security has been roundly criticized for not assisting Dziekanski during his many hours in the airport. Once he became agitated, security guards made little attempt to communicate with him or defuse the situation. The Canada Border Services Agency reported it is reviewing its procedures at airports.

Political Reaction

The incident has had significant coverage in Poland. The Polish consul general demanded answers about Dziekanski's death. Canada's ambassador in Poland was invited to discuss the incident with officials in Warsaw, and one Polish official stated in the weeks after the incident that "we want the matter clarified and we want those guilty named and punished." On December 12, 2008 the Polish embassy in Ottawa issued a statement stating that the Crown's decision not to charge the RCMP officers was "most disappointing". In February 2009 it was reported that Canada had unilaterally suspended its mutual legal assistance treaty with Poland, thus blocking Poland's own investigation of the Dziekanski Taser incident.

Canada's Public Safety Minister, Stockwell Day, said that he has asked the RCMP for a review on Taser use and that a report is being prepared, and pointed out that several investigations of the incident are already underway. Liberal Public Safety Critic Ujjal Dosanjh said that what was needed was an independent body to conduct a national and public review of the issue, which would lead to national guidelines for Taser use by law enforcement officers. BC NDP Public Safety Critic and Port Coquitlam MLA Mike Farnworth called for a special prosecutor to be appointed to investigate the incident, citing concerns of police investigating themselves.

Law Enforcement Response

The response from law enforcement has been mixed. Law enforcement professionals have featured prominently in the media criticizing the RCMP's handling of the situation and the aftermath. The Ottawa Police, the first Ontario police force to adopt the Taser, held a Taser demonstration for reporters to illustrate their safety. Both the Toronto Police and the Royal Newfoundland Constabulary, meanwhile, have put large orders of Tasers for their front-line officers on hold.

Public Inquiry

The Braidwood Inquiry was established by the Provincial Government of British Columbia and headed by retired Court of Appeal of British Columbia and Court of Appeal of the Yukon Territory Justice The Honourable Thomas R. Braidwood, Q.C. to "inquire into and report on the use of conducted energy weapons" and to "inquire into and report on the death of Mr. Dziekanski." After two delays, the Braidwood Commission began proceedings on January 19, 2009, investigating the circumstances surrounding Dziekanski's death. Commission counsel Art Vertlieb said that the involved RCMP officers, Constable Millington, Constable Bentley, Constable Rundel, and Corporal Robinson, will be summoned to appear before the inquiry and could face findings of misconduct. Constable Gerry Rundel and Constable Bill Bentley testified at the Inquiry the week of February 23, 2009 and Constable Kwesi Millington testified there the following week. The fourth and commanding RCMP officer, Corporal Benjamin Robinson, testified beginning March 23, 2009.

Aqsa Parvez Honour Killing

From Wikipedia: (lightly edited and formatted)
http://en.wikipedia.org/wiki/Aqsa_Parvez

Aqsa Parvez
Born April 22, 1991
Died December 10, 2007 (aged 16)
Mississauga, Ontario, Canada
Education High school student at Applewood Heights Secondary School

Aqsa "Axa" Parvez (April 22, 1991 – December 10, 2007) was the victim of an alleged honour killing in Mississauga, Ontario, Canada. Her father, Muhammad Parvez is accused of strangling his daughter, then calling police to turn himself in. Apparently, she was killed after she refused to wear the hijab, a traditional Islamic head scarf for women, and declared her desire to dress like other Western girls. However, her closest friend Lubna Tahir asserted that the hijab issue was just one of many clashes between the victim and her father and that the other women in the family do not wear the Hijab. Parvez's death was reported internationally and sparked a debate about the status of women in Islamic communities. Parvez was a student of Applewood Heights Secondary School in Mississauga, Ontario, Canada. Her father, Muhammad Parvez, was a taxicab driver.

Background

Growing up in a Muslim family of Pakistani origin, she was required to wear a hijab while out of the house. However, many friends claimed that she refused to wear the veil and would often change her clothing once she got to school and then would change back before going home. Her friends also claimed that she was drawn to Western culture though her family adhered to a devout form of Islam and that she was not getting along well with her family. A week before her death, she had moved in with her friend, Lubna Tahir, to escape tension with her family.

Incident

Around 8 am (EST) on December 10, 2007, Peel Regional Police responded to a 911 call from a man who had said he had just killed his daughter. When officers arrived at a single-family detached home, they found Parvez suffering from life threatening injuries. She was immediately taken to Credit Valley Hospital and later transferred in critical condition to the Hospital for Sick Children where she died. Her father, Muhammad Parvez, had allegedly strangled her, causing her to die from neck compression. One student reported that her father was threatening her, causing her to fear for her life. Parvez's friends also said she wanted to run away from her family to escape the conflicts with them.

Reaction

Muhammad Parvez was charged with second degree murder and denied bail. Aqsa's older brother Waqas Parvez was ordered by his father not to communicate with police, faced a charge of obstructing police and was in custody. He was released on bail and ordered to reside with his surety and surrender his passport. Parvez's death revived the story of the similar honour killing in 1989 in which Zein Isa killed his 16 year old daughter Tina.

On June 27, Waqas Parvez was charged by Peel Regional Police with first degree murder. Some people consider her murder to be a case of an honour killing, while Islamic leaders state this is a case of domestic violence. Her death has also sparked a debate about the status of women in Islamic communities. Lubna Tahir, at whose home Aqsa Parvez had been living before her death, asserted that the hijab was not a major factor and that other girls in the family did not wear the hijab. She branded as "rumours" news stories that Parvez's father allegedly killed her for not wearing the hijab.

A public funeral was to take place for Parvez at 1:30 pm (EST) at a Mississauga mosque on December 15, 2007. However, hours before the funeral, her family decided instead to have a private funeral. Parvez was buried in an unmarked grave at the Meadowvale Cemetery in Brampton; her family refused a donation of a gravestone and a memorial.

Syed Soharwardy, the head imam at the Calgary Islamic Centre and national president of Islamic Supreme Council of Canada, went on a hunger strike on December 15 and 16 to denounce family violence, which he described as completely against the teachings of Islam. Sheik Alaa El-Sayyed, imam at Mississauga's Islamic Society of North America, said Islam, like all other beliefs, denounces and condemns such acts. Mohammad Alnadui, vice-chairman of the Canadian Council of Imams, called the murder "un-Islamic", and denounced the act "without any reservation".

Honour Killings in Canada 2009

Canwest News Service 2009/07/23 By Shannon Proudfoot,

'Honour killings' of females on rise in Canada: Expert

As many as 5,000 women and girls lose their lives, most at the hands of family members in "honour killings", around the world each year according to the United Nations. Up to a dozen have died for the same reason in Canada in the last decade, and it's happening more often, says Amin Muhammad, a psychiatrist who studies honour killings at Memorial University in Newfoundland. "There are a number of organizations which don't accept the idea of honour killing; they say it's a Western propagated myth by the media. But that's not true," he says. "Honour killings are there, and we should acknowledge it, and Canada should take it seriously."

Kingston, Ontario, police are now investigating that as a motive in the deaths of three teenage sisters and an older female relative who were found in a car submerged in the Rideau Canal in Kingston on June 30. The girls' mother, father and brother were arrested on Wednesday and charged with first degree murder. "In our Canadian society, we value the cultural values of everyone that makes up this great country, and some of us have different core beliefs, different family values, different sets of rules," Kingston Police Chief Stephen Tanner said at a news conference on Thursday. "Certainly, these individuals, in particular the three teenagers, were Canadian teenagers who had all the freedom and rights of expression of all Canadians." He added that he'd received an email from an extended family member of the girls, suggesting honour killing was to blame for their deaths.

Honour killings can be sparked by a woman talking to a man, having a boyfriend, wearing makeup or revealing clothing, or even seeking a divorce, says Diana Nammi, founder of the London based International Campaign Against Honour Killings. Nammi, originally from Iran, says children of immigrants who grow up in western nations take those freedoms for granted, which can throw them into conflict with their parents' rigid standards.

"When people are moving to another country, they leave everything they have, all their possessions, behind. But what they can bring with them is what they believe, their culture, their traditions, their religion," she says. "Unfortunately, they are choosing to show the worst part of that, and the worst and criminal part of that is controlling women."

One of the earliest honour killings involving a Canadian occurred in 2000, when Maple Ridge, BC, resident Jaswinder Sidhu was murdered in India in what police called a contract killing, after she married a man she met while travelling.

In 2003, Amandeep Atwal, 17, died after her father stabbed her 17 times. The Kitimat, BC, teen had been secretly seeing a boyfriend.

Sixteen year old Aqsa Parvez's father and brother are currently awaiting trial for her strangulation death in 2007, and friends said the Brampton, Ontario teen had been clashing with her family over her refusal to wear the hijab.

In May, an Ottawa man was sentenced to life in prison for killing his sister, Khatera Sadiqi, 20, and her fiancé.

"We cannot say there's a huge number of cases, but now the cases are increasing, and very soon we'll have a problem in Canada," says Muhammad. Men occasionally die in honour killings, he says, but young women are almost always the victims in western countries. Honour killing is most prevalent in nations with large Muslim populations, but Aysan Sev'er, a professor of sociology at University of Toronto, Scarborough and author of an upcoming book on the subject, says there's nothing in Islam that sanctions the practice. Some perpetrators use religion as a "cloak" she says, but honour killing is about patriarchy, not religion.

"A few women are sacrificed to terrorize all women, to push them into submission, where they are not in the position to defend themselves or even their daughters or sisters," Sev'er says. It's wrong-headed to blame particular cultures or further stereotype the Middle East, she emphasizes, but Canada cannot overlook the motivation for these "heinous crimes." "In Canada, we have been extremely culturally sensitive, and that's a good thing," she says. "But in this particular case, we may have pushed the pendulum a little to the other side, in the sense that there are cultural components in these types of crimes which we cannot ignore."

Honour killings or Domestic Abuse

From The Canadian Broadcasting Corporation: (lightly edited and formatted)
http://www.cbc.ca/canada/story/2009/07/24/f-honour-killings.html

Honour killings: domestic abuse by another name?
By Amber Hildebrandt, CBC News

Flowers sit near the Kingston Mills locks on the Rideau Canal where three teenage sisters and their father's first wife died on June 30. It has been suggested that the women's death was an honour killing. Flowers sit near the Kingston Mills locks on the Rideau Canal where three teenage sisters and their father's first wife died on June 30. It has been suggested that the women's death was an honour killing.
(Sunny Freeman/Canadian Press)

The term "honour killing" muddies the issue of domestic abuse with religious connotations. For others, it's an important designation of a cultural phenomenon distinct from domestic violence. Believed to have originated as a patriarchal tribal custom, so called honour killings aimed at restoring a family's or community's reputation, are today a worldwide problem. Though often associated with Muslim cultures, they also happen among Sikhs and Hindus.

A 2000 report by the United Nations Population Fund estimated as many as 5,000 women and girls are killed each year by relatives for dishonouring their family. Many of the cases involve the "dishonour" of having been raped. Though often linked to sexual issues such as adultery and premarital sex, the perceived "offences" that have prompted honour killings have come to include a woman's push for independence.

Mourners gather to remember Aqsa Parvez in Mississauga in 2007.

The teen was found strangled in her family's Mississauga home, and her brother and father have been charged with first degree murder. Mourners gather to remember Aqsa Parvez in Mississauga in 2007. The teen was found strangled in her family's Mississauga home, and her brother and father have been charged with first degree murder. (J.P. Moczulski/Canadian Press)

Alleged honour killings in Canada

It's unknown how many cases of honour killings have happened in Canada, but the following is a selection of deaths reported as such:

Farah Khan, 5
Her father beat the Toronto girl to death and dismembered her in 1999 while her stepmother watched. The father is said to have killed the little girl because he believed she wasn't biologically his.

Jaswinder Kaur Sidhu, 25
The BC born woman was found dead in 2000 after moving to India to live with her new husband, who was also beaten a day earlier. Her mother and uncle were among nine people charged in India with conspiracy to kill Sidhu.

Amandeep Atwal, 17
Her father was convicted in her stabbing death in 2003 in BC. He apparently disapproved of her relationship with her high school sweetheart, who was from a different ethnic group.

Khatera Sadiqi, 20
Sadiqi and her fiancé were shot to death in 2006 while parked in a car outside an Ottawa shopping plaza. Her brother was found guilty of murdering them. He told the court that he wanted his sister to respect their father.

Aqsa Parvez, 16
The teen was found strangled in her family's Mississauga home in 2007. Her brother and father have been charged with first degree murder.

Parvez's friends said she'd been having arguments with her father about wearing a traditional hijab.

The Shafia family
The Shafia sisters, Zainab 19, Sahar 17, and Geeti 13, were found dead in a submerged car in Kingston, Ontario, on June 30, 2009, along with their father's first wife, Rona Mohammed 50. The sisters' parents and 18 year old brother have been charged with four counts of first degree murder. Although police have not released an official motive for the killing, they have hinted at cultural undertones in the case and are investigating the possibility that the deaths were honour killings.

In Canada, the issue was most recently raised when police in Kingston, Ontario, revealed that they are investigating the possibility that the deaths of three teenage girls and a woman found in a car submerged in a Rideau Canal lock were a case of honour killings. The parents and 18 year old brother of the girls have been charged with first degree murder and conspiracy to commit murder in the deaths. The family had recently moved to Montreal after living in Dubai for 15 years but originally came from Afghanistan, the majority of whose population is Muslim.

At a press conference, Kingston police Chief Stephen Tanner acknowledged he'd received an email from a likely relative of the older victim claiming it was an honour killing. Though tight lipped about a motive for the killings, he alluded to cultural undertones. "These three teenagers were Canadian teenagers who have all the freedom and rights of expression of all Canadians," he said. "So, whether that was a part of a motive within the family based on one of the girls' or more of the girls' behaviour is open to a little bit of speculation."

Characteristics of an honour killing

Debate rages over whether honour killings are simply cases of domestic abuse by another name. Many Muslim groups say the term "honour killing" is a misnomer that stigmatizes their religion and are quick to denounce the label.

Writing in the spring edition of the U.S. policy journal Middle East Quarterly, American feminist writer Phyllis Chesler argues that honour killings are distinct from domestic violence. In her article, Chesler accuses law enforcement officials in the U.S. and Canada of too often mistakenly chalking deaths up to domestic violence when they are the result of honour killings. "The frequent argument made by Muslim advocacy organizations that honour killings have nothing to do with Islam and that it is discriminatory to differentiate between honour killings and domestic violence is wrong," said Chesler, a professor emerita of psychology and women's studies at the Richmond College of the City University of New York

She listed several distinctions between the two forms of violence:

- Planning — Honour killings are planned in advance. The perpetrator's family may repeatedly threaten the victim with death if she dishonours her family. Domestic abuse cases tend to be spontaneous.

- Family complicity — Domestic abuse cases rarely see more than one family member involved in the killing whereas honour killings can include multiple family members, even brothers and cousins.

- Stigma — Where domestic abusers are often ostracized, perpetrators of honour killings don't face the same stigma.

Chesler says the idea of honour killing needs to be recognized by governments, police forces and Islamic organizations so society can begin to tackle the problem.

Obscuring real motives

Mohammad Shafia and his wife Tooba Mohammad Yehya have been charged, along with their 18 year old son, with killing their three daughters and Shafia's first wife in Kingston, Ontario.

Amin Muhammad, a psychiatry professor with Newfoundland's Memorial University who studies honour killings, agrees that the term needs to be acknowledged. "I think everybody is scared of this term, but I think it is important to accept that this term is there," Muhammad told CBC Radio's The Current. "I would say, never dodge the difficulties: meet, greet and defeat." He stresses, though, that the label can cause other complicating factors, such as financial issues and mental health troubles, that might play a role in a killing to be overlooked.

Others, though, would like the term obliterated. "I get really distressed by the idea that a really terrible violence that has been done to girls and women is now getting framed as a kind of hate fest, something about Islam and Muslims," says Sherene Razack, professor of sociology and equity studies at University of Toronto's Ontario Institute for Studies in Education. Razack says the term also detracts from the real issue, which, in the end, simply boils down to violence against women.

Light Sentence for Killers

From the National Post 2009/12/05 by Canwest News Service

Killer's Parole Extended for Six Months

Victoria, BC: A man convicted of murdering a Victoria area teenager has had his day parole extended for another six months. In 1999, Warren Glowatski was convicted of second degree murder in the swarming and drowning death of 14 year old Reena Virk on Nov 14, 1997. He was sentenced to life in prison with no chance of parole for seven years. Glowatski was granted day parole in June 2007. The parole board decided in late last month to grant Glowatski, now 28, another six months on day parole so long as he abstains from alcohol and drugs, has no contact with people involved in criminal activity or substance abuse, and returns to his halfway house every night. His parole will be reviewed in another six months.

Caledonia Land Dispute

From Wikipedia: (lightly edited and formatted)
http://en.wikipedia.org/wiki/Grand_River_land_dispute

The current Grand River land dispute came to the attention of the general public of Canada on February 28, 2006. On that date, protesters from the Six Nations of the Grand River began a demonstration to raise awareness about First Nation land claims in Ontario, Canada, and particularly about their claim to a parcel of land in Caledonia, Ontario, a community within the single tier municipality of Haldimand County, roughly 20 kilometres southwest of Hamilton. Soon after this demonstration, the demonstrators assumed control of the disputed land.

The land at the centre of the dispute in Caledonia covers 40 hectares which was to be developed by Henco Industries Ltd. into a residential subdivision known as the Douglas Creek Estates. It is part of a 385,000 hectare plot of land known as the "Haldimand Tract", which was granted, in 1784, by the Crown to the Six Nations of the Grand River, for their use in settlement. Henco argues that the Six Nations surrendered their rights to the land in 1841, and Henco later purchased it from the Crown. The Six Nations, however, maintain that their title to the land was never relinquished.

Former Nazi Deportations

Michael Seifert

From Wikipedia; (lightly edited and formatted)
http://en.wikipedia.org/wiki/Michael_Seifert_%28SS_guard%29

Michael Seifert (born 16 March 1924) was an SS guard in Italy during World War II. Dubbed the "Beast of Bolzano", he was convicted in absentia in 2000 by a military tribunal in Verona, Italy, on nine counts of murder, committed while he was an SS guard at a prison transit camp in Bolzano, northern Italy. He was sentenced to life in prison and extradited on February 15, 2008 from Canada to Italy. His crimes involved actions taken in a prison camp in Bolzano, Italy, from 1944 to 1945.

At his trial, people testified that Seifert starved a 15-year-old prisoner to death, gouged out a person's eyes and tortured a woman before killing her and her daughter.

Avi Benlolo, president of the Friends of Simon Wiesenthal Center for Holocaust Studies in Canada, noted that Seifert's imprisonment "sets an example for other war criminals, not only Nazi war criminals, but war criminals related to Rwanda, Bosnia, Darfur or any other genocide, that there's no time limit to justice."

After his extradition to Italy, Seifert was held in a Italian military prison in Santa Maria Capua Vetere. Prosecutors from Italy and Germany intended to interview him regarding other war crimes that may have taken place at Bolzano

Helmut Oberlander

From Wikipedia; (lightly edited and formatted)
http://en.wikipedia.org/wiki/Helmut_Oberlander

Helmut Oberlander (born 1924) is a Canadian citizen who has been at the center of a Canadian government process regarding his Canadian citizenship. As an ethnic German born and living in the Ukraine during WWII, he was conscripted into the German forces at the age of 17 to serve as an interpreter for the EK10A (Einsatzkommando) when they entered Ukraine in 1941. His duties included listening to and translating Russian radio transmissions, acting as an interpreter during interactions between the military and the local population, and the guarding of military supplies.

After immigrating to Canada with his wife Margaret in 1954, he ran a construction business and lived in Kitchener-Waterloo, Ontario. He became a Canadian citizen in 1960. In 1995 the Government of Canada initiated a denaturalization and deportation process against him. On February 28, 2000, Judge Andrew MacKay reported his findings: He concluded that there is no evidence that Oberlander was involved, directly or indirectly, in committing any war crimes or any crimes against humanity. However he might not have disclosed his wartime record during his immigration interview in 1953 in Karlsruhe, Germany. The Canadian government determined that withholding this information was sufficient reason to strip Oberlander of his Canadian Citizenship. In October 2008, the government revoked his citizenship. In November 2009 the Federal Court of Appeal struck down this decision thus reinstating his citizenship.

His supporters say that he was not a German citizen during WWII, a Nazi Party member or ever politically active, and never attained a rank which put him in a position to affect the actions of his unit or direct any of its wartime activities. They say that Oberlander was just a 17-year old student when he was forced by threat of death to serve as an interpreter for German occupation units in Ukraine in 1941. They state that the judicial finding that he failed to disclose his wartime record when applying for immigration to Canada was based on the balance of probabilities and that he was not likely to have been asked. They also show that Oberlander has been a model citizen since coming to Canada in 1954, and that his removal or stripping of citizenship serves only partisan political purposes and unfairly targets an innocent man.

Oberlander's critics say that even though his contributions to the German forces were minor, the government was justified in proceeding against him because the unit he was conscripted into committed war crimes. Wartime documents show that Oberlander was an ethnic German from the vicinity of Halbstadt in Ukraine, and served in the SD (the Security Service of the SS) from 1941 until 1943. The unit in which he served, Detachment 10a of Einsatzgruppe D, was composed of 100 to 120 men and was responsible for annihilating persons in its areas of operation who were considered "undesirable" by the Nazi regime, particularly the Jewish, Sinti and Roma (so-called Gypsy) inhabitants. There is no evidence that Oberlander participated or was present at any war crimes.

Polygamy in British Columbia

From Wikipedia: (lightly edited and formatted):
http://en.wikipedia.org/wiki/Bountiful,_British_Columbia

Bountiful is a settlement located in the Creston Valley of southeastern British Columbia, Canada, near Cranbrook and Creston. The closest community is Lister, British Columbia. Bountiful's community is made up of members of a polygamist Mormon fundamentalist group. The polygamists live in a commune style compound outside of Lister. The settlement is named after Bountiful in the Book of Mormon.

History

The first member of the group that purchased property near Lister was Harold (aka) Michael Blackmore, who moved there with his family in 1946. Other members of the church who believed in the principles of plural marriages soon followed. After Winston Blackmore became the bishop in the 80's, the group took the name of Bountiful. In 1998 the estimated population was 600 and has since grown to about 1,000. Most of the residents are descended from only half a dozen men.

The Mormon fundamentalists in Bountiful have divided into two groups: about half are members of the Fundamentalist Church of Jesus Christ of Latter Day Saints (FLDS Church), and the other half are members of an FLDS offshoot based on the teachings of their bishop, Winston Blackmore, who split with the FLDS Church after concluding the president of the church, Warren Jeffs, had exceeded his authority and become too dictatorial.

Rumours of abuse

On April 19, 2005 Bountiful's leaders held an extensive press conference in an effort to dispel many of the rumours of abuse that had surrounded their community.

Bountiful has come under intense scrutiny for its involvement in the polygamous sect. Warren Jeffs, who was considered one of the FBI's Ten Most Wanted Fugitives, is thought to have visited a dozen or so times in 2005. The Vancouver Sun on January 28, 2006, released information stating that Utah's Attorney General is collaborating with British Columbia's Attorney General in attempting to deal with polygamy and the alleged abuse in these communities. Jeffs was captured by the authorities outside Las Vegas during August 2006 during a routine traffic stop. On September 25, 2007 Jeffs was found guilty of being an accomplice to rape. Prosecutors said Jeffs forced a 14 year old girl into marriage and sex with her 19 year old first cousin. Jeffs faces five years to life in prison on each of two felony charges. Utah Attorney General Mark Shurtleff said,"Everyone should now know that no one is above the law, religion is not an excuse for abuse and every victim has a right to be heard."

Winston Blackmore's family invited the media to visit on May 16, 2006 in response to a recent visit by the Royal Canadian Mounted Police, indicating that they feel persecuted. Three of his wives may face deportation, as they are U.S. citizens and would not be considered legally married to a Canadian.

On June 6, 2007, the province of British Columbia announced the appointment of high-profile Vancouver criminal lawyer Richard Peck as a special prosecutor to review the results of a police investigation into possible polygamous activity or other offences by members of the community. On August 1, 2007, Richard Peck concluded that there isn't enough evidence to charge the group with sexual abuse or exploitation charges as it has been extraordinarily difficult to find victims willing to testify and the defendants are likely to claim "religious freedom" as a defense.

Peck suggested that British Columbia ask the courts whether the current laws concerning polygamy are constitutional. Peck said that it's time to find out once and for all if Canada's laws against polygamy will stand. He stated that, "If the law is upheld, members of the Bountiful community will have fair notice that their practice of polygamy must cease."

Lawyer Leonard Doust said the court should be asked whether Canada's laws against polygamy are constitutionally valid, and whether they could withstand a court challenge on the grounds that multiple marriages fall under the right of religious freedom. Attorney General Wally Oppal said it's no secret he favours a more aggressive approach to the issue, but he must consider the opinions given by two highly respected lawyers, Doust and the special prosecutor who gave the same advice earlier.

Opposition justice critic Leonard Krog said the time for studying the issue is over and the government should lay charges, saying a prosecution would send a message that it's unacceptable to have children being married to old men.

YFZ Ranch Raid

The settlement has close ties to the YFZ Ranch in Texas, which was the subject of a child abuse investigation and mass removal of its children due to speculation of a culture of underage marriage similar to those rumoured in Canada. Two Canadians from Bountiful travelled to Texas shortly after their daughter was removed in the raid of 2008. They told authorities that their 17 year old daughter was visiting her grandmother, and wanted to take her home. An observer who has compiled genealogical maps of the families says that her father helped build the YFZ compound in Texas, but her grandmother does not live there, and speculates she might have been placed in a "spiritual marriage".

IRB and Refugee Backlogs 2009

From The CBC News 2009/12/04 (& posted on the internet)

by David McKie

http://www.cbc.ca/politics/story/2009/12/04/refugee-claims-delay-conservatives.html

The backlog of people waiting to have their refugee claims heard has tripled since the Conservatives came to power, statistics show. The wait times have increased despite the government's criticism that delays open the door for bogus refugees to stay in the country. When the Conservatives came to power in January 2006, the backlog of people waiting for their claims to be heard by members of the Immigration and Refugee Board (IRB) was slightly less than 20,000. Since then, the number of people on the waiting list has grown to 62,000.

As the backlog increased, the number of board members available to hear cases decreased. As a result, the average time refugees wait to have their cases heard has increased by 44 per cent since 2006, and critics predict that percentage might continue to climb. "It's hypocritical," said Peter Showler, a former chairman of the IRB who teaches refugee law at the University of Ottawa, "because (the Conservative government), to a significant degree, is the author of the increased backlog and the delays."

When the Conservatives took power, the IRB had 164 members to hear cases. By March 31, 2008, that number dipped to 106. IRB members are appointed by the government, and Showler and other critics say the Conservatives have politicized that appointment process, taking too long to fill vacancies while the backlog continues to grow.

Claims of partisan appointments predate Tories. Advocates for a more efficient refugee determination system have blamed governments for playing politics with the board ever since its creation in 1989. Former prime ministers Brian Mulroney and Jean Chrétien faced criticism that they used the board as a cushy landing place for the people to whom they wanted to give partisan patronage appointments. Some of those people were ill equipped to make life and death decisions about who got to stay in Canada the critics alleged.

When the Liberals were still in power earlier this decade, they made changes to the IRB, reducing the number of board members hearing cases from two to one and promising to create an appeal board. The aim of the appeal body would be to catch the inevitable mistakes that would happen with only one person presiding over the original hearings. Politicians from all parties also vowed to take the politics out of the appointment process. But advocates are still waiting for an appeal board, and they're still complaining about an appointment process dominated by politics.

Even the auditor general criticized the Conservatives for dithering instead of appointing board members quickly. In her report last spring, Sheila Fraser said that in some instances, board members didn't find out they were being re-appointed until their term ended. "In our view, these individuals should be treated in a more respectful manner," Fraser wrote in her report.

This week, Immigration Minister Jason Kenney announced that he has filled most of the vacant board positions and expects to have a full complement by Christmas. A more complete board will help reduce the backlog, which was created in part by an influx of refugee claimants from Mexico and the Czech Republic. In the summer, the government imposed visa restrictions on individuals from those countries.

Still, critics don't expect the backlog to go away and say it could even increase. That's because many of the board members the government has appointed are new and lack experience. The auditor general noted that from January 2006 to March 2008, the Conservatives re-appointed 43 out of the 99 candidates the IRB suggested should be kept.

Showler says it takes about a year to train a new board member. So newer members can't always work as efficiently and quickly as individuals who have been around longer. "We're talking about deciding whether someone is or is not sent back to persecution," he said. The Provinces bear the brunt of backlog. As for the people who must wait and endure the backlogs, their lives can be frustrating.

Alexandra Mendes, the Liberal MP from the Quebec riding of Brossard La Prairie, hears many of their concerns about the long waits and the uncertainty of life in Canada. These concerns prompted her to ask the immigration minister to provide details about the average time it takes the IRB to hear claims. In a formal, written response, the minister sent Mendes a breakdown of wait times from 2005 to the end of August 2009. In 2006, the average wait was 11.7 months while by the end of August 2009, it was 17.7 months. Since then, the average wait time has climbed to 18 months.

The refugee claim is only the beginning of the process of gaining refugee status. Traditionally, the board has rejected about half of all claims. If the initial claim is rejected, the applicant can ask the federal court to review the case. "Leave to appeal," as the process is called in legal jargon, is only granted in about 10 per cent of cases, according to Showler.

If the claimant is one of the majority of people whose request has failed, the individual can apply to the Department of Citizenship and Immigration for what's called a "pre-removal" hearing. But here, too, the backlog can push the wait to two years. Finally, there is the option of appealing to the minister to stay in Canada based on humanitarian grounds.

Showler says in many cases, the person is able to stay, but the precise numbers are unknown because the department withholds that information. While refugee claimants wait for the process to unfold, they qualify for health care, education and legal aid . . . and the costs borne by the lower levels of government, especially the provinces. There is some evidence that provincial and municipal authorities are growing weary of paying for these services. In a letter to the immigration minister sent in May, the Quebec government complained about the backlog, claiming that its costs had doubled since the Conservatives have been in power.

Ontario Court Backlog 2003 - 2009

From the Globe & Mail 2009/11/30 by Kirk Makin

The justice system of Ontario has fallen into a state of disrepair highlighted by a flurry of punitive federal legislation and a legion of accused criminals who languish behind bars awaiting trial, according to an influential Ontario Court of Appeal judge.

Mr. Justice Marc Rosenberg, widely regarded as the finest criminal law mind in the country, said that Canadians must take stock of the shambles that has been created through indiscriminate use of imprisonment. "Something has gone terribly wrong," Judge Rosenberg told a Toronto legal conference. "On any day in Canada, we have more people in pretrial custody than actually serving sentences. The constitutional guarantees of the presumption of innocence and reasonable bail seem illusory."

Judge Rosenberg's comments come at a time when the federal government is legislating a profusion of tough on crime bills that create mandatory sentences for some offences, eliminate reduced sentences for those who serve pre-trial custody, limit parole and drastically restrict conditional sentences. "It is Parliament's right to be prescriptive," Judge Rosenberg said. "And, subject to the limits of cruel and unusual punishment, it is also their right and, indeed, their responsibility to respond to public anxiety about crime. But this increasingly punitive approach places an immense burden on you to protect your clients from unjust punishments."

Coming from a judge who is known for reticence and for adhering to the judicial code of rarely speaking out, his remarks shocked the 400 lawyers at a Criminal Lawyers Association luncheon. Judge Rosenberg was particularly critical of harsh mandatory minimum prison sentence. He also mourned the fact that conditional sentences, which allow for house arrest and other sanctions that fall short of prison, "are narrowing almost to the vanishing point".

Ottawa lawyer Norm Boxall said, "as Canada's foremost authority on criminal law, a former Crown, defence counsel and policy maker, Justice Rosenberg is our conscience. When someone of his stature makes an impassioned plea to reverse the direction we are travelling on, with the increased use of incarceration both pre- and post-trial, everyone should listen."

As a lawyer, Judge Rosenberg worked closely with his more famous partner, defence counsel Edward Greenspan, for 20 years. A fixture in appellate courts, he later became Ontario's assistant deputy attorney general and was appointed straight to the Court of Appeal. He has written more than 2,000 judgments, and is widely touted as a top candidate whenever a Supreme Court of Canada vacancy arises. In his speech, he told the CLA that the justice system has become "increasingly risk averse" as a result of the amount of misinformation about crime and justice that permeates an increasingly ill-informed public debate.

Judge Rosenberg also took a swing at the under funding of legal aid programs: "Ensuring adequate funding for legal aid has been an ongoing struggle for decades," he said. "Legal aid is a cornerstone of our system. We cannot continue to bring the most vulnerable in our society to the precipice every few years." Coming at a time when virtually all experienced defence lawyers are boycotting the legal aid plan to protest its low fee structure, Judge Rosenberg's endorsement of legal aid "cannot be ignored," said Mr. Boxall.

Legal Aid Salaries in Ontario 2009

Excerpt from the National Post 2009/12/05 by Shannon Kari

An Ontario Superior Court judge has turned down a request from three men charged with murder to order the province to pay their lawyers at least $170 per hour, which would be 70% higher than the legal aid rate. The decision by Justice James Ramsay was issued yesterday during the seventh month of a boycott of major cases by criminal lawyers in Ontario, who are protesting against legal rates that have increased by only 15% since 1987. The lawyers that Ronald Cyr, Zdenek Zvolensky and Nashat Qahwash want to hire as defence counsel have said they will not handle the case for the fees that Legal Aid Ontario is willing to pay. Legal Aid Ontario has found two lawyers willing to represent the defendants, although one is 73 years old and the other has never handled a murder trial.

Ponzi Schemes & Earl Jones

From the Montreal Gazette, 2009/12/04 By Anne Sutherland

The next court date for besieged Montreal investment adviser Earl Jones could bring more charges added to the four each for theft and fraud he already faces, his lawyer suggested Friday. Lawyer Jeffrey Boro said Quebec provincial police investigators have interviewed 159 people, and that the possibility of more charges is very real. "Obviously and logically, there will be more," Boro said outside the Montreal courtroom where Jones's scheduled hearing date was postponed to Jan. 15. Financial adviser Earl Jones could face more charges, the lawyer says. As expected, Jones was not in court Friday. He was arrested July 27 and charged the following day with four counts of theft and four of fraud. He remains free on $30,000 bail.

"He had trouble finding lodging; as soon as he gave his name, people refused to rent to him," Boro said of his client. "He's quite a marked man; there are days when he attempts to take a taxi and he's recognized and the driver won't take him." Like everyone over 65, Jones gets a government pension but Boro said his client has trouble paying the rent. When questioned as to how Jones was paying Boro's fees, the lawyer replied: "That could be problematic." Asked if he would drop Jones, Boro replied: "I started the file, and I will finish the file."

Unlike Friday's court appearance, Jones must show up — some time next week — to testify at bankruptcy hearings into the demise of Earl Jones Consultant & Administration Corporation. "This is not discretionary," said Gilles Robillard, with trustee RSM Richter. "He has been subpoenaed and he has no choice, lawyer or not."

After former employees and his wife have given depositions before the trustee handling the bankruptcy, Jones is expected to have his turn. Any information Jones gives in his deposition to the trustee handling the bankruptcy cannot be held against him in criminal proceedings, Robillard confirmed. "I think he'll show up, but I don't follow him around 24 hours a day," Boro said Friday. Two and possibly three days of testimony are scheduled. Meantime, a select few got an inside look Friday at the formerly luxurious lifestyle long enjoyed by Jones.

Real estate agents mandated to sell a condo in Dorval, a Montreal suburb, which served as the main residence of the Jones family from 1999 until his downfall last summer, were to conduct media tours of the residence. The posh two bedroom waterfront condo, with an asking price of $925,000, offers lavish 180 degree views of Lake St. Louis, in addition to a renovated kitchen, two bathrooms and indoor parking. Trustee RSM Richter seized the home from Jones Sept 11. A relatively small proportion of the sale proceeds will apparently be going to clients Jones is alleged to have bilked of some $75 million over the years.

In late 2006, Jones took a $558,750 second mortgage on the condo, which he had jointly owned with his wife. At Jones' condo in Boca Raton, Fla., the locks have been changed and photographs have been taken of the interior. Chris Frohock, a real estate agent who also works for the condo association where Maxine and Earl Jones have a two-bedroom unit, confirmed that bailiffs representing RSM Richter visited the property and asked if she were interested in listing the condo. "I told them no, the market is so bad here with bankruptcies and foreclosures, you often get stiffed for the commission," Frohock said.

She also said that Maxine Jones called last month to inquire about her car, a Toyota, that is parked in the garage under the condo building.

Bailiffs towed away her Audi Quattro SUV in July. "She was practically in tears because she heard her car was gone, but I said 'Honey, you're mistaken, it's still here", Frohock said.

More about Earl Jones

From the Gazette Justice Reporter 2009/07/15 By Sue Montgomery

The phone company has cut Peter Kent's mother's service for non-payment. The nursing home where the 84 year old stays hasn't been paid in three months. Now Kent and his siblings are scrambling to find a home for her, after the sickening discovery that her once trusted financial adviser, Earl Jones, appears to have disappeared with all her money. "My sister is talking about renovating and putting in a wheelchair ramp," he said. "We're talking about who can take her in if necessary."

A few of Jones's victims were in Quebec Superior Court Wednesday where an extension to RSM Richter Inc.'s mandate as interim receiver was granted to July 29, when a hearing will be held to declare Jones bankrupt. But in the meantime, some of Jones's alleged victims are worried about how they'll put food on the table after discovering the smooth talker they'd entrusted with their life savings appears to have been running a Ponzi scheme.

Dominique Jackson said her mother, Christiane Jackson, entrusted everything to Jones, then received a monthly cheque of $4,000. The last one arrived July 2. She's gone from believing in April that she had more than $2 million to discovering payments hadn't been made on her mortgage, she now owes $30,000 and is being forced to sell her home. Jones, of Dorval, was also handling Christiane Jackson's late spouse's estate, of which a large sum of money was to go to the charity Doctors Without Borders. On the advice of her mother, Dominique, 34, took all her money out of a reputable U.S. investment firm and handed it over to Jones.

A small group of victims is trying to gather information about food banks and other social services to which some of the elderly among them may be forced to turn, she said. A meeting is tentatively set for Friday at the Pointe Claire Holiday Inn. They also want to know how to get Revenue Canada and Revenue Quebec off their backs for taxes that Jones was supposed to be paying on their behalf. Notices about the upcoming bankruptcy hearing will be placed in Saturday's Gazette and La Presse, as well as at Jones's vacated Pointe Claire office. The goal is to seize assets from Jones's company, Earl Jones Consultant and Administration Corp., and distribute it among creditors.

Neil Stein, who is representing the victims, said Wednesday there are three groups of creditors: those who are beneficiaries of wills that were being administered by Jones; those who entrusted Jones to take care of their money; and those who lent money to successors of wills, using assets listed on the will as collateral. "He was saying it was a bridge loan, that the succession needed money on a temporary basis because it can't sell off the assets quick enough and wants to provide liquidity to the beneficiaries," Stein explained.

But none of the so called borrowers were ever aware that money was being lent for their alleged benefit. All the money, he said, seems to have disappeared. Stein said they aren't sure how many people were swindled by Jones, but about 100 wills were found in his office. Another 30 people, such as Peter Kent's mother, had put Jones in charge of all their finances, from paying the phone bill to paying their taxes. "In addition to that, there are people who have lent money," Stein said. Jones "appears to be hopelessly insolvent and appears to be involved in a major fraud of the nature of a Ponzi scheme, which has now collapsed due to the fact its clients all want their money back," Stein's motion reads. In all, the loss reaches into the millions of dollars.

Kevin Curran says his mom is "77 going on 100" after the shock of learning that her bank account is empty. "We found out that the property taxes and mortgage for three months hadn't been paid," he said. "And she has no income."

Court documents show that Mary Sue and Robert Gibson, who knew Jones for more than a decade, had socked away $78,000 for their children's education, which was placed in personal accounts named Earl Jones In Trust. In June, cheques totalling $3,500 from Jones were returned to the Gibsons because of insufficient funds. According to court documents, Jones also forged Gibson's signature on an agreement for another of his clients for a $125,000 loan. Another couple, Johanna and Robert Earle, had close to $1 million in a personal account named Earl Jones In Trust. According to court documents, their combined annual income is $52,589, mostly from pensions.

Ponzi Schemes & Pension Plans

From the National Post 2009/04/08 by the Editor, Kelly McParland

Canada's giant Ponzi pension swindle

Nobody worries much about pensions other than people who are about to receive one, or are old enough to realize they should have thought about it sooner. That's probably why reports on the general disarray of the Canadian pension industry tend to get tucked away in the back of the financial section, where grumpy old editors chew bitterly over the fact they ignored their father's advice to become an accountant.

The aging of Canada's population, and simultaneous disappearance of all the money they planned to use to finance their old age, means the ranks of crabby editors are likely to get a bunch of new friends, and soon. Ottawa hasn't paid a lot of attention to this yet, but that's because the money only disappeared recently. Boomers aren't used to being shafted, and you know what happens when they feel their inborn right to the best of everything has been violated. The bitching will know no end. And with considerable justification.

The details of the shafting have been amply documented. Large numbers of Canadians who have spent their working lives putting money aside for their old age have suddenly discovered it was a waste of effort. The odds on a private sector employee having a decent pension are about one in five. That's the percentage of Canadians who can boast of a defined benefit plan, the kind that pays a set amount based on salary level and years of service.

Companies don't like defined benefit plans because they're expensive and force companies to play nanny to aging non workers. So a lot of them switched to "defined contribution" plans, which promise nothing except regular deductions from your pay cheque. The money goes into the markets, and if the markets tank, well . . . tough. How do you like your dog food?

People with defined contribution pensions are looking at a long, bleak old age. Retirement? Forget it. The only question is whether you keep your existing job, or get forced out and find yourself bagging groceries at the Price Chopper, where your retiree friends are forced to shop.

People on defined benefit plans are a little better off, if their company didn't go bankrupt, or threaten to go bankrupt, the better to convince Ottawa to let them out of paying employees what they promised. Auto workers, Air Canada employees and Nortel retirees know how it feels to discover all those promises about a decent retirement aren't worth last year's Pontiac.

Public employees are a different matter, safe in the knowledge taxpayers will have to foot the bill to ensure they don't suffer unduly. But they're not entirely immune. Ontario Teachers' Pension Plan, one of Canada's biggest, sent a newsletter to members this week noting cheerfully that while it lost $19 billion last year, it "tied for first place in service delivery among 58 international pension plans." Teachers already pay 11% of their salary into the plan, which has nonetheless cut benefits and increased contributions to offset earlier shortfalls. When the latest losses are accounted for in 2011, according to the report, the plan has the option of further cuts, higher contributions, or both. See? Something to look forward to.

There's talk of pension reform in Ottawa, but it's mainly focussed on finding ways to take even more burden off companies that can't pay what they owe. The global financial crisis means even the biggest funds have multi-billion dollar holes in their account books. They're pressing the government for "relief", which in this instance means "please don't make us pay all those employees from whom we took money."

All this might be more bearable if Ottawa didn't make it so difficult for individuals to look after themselves. Saving is still discouraged by high tax rates. The safer the investment, the higher the tax, encouraging people to take higher risks than they would like to. RRSPs have limits on contributions, and anyone in a job that theoretically includes a pension, no matter how unlikely they are ever to collect it, is blocked from contributing more than a fraction of the maximum. Some retirees did well on income trusts for a while, but then Ottawa caught on and taxed them to death, taking many seniors' savings with them. The new tax free savings accounts may make a small dent, but they're a bit late in the game for most boomers.

Given the mess they've been dumped into, a lot of people would have been better off if they'd been allowed to take their pension contributions, and those of their employer, and stick it in something safe, with a small but reliable return, without Ottawa taking it all back in taxes. Or if the money had been added to the Canada Pension Plan, in return for a higher payback. Or something, anything, slightly brighter than exposing the security of the country's retirees to the good graces of the stock market.

Wholesale changes seem inevitable. It's hard to imagine another generation of workers being subject to similar Ponzi schemes. Madoff took billions of dollars, made lots of promises, and reneged on them all. That's OK for a crook, but not for what passes as a pension industry. Now that it's been exposed, it shouldn't be allowed to continue bilking Canadians of their money and their aspirations.

Corruption in Quebec Courts

From a Publication of Hillsdale College 2008/01 by Mark Steyn

All that being said, if you remove health care from the equation, the differences between our two economies become relatively marginal. The Fraser Institute's "Economic Freedom of the World 2007 Annual Report" ranks the U.S. and Canada together, tied in fifth place along with Britain. And here's an interesting point. The top ten most free economies in this report are Hong Kong, Singapore, New Zealand, Switzerland, United States, United Kingdom, Canada, Estonia, Ireland, and Australia: With the exception of Switzerland and Estonia, these systems are all British derived. They're what Jacques Chirac (a former French President) dismissively calls *les anglo-saxon.* And he and many other Continentals make it very clear that they regard free market capitalism as some sort of kinky Anglo-Saxon fetish.

On the other hand, Andrew Roberts, the author of *A History of the English-Speaking Peoples since 1900*, points out that the two most corrupt jurisdictions in North America are Louisiana and Quebec . . . both French derived. Quebec has a civil service that employs the same number of people as California, even though California has a population nearly five times the size.

In the province of Quebec, it's taken more or less for granted by all political parties that collective rights outweigh individual rights. For example, if you own a store in Montreal, the French language signs inside the store are required by law to be at least twice the size of the English signs. And the government has a fairly large bureaucratic agency whose job it is to go around measuring signs and prosecuting offenders. There was even a famous case a few years ago of a pet store owner who was targeted by the Office De La Langue Francaise for selling English-speaking parrots. The language commissar had gone into the store and heard a bird saying, "Who's a pretty boy, then?" and decided to take action. I keep trying to fi nd out what happened to the parrot. Presumably it was sent to a re-education camp and emerged years later with a glassy stare saying in a monotone voice, "Qui est un joli garçon, hein?".

The point to remember about this is that it is consonant with the broader Canadian disposition. A couple of years ago it emerged that a few Quebec hospitals in the eastern townships along the Vermont border were, as a courtesy to their English speaking patients, putting up handwritten pieces of paper in the corridor saying "Emergency Room This Way" or "Obstetrics Department Second on the Left." But in Quebec, you're permitted to offer health care services in English only if the English population in your town reaches a certain percentage. So these signs were deemed illegal and had to be taken down. I got a lot of mail from Canadians who were upset about this, and I responded that if you accept that the government has a right to make itself the monopoly provider of health care, it surely has the right to decide the language in which it's prepared to provide that care. So my point isn't just about Quebec separatism. It's about a fundamentally different way of looking at the role of the state.

Report on RCMP re Dziekanski

From the National Post 2009/12/09 by Brian Hutchison

Taser Report Slams RCMP

Officers' accounts of Dziekanski death found not credible

VANCOUVER: Paul Kennedy wanted more oversight powers. Instead, he's getting pink slipped. But the chairman of the Commission for Public Complaints Against the RCMP seems determined to leave office with a bang and a bite. Yesterday, in one of his last major acts as the country's federally appointed RCMP watchdog - his contract was not renewed and he's out of a job at year's end - Mr. Kennedy offered a bruising assessment of the way four Mounties handled Polish immigrant Robert Dziekanski at Vancouver International Airport in 2007.

To no one's surprise, the CPC chairman found fault with the four officers and with the subsequent RCMP investigation of the Dziekanski fatality. But Mr. Kennedy went much further than expected, using yesterday's news conference in Vancouver to take some well aimed verbal shots at stagnant RCMP culture, especially its notorious, self-destructive resistance to change. It is a "massively inert" organization, he said, and that must not stand.

He used the opportunity to castigate RCMP Commissioner William Elliott. They have not seen eye to eye on several issues, including Mr. Kennedy's previous, bleak assessments of internal police investigations and his request for more oversight powers; that has gone nowhere.

Yesterday, Mr. Kennedy called out Commissioner EIliott for not responding to his Dziekanski report. "It has not impressed me at all," he told reporters. Mr. Elliott's intentional disregard for his work is "bizarre to the extreme." A slim but detailed executive summary of his 208 page report was made public in Vancouver yesterday. Mr. Elliott received the full document six weeks ago. He was invited to respond to it. He has chosen not to, for reasons that Mr. Kennedy says are unacceptable.

His report describes how Mr. Dziekanski died at the airport immediately after receiving five Taser shots to his body and being wrestled with on the ground by the four officers. The incident was captured on video by an airport passerby, Paul Pritchard, and its release brought international condemnation and shamed the Mounties. A subsequent public inquiry into the matter led by retired judge Thomas Braidwood has only sharpened criticism of the RCMP.

Mr. Kennedy reminded reporters yesterday that the CPC took the matter seriously; in fact, he had his own people in Vancouver examining the Dziekanski fatality within 24 hours of the incident. Based on dispatch information the four officers were given, Mr. Kennedy writes, "the decision to approach Mr. Dziekanski to deal with the complaints was not unreasonable". Unfortunately, just about everything that followed at the airport was (unreasonable).

The senior Mountie in charge, Corporal Benjamin "Monty" Robinson, failed to take control of the situation and the result was chaotic, writes Mr. Kennedy. Each officer who approached Mr. Dziekanski responded to him differently "because there was no direction," he told reporters yesterday. One officer circled; one flexed his baton; one gave the befuddled Mr. Dziekanski directions by pointing his finger; one, of course, pointed his Taser and fired.

Const. Kwesi Millington should have issued a required warning before deploying his Taser, Mr. Kennedy concluded in his report. "No significant attempts were made to communicate with Mr. Dziekanski" he noted. The multiple cycles of the Taser on Mr. Dziekanski were not appropriate. And the four officers "demonstrated no meaningful attempt to de-escalate the situation, nor did they approach the situation with a measured, coordinated and appropriate response." The Taser was used too quickly, he concluded. Furthermore, wrote Mr. Kennedy, the handcuffs used on Mr. Dziekanski should have been removed as soon as the officers determined that he had lost consciousness and was in distress.

He rejected the officers' credibility. "I do not accept as accurate any of the versions of events presented by the involved members because I find considerable and significant discrepancies in the detail and accuracy of the recollections of the members when compared against the otherwise uncontroverted video evidence".

Their notes of the incident were inadequate, he found. Mr. Kennedy went on to suggest that the RCMP led fatality investigation was compromised because Cpl. Robinson was allowed to attend an investigators' briefing within hours of Mr. Dziekanski's death. Moreover, the four officers should not have met "alone at the YVR (Vancouver airport) sub-detachment office following the death of Mr. Dziekanski". In all, Mr. Kennedy made 23 findings of fact, and 16 recommendations that seem to make sense. He wishes they were acted on, now.

Mr. Kennedy invited the RCMP brass in October to respond to his findings and recommendations; specifically, he asked Commissioner

Elliott to share his opinion of the report. He (Commissioner Elliott) would not. In a letter written to Mr. Kennedy last week, which Mr. Kennedy copied and handed to reporters yesterday, Commissioner Elliott says "it would not be appropriate, in our view, to provide you with our response prior to receiving the final (Braidwood) report of the inquiry".

Of course, Mr. Braidwood is not expected to deliver his final report until March 2010, at the earliest. By then, Mr. Kennedy will be long gone from the RCMP Complaints Commission; however, should anyone wish to discuss with him his turbulent four year run as complaints chairman, he promises to be available. And to be "as outspoken and as candid as possible".

Tarnished Justice

From the National Post 2009/12/08 by Matt Gurney

Canadians take pride in living in a peaceful, safe country. We take particular pride in our police and courts. We have faith in the judicial system; in this land, you never need to fear being pulled over by a corrupt police officer at night, or worry that you don't have enough money to bribe your way out of a false charge.

Recent events, however, are increasingly tarnishing the shining reputation of these vital civil servants. In Ontario, an ongoing lawsuit has provided devastating testimony that shows that the Provincial Police utterly abandoned a family to lawless chaos behind native barricades in Caledonia. In Toronto, David Chen was charged with assault and forcible confinement after he tackled and tied up a man who'd just robbed his store, holding him until police could arrive.

As if that weren't bad enough, the Crown prosecutors made a deal with the thief, reducing his sentence in exchange for testifying against the man he'd robbed!

It's not just Ontario. In British Columbia, the public's confidence in the RCMP has been rocked not only by the unnecessary death of Robert Dziekanski after being stun-gunned by a quartet of officers, but by the refusal of the Crown to press charges against one of those very same officers following a suspicious death on the roads. After running down motorcyclist Orion Hutchinson, the officer - Benjamin Robinson - tested over the legal blood alcohol limit on a breathalyzer test. Corporal Benjamin Monty Robinson of the Royal Canadian Mounted Police was testifying at an inquiry into the death of Robert Dziekanski. Robinson was the senior officer in charge when Dziekanski was tasered. But he claimed this was because he'd begun drinking vodka immediately after hitting the victim. Incredibly, the Crown bought it, and Robinson will not face impaired driving causing death charges.

Pleas and early parole should never be used to alleviate overcrowded prisons.

The examples above are bad. This one is worse. In Calgary, a judge has thrown out sexual assault charges against two men arrested for a gang rape of a 15 year old girl because the Crown and police couldn't get their act together. The case languished for a full five years, and the judge ruled that the delay violated the right of the accused to receive a speedy trial. There was obviously a good case to be made; two other men involved in the same incident, whose cases were brought to trial in a timely fashion, were found guilty and given sentences of 27 and 30 months, respectively. So clearly lack of evidence wasn't the problem. Somewhere along the line, the police and the prosecution simply dropped the ball. The judge said as much when throwing out the charges, noting that the long delay was "in large part unexplained and unjustified." No kidding.

Most cops are honourable, and most prosecutors are dedicated professionals. Even so, there are signs the system itself is overburdened and cracking under the strain. The latter example from Calgary, in particular, is the logical result of a system so clogged with cases that suspects routinely plead to lesser charges, not because it's just or promotes the public good, but because the system would collapse if forced to actually bring each person arrested to a trial.

The justice system needs more of everything. More prosecutors to stay on top of the case load, more courtrooms in which to conduct the trials. Our prison system needs expansion, not because the government is about to start throwing petty criminals in jail for life (as some bleeding hearts would have you believe) but because overcrowded prisons are a lousy reason to not jail a convicted criminal. Plea bargains and early parole should never have to be used to alleviate living conditions in our penitentiaries.

Being tough on crime means more than just catching criminals. It means having police and courts that have the staffing and funding necessary to do their jobs. It means having the prison infrastructure to rehabilitate those who can be redeemed while locking away the rest; . . . forever, if necessary. Canadians have rested too long on our reputation for having a just society. It's time to demand improvements in our fraying system, before it gets any worse.

National Post mgurney@nationalpost.com

Reduced Sentence - Alvin Persaud

From The Ottawa Citizen, 2009/12/08 by Andrew Seymour,

A jealous boyfriend who shot his girlfriend in the throat with a semi-automatic handgun, leaving her paralyzed from the waist down, pleaded guilty to attempted murder Tuesday. Alvin Persaud, who was then 29, admitted putting the gun to the throat of 44 year old Cathleen Lavoie and pulling the trigger just after 3 a.m. on July 22, 2008, in the living room of her Marlin Private home. Lavoie later told police that Persaud called her a "cheating whore" and "went into his own world" before pulling out the gun and shooting her. Lavoie said she didn't believe the shooting was an accident, as Persaud insisted when a neighbour who came to her aid. While the bullet did not hit any major arteries in Lavoie's neck, it did leave Lavoie a paraplegic.

Lavoie told police Persaud "went nuts" the day of the shooting after asking Lavoie if she liked a male singer more than she liked him. Persaud had also become "possessive" in the days before the shooting, and wanted Lavoie to have his baby. Lavoie didn't want another child at her age. Persaud was "very disappointed" and "got angry and mad" when she wasn't pregnant and told her it was her he chose to have his child with. He was also upset about her ex-boyfriends.

Persaud's lawyer, Pat McCann, said his client admitted intending to kill Lavoie at the moment he pulled the trigger, but immediately regretted his actions and called 911. A distraught Persaud was arrested at the scene. McCann added Persaud believes he is an alcoholic and his actions were a result of his drinking the day of the shooting. He did not agree to Lavoie's characterization of their relationship. Court heard the handgun Persaud used to shoot Lavoie was registered to him. McCann said Persaud won't oppose the Crown's call for 10 years in prison when he is sentenced next week.

Reduced Sentence - Brett Flaten

From Newstalk980, Radio Station CJME 980, 2009/12/16

By Murray Wood

http://www.newstalk980.com/story/20091216/26851

A Regina man who lured his ex-girlfriend from her home and shot her in the head, is getting what amounts to an early Christmas gift. The Saskatchewan Court of Appeal has reduced the sentence for Brett Corbin Flaten.

Flaten had been tried under the Youth Criminal Justice Act (YCJA), but was sentenced last year as an adult, even though he was 16 at the time of the offence in October of 2007. He was almost 18 when he was convicted of attempted murder and sentenced to nine years. The trial judge reduced it to eight years and two months, after counting time spent on remand.

Flaten appealed, saying the judge should not have sentenced him as an adult and should have considered his low risk to re-offend. Even if he was to be sentenced as an adult, Flaten's lawyer contended the sentence was too severe under the principles of the YCJA. They argued instead for a sentence of six years. The Court of Appeal agreed Flaten should be tried as an adult but reduced his sentence to seven years, saying that was the appropriate term for the crime. It also increased the credit for remand time, meaning his sentence is effectively five years and nine months. Flaten will remain in a youth facility until he's 20. At that time, he'll be transferred to an adult institution.

Flaten had been dating the 16 year old girl for over a year before she broke off the relationship about a month before the shooting. Flaten stole a .22 calibre rifle from a locked cabinet on his family farm about two weeks before the shooting. He gave it to a friend to store, but got it back the night of the shooting, saying he wanted to return it before it was missed. Instead, he went to the girl's house, texted her that he had left her something on the porch, then waited on one knee, described as 'sniper style' in court documents and waited for her to emerge. When she did, he aimed at her forehead and shot her in the face. He later indicated to police that he intended to kill her.

The girl's mother found her lying in front of the door, bloody and moaning. The bullet had entered her right eye socket, shattering the orbital bone and entering the brain. She underwent brain surgery for swelling, as well as reconstructive surgery. Some bullet fragments remain in her brain. Part of her right temporal lobe had to be removed. The girl lost her right eye, the hearing in her right ear and suffered facial paralysis, disfigurement and cognitive impairment. She has had to learn to walk, speak, chew and swallow; a recovery described as painful and arduous. She is still receiving treatment from a number of specialists.

No Reduction - Robert Latimer

From Wikipedia; lightly edited and formatted: http://en.wikipedia.org/wiki/Robert_Latimer

Robert Latimer

Robert William "Bob" Latimer (born March 13, 1953), a Canadian canola and wheat farmer, was convicted of second degree murder in the death of his daughter Tracy (November 23, 1980 – October 24, 1993). This case sparked a national controversy on the definition and ethics of euthanasia as well as the rights of people with disabilities, and two Supreme Court decisions, R. v. Latimer (1997), on section 10 of the Canadian Charter of Rights and Freedoms, and later R. v. Latimer (2001), on cruel and unusual punishments under section 12 of the Charter. Latimer was released on day parole in March 2008 and will be eligible to apply for full parole in December 2010. Before his imprisonment, Bob Latimer lived near Wilkie, Saskatchewan on a 1,280 acres (520 ha) wheat and canola farm with his wife Laura, and their four children.

Tracy Latimer

Tracy Latimer was born November 23, 1980. An interruption in Tracy's supply of oxygen during the birth caused cerebral palsy, leading to severe mental and physical disabilities including seizures that were controlled with seizure medication. She had little or no voluntary control of her muscles, wore diapers, and could not walk or talk. Her doctors described the care given by her family as excellent.

The Supreme Court judgment of 1997 noted, "It is undisputed that Tracy was in constant pain." In her medical testimony Dr. Dzus, Tracy's orthopaedic surgeon, noted "the biggest thing I remember from that visit is how painful Tracy was. Her mother was holding her right leg in a fixed, flexed position with her knee in the air and any time you tried to move that leg Tracy expressed pain and cried out". She also noted that despite having a hip that had been dislocated for many months Tracy could not take painkillers because she was on anti-seizure medication which, in combination with painkillers, could lead to renewed seizures, stomach bleeding, constipation, aspiration and aspiration pneumonia. Robert Latimer reported that the family was not aware of any medication other than Tylenol that could be safely administered to Tracy. Considering it too intrusive, the Latimers did not wish a feeding tube to be inserted, though according to the 2001 Supreme Court judgment it might have allowed more effective pain medication to be administered, as well as improve her nutrition and health. During her life, Tracy underwent several surgeries, including surgery to lengthen tendons and release muscles, and surgery to correct scoliosis in which rods were inserted into her back.

Despite her medical condition, Tracy attended school regularly in Wilkie. People who worked with Tracy in group homes and schools described her smile, love of music and reaction to horses at the circus. According to the Crown prosecutors' brief presented at the second trial, "She also responded to visits by her family, smiling and looking happy to see them. There is no dispute that through her life, Tracy at times suffered considerable pain. As well, the quality of her life was limited by her severe disability. But the pain she suffered was not unremitting, and her life had value and quality." In October 1993, Dr. Dzus recommended further surgery on November 19, 1993 in the hope that it would lessen the constant pain in Tracy's dislocated hip. Depending on the state of her hip joint, the procedure might have been a hip reconstruction or it might have involved removing the upper part of her thigh bone, leaving the leg connected to her body only by muscles and nerves. The anticipated recovery period for this surgery was one year. The Latimers were told that this procedure would cause pain, and the doctors involved suggested that further surgery would be required in the future to relieve the pain emanating from various joints in Tracy's body." Dr. Dzus reported that "the post operative pain can be incredible", and described the only useful short term solution being the use of an epidural to anaesthetize the lower part of the body and help alleviate pain while Tracy was still in hospital.

Tracy's death

On October 24, 1993, Laura Latimer found Tracy dead. She had died under the care of her father while the rest of the family was at church. At first Robert Latimer maintained that Tracy had died in her sleep; however, when confronted by police with autopsy evidence that high levels of carbon monoxide were found in Tracy's blood, Latimer confessed that he had killed her by placing her in his truck and connecting a hose from the truck's exhaust pipe to the cab. He said he had also considered other methods of killing Tracy, including Valium overdose and "shooting her in the head".

Robert Latimer said his actions were motivated by love for Tracy and a desire to end her pain. He described the medical treatments Tracy had undergone and was scheduled to undergo as "mutilation and torture". "With the combination of a feeding tube, rods in her back, the leg cut and flopping around and bedsores, how can people say she was a happy little girl?" Latimer asked.

Murder trials and appeals

On November 16, 1994, a jury convicted Latimer of second degree murder. However, the Supreme Court of Canada ordered a retrial, because of jury interference as the prosecutor had questioned potential jurors about religion, abortion, and mercy killing during jury selection. (See R. v. Latimer (1997) for more information on this decision.) On November 5, 1997, the jury at the second trial again found Latimer guilty of second degree murder. Although the minimum sentence for second degree murder is life with no chance of parole until after 10 years, the jury recommended that Latimer be eligible for parole after one year. Because he believed Latimer was motivated by compassion, Judge Ted Noble argued that a "constitutional exemption" could apply, and sentenced him to one year in jail, and one under house arrest.

The Crown appealed the decision because Latimer had not received the minimum sentence for his crime. The Saskatchewan Court of Appeal ruled that Latimer would have to serve a life sentence. Latimer appealed this decision to the Supreme Court of Canada, asserting that he had not been allowed to argue that he had no choice but to kill Tracy, and that a life sentence was cruel and unusual punishment. The Supreme Court unanimously upheld Latimer's conviction and life sentence holding that Latimer had other options available to him and that the minimum 10 year sentence was not excessive.

Prison

Robert Latimer began serving his sentence on January 18, 2001 and was incarcerated at William Head Institution, a minimum security facility located 30 kilometres west of Victoria, BC, on Vancouver Island. While in prison, he completed the first year of carpentry and electrician apprenticeships. He continued to run the farm with the help of a manager.

Parole

On December 5, 2007 Robert Latimer requested day parole from the National Parole Board in Victoria, BC. He told the parole board that he believed killing his daughter was the right thing to do. The board denied his request, saying that Latimer had not developed sufficient insight into his actions, despite psychological and parole reports that said he was a low risk to re-offend unless he was put into the same situation again. In January 2008, lawyer Jason Gratl filed the appeal on Latimer's behalf, arguing that in denying parole the board had violated its own rules by requiring admission of wrongdoing and by ignoring the low risk for re-offending. In February 2008, a review board overturned the earlier parole board, and granted Latimer day parole stating that there was low risk that Latimer would re-offend. Latimer was released from William Head Prison and began his day parole in Ottawa in March. On his release he expressed his plan to press for a new trial and for identification of the pain medication that the 2001 Supreme Court ruling suggested he could have used instead of killing his daughter.

Public debate

Support for Latimer

A 1999 poll found that 73% of Canadians believed that Latimer acted out of compassion and should receive a more lenient sentence. The same poll found that 41% believe that mercy killing should not be illegal. Ethicist Arthur Schafer argued that Robert Latimer was "the only person in Canadian history to spend even a single day in prison for a mercy killing" and that compassion and common sense dictated a reduced sentence and the granting of parole. In their book, "The Elements of Moral Philosophy", James Rachels and Stuart Rachels present Robert Latimer's actions sympathetically.

Support for Latimer's conviction and sentence

Numerous disability rights groups obtained intervenor status in the Latimer's appeal to the Supreme Court of Canada, arguing that killing a severely disabled child like Tracy is no different than killing a non-disabled child and should carry the same penalty. To do otherwise, they argued, would devalue the lives of disabled people and increase the risk of more such killings by their caregivers. Religious groups representing the Roman Catholic church and the Evangelical Fellowship also appeared as intervenors in Latimer's Supreme Court appeal.

Latimer's 2007 application for day parole was rejected primarily because he still denied any wrongdoing. Maclean's columnist Andrew Coyne argued that the National Parole Board was right to expect remorse on Latimer's part, because to do otherwise might inspire others to similar actions.

Cost of Justice - John Howard Society

From Wikipedia: (lightly edited and formatted)
http://www.johnhoward.ab.ca/PUB/C48.htm

Executive Summary - The John Howard Society

In 1994-95, the administration and operation costs of criminal justice services in Canada totalled almost $10 billion, broken down as follows:

Service	Total	Per Capita
Police	$ 5,783,656,000	$198
Courts	$ 835,404,00	$ 29
Adult Corrections	$ 1,893,530,000	$ 65
Youth Corrections	$ 525,545,000	$ 18
Legal Aid	$ 646,433,000	$ 22
Prosecutions	$ 257,855,000	$ 9
Total	$ 9,942,423,000	$340

Source: Canadian Centre for Justice Statistics (1997, January, p. 9)

The above presents only the economic costs associated with maintaining the criminal justice system. However, there are other costs associated with crime and delinquency that impact greatly upon society. Physical injury, psychological trauma, feelings of mistrust, vulnerability and fear are social costs that damage the individual victim and society. The subjective nature of social costs of crime makes it very difficult to assess the damage inflicted on a crime victim.

The incredible costs of crime, both economic and social, suggest the need for a more pro-active, rather than re-active, stance toward crime fighting. This would significantly reduce crime levels and current justice expenditures by preventing crimes from ever occurring.

Crime prevention through social development (CPSD) is an approach committed to reducing the future risk of crime by alleviating both the social and economic problems associated with criminal behaviour.

Introduction

The cost of criminal justice in Canada is astronomical. In 1994-95, the administration and operation costs of criminal justice services in Canada totalled almost $10 billion (Canadian Centre for Justice Statistics (CCJS), 1997, January, p. 1). This amounts to a cost to each Canadian of about $340 a year.

Each level of government in Canada has a different mandate and, therefore, each have their own responsibilities within the criminal justice system. The federal government is comprised of two justice related departments: the Ministry of the Solicitor General and the Department of Justice. These departments further divide into specific sectors responsible for various operations within the justice system. The Ministry of the Solicitor General is responsible for policing, corrections and parole. The Ministry of the Solicitor General includes the Royal Canadian Mounted Police (RCMP), the Correctional Service of Canada (CSC), a Secretariat, the National Parole Board and the Canadian Security Intelligence Agency. The federal Department of Justice is responsible for policy making (Canadian Criminal Code) and the administration of justice at the federal level. The federal government, or more correctly the Correctional Service of Canada, is responsible for providing custodial services for offenders sentenced to imprisonment of two years or more.

Provincial governments are responsible for creating and enforcing "quasi criminal" laws. Examples include the Highway Traffic Act and the Liquor Control Act. Each province is also responsible for providing custodial services to those offenders sentenced to prison terms of less than two years. Only three provinces (Ontario, Quebec and Newfoundland) operate independent provincial police forces. In the remaining provinces and territories, the RCMP have exclusive authority.

At the municipal level, all laws relating to the Criminal Code, provincial statutes and municipal bylaws are enforced. Policing services are carried out by independent municipal police forces or by the RCMP under contract.

This paper will examine the total costs of criminal justice in Canada, and will also show how the justice dollar is divided and spent by the provincial/territorial and federal government departments responsible for services such as policing, adult and youth corrections, courts, legal aid and prosecutions. Most figures are for 1994-95; otherwise, the most current figures available are provided.

The Cost of Criminal Justice - An Overview

The administration of justice by the federal, provincial and municipal governments in Canada makes up one of the more significant government expenditures. The 1994-95 total annual cost of almost $10 billion for policing, adult and youth corrections, courts, legal aid and prosecutions accounted for approximately 3% of the total annual expenditures by all levels of government combined (CCJS, 1997, January, p. 1). After adjusting for inflation, this figure represents a 13% increase over 1988-89 expenditures (CCJS, 1997, January, p. 1). This increase is comparable to increases in government spending on all other services. A breakdown of the justice dollar by sector reveals that policing services use the majority of justice dollars (58%), followed by adult corrections (19%), courts (8%), legal aid (7%), youth corrections (5%) and prosecutions (3%) (CCJS, 1997, January, p. 1).

Security of the Economy

Canada's Banks

From Bank of Canada: (lightly edited and formatted):
http://www.bankofcanada.ca/en/about/are.html

The Bank of Canada

The Bank of Canada is the nation's central bank. We are not a commercial bank and do not offer banking services to the public. Rather, we have responsibilities for Canada's monetary policy, bank notes, financial system, funds management. Our principal role, as defined in the Bank of Canada Act, is "to promote the economic and financial welfare of Canada."

The Bank was founded in 1934 as a privately owned corporation. In 1938, it became a Crown corporation belonging to the federal government. Since that time, the Minister of Finance has held the entire share capital issued by the Bank. Ultimately, the Bank is owned by the people of Canada.

The Bank is not a government department and conducts its activities with considerable independence compared with most other federal institutions. For example:

- The Governor and Senior Deputy Governor are appointed by the Bank's Board of Directors (with the approval of Cabinet), not by the federal government.

- The Deputy Minister of Finance sits on the Board of Directors but has no vote.
- The Bank submits its expenditures to its Board of Directors. Federal government departments submit theirs to the Treasury Board.
- Bank employees are regulated by the Bank itself, not by federal public service agencies.
- The Bank's books are audited by external auditors appointed by Cabinet on the recommendation of the Minister of Finance, not by the Auditor General of Canada.

Canadian Commercial Banks

From Google: (lightly edited and formatted)
http://www.canadabanks.net/

Canada has stable and very well developed banking system and Canadian banks play important role in Canadian economy and society. Canadian banks are amongst the top Canadian employers, employing over 200,000 people. Canadian banks are among the top tax payers too. Canadian Banks have created widespread financial network consisting of over 8,000 bank branches and over 18,000 ABMs (automated banking machines). Canadian banks offer many electronic services like online banking and debit cards.

The "Big Five" Canadian banks are Royal Bank of Canada, Toronto Dominion Bank, Bank of Nova Scotia, Canadian Imperial Bank of Commerce, Bank of Montreal. The big five Canadian banks and the federal Bank of Canada, are frequently called the "Big Six Banks" account for 90% of the assets of the Canadian banking business. The "big five" Canadian Banks have significant presence outside of Canada most notably in United States, Latin America, the Caribbean region and Asia.

Corporations & Investment Canada

From Industry Canada; Frequently asked Questions; (Abridged and lightly edited):

http://www.ic.gc.ca/eic/site/ica-lic.nsf/eng/h_lk00007.html

Investment Canada Act

Question: When will an investment be reviewable?

1. An investment is subject to review if there is an acquisition of a Canadian business and the asset value of the Canadian business being acquired equals or exceeds the following thresholds:

   a. For non-WTO (World Trade Organization) investors, the threshold is $5 million for a direct acquisition and over $50 million for an indirect acquisition; the $5 million threshold will apply for an indirect acquisition if the asset value of the Canadian business being acquired exceeds 50% of the asset value of the global transaction.

   b. Except as specified in paragraph © below, a threshold is calculated annually for subject to review direct acquisitions by or from WTO investors. The threshold for 2009 is $312 million. Pursuant to Canada's international commitments, indirect acquisitions by or from WTO investors are not subject to review.

   c. The limits set out in paragraph (a) a apply to all investors for acquisitions of a Canadian business that:
      i. engages in the production of uranium and owns an interest in a producing uranium property in Canada;
      ii. provides any financial service;
      iii. provides any transportation service; or
      iv. is a cultural business.

2. Notwithstanding the above, any investment which is usually only notifiable, including the establishment of a new Canadian business, and which falls within a specific business activity listed in Schedule IV of the Regulations Respecting Investment in Canada, may be reviewed if an Order in Council directing a review is made and a notice is sent to the Investor within 21 days following the receipt of a certified complete notification.

Question: Under what circumstances will the acquisition of a business which owns pipelines trigger an application for review?

Pursuant to subsections 14(1), (3) and 14.1(5) of the Investment Canada Act (the "Act"), the direct acquisition of a Canadian business which provides transportation services is subject to review where the asset value of the business acquired, calculated according to the Investment Canada Regulations (the "Regulations"), is $5 million or more. Pursuant to subsections 14(1), (4) and 14.1(5) of the Act, the indirect acquisition of such a business is subject to review where the asset value is $50 million or more.

"Transportation services" are defined in section 2.2 of the Regulations as follows:

> 2.2 For the purposes of paragraph 14.1(5)© of the Act, "transportation services" means a Canadian business directly or indirectly engaged in the carriage of passengers or goods from one place to another by any means, including, without limiting the generality of the foregoing, carriage by air, by rail, by water, by land and by pipeline."

The oil & gas industry makes extensive use of pipelines. By this definition, the transportation of gas or oil through a pipeline constitutes a transportation service. Thus, an entity the sole purpose of which is to operate a pipeline will be a transportation service. However, where the transportation service provided through a pipeline is an ancillary or incidental portion of a type of business other than a transportation service, the Investment Review Division ("IRD") may deem the business not to be a transportation service. To determine the extent, if any, to which the transportation service is ancillary or incidental to the business being acquired, IRD will consider a number of factors, including:

1. The assets being acquired (wells, plants, pipelines) and their corresponding values.
2. The ownership and control of the various assets being acquired.
3. The nature of the assets or facilities connected by the pipeline and the ownership or control of these assets or facilities.
4. The extent to which third party oil or gas is being transported through the pipeline (e.g. volume and percentage of overall throughput), and the business reason(s) for this.
5. The amount and percentage of the overall business revenues derived (a) from the pipeline activity and (b) the transportation of third party gas or oil.

This list is not exhaustive and other factors may be considered. IRD will consider each transaction on a case by case basis. This statement sets out a general approach and is not intended to be a binding statement of how IRD will interpret the Act for a particular transaction and should not be taken as such, nor is it intended to restate the law. Guidance regarding a specific transaction may be requested from the IRD. A formal written opinion under section 37 of the Act may be requested through a formal written opinion request.

Amendments to the Investment Canada Act

From Davies, Ward, Phillips, & Vineberg; (Lightly edited and formatted) http://www.dwpv.com/en/17620_23425.aspx

March 13, 2009: The enactment of Bill C-10 introduces significant changes to the Investment Canada Act. Below is a summary of the key amendments and their implications.

Key Changes

1. The usual thresholds for review for direct acquisitions of Canadian businesses (other than acquisitions of cultural businesses) by foreign investors will change as of a date to be determined by the federal Cabinet. These transactions are now subject to review if the book value of the assets of the Canadian business exceeds $312 million, but will shortly be subject to a general net benefit review only if the "enterprise value" of the assets of the Canadian business is equal to or greater than (a) $600 million, in the case of investments made during the first two years after the amendments come into force; (b) $800 million, in the case of investments made during the third and fourth years after the amendments come into force; and © $1 billion, in the case of investments made between the fifth year after the amendments come into force and December 31 of the sixth year after the amendments come into force. This threshold will thereafter be adjusted annually. In addition, the lower threshold ($5 million) currently applicable to the transportation, financial services, and uranium sectors is repealed.

2. There is now a new review process for investments that could be *"injurious to national security"*. The federal Cabinet is authorized to take any measures that it considers advisable to protect national security, including the outright prohibition of a foreign investment in Canada.

Implications

1. The apparent intention of amending the threshold for direct acquisitions is to reduce the number of foreign investments subject to a general net benefit review under the Investment Canada Act. Unfortunately, no definition has yet been provided for the new benchmark, i.e., "enterprise value", so it is difficult to assess the extent to which this goal is likely to be achieved.

2. There is a similar lack of clarity with respect to the new "national security" review process. No definition of "national security" has

been provided. The applicable standard, "could be injurious to national security", is ambiguous, and potentially open to wide interpretation. As a result, the Minister of Industry and the federal Cabinet will have wide discretion to decide which transactions they will review.

3. The Investment Review Branch of Industry Canada may now require that foreign investors provide any information considered necessary for an Investment Canada Act review, which may extend the scope of reviews and raise issues about the Branch's use of such information.

Corporate & Regional Subsidies

From the National Post 2010/02/23, (Abridged and formatted)

by Terence Corcoran

Is there any economic activity in Canada that doesn't get a handout from Government? Doesn't seem like it; No project is too big or too small that it cannot be rolled onto the backs of taxpayers. Loblaw, for example, announced recently that Ottawa would help bail the food giant out of a Toronto superstore miscalculation. In a 2004 bidding war against Home Depot and Wal-Mart, Loblaw took control of Maple Leaf Gardens, the former home of Toronto's NHL franchise. Turning the hockey palace into a food store proved to be uneconomic, so the company hooked up with nearby Ryerson University to land a $10 million federal subsidy.

On a still smaller scale, the Diamond Bourse of Canada recently opened in Toronto as a market for trading some of the $2.8 billion in diamonds produced in Canada. To help it open, the bourse received a $140,000 government grant. Not a large subsidy, but good evidence that Canadian business has yet to come across an objectionable government handout.

There are hundreds of corporate welfare items in Ottawa, too many to list or even count. Programs are buried within programs with grants and loans vying with tax credits and direct subsidies to relieve Canada's capitalists of risk and transfer it over to taxpayers. Many of these could be cut without the least disturbance to Canada's economic performance. More likely, Canadians would benefit if the distortions caused by these tax and spending programs were removed from the market.

The Chopping Block, in its quest to trim $20 billion from federal spending by 2013 and eliminate the federal spending deficit, will identify other prime cuts in the corporate welfare portfolio over the next few days, but let's carve off $1 billion or more worth of annual spending and tax expenditures just to get the hang of it.

On The Chopping Block:

• Labour Sponsored Venture Capital Corporations	$120 million
• Flow through shares	$100 million
• Canadian Film or Video Production Tax Credit	$200 million
• Film and Video Production Services Tax Credit	$100 million
• Atlantic Investment Tax Credit	$250 million
• Atlantic Canada Opportunities Agency	$350 million
• Western Economic Diversification	$250 million

Cumulative Budget saving to 2013 - 14:

Approximately $6 billion; in the 2013 - 14 fiscal year, $1.35 billion. This is, admittedly, a hodge podge of tax credits and actual cash dispensing operations, but they're all part of the federal government's vast array of political handouts that take money from once set of taxpayers and give it to others. The last two items (the Atlantic and Western development agencies), are straight money out the door schemes that give MPs and cabinet ministers a reason to visit tidings and deliver cheques while posing for local media photo opportunities. Another such agency, the Southern Ontario Development Agency, was recommended for The Chopping Block earlier in our series. Sometimes described as regional development vehicles, they have long been recognized among economists as sources of economic distortion and dependency.

There is no end to the demand for subsidy, and no end to the rationale for more from Canada's regional development specialists. The Atlantic agency, for example, is very effective in simultaneously claiming great achievement while warning that "significant challenges remain." In any economy, no matter how successful, there will always be significant challenges. Subsidies do not fix challenges, they entrench them at taxpayer expense.

The Labour Sponsored Venture Capital Corporation funds receive investment money from Canadians who receive a tax credit from Ottawa. Numerous studies have shown the LSVCC's create problems in the venture capital industry and for investors. As the C. D. Howe noted in its shadow budget plan last week, the fact that these LSVCC's "would likely not survive in the absence of the tax credits is evidence that these resources are likely not routed to their best uses."

The same could be said for just about everything government does to stimulate and artificially shape the economy. The federal flow through share program, which benefits resource companies, is vigorously defended by industry. As are the various government incentives to "cultural" industries, especially the film and video makers who are notoriously aggressive in defending their vital contribution to Canadian culture. Such tax credits may make film makers richer by $350 million a year, but how much greater is their value to Canada than the work of newspaper columnists?

One big cultural item is the $1 billion annual CBC subsidy, a popular target among The Chopping Block's contributors. To get at least some of that off Ottawa's annual spending, Andrew Coyne has recommended collecting $500 million or half the subsidy directly from television viewers. A good idea in some ways, but essentially a tax increase on TV viewers.

Increasing taxes to cut the CBC portion of the deficit would not be a first choice. There are plenty of other options around.

Also from the National Post 2010/02/24 by Terence Corcoran

The head of the Canadian Olympic Committee, Chris Rudge, is having second thoughts about the Own the Podium program, although not so much about the program as the name of the program. Maybe, he suggested, there's too much "braggadocio" in Own the Podium. "Should we change the name now? Maybe that's one of the things we should consider".

Now there's a man who knows how governments work, or don't work. When a $110 million program fails to produce results, rename the program to avoid continued criticism and attention. The last thing you want to do is kill the program itself, no matter how ineffective. Best to come up with a dense purposeless name that doesn't imply grand results or even any results at all. Ottawa has a lot of these. There's the $500-million Sustainable Development Technology Canada Fund, the $500 million NextGen Biofuels Fund, $145 million Agricultural Bioproducts Innovation Program. Do we get world class champions out of these efforts? Nobody even asks.

The Sustainable Development Fund is typical: nobody will ever know (or even wonder) whether the $500 million it receives will produce value for money. There are no medals to count. There isn't even a definition for "sustainable development." The national grand master of program policy nomenclature obfuscation is the federal Scientific Research and Experimental Development, (SR&ED) investment tax credit regime. Ottawa gives up about $3 billion a year in corporate tax credits through the SR&ED program, even though it produces results that make the Olympic "Own the Podium" program look like a huge success.

Let's cut the business equivalent of "Own the Podium"

If the COC wants a new name, it could take a tip from the SR&ED folks. How bout the Sports Research and Athletic Improvement & Development Tax (SRAIDTC) Credit. Clean. Generally meaningless. Best of all the SRAIDTC contains not a hint of a specific objective or target let alone braggadocio.

It works for the R&D community. Canada's R&D tax holidays, the target of today's edition of The Chopping Block, are universally acknowledged to be among the most generous in the world. As for gold medal production, measured in actual R&D generated in Canada, it's a dud. Among OECD countries, when it comes to producing R&D gold, Canada ranks 16th, with R&D spending equal to only 1% of GDP. Countries with much less generous subsidies get more gold. There even seems, be something of an inverse relationship between subsidy and results.

According to a finance department study published with the 2009 annual Tax Expenditures and Evaluations data, Canada provides subsidies worth 30% of the capital cost of research and development (46% for small firms). But OECD numbers show Canada gets half the R&D spending of the United States, which has a subsidy rate of 9.2%. Sweden, which essentially doesn't even bother subsidizing R&D, is the top R&D performer. Japan, with about half the subsidy rate of Canada, is the R&D silver winner. (See tables).

The trouble with subsidies of this kind is that, once in place, they are almost impossible to remove. The "Own the Podium" program has now turned the Canadian Olympic Committee into an even greater dependent on government funding. If the program were to be cut, Olympic athletes would be left in the lurch. Subsidies, once in place, become politically impossible to cut, even when they don't produce measurable results.

Ottawa's SR&ED regime, despite its obvious inadequacies, remains untouchable for the same reason. Cutting it seems impossible. But suppose we tried, as an experiment, cutting the R&D subsidy rate in half, down to the global average of 15%. Maybe the amount of R&D would remain at 1%, but at east taxpayers would save $1.5 billion a year. Given the perverseness of the relationship between subsidy and spending results, Canadian business R&D spending might even go up.

The Chopping Block From National Post 2010/02/27 by Terence Corcoran

This table is the final tabulation of federal spending cuts proposed by *FP Comments* four week feature, The Chopping Block. The objective was to find $20 billion in federal spending to balance the budget by 2013 or sooner.

On the Chopping Block	Savings 2010-11	Savings 2011-12	Savings 2012-13	Savings 2013-14	Four Year Total
Southern Ontario Development Agency	$300M	$200M	$200M	$200M	$900M
Agriculture Canada	$1B	$1B	$1B	$1B	$4B
Fed Transfers to Provinces	$2.6B	$5.3B	$8.9B	$8.9B	$25.7B
Public Transit Tax Credit	$130M	$140M	$140M	$150M	$560M
First Time Home Tax Credit	$200M	$200M	$200M	$200M	$800M
Fed Carbon Capture Program	$250M	$250M	$250M	$250M	$1B
Labour Venture Capital Funds	$120M	$120M	$120M	$120M	$480M
Flow-Through Shares	$255M	$255M	$255M	$255M	$1.02M
Film/Video etc Tax Credit Production & Services	$300M	$300M	$300M	$300M	$1.2B
Scientific Research & Experimental Development Investment Tax Credit	$1.6B	$1.6B	$1.6B	$1.6B	$6.4B
Atlantic Investment Tax Credit Atlantic Opportunities Agency Western Eco Diversification	$850M	$850M	$850M	$850M	$3.4B
Canada Health Infoway	$500M		$500M	$500M	$1.5B
Federal Civil Service Employment & Wages	$1B	$2.2B	$2.8B	$3.4B	$9.4B
Equalization & Cost Sharing of Public Service Pension Plans 50% Employer/50% Employee	$177M	$363M	$555M	$850M	$1.95B
Military Spending	$500M	$966M	$1.4B	$1.5B	$4.33N
Chopping Block Initial Total	$9.8B	$13.74B	$19.03B	$20.1B	$62.64B
Fed Deficit Projection Sept 09	-$45.3B	-$27.4B	-$19.4B	-$11.2B	-$103.3B
Chopping Block Revision	-$35.3B	-$13.59B	-$322M	-$8.85B	-$40.54B

Venture Capital Enhancements

From The National Post 2010/03/16 by Stephen A. Hurwitz

An Example of Good Governance

In a tax "master stroke", the Canadian government has just announced proposed legislation in its 2010 budget that would remove the "Section 116" barrier to the flow of international investment capital to Canadian technology companies. The new legislation will remove formidable administrative and economic burdens that have hampered the flow of potentially hundreds of millions of dollars in capital that is critically needed by Canadian technology companies. This change could alter the future of Canadian innovation.

In the past, Section 116 had required international investors, the vast majority of whom were already exempt from federal taxes on the sale of Canadian investments under Canada's broad network of tax treaties, to go through burdensome administrative hurdles before funds could freely flow to them. Documentation was required for every investor in a foreign venture capital fund, and many funds have hundreds of investors. A single sale could involve preparing and filing hundreds of pages of documents and signatures, including tax returns, even though invariably no taxes were due. This process often translated into months of delay, significant costs and sometimes major financial loss for the international investor.

The new legislation Will eliminate all of these bureaucratic hurdles, making it easier for international investment capital to invest in Canadian technology companies. The likely results for Canada's innovation industries and economy are extremely promising:

- Canada's emerging technology companies will now have access to deep pools of international capital and the vast global customer markets to which those pools are connected.
- Over time, the increased flow of international capital could help propel Canada's technology into global industry leadership in

numerous markets, resulting in significant increases in Canadian jobs, exports and tax revenues.
- The Harper government has given a clear signal that Canada is "open for business" and welcomes international capital, making Canada and its technology companies a more attractive place to invest.
- The government has demonstrated its commitment to ending unnecessary paperwork.
- Most remarkable of all, these impressive accomplishments are being achieved with minimal cost to Canada.

It's important to remember that the Section 116 problem was not one of the Harper government's making. It was inherited. The Canadian government deserves high praise for taking this unprecedented action to fix it.

Yet there is much work still to be done to put the Canadian venture capital industry back on its feet. Without doubt, 2009 was the worst year since the mid-1990s for venture capital investing in Canada and for fundraising by its venture capital firms. There is a need for the government to consider additional steps to resuscitate the venture capital industry. These may include expanding and liberalizing tax credits for emerging technology companies, as well as creating innovative incentives for institutional investors and individuals to invest in VC firms and for angel investors to invest in seed financing. In the short run and on at least a temporary basis, government may have to further intervene as an investor catalyst to help jump start the VC industry. But there is now light at the end of the tunnel, and we are closer to turning the corner than we've been before.

Given Canada's highly educated population, world class universities and research centres, major outlays of R&D, and proximity to the huge U. S. market, Canada has the potential in its technology and innovation to pack a global punch well beyond the relatively small size of its population and GDP. If the Harper government continues to make the right moves to bolster the VC industry in the bold and innovative way it did with Section 116, it could earn its place in history. It would be remembered as the government that set the stage for a truly dazzling global future for Canadian innovation and positioned Canada to blow the socks off the rest of the world.

Financial Post: Stephen A. Hurwitz, a partner in the law firm of Choate Hall & Stewart LLP, Boston, specializes in Canada - U.S. cross border transactions involving venture capital, private equity and technology companies. He is co-founder and chairman of the Quebec City Conference, a leading international VC, PE and LP conference.

The Federal Debt & GDP in 2010

From the National Post 2010/03/04 (lightly edited) by Livio Di Matteo

Act now to stop the return of the debt Leviathan

Today, Ottawa will move to bring its $56 billion deficit under control, to avoid a repeat of the fiscal crisis that engulfed Canada during the period 1973-1996.

From 1961 to 1973, Canada enjoyed robust economic growth, rising tax revenues and rising expenditures with which it put in place the last bricks of a comprehensive welfare state: namely Medicare, Unemployment Insurance and the Canada Pension Plan. Real per capita revenues grew at an astounding 7% a year while real per capita spending grew at only a slightly less astounding rate of 6%.

During this autumn of the post war boom, program spending accounted for nearly 90% of total federal government spending while the debt to GDP ratio fell to 20%. All this ended with the oil price shock and the 1973-74 recession, which ushered in an era of slower economic growth, stagflation and budget deficits.

The slowdown of the 1970s at first seemed like a temporary phenomenon. The Keynesian prescription of fiscal stimulus combined with the era's regional development inclinations produced seemingly modest deficits intended to mitigate the downturn. Unfortunately, the road to fiscal crisis runs parallel to the road to hell, which is also paved with good intentions.

What started out as deficits of $1 billion to $3 billion in the early 1970s reached $29 billion by 1982 and then continued to grow, peaking at nearly $40 billion by the early 1990s. The early deficits rapidly took on a life of their own as the high interest rates of the 1980s compounded the accumulated deficits into a debt leviathan. From 1973 to 1996, real per capita revenue grew at about 1% while per capita expenditures grew at 2%, resulting in a growing fiscal gap.

Debt service costs crowded out program spending and the share of total expenditures devoted to government programs fell to 70% by 1991. The accumulated federal deficit in 1961 of just under $15 billion had grown to $108 billion by 1982 and then soared to $563 billion by 1996. The concerted expenditure restraint of the mid-1990s combined with a booming economy brought the federal deficit and debt situation under control as deficits were converted to surpluses and both the absolute level of debt and the debt to GDP ratio fell. Substantial fiscal pain was felt in federal health and education transfers to the provinces.

By 2007, the federal debt had fallen to well below $500 billion, the debt to GDP ratio had declined to 30% and the budget had seen nearly a decade of consecutive surpluses. In many respects the period from 2000 to 2007 had come to resemble the golden autumn of the post war boom. While the growth rates of real per capita revenues and expenditures were lower than the 1960s, the real fiscal driver became the dividend from falling debt service costs, which allowed program spending to rise faster than per capita tax revenues, tax rates to be lowered and still generate surpluses. However, every boom must end, the question is never if but when, and the onset of the Great Recession saw the return of deficits.

With the rediscovery of Keynesian stimulus spending and declining government revenues, surpluses ended and a deficit of about $6 billion dollars in 2008-09 has been followed by an estimated $56 billion deficit in 2009-2010. Once again, we are on the verge of a giant gap between revenues and expenditures continuing.

To date we have been spared the full onslaught of the debt leviathan because it is early on and interest rates have remained at historically low rates. A drop in debt service costs fuelled by falling interest rates is unlikely to repeat itself. Interest rates cannot remain at historic lows forever and if deficits are not converted to surpluses by some combination of revenue increases and/or expenditure reductions, the power of compound interest will eventually and undo all the work that was done to restore the country's fiscal health since the mid-1990s.

We may wish to debate if the deficit is structural or cyclical but the solution remains the same in either case. Our fiscal history suggests that the best remedy to restore fiscal health is to ensure that expenditures not rise faster than revenues.

Financial Post, Livio Di Matteo is Professor of Economics at Lakehead University.

Pension Security

From the Globe & Mail 2009/10/19 Editorial article / page A22

Canadians can no longer assume they will retire with security.

Many are seeking increasingly scarce work while others flail as their once flush retirement accounts haemorrhage. A Globe and Mail series beginning today shows that the crisis in Canadian pensions is not looming; it is here, and has been for some time. A concerted national effort, involving changes in policy, behaviour and mindset from governments, businesses, unions, pension overseers and individual Canadians, is needed to repel the crisis.

The financial crisis is just the public face of the pension crisis. Stock market plunges have devalued everyone's savings in the short term, draining retirement accounts by $50-billion, according to one estimate.

When companies started toppling, apparently secure pensions were thrown into bankruptcy court (where they were put at the back of the creditors' queue, as with Nortel); or they were thrown into rescuing arms; General Motors had received pension funding exemptions because it was deemed too big to fail, and this year governments decided that it was also too big to be allowed to fail.

But the gestation period for the pension crisis has been long. Private sector participation in workplace pension plans has been falling. Defined benefit plans that deliver a guaranteed income benefit amount are disappearing, covering 41 per cent of all workers in 1991 but only 30 per cent in 2006. Pensioners in the steel and forestry industries have"already met the fate now being meted out to Nortel retirees. The mentality that informed the too big to fail policy, defer or forget about the problem, because it will eventually get fixed or fix itself, afflicted policy makers, pension administrators and beneficiaries of all sizes. Infrequent assessments of pension plans, done only every three years, predicated on unreasonable assumptions about investment returns, made pools of savings look more enduring than they were. Employers and employees failed to strike deals to re-balance plans, even when the number of retirees started to exceed the number of workers.

Another set of poorer Canadians should never have had the illusion of security in the first place. A large proportion of workers, 44 per cent, or eight million Canadians, have neither an RRSP nor an employer based registered pension plan. A growing proportion is self-employed. They will depend on the Canada and Quebec Pension Plans and government backstops like Old Age Security. These provide basic assistance, but little more. The maximum CPP monthly payment for a 65 year old is $908.75. Unless blessed with other assets, a senior who relies on the public system alone lives a life of poverty.

Meanwhile, government finances are getting squeezed in two ways. More than five in six public sector workers are in registered pension plans, usually requiring significant government co-payments; unlike their private sector counterparts, these workers have successfully maintained relatively expensive benefits during collective bargaining.

Second, an aging population means governments are spending more on health care, while the proportion of taxpaying workers falls. Increasing taxes, and increasing public spending on retirement income, are not solutions to the pension crisis.

With so many Canadians at personal financial risk, a new approach is needed.

Regulators must be more active in monitoring plans between official evaluations. Governments should facilitate the creation of multi-employer pension plans, whose scale can help spread risk and attract workers from smaller workplaces; new plans could get tax credits to encourage their growth. Commitments inherent in existing defined benefit plans should be legislatively enshrined, so that they cannot be lost in bankruptcy or squandered when good times make plan administrators succumb to the temptation to reduce incoming payments. The principle, outlined by University of Toronto professor Keith Ambachtsheer in an unpublished paper, is that "accruing pension promises must be fully costed and fully funded at all times." But employers do not need to wait for the government's hand. They can ensure their plans are better funded by setting higher default contribution rates from employees.

Other employers can facilitate payroll deductions to the savings account of the employee's choice. As long as these schemes, or "nudges," as described by the economists Cass Sunstein and Richard Thaler, still leave the ultimate choice on whether to participate in the hands of individual workers, they should be pursued widely. And employers must see the larger public benefits that come with their sponsorship of pensions. Without their participation, families and governments will buckle under the pressure to provide for Canada's retirees.

Institutions can only do so much; pensions are just part of a larger process of retirement planning incumbent on every Canadian. No amount of alchemy, short of another stock market boom, will make the lost assets return. Individuals need to make their own contribution to build or rebuild their savings. And they need to embrace financial literacy as a competency for life, just as they learn safe driving.

As a society, Canada decided many years ago that its older people and retirees should not have to depend purely on family, charity or their own devices to live. But the promise inherent in our patchwork pension framework has become unravelled. National will must be summoned to repair it.

Retirement Lost

From Globe & Mail 2009/10/17 by Jacquie McNish

Charles Walker spent his summer overseeing the death of 1,167 retirement dreams.

After 22 years as vice-president of finance at a perennially struggling aluminum mill in Cap de la Madeleine northeast of Montreal, Mr. Walker was accustomed to tough assignments. But nothing prepared the retiree for his comeback task: assessing the health of the mill's three pension plans after the company was forced into liquidation proceedings in March by its bankrupt Ohio parent, Aleris International Inc.

For three sweltering months, Mr. Walker, 65, toiled in the mill's abandoned, airless offices, making calculation after calculation. His final tally: $46.2 million of pension deficits. That tab, he estimates, will erase between 30 and 40 per cent of the pensions owed to him and his fellow retirees and employees. "I felt like I was in a morgue," Mr. Walker says.

"You look at this and you say, 'Jesus, this is painful . . . I know people in the plant, I know their families. So it is very, very agonizing to see these people who have worked all their life to try and get a pension - and, all of a sudden, it falls apart." Canadians are facing a national pension meltdown. Decades in the making, it has worsened dramatically during the recession.

Businesses are shredding pension promises, retirement savings are shrinking, employees are working longer and the elderly are selling homes and returning to the work force. As the retirement dream fades, policymakers seem unwilling to tell Canadians they have not saved enough to retire.

"We have overestimated our capacity to protect the needs of retirees," says Harry Arthurs, former head of an Ontario commission that identified numerous flaws in the province's pension regime. "We now know there is no such thing as a pension or retirement promise," Mr. Arthurs says. "There is no certainty."

A slow retreat by companies from their pension obligations turned into a gallop this year after a severe global recession laid bare the frailties of the promises made to employees. The withdrawal is a major factor behind a startling statistic: eleven million Canadian workers, about 60 per cent of the work force, do not have a pension plan.

Those corporate pension plans left standing also face unprecedented stresses. Market turmoil has punched an estimated $50 billion deficit hole into Canada's corporate pension funds, according to experts who have crunched what little current data is available.

The cost of replenishing the deficit is squeezing businesses when they can least afford it. Pension costs areA spiralling as retirees live longer and the baby boom generation heads for the exits: more than 40 per cent of workers will reach retirement age in the next two decades.

A crisis this large isn't just financial. It's also tearing the fabric of Canadian society. Retirement anxiety is changing our notion of personal wealth. Where once a house and two cars were symbols of success, today the measure is more likely to be the size of your nest egg. And as with any wealth metric, there is a class system. At the top of the system is a shrinking royalty.

Most of them are public servants. About 84% of public sector workers are pension plan members, most of whom have gold plated pensions designed to guarantee retirees fixed incomes. At the bottom are the pension paupers, the millions of workers who never had an employee retirement plan, and whose taxes contribute to public sector pensions that they can only dream about.

Apart from fraying Canada's social fabric, the growing ranks of pension wounded pose long term challenges for an economy that depends on consumer spending. Aleris's Mr. Walker, who stands to lose 30% of his pension income, plans to survive by simply spending less.

While the casualties mount, businesses are stepping up their lobbying of federal and provincial governments for more latitude to ease pension burdens. "Existing deficit funding rules may threaten the sustainability of many Canadian companies and ultimately the pensions of their retirees and employees," Calin Rovinescu, CEO of Air Canada, told The Globe and Mail. In July of this year, the airline won a special 21 month reprieve from its employees and the federal government to delay repairing its $2.9 billion pension deficit. It is one of seven companies lobbying Ottawa to allow businesses more time and discretion to replenish pension deficits.

Federal and provincial governments, which divide responsibility for pension regulation, have responded to the pension crisis by granting businesses like Air Canada extra breathing room to replenish underfunded pensions. But these measures are little more than Band Aids applied to a critically injured system. No policy maker seems willing to admit that the corporate pension promise is broken and Canadians need to save more to survive retirement.

While governments watch from the sidelines, bankruptcy courts have become the de facto policy maker. The fate of thousands of elderly workers and retirees is being decided in court supervised restructuring. The narrow lens of the commercial court judges has produced some recent decisions that have weakened employees' pension rights.

"No one is doing anything for us," says LeRoy Pickett, a 67 year old retiree. When Slater Steel Inc., his employer of 39 years, declared bankruptcy in 2003, he lost nearly 30 per cent of his pension. His wife had to return to work and the couple were forced to sell their house in

Hamilton. "It makes you feel like a horse being sent to the glue factory after a long time off work," Mr. Pickett says.

Disaster Long in the Making

The surprising thing about Canada's pension crisis is that it has caught anyone by surprise. Like a volcano that has been spewing ominous clouds for years, the crisis has been foretold by countless academics, consultants and government panels. Four provinces British Columbia, Alberta, Ontario and Nova Scotia, have recently had commissions report on pension woes. Ottawa has created a joint federal provincial task force that will report in December.

For all this seeming attention, however, there has been little meaningful change in the country's fragmented pension regime for nearly two decades. "Our politicians don't want to talk about this. They always hope that someone else will deal with it," says Claude Lamoureux, former head of the Ontario Teachers' Pension Fund, one of the country's largest public sector pension pools.

The crisis is making for some unlikely rebels. Next week Nortel Networks Corp's highly organized fraternity of 11,000 retirees is demonstrating on Parliament Hill, two weeks after a similar rally at Queens Park. Among the leaders is Robert Ferchat, a former president of Nortel Canada, who retired in 1991 and saw his pension cheques frozen after Nortel's collapse. He never imagined he would one day march arm in arm with union leaders.

"When I worked at Northern Telecom, it was king of the world," he says. "Today its pensioners are victims of years of mistakes and bad luck. It is outrageous to me that during this time the executive compensation rose dramatically, while the pensioners became more vulnerable."

Some workers have been able to ease the sting of lost pension income with savings invested in registered retirement savings plans (RRSPs). But workers with company pensions can only take limited advantage of the tax break on RRSP contributions. Stock market volatility and high management fees on many popular retirement funds also point to the drawbacks of these investments. "It turns out the private savings in RRSPs were not as good as we thought it would be, because those that did save have been hurt," says Bob Brooks, recently retired vice chairman with Bank of Nova Scotia.

Historians believe that Hudson's Bay Co. pioneered Canada's first pension plan in the 1840s as an incentive to lure managers to desolate trading posts. Soon, rapidly growing railroads, banks and department stores were dangling pensions to cement the loyalty of the skilled workers they badly needed for expanding empires.

The genius of these early plans was that costs were minimal. Only a lucky few employees would live long enough to collect benefits, up until 1950 the average Canadian life expectancy was under 65. Ottawa joined the pension movement in 1927 with a plan that helped provinces ensure every Canadian over 70 would receive $20 a month.

As the economy grew and prospered after the Second World War, pensions came to be seen as a worker's birthright. The federal government's Old Age Security program and Canada Pension Plan, as well as the Quebec Pension Plan, were created to ensure that no retired employee fell below the poverty line.

Supplementing these Spartan plans were increasingly rich company pensions that promised a comfortable retirement. By 1977, 46% of the work force was enrolled in employment pension plans. The public/private split was already clear: 75% of public sector workers were registered in plans, compared with 35% in the private sector, according to Statistics Canada.

Since then, the pension blanket has slowly unravelled. Core manufacturing sponsors transferred operations to lower wage countries or switched to cheaper defined contribution plans. By 2007 this shift was so pronounced that the percentage of companies offering defined benefits had dropped by half to 15.7%. And by that year, 84% of public sector workers had rock solid defined benefit plans.

Many business leaders privately grumble that unions are to blame for demanding unrealistic pension benefits. But Mr. Arthurs, head of Ontario's commission, says this is not the whole picture. "There has been an element of willful deception. Companies knew they would not be able to deliver their pension promises," he says.

Compounding the crisis, pension investment strategies have foundered. After decades of successfully covering pension costs with returns from securities with fixed interest payments, pension managers facing declining returns in the 1990s pushed into riskier stocks and derivatives such as asset backed commercial paper. At first, the strategies were wildly successful.

The heady returns led to a complacency that blinded workers, employers and governments to the fault lines. During these good times, some businesses siphoned off a portion of pension surpluses while others took pension contribution holidays, in part because Canada's tax laws penalize companies that plow extra savings into plans. Adding to the environment of complacency was the unchecked optimism of actuaries, the gatekeepers who are required by law to test the solvency of pension funds. As markets inflated, actuaries continued to assume that abnormal investment gains would deliver sufficient returns over the long term to cover rising pension costs. "We tended to think this was tomorrow's problem, but tomorrow's problem is here today," says Mr. Lamoureux.

The Breaking Point

The crisis erupted with a bang last fall when the global financial meltdown knocked the stuffing out of pension portfolios and retirement savings. Almost overnight, the rosy investment forecasts of actuaries and pension managers began to look delusional.

Taking the pulse of corporate pension plans is no easy matter in Canada. Pension oversight is divided among federal and provincial regulators that rely on outdated data to monitor pension fund health. Typically, pension funds are subject to actuarial assessments of their solvency only every three years. Thus the full impact of the market collapse will not be known at many funds for several months.

Still, a number of pension experts have made some educated guesses about the hit that funds have taken. RBC Dexia, a pension services company, estimates major Canadian pension plans with more than $1 billion of assets saw assets swoon by an average of 18% last year.

The carnage was particularly gruesome in the private sector, where pension managers are significantly less experienced than their public sector counterparts. "The pension burden has proven to be too great," says Ian Markham, a director with pension consultant Watson Wyatt Worldwide, who estimates the average Canadian corporate plan is 20 per cent short of the assets it needs to fund its long term pension obligations. That deficit adds up to about $50 billion, a staggering IOU that is crippling a number of companies.

The overall impact of the recession has forced a record number of Canadian companies to liquidate or restructure their operations. Hidden behind these bankruptcy statistics are a growing number of crippled companies with pension deficits. Again, there are no precise current data, but pension professionals say they have never seen so many companies land in bankruptcy proceedings with broken pensions.

"We are witnessing an unprecedented pension crisis," says Brett Ledger, a corporate pension litigator with Osler Hoskin & Harcourt LLP. "It's going to get a whole lot worse," he predicts, because another wave of struggling companies is drawing closer to bankruptcy.

It is in these proceedings that the worst of Canada's pension flaws are revealed. Many retirees and employees have no idea that their pension funds have deficits until their companies land in court. Several former workers at Slater Steel learned the company was in bankruptcy in 2003 only when their pharmacists informed them that their benefits had been cut off. There are so few warning signs because actuarial checkups are so infrequent. But even these infrequent analyses, experts warn, can be subjective and sometimes very wrong.

In early 2002, only a few months before Slater Steel filed for bankruptcy protection, two pension funds at subsidiary Slater Stainless Corp. received a stamp of approval from Melvin Norton, a veteran actuary with Aon Consulting Inc. The Ontario Superintendent of Financial Services, the province's pension regulator, later concluded the funds were in fact 40 percent underfunded. It sued Mr. Norton for allegedly filing a false actuarial report. The charges against Mr. Norton were dismissed by an Ontario judge. In 2008, the Canadian Institute of Actuaries fined Mr. Norton $15,000 and placed him under supervision for six months after it found that he had failed to perform professional services with "skill and care."

Mr. Norton says he was not responsible for the pensioners' losses. "It was the fact that the company didn't put enough money in the plan." "We need an early warning system," says Mr. Arthurs, who headed the Ontario commission. "There is a wide zone of discretion left to actuaries who are making judgments about the health of pensions."

Justice can seem selective for pensioners whose funds become entangled in bankruptcy proceedings. In court, workers, unions and even pension regulators have been locked in losing battles against creditors. In two recent cases, creditors offering new financing have successfully demanded the courts suspend payments owed to repair pension deficits.

By trumping pension laws, the judges in these cases are seeking to strike a reasonable commercial solution that can help the companies survive and possibly one day prosper sufficiently to repair ailing pensions. But these decisions come with risks. If restructuring efforts fail and company assets are liquidated, pensioners have little hope of recouping owed pensions, because they are outranked by most other creditors.

"Everyone feels like a victim here," says Carol Kirton 52, who has worked for 32 years at one of the companies, the Port Hope, Ont. based branch plant of D. S. auto parts maker Collins & Aikman Corp. Ms. Kirton says company officials have disclosed that the pension has a 30% shortfall. After two years of bankruptcy protection, she says hope is fading that the company will survive.

Concerns are rising among labour groups and their legal advisers that bankruptcy proceedings are becoming a place were companies can too easily amputate their infected pensions. "Bankruptcy, or the threat of bankruptcy, is being used to eviscerate pension funding," says Murray Gold, an adviser to Ontario's Arthurs commission and a Koskie Minsky LLP lawyer who specializes in representing labour groups.

"Bankruptcy court . . . is not the right place to make social policy.

Attention Must Be Paid

There are other places besides bankruptcy court to reform a damaged pension regime. But these court room tug of wars will likely continue until governments, businesses and workers adopt what former Ontario pension commissioner Mr. Arthurs calls "a new mindset." That new approach would recognize that battles over shrinking corporate pension plans have, at best, only fixed the system at the margins and, at worst, delayed momentum for change.

Turning the Band Aid solutions into a blanket fix for Canadian retirees would require Ottawa and the provinces to take a difficult and politically unattractive first step: recognizing that the century old business promise of a comfortable retirement is vanishing like the trading companies, retailers and railroads that first introduced them. Until that happens, the courts will continue to be the graveyards of broken retirement dreams.

Just ask Mr. Walker, the former Aleris executive. "This is a dream buster .... People have really been caught short."

With a report from reporter Greg Keenan

Their Stories

"I never imagined this would happen." John Mlacak ended his career at Canada's most admired technology company in 1994 with a pension that he figured would make retirement easy. There would even come a time when he and his wife, Beth could pull their three children together to advise them of a modest inheritance. He figured wrong.

When the 73 year old former technology manager with Nortel Networks did talk to his adult children this summer, it was to tell them that his pension cupboard is running low. Nortel had collapsed into bankruptcy proceedings. Over $200,000 of retirement savings he invested in a company plan had vanished. His medical, dental and insurance benefits looked like toast.

And the company's pension plan is so underfunded that he stands to lose as much as 30 per cent of his monthly $3,000 pension. If that happens, the elderly couple risks losing their house of 34 years in Kanata, Ontario. "We used to always talk about how much we were going to leave our children . . . now we may need to rely on them for help. I never imagined this would happen," he said. On dark days, he said he still struggles to understand how a company that became the envy of the world during his 35 year career could have stranded him 13 years after he retired.

"It is extremely discouraging to know at this stage in one's life that everything that you invested your life for . . . is endangered," he said. He sometimes thinks of returning to work, but worries that heart and blood pressure conditions might be a handicap. "I'm thinking of trying to get a job at 73, but I have to have a nap every day at noon," he said.

Vital Statistics

84% of public service workers have pensions
78% of these plans are gold plated defined benefit pensions

25% of private sector workers have a pension plan
16% of these plans are gold plated defined benefit pensions

11 million workers, or 60%, of Canada's workers have no pension at all
8 million or 45% have no pensions or RRSPs

Security of Transportation

Transportation in Canada

From Wikipedia; (Lightly edited and formatted):
http://en.wikipedia.org/wiki/Transportation_in_Canada

Canada is a developed country whose economy includes the extraction and export of raw materials from its large area. Because of this, it has a transportation system which includes more than 1,400,000 kilometres (870,000 mi) of roads, 10 major international airports, 300 smaller airports, 72,093 km (44,797 mi) of functioning railway track, and more than 300 commercial ports and harbours that provide access to the Pacific, Atlantic and Arctic oceans as well as the Great Lakes and the Saint Lawrence Seaway. In 2005, the transportation sector made up 4.2% of Canada's GDP, compared to 3.7% for Canada's mining and oil and gas extraction industries.

The federal department of Transport Canada oversees and regulates most aspects of transportation within Canadian jurisdiction. Transport Canada is under the direction of the federal government's Minister of Transport. The Transportation Safety Board of Canada is responsible for maintaining transportation safety in Canada by investigating accidents and making safety recommendations.

Gross domestic product, transport industries, 2005

Industry	% of Transport GDP
Air Transportation	9
Rail Transportation	13
Water Transportation	3
Truck Transportation	35
Transit and ground passenger transportation	12
Pipeline Transportation	11
Scenic and sightseeing transport & support	17
Total Transportation	100

Road Transportation

There are a total of 1,042,300 kms (647,700 mi) of road in Canada, of which 413,600 kms (257,000 mi) are paved, including 17,000 kms (11,000 mi) of expressways). As of 2006, 626,700 kms (389,400 mi) were unpaved.

In 2006, there were 19,499,843 road vehicles registered in Canada, of which 96.1% were vehicles under 4.5 tonnes, 2.3% were vehicles between 4.5 and 15 tonnes, and 1.6% were 15 tonnes or greater.

These vehicles travelled a total of 326.14 billion kilometres, of which 296.9 billion were for vehicles under 4.5 tonnes, 7.4 billion were for vehicles between 4.5 and 15 tonnes, and 21.8 billion were for vehicles over 15 tonnes.

For the 4.5 to 15 tonnes trucks, 92.2% of vehicle-kilometres were intra-provincial trips, 4.5% were inter-provincial, and 3.2% were made between Canada and the US. For trucks over 15 tonnes, 58% of vehicle-kilometres were intra-provincial trips, 18.4% inter-provincial trips, 15.4% Canada-US trips, and 8.4% trips made outside of Canada. The Ambassador Bridge between Windsor and Detroit, Michigan has a quarter of US-Canada trade cross over it.

Canada's vehicles consumed a total of 31.1 million cubic metres (196 Mbbl) of gasoline and 10.1 million cubic metres (64 Mbbl) of diesel. Trucking generated 35% of the total GDP from transport, compared to 25% for rail, water and air combined (the remainder being generated by the industry's transit, pipeline, scenic and support activities). Hence roads are the dominant means of passenger and freight transport in Canada.

Roads and highways were managed by provincial and municipal authorities until construction of the Alaska Highway, and the Trans-Canada Highway project initiation. The Alaska Highway of 1942 was constructed during World War II for military purposes connecting Fort St. John, British Columbia with Fairbanks, Alaska. The transcontinental highway, a joint national and provincial expenditure, was begun in 1949 under the initiation of the Trans Canada Highway Act in December 10, 1949. The 7,821 km (4,860 mi) highway was completed in 1962 at a total expenditure of $1.4 billion.

Internationally, Canada has road links with both the lower 48 U.S. states and Alaska. The Ministry of Transportation maintains the road network in Ontario and also employs Ministry of Transport Enforcement Officers for the purpose of administering the Canada Transportation Act and related regulations. The Department of Transportation in New Brunswick performs a similar task in that province as well.

Regulations enacted in regards to Canada highways are the 1971 Motor Vehicle Safety Act and the 1990 Highway Traffic Act. The safety of Canada's roads is moderately good by international standards, and is improving both in terms of accidents per head of population and per billion vehicle kilometres.

Air Transportation

Air transportation made up 9% of the transport sector's GDP generation in 2005. Air Canada is the world's 8th largest passenger airline by fleet size (2008), and the airline is a founding member of Star Alliance, an alliance of 21 member airlines formed in 1997. Air Canada had 34 million customers in 2006 and operated 368 aircraft, including Air Canada Jazz. With the advent of larger aircraft in 2009, the fleet had been reduced to 202 aircraft, plus 37 Boeing 787 Dreamliners on order for 2013. WestJet is a low cost carrier formed in 1996, and has 85 aircraft, plus another 50 on order. It is a rarity in the airline industry as it is a non-union, profit sharing operation. WestJet has made significant gains in domestic market share against Air Canada. In 2000 it held only 7% to Air Canada's 77%, though by 2009 WestJet has risen to 36%, against Air Canada's 57%. WestJet plans to be one of the world's top five most profitable international airlines, by 2016. CHC Helicopter is the world's largest commercial helicopter operators with 320 aircraft in 2008. Canada's airline industry saw significant change in 1995, when the marketplace became less regulated and more competitive.

The Canadian Transportation Agency employs transportation enforcement officers to maintain aircraft safety standards, and conduct periodic aircraft inspections, of all air carriers. The Canadian Air Transport Security Authority is charged with the responsibility for the security of air traffic within Canada. In 1994 the National Airports Policy was enacted.

Principal Airports

Further information: National Airports System, List of the busiest airports in Canada, List of heliports in Canada

Of over 1,700 registered Canadian aerodromes, certified airports, heliports, and floatplane bases, 26 are specially designated under Canada's National Airports System (NAS): these include all airports that handle 200,000 or more passengers each year, as well as the principal airport serving each federal, provincial, and territorial capital. However, airports such as Montréal Mirabel International Airport, which has fewer that 200,000 passengers has not been removed from the list. The Government of Canada retains ownership of these airports and leases them to local authorities. The next tier consists of 64 regional / local airports formerly owned by the federal government, most of which have now been transferred to other owners (most often to municipalities).

Below is a table of Canada's ten biggest airports by passenger traffic in 2009. Toronto Pearson International Airport, is the busiest airport in Canada, and was also the only Canadian airport ranked in the top 30 airports in the world by number of passengers in 2006 (although it dropped off the list in 2007). In 2009, 95.9 million passengers travelled through Canada's ten largest airports. Future projections see Toronto Pearson International Airport handling 55 million passengers annually by 2020.

As of November 2008 NAV CANADA reported that there were 41 airports with an air traffic control tower and 59 airports with a flight service station (FSS).

Passengers Statistics for Canada's Busiest Airports - 2008

Rank	Name and Location	Total Passengers	Annual Increase %
1	Toronto Pearson International Airport	32,334,831	2.8
2	Vancouver International Airport	17,852,459	2.0
3	Calgary International Airport	12,379,843	2.0
4	Montréal-Pierre Trudeau International Airport	12,506,893	-0.2
5	Edmonton International Airport	6,437,334	6.1
6	Ottawa International Airport (est)	4,320,000	5.5
7	Edmonton International Airport	3,578,931	3.2
8	Winnipeg James Armstrong Richardson International Airport	3,570,033	0.1
9	Victoria International Airport	1,538,417	3.8
10	Kelowna International Airport	1,389,883	1.9

Rail Transportation

In 2007, Canada had a total of 72,212 km (44,870 mi) of freight and passenger railway, of which 31 km (19 mi) is electrified. While intercity passenger transportation by rail is now very limited, freight transport by rail remains common. Total revenues of rail services in 2006 were $10.4 billion, of which only 2.8% was from passenger services. The

Canadian National and Canadian Pacific Railway are Canada's two major freight railway companies, each having operations throughout North America. In 2007, 357 billion tonne-kilometres of freight were transported by rail, and 4.33 million passengers travelled 1.44 billion passenger-kilometres (an almost negligible amount compared to the 491 billion passenger-kilometres made in light road vehicles). 34,281 people were employed by the rail industry in the same year.

Nation wide passenger services are provided by the federal crown corporation Via Rail. Three Canadian cities have commuter rail services: in the Montreal area by AMT, in the Toronto area by GO Transit, and in the Vancouver area by West Coast Express. Smaller railways such as Ontario Northland, Rocky Mountaineer, and Algoma Central also run passenger trains to remote rural areas. In Canada railways are standard gauge rails 1,435 mm (4 ft 8 ½ in).

Canada has rail links with the lower 48 U.S. States, but no connection with Alaska other than a train ferry service from Prince Rupert, British Columbia, although a line has been proposed. There are no other international rail connections.

Waterway Transportation

In 2005, 139.2 million tonnes of cargo was loaded and unloaded at Canadian ports. The Port of Vancouver is the busiest port in Canada, moving 68 million tonnes or 15% of Canada's total in domestic and international shipping in 2003.

Transport Canada oversees most of the regulatory functions related to marine registration, safety of large vessel, and port pilotage duties. Many of Canada's port facilities are in the process of being divested from federal responsibility to other agencies or municipalities. The inland waterways comprise 3,000 km (1,900 mi), including the Saint Lawrence Seaway. Transport Canada enforces acts and regulations governing water transportation and safety.

Container Traffic in Canadian Ports 2006

Rank	Port	TEUs "Twenty-foot Equivalent Units"	Boxes	Containerized
1	Vancouver BC	2,207,730	1,282,807	17,640,024
2	Montréal PQ	1,288,910	794,735	11,339,316
3	Halifax NS	530,722	311,065	4,572,020
4	St. Johns NL	118,008	55,475	512,787
5	Fraser River BC	94,651	N/A	742,783
6	Saint John NB	44,566	24,982	259,459
7	Toronto ON	24,585	24,585	292,834

Ferry Transportation Services

Passenger ferry service
- Vancouver Island to the mainland
- several Sunshine Coast communities to the mainland and to Alaska.
- Internationally to St. Pierre and Miquelon

Automobile ferry service
- Nova Scotia to Newfoundland and Labrador,
- Quebec to Labrador
- Labrador and the island of Newfoundland.

Train ferry service
- British Columbia to Alaska or Washington state.

Canals

The St. Lawrence waterway was at one time the world's greatest inland water navigation system. The main route canals of Canada are those of the St. Lawrence River and the Great Lakes. The others are subsidiary canals.

- Saint Lawrence Seaway
- Welland Canal
- Soo Locks
- Trent-Severn Waterway
- Rideau Canal

Ports and harbours

The National Harbours board administers Halifax, Saint John, Chicoutimi, Trois-Rivières, Churchill, and Vancouver. Over 300 harbours across Canada are supervised by the Department of Transport.

West coast
- Victoria, British Columbia
- Vancouver, British Columbia
- New Westminster, British Columbia
- Prince Rupert, British Columbia

East coast
- Halifax, Nova Scotia
- Saint John, New Brunswick
- St. John's, Newfoundland and Labrador
- Sept-Îles, Quebec
- Sydney, Nova Scotia
- Botwood, Newfoundland and Labrador

Northern and central
- Churchill, Manitoba Seaport
- Bécancour, Quebec
- Churchill, Manitoba
- Hamilton, Ontario
- Montreal, Quebec
- Quebec City, Quebec
- Trois-Rivières, Quebec
- Thunder Bay, Ontario
- Toronto, Ontario
- Windsor, Ontario

Merchant marine

Canada's merchant marine comprised a total of 173 ships (1,000 gross register tons (GRT) or over) 2,129,243 GRT or 716,340 metric tons deadweight (DWT) at the end of 2007.

Pipelines

Pipelines are part of the energy extraction and transportation network of Canada and are used to transport natural gas, natural gas liquids, crude oil, synthetic crude and other petroleum based products. Canada has 23,564 km (14,642 mi) of pipeline for transportation of crude and refined oil, and 74,980 km (46,590 mi) for liquefied petroleum gas.

Profiling Acceptable in Canada & USA

From the National Post 2009/01/07 (Lightly edited and formatted)
Editorial

Yes, the so called "naked" scanners, 44 of which will be installed at Canadian airports by spring, are intrusive. While passengers need not fear that they take a picture of a passenger's body under his or her clothes, they do give screeners a pretty good idea of one's body shape, the sort of image once reserved for spouses, doctors and locker room chums.

But the revealing nature of the images isn't their biggest drawback. The problem is that they perpetuate our obsession with keeping bad things off airlines, guns, blades, explosives, etc., rather than keeping off bad people.

Authorities don't need to search every passenger for 100 millilitres of hand lotion just because a cadre of Islamic extremists in Britain planned to use sports drinks and toothpaste to blow up as many as 10 jetliners simultaneously in 2006. They don't need to have every elderly lady take off her shoes to be X-rayed either, or have every rotund Caucasian male remove his belt and hobble through the metal detector with one hand on his waistband.

Screening efforts must focus on the groups that contain the most dangerous radicals.

What is needed is profiling of passengers, their behaviour, travel history, sex, ethnicity, travel companion status and outward religious aspect. Men are far more likely to be terrorists than women, so men should receive greater scrutiny. Young adults are more likely to be terrorists than the aged. Religious Muslims who've travelled frequently to Yemen or Nigeria or Pakistan are statistically more likely to be terrorists than Sikhs, nuns and Quakers.

Men travelling alone are more likely to be terrorists than men travelling with children. None should be treated as a presumptive terrorist. But only the blind may ignore the fact that almost the entire terrorist threat originates with a small subset of the travelling population.

The federal government's announcement on Tuesday that it will step up security for flights going from Canada to the United States was a mixed effort, then. On the one hand, it again focuses on interdicting dangerous objects, which is hit and miss at best. But for the first time, it does also acknowledge that more profiling is necessary.

Ottawa will spend $11 million installing full body scanners at airports in Vancouver, Calgary, Edmonton, Winnipeg, Toronto, Montreal, Ottawa and Halifax, the cities from which most U.S. bound Canadian flights originate. To what end though? U.S. security experts have told several American newspapers that even these naked scanners would not have detected the explosives in Umar Farouk Abdul Mutallab's shorts when he boarded a Detroit bound flight in Amsterdam on Christmas Day. Only thermal imaging scanners could have done that. So once again, federal officials are reacting to a terror threat by inconveniencing the entire travelling public in a way that does little to heighten security.

On the other hand, transportation Minister John Baird will also instruct Canadian airport security screeners to use "passenger behaviour observation" techniques (i.e. profiling) for any number of unusual behaviours such as excessive sweating, anxious movements and the wearing of clothing too heavy for the weather. Anyone exhibiting these behaviours would be singled out for further screening, such as an interview with a screener or a full body scan.

This is not that different from what screeners are doing now, but it is one of the clearest indications yet that Ottawa recognizes that not all passengers are an equal threat to air safety. The federal government needs to go several steps further though: it needs to look beyond mere behaviour and match screening efforts to the groups in society that contain the most dangerous radicals. Right now, of course, that principle leads us to profiling young Muslim males, since nearly all the successful and unsuccessful attacks carried out against airliners in recent decades have come from this group.

But it should be emphasized that this is an equal opportunity principle: If Jews start blowing up aircraft, then we should start targeting anyone with a yarmulka, a Jewish name or an Israeli stamp on their passport. Ditto for anyone named Singh, if a reprise of Air India Flight 182 seems likely. And if the drug gangs, kidnappers and terrorists of Mexico start infiltrating our airspace, well then, Mr. Gomez, please step to one side and raise your arms. It goes without saying that 99.999% of Muslim males are no more of a threat to hijack or blow up a plane than anyone on this editorial board. But security isn't about the 99.999%. It's about the other 0.001%. There can be no indulgence of political correctness. when it comes to protecting our airspace. Profiling must match the threat.

Muslim Male Extremists Age 17-40

(Received by frequently forwarded email; original author unknown)

Why not try this for a decade and see how they get around profiling. A lot of Americans have become so insulated from reality. Absolutely No Profiling! Pause a moment, reflect back, and take the following multiple choice test. These events are actual events from history. They really happened! Do you remember? (*Note: choices a, b, c, were irrelevant in every case*)

1. 1968 Bobby Kennedy was shot and killed by:

d. A Muslim male extremist between the ages of 17 and 40

2. In 1972 at the Munich Olympics, athletes were kidnapped and massacred by:
d. Muslim male extremists mostly between the ages of 17 and 40

3. In 1979, the U.S. embassy in Iran was taken over by:
d. Muslim male extremists mostly between the ages of 17 and 40

4. During the 1980's a number of Americans were kidnapped in Lebanon by:
d. Muslim male extremists mostly between the ages of 17 and 40

5. In 1983, the U.S. Marine barracks in Beirut was blown up by:
d. Muslim male extremists mostly between the ages of 17 and 40

6. In 1985 the cruise ship Achille Lauro was hijacked and a 70 year old American passenger was murdered and thrown overboard in his wheelchair by:
d. Muslim male extremists mostly between the ages of 17 and 40

7. In 1985 TWA flight 847 was hijacked at Athens, and a U.S. Navy diver trying to rescue passengers was murdered by:
d. Muslim male extremists mostly between the ages of 17 and 40

8. In 1988, Pan Am Flight 103 was bombed by:
d. Muslim male extremists mostly between the ages of 17 and 40

9. In 1993 the World Trade Center was bombed the first time by:
d. Muslim male extremists mostly between the ages of 17 and 40

10. In 1998, the U.S. embassies in Kenya and Tanzania were bombed by:
d. Muslim male extremists mostly between the ages of 17 and 40

11. On 9/11/01, four airliners were hijacked; two were used as missiles to take out the World Trade Centres and one crashed into the U.S. Pentagon
d. Muslim male extremists mostly between the ages of 17 and 40

12. In 2002 the United States fought a war in Afghanistan against:
d. Muslim male extremists mostly between the ages of 17 and 40

13. In 2002 reporter Daniel Pearl was kidnapped and murdered by:
d. Muslim male extremists mostly between the ages of 17 and 40

14. A North West Delta Jet destined for Detroit carried a terrorist, who was grabbed by a fellow passenger before he blew it up.
d. Muslim male extremist between the ages of 17 and 40

Security of Communications

Spectrum Policy of Canada 2007

From Industry Canada: (Lightly edited and formatted)
http://www.ic.gc.ca/eic/site/smt-gst.nsf/eng/sf08776.html

Executive Summary

In 2006, the Minister of Industry received the Telecommunications Policy Review Panel report. In acknowledging receipt of the report, the Minister stated that, "The telecommunications sector is of critical importance to Canada's economy and our future well being. I intend to work, along with my Cabinet colleagues, to ensure that Canada has a policy and regulatory framework that provides Canadians with access to telecommunications services that are, in every sense, world class." The Minister then tabled in Parliament a proposed policy direction to the Canadian Radio-television and Telecommunications Commission (CRTC) signalling the government's intention to direct the CRTC to rely on market forces to the maximum extent feasible under the Telecommunications Act and to regulate where there is still a need to do so in a manner that interferes with market forces to the minimum extent necessary.

In this context, the Department has taken the opportunity, within the existing legislative authorities, to combine over eighteen months of public consultation and industry discussion with these new broad policy orientations, to create an even more progressive and renewed Spectrum Policy Framework for Canada.

The Department has been able to streamline the renewed Spectrum Policy Framework for Canada even more than initially proposed. The new Framework moves from the previous seven core policy objectives and fifteen guidelines that had blurred the line between "ends and the means" toward a single policy objective with a set of concise guidelines. During Consultation discussions with industry, the desire for such a progressive approach had been expressed. This document guides the reader through the changes to the Framework that the Department initially proposed, and the rationale upon which a more progressive and renewed Spectrum Policy Framework for Canada is established herein.

The proposed version of the renewed Framework also contained a second part that explored topical spectrum issues related to new radio technologies and approaches to spectrum management that the Department was considering. In this regard, this edition of the Spectrum Policy Framework for Canada will serve the Spectrum Management Program in dealing with these issues into the foreseeable future.

This renewed Spectrum Policy Framework for Canada is the third edition. The first was the 1992 benchmark edition that for the first time brought all the Spectrum Management Program radio policy, technical and licensing objectives and guidelines together in one document, to guide the wireless industry through a decade of rapid radiocommunication technology growth and challenges. The second edition, released in 2002, sought to update all of the ongoing advancements made to the Spectrum Management Program in the intervening time.

The rapid change in technology remains unabated. Like other similar administrations around the world, the Department faces constant change as it deals with spectrum stewardship challenges. The Department is establishing this third renewed Spectrum Policy Framework for Canada to continue on its course to meet these challenges with effective spectrum policy and management that serves the social and economic interests of all Canadians.

Introduction

This document is the renewed Spectrum Policy Framework for Canada (the Framework), which is the policy foundation for the Canadian Spectrum Management Program (the Program). This revised Framework provides a policy objective and enabling guidelines that will guide the Department in managing the radio frequency spectrum resource in Canada.

The radio frequency spectrum is a unique resource from which all aspects of society benefit. It provides access for Canadians to a range of private, commercial, consumer, defence, national security, scientific and public safety applications. The radio frequency spectrum is divided into different bands which are used by a variety of communications services including; broadcasting, cellular, satellite, public safety and two way radio. It is the only resource that can support practical wireless communications in every day situations. The Department recognizes that there are a number of factors; rapidly evolving technology, changing market demands, globalization and an increased focus on public safety and security, which need to be taken into account in an effective spectrum management program.

The wireless telecommunications sector plays an important role in the Canadian economy, accounting for 25,000 jobs, over $9.5 billion in revenue, and a $4.1 billion investment in infrastructure. In recent years, the number of wireless subscribers has increased at a compound annual growth rate exceeding 17% to reach 14.9 million while revenue has grown at a rate of 14% to reach $9.5 billion.

Over the past 15 years, Industry Canada has licensed considerable spectrum for Canadian use. The use of this spectrum by the wireless telecommunications industry has had a significant impact on the companies that manufacture cell phones and other devices designed to operate on wireless networks. Its use has created many opportunities for innovation by Canadian industry.

Effective management of the radio frequency spectrum is essential to the future growth of the communications in Canada. From phones, to broadcasting, to satellite services, to air traffic control, and to reaching out to remote communities, Canadians expect these services to be available, free of interference, and properly managed.

The Minister of Industry has the statutory responsibility for Canada's radio frequency spectrum. The radio frequency spectrum is managed on the Minister's behalf by staff in the Program who — under the umbrella of the International Telecommunication Union (ITU) — obtain, plan, and authorize its use, and use sophisticated equipment and automated systems to ensure that harmful radio signals do not hamper its use by licensed and essential communications services. Without clear radio channels, all communications services would experience difficulty in carrying out their operations. For safety services, the inability to communicate can lead to serious injury including loss of life.

The Program has been crucial to the orderly development of Canada's wireless and broadcasting services. By establishing the proper policy and regulatory environment, the government has enabled a very vibrant wireless sector that is growing at twice the rate of the Canadian economy and significantly contributing to Canadian jobs and prosperity.

The Program supports the effective management of the radio frequency spectrum including: securing Canada's access to it; the use of auctions to assign it; the development and implementation of Mutual Recognition Agreements for the approval of radio equipment; the determination of client needs and improved services; and addressing emerging priorities in response to new applications of technology, client expectations and government objectives.

The pace of global economic growth in wireless technologies and services imposes increased pressure on the resources currently available to the Program. Each year more and more demand for radio frequency spectrum is placed on the Program by an expanding client base. In this context, managing the radio frequency spectrum is becoming more complex, driven by continuous improvements in technology that foster the marketing of new communications products and services for industrial and consumer applications that are increasingly spectrum dependant. A more progressive Framework with enabling guidelines will enable the Department to meet these global and domestic challenges into the foreseeable future.

Background

First released in 1992, the Framework is based on the provisions of the Radiocommunication Act and provides the fundamental policy basis for the planning and management of the radio frequency spectrum by Industry Canada. The Framework was revised in 2002 to reflect the evolution of government and departmental policy as well as the changing use of radio frequency spectrum over the intervening years. At the time, Industry Canada recognized that studies had been initiated in other countries which examined the principles of spectrum management. The Department determined that further review and revision to the Canadian Framework was warranted to ensure that it remains relevant and continues to be the appropriate policy foundation for the Program.

The Department initiated a second review of the Framework in May 2005, announced in DGTP-001-05, and entitled Consultation on a Renewed Spectrum Policy Framework for Canada and Continued Advancements in Spectrum Management (the Consultation). The Department received twenty-seven submissions in response. Generally, these comments were supportive of the proposed changes, although some issues with specific aspects of the proposal were raised. This renewed Framework responds to the substantial public comments received.

A number of other countries are also undertaking reviews and making fundamental changes to their spectrum management programs to address similar challenges. A common finding of these reviews has been the benefit of moving from a prescriptive form of spectrum management to one that embraces more flexibility and a greater reliance on market forces, particularly with respect to spectrum used for commercial purposes.

On March 22, 2006 the Minister of Industry, received the Telecommunications Policy Review Panel (TPRP) report. In acknowledging receipt of the report, the Minister stated that, "The telecommunications sector is of critical importance to Canada's economy and our future well-being. I intend to work, along with my Cabinet colleagues, to ensure that Canada has a policy and regulatory framework that provides Canadians with access to telecommunications services which are, in every sense, world class". This focus is reflected in the renewed Framework and the changes that are being adopted.

On December 14, 2006 the Governor in Council issued a policy direction to the Canadian Radio-television and Telecommunications Commission (CRTC) directing the CRTC to rely on market forces to the maximum extent feasible under the Telecommunications Act, and to regulate where there is still a need to do so in a manner that interferes with market forces to the minimum extent necessary. This renewed Framework reflects this broad policy orientation in the context of existing legislation.

The Department anticipates that this renewed Framework will continue to provide an effective policy and regulatory foundation for the Program to accommodate the evolving delivery of telecommunications, broadcasting and new media.

Context for the Spectrum Policy Framework

Government Mandate

The Minister of Industry, through the Department of Industry Act, the Radiocommunication Act and the Radiocommunication Regulations, with due regard to the objectives of the Telecommunications Act, is responsible for spectrum management in Canada. As such, the Minister is responsible for developing national policies and goals for spectrum resource use and ensuring effective management of the radio frequency spectrum resource.

Impact on Access to Spectrum

The communication spectrum is a finite resource. Many factors affect access, such as:

- new and rapidly changing technology and accompanying market demands which are expected to challenge the Department's ability to anticipate and respond to requirements for access to spectrum in a timely manner;
- globalization, which elevates the need to ensure that there is a regulatory environment conducive to the efficient assignment of spectrum among competing uses that is internationally harmonized to the greatest extent feasible; and
- the increased focus on public safety and security, which is reflected in an array of emerging issues.

Developments in Other Countries

The spectrum management programs of other countries are facing similar challenges to those in Canada. A number of countries, such as Australia, the United Kingdom and the United States have undertaken extensive reviews of their spectrum management programs, and are currently implementing changes. A common finding in these reviews is that traditional methods of spectrum management have often impeded access to spectrum and are slow to adapt to changes in technology and markets. As a result of these reviews, these countries are taking steps to evolve from a prescriptive style of spectrum management to an approach that embraces more flexibility and a greater reliance on market forces.

Recent Developments in Canada

In Canada, an extensive review of government regulation of telecommunications was recently completed by the TPRP. In its report the TPRP commented on and supported the Department's ongoing review of the Framework. The TPRP also noted the significant steps that the Department has taken to adapt the Program such as the use of spectrum auctions and a form of spectrum trading for certain licences. In the opinion of the TPRP, "Canada needs a policy framework that supports a strong and vibrant industry, enhances the efficient use of spectrum and facilitates the adoption of wireless". A number of the TPRP recommendations bear directly and indirectly on the role of the Framework in setting out policy and guidelines for the Program. The government has expressed general support for the broad thrust of the TPRP report, in particular toward reliance on market forces to the maximum extent feasible.

The Department continues to explore and implement new approaches and techniques in spectrum management to ensure the greatest access to spectrum in a competitive marketplace and the availability of spectrum for public interest needs such as security and public safety. In this context, the Framework must serve as the appropriate policy vehicle to support the ongoing modernization of the Program.

The Public Consultation Context

The Consultation, the Department's second review of the Framework, resulted in extensive and varied comments (in all, twenty-seven submissions were received) primarily from service providers, manufacturers and associations representing various interest groups. Generally, the comments received were supportive of the proposed changes, although some respondents disagreed with certain aspects.

It is important to note that the public feedback provided to the Department has been very helpful in preparing this revision of the Framework. The Department anticipates that this renewed Framework will continue to provide an effective policy foundation for the Program and will accommodate the evolving delivery of telecommunications, broadcasting and new media in the near to mid term. A number of themes emerged in the public comments and are presented as follows.

Market Forces in Spectrum Management

A particular focus that emerged in the comments on the proposed revision to the Framework was the appropriate balance in spectrum management between the use of economic incentives and market forces compared to government intervention. Some large service providers offered unqualified support for the application of market forces. Many other respondents offered support in principle, but subject to the caveat that reliance on market forces does not threaten use of the spectrum for public interest requirements. For example, many specific interest groups such as public safety and scientific entities argued that their access to spectrum should be exempted from the application of market forces. There were also calls for government intervention to support interoperability standards for public safety services, availability of licence-exempt spectrum and its impact on incumbents, set asides for linguistic minorities and for facilitating communications in rural areas.

Facilitating the use of Spectrum

There was overwhelming support for the introduction of a third-party access scheme and many specific comments and proposals were made regarding its implementation. As well there was considerable support for allowing flexibility in the application of domestic frequency allocations, although there was concern expressed about the windfall that might accrue to current licensees of spectrum.

Roll-out Licence Conditions

Some incumbent service providers expressed the view that licensing conditions requiring the rollout of radio systems were inappropriate as the Department moves towards a greater reliance on market-based mechanisms in licensing. Consequently they proposed the deletion of that matter from the proposed Policy Guidelines. Others stated that at least rollout requirements should not apply to spectrum that has been licensed through an auction.

Others were of the view that rollout requirements should be retained as a means of encouraging the deployment of spectrum. Several specific suggestions were made for modification of the wording. One suggestion was to temper the wording of the Policy Guidelines to take into account "... the market, technology development, manufacturing, implementation and roll out time for the service." Another suggestion proposed wording that would require the Department to periodically review licensed spectrum holdings and take appropriate steps in cases of non-compliance with licence conditions.

Spectrum for Licence Exempt Operations

There was general consensus that the Department should not create unique licence-exempt bands for Canada but should rely on the larger market forces associated with regional or global designations.

However, concern was expressed by a number of service providers using licensed spectrum that a "tragedy of the commons" was occurring in frequency bands designated for licence exempt operations whereby competing uses and inefficient practices were undermining the value of the spectrum. In addition, one comment stated that the creation of additional licence exempt bands should be temporarily suspended until this issue is clarified. These service providers also believe that the Department should adopt measures to ensure that adequate protection is afforded to licensed operations in frequency bands adjacent to licence exempt applications. Various commentators offered suggestions for the means of ensuring that licence exempt equipment operates within defined limits.

Advances in Technology

The Consultation elicited some positive response regarding the benefits of the future role of software-defined radio and cognitive radio. However, the general consensus was that these particular technologies would be introduced in an incremental fashion and the benefits would accrue slowly. Certain interest groups expressed concerns about the potential for interference from underlay techniques or the application of the concept of Interference Temperature in spectrum management.

Several ideas were advanced regarding the establishment of research and development (R&D) requirements in licensing. Some respondents favoured the exemption of smaller licensees from R&D requirements, applying R&D requirements only to licences awarded by first come, first served process and also considering equivalent expenditures of contributions in kind.

Communications in Rural and Remote Areas

There was general support for the provisions of the Framework that facilitate access to communications in rural areas. There were specific proposals for modifications of the wording. In the discussion topics, there was considerable support for the use of flexible spectrum management tools which would facilitate the deployment of communications in rural areas. Another idea advanced was to apply R&D expenditures to fund rural / remote communications deployment. There was limited comment on the topic of a definition for rural areas, and most of that opposed the use of a population density as a measure. Another alternative was offered to define rural based on the availability of types of communications facilities in those areas.

Public Safety

Respondents were generally supportive or silent on the Framework provisions which ensure access to spectrum for security, sovereignty and public safety needs. However, a number of respondents pointed out that public safety and security communications are often carried by commercial systems, and that this should be recognized in the Framework, and the priority for access to spectrum should be afforded for all systems regardless of ownership. There was also considerable support for the adoption of interoperability standards for public safety. Most respondents felt that these standards should be derived by industry consensus.

Canada's Wireless Oligopoly

From the National Post 2009/12/15 by Terence Corcoran

It is deeply entrenched conventional wisdom that Canada's wireless market is an oligopoly that lacks competition and therefore leaves consumers with over priced cellphone service that is not up to global standards. On the coattails of that widely held view, Industry Minis. ter Tony Clement last week managed to turn his government's Globalive policy retreat into victory.

It's not often that weasling out of a policy blunder gets paraphrased as an achievement; even better is to get the blunder passed on to a sitting duck agency. In its news release on Friday, Industry Canada said "The Government of Canada has varied a Canadian Radio-television and Telecommunications Commission (CRTC) decision. The variance is effective immediately so that Globalive can enter the wireless telecommunications market without delay." The government, in other words, is saving Canadian cellphone users from the CRTC.

Allowing new entrants into a market is a cornerstone of a free enterprise system, so it will be good to see Globalive unleash its Wind wireless brand on the Canadian public. For that, the government deserves credit. Finally, the activist and consultant claims that Canada is an under serviced and overpriced wireless market dominated by three fat cats; Rogers, Bell and Telus, is about to be put to the test. If Peru has a better system than Canada, as claimed by critics, then presumably Globalive will quickly scoop up all those gigantic excess profits the incumbents are collecting. We shall see.

While that improbable scenario unfolds, the policy mess remains unresolved. The main issue is the tortuous route Globalive, backed by a foreign telecom, had to go through to get to the point where it could compete. Even more elaborate and contrived are the foreign ownership rules that now hang in confusion over the Canadian telecom industry.

"Globalive is a Canadian company", declared Mr. Clement on Friday, with a straight face. He didn't get into the definition of "Canadian." For the record, here it is: Under the law, determination of Canadian control is "not determined by whether a telecommunications common carrier is controlled by Canadians but rather that it not be controlled by persons that are not Canadian."

In 2008, after Globalive paid $442 million cash to Ottawa following a wireless spectrum auction, Industry Canada gave its first approval of Globalive as a Canadian company. That approval was given even though Orascom, the global telecom giant controlled by Egyptian telecom magnate Naquib Sawiris, was putting up 99% of Globalive's equity and debt, and providing all of its technology. While that might seem like the kind of structure that should give one control, Industry Canada approved Globalive as Canadian on the grounds that voting control, not monetary control, would be 66% Canadian. As a result, while not Canadian controlled per se, Globalive would be controlled in fact by persons who were Canadian, or as the law requires, were not non-Canadian.

The CRTC, at hearings earlier this year, looked at what Industry Canada had approved last year and declared the provisions inadequate. In response, several key changes were made. The board of directors that Industry Canada had approved was revamped, various covenants on the Orascom debt were removed, and several other changes to liquidity and other agreements were watered down to reduce Orascom's influence or ability to influence strategic and day to day operations at Globalive.

And so, when Mr. Clement declared Globalive a Canadian company on Friday, he was backtracking on key elements Industry Canada had agreed to when it declared it Canadian last year. The government had already reversed itself. To that extent, the CRTC forced the government's hand. There were however, some other CRTC demands that the government rejected. It did not insist that Orascom be forced to offload its hundreds of millions in debt to banks and third parties, thereby removing a major source of influence over Globalive's operations. The annual interest on that debt in the initial agreements ran to 18%.

In summary, the outcome of this battle between Industry Canada and the CRTC is essentially a draw. The CRTC successfully forced Globalive and Industry Canada to redraft key parts of Globalive's ownership structure, but the government did not force the company to adopt all of the CRTC's demands. The result, however, is a policy shambles, with key decisions subject to strategic wars between the government and the regulator. All because Canada's politicians refuse to remove Canadian control as a condition to operate telecom services in Canada.

The absurdities remain. Here's how the CRTC described a revised composition of the board of directors of Globalive, under a holding company called GIHC. "The GIHC board is now composed of eleven directors; four nominated by AAL (representing CEO Anthony Lacavera), four by Orascom, and three Independent Directors. The first Independent Director is selected by AAL with subsequent Independent Directors chosen by a selection committee composed of three members: the longest serving Independent Director, one director nominated by AAL, and one director nominated by Orascom."

The CRTC, in its ruling, said this arrangement was unsatisfactory and would still leave Orascom with too much influence. Mr. Clement and the government say Orascom would not have control over Globalive under this arrangement. The current government agreement protects Globalive from becoming controlled by non-Canadians because "The influence of the non-Canadians can be offset by a combination of Canadian shareholder board nominees and directors that are independent from the non-Canadian, as long as they are Canadian residents." One day, Canada will become an adult country and companies like Orascom would be able to start up a business without encountering such childishness.

Broadband Internet Access

From Wikipedia; (Lightly edited and formatted):
http://en.wikipedia.org/wiki/Broadband_Internet_access

Broadband Internet access, often shortened to just broadband, is a high data rate Internet access, typically contrasted with dial up access using a 56k modem. Dial-up modems are limited to a bit rate of less than 56 Kbit/s (kilobits per second) and require the full use of a telephone line . . . whereas broadband technologies supply more than double this rate and generally without disrupting telephone use.

Although various minimum bandwidths have been used in definitions of broadband, ranging from 64 Kbit/s up to 2.0 Mbit/s(1), the 2006 OECD report is typical by defining broadband as having download data transfer rates equal to or faster than 256 Kbit/s, while the United States (US) Federal Communications Commission (FCC) as of 2009, defines "Basic Broadband" as data transmission speeds exceeding 768 kilobits per second (Kbps), or 768,000 bits per second, in at least one direction: downstream (from the Internet to the user's computer) or upstream (from the user's computer to the Internet). The trend is to raise the threshold of the broadband definition as the marketplace rolls out faster services.

Data rates are defined in terms of maximum download because common consumer broadband technologies such as ADSL are "asymmetric", supporting much slower maximum upload data rate than download. "Broadband penetration" is now treated as a key economic indicator.

Broadband is often called "high speed" Internet, because it usually has a high rate of data transmission. In general, any connection to the customer of 256 Kbit/s or greater is more concisely considered broadband Internet. The International Telecommunication Union Standardization Sector (ITU-T) recommendation I.113 has defined broadband as a transmission capacity that is faster than primary rate ISDN, at 1.5 to 2 Mbit/s. The FCC definition of broadband is 768 Kbit/s (0.8 Mbit/s). The Organization for Economic Cooperation and Development (OECD) has defined broadband as 256 Kbit/s in at least one direction and this bit rate is the most common baseline that is marketed as "broadband" around the world. There is no specific bit rate defined by the industry however, and "broadband" can mean lower bit rate transmission methods. Some Internet Service Providers (ISPs) use this to their advantage in marketing lower bit rate connections as broadband.

In practice, the advertised bandwidth is not always reliably available to the customer; ISPs often allow a greater number of subscribers than their backbone connection or neighbourhood access network can handle, under the assumption that most users will not be using their full connection capacity very frequently. This aggregation strategy works more often than not, so users can typically burst to their full bandwidth most of the time; however, peer-to-peer (P2P) file sharing systems, often requiring extended durations of high bandwidth, stress these assumptions, and can cause major problems for ISPs who have excessively over booked their capacity. For more on this topic, see traffic shaping. As take up for these introductory products increases, telcos are starting to offer higher bit rate services. For existing connections most of the time, this simply involves reconfiguring the existing equipment at each end of the connection.

As the bandwidth delivered to end users increases, the market expects that video on demand services streamed over the Internet will become more popular, though at the present time such services generally require specialized networks. The data rates on most broadband services still do not suffice to provide good quality video, as MPEG-2 video requires about 6 Mbit/s for good results. Adequate video for some purposes becomes possible at lower data rates, with rates of 768 Kbit/s and 384 Kbit/s used for some video conferencing applications, and rates as low as 100 Kbit/s used for videophones using H.264/MPEG-4 AVC. The MPEG-4 format delivers high-quality video at 2 Mbit/s, at the low end of cable modem and ADSL performance.

Increased bandwidth has already made an impact on newsgroups: postings to groups such as alt.binaries.* have grown from JPEG files to entire CD and DVD images. According to NTL, the level of traffic on their network increased from a daily inbound news feed of 150 gigabytes of data per day and 1 terabyte of data out each day in 2001 to 500 gigabytes of data inbound and over 4 terabytes out each day in 2002.

Technology

The standard broadband technologies in most areas are DSL and cable modems. Newer technologies in use include VDSL and pushing optical fibre connections closer to the subscriber in both telephone and cable plants. Fibre optic communication, while only recently being used in fibre to the premises and fibre to the curb schemes, has played a crucial role in enabling Broadband Internet access by making transmission of information over larger distances much more cost effective than copper wire technology. In a few areas not served by cable or ADSL, community organizations have begun to install Wi-Fi networks, and in some cities and towns local governments are installing municipal Wi-Fi networks. As of 2006, broadband mobile Internet access has become available at the consumer level in some countries, using the HSDPA and EV-DO technologies. The newest technology being deployed for mobile and stationary broadband access is WiMAX.

DSL (ADSL/SDSL) Asymmetric Digital Subscriber Line

Multi-linking Modems

Roughly double the dial-up rate can be achieved with multi-linking technology. What is required are two modems, two phone lines, two dial up accounts, and ISP support for multi-linking, or special software at the user end. This inverse multiplexing option was popular with some high end users before ISDN, DSL and other technologies became available.

Diamond and other vendors had created dual phone line modems with bonding capability. The data rate of dual line modems is faster than

90 Kbit/s. The Internet and phone charge will be twice the ordinary dial up charge.

Load balancing takes two Internet connections and feeds them into your network as one double data rate, more resilient Internet connection. By choosing two independent Internet providers the load balancing hardware will automatically use the line with least load which means should one line fail, the second one automatically takes up the slack.

ISDN

Integrated Service Digital Network (ISDN) is one of the oldest broadband digital access methods for consumers and businesses to connect to the Internet. It is a telephone data service standard. Its use in the United States peaked in the late 1990s prior to the availability of DSL and cable modem technologies. Broadband service is usually compared to ISDN-BRI because this was the standard broadband access technology that formed a baseline for the challenges faced by the early broadband providers. These providers sought to compete against ISDN by offering faster and cheaper services to consumers.

A basic rate ISDN line (known as ISDN-BRI) is an ISDN line with 2 data "bearer" channels (DS0 - 64 Kbit/s each). Using ISDN terminal adapters (erroneously called modems), it is possible to bond together 2 or more separate ISDN-BRI lines to reach bandwidths of 256 Kbit/s or more. The ISDN channel bonding technology has been used for video conference applications and broadband data transmission.

Wired Ethernet

Where available, this method of broadband connection to the Internet would indicate that Internet access is very fast. However, just because Ethernet is offered doesn't mean that the full 10, 100, or 1000 Mbit/s connection can be utilized for direct Internet access. In a college dormitory, for example, the 100 Mbit/s Ethernet access might be fully available to on-campus networks, but Internet access bandwidths might be closer to 4xT-1 data rate (6 Mbit/s). If you are sharing a broadband connection with others in a building, the access bandwidth of the leased line into the building would of course govern the end-user's data rate.

In certain locations, however, true Ethernet broadband access might be available. This would most commonly be the case at a POP or a data center, and not at a typical residence or business. When Ethernet Internet access is offered, it could be fibre-optic or copper twisted pair, and the bandwidth will conform to standard Ethernet data rates of up to 10 Gbit/s. The primary advantage is that no special hardware is needed for Ethernet. Ethernet also has a very low latency.

Rural broadband

One of the great challenges of broadband is to provide service to potential customers in areas of low population density, such as to farmers, ranchers, and small towns. In cities where the population density is high, it is easy for a service provider to recover equipment costs, but each rural customer may require expensive equipment to get connected.

Several rural broadband solutions exist, though each has its own pitfalls and limitations. Some choices are better than others, but are dependent on how proactive the local phone company is about upgrading their rural technology.

Wireless Internet Service Provider (WISPs) are rapidly becoming a popular broadband option for rural areas, although the technology's line-of-sight requirements hamper connectivity in areas with hilly and heavily foliated terrain. In addition, compared to hard wired connectivity, there are security risks (unless robust security protocols are enabled); speeds are significantly slower (2–50 times slower); and the network can be less stable, due to interference from other wireless devices, weather, and line-of-sight problems.

Satellite Internet

Satellites in geostationary orbits are able to relay broadband data from the satellite company to each customer. Satellite Internet is usually among the most expensive ways of gaining broadband Internet access, but in rural areas it may only compete with cellular broadband. However, costs have been coming down in recent years to the point that it is becoming more competitive with other broadband options.

Broadband satellite Internet also has a high latency problem due to the signal having to travel to an altitude of 35,786 km (22,236 mi) above sea level (from the equator) out into space to a satellite in geostationary orbit and back to Earth again. The signal delay can be as much as 500 milliseconds to 900 milliseconds, which makes this service unsuitable for applications requiring real time user input such as certain multiplayer Internet games and first person shooters played over the connection. Despite this, it is still possible for many games to be played, but the scope is limited to real time strategy or turn based games. The functionality of live interactive access to a distant computer can also be subject to the problems caused by high latency. These problems are more than tolerable for just basic email access and web browsing and in most cases are barely noticeable.

For geostationary satellites there is no way to eliminate this problem. The delay is primarily due to the great distances travelled which, even at the speed of light (about 300,000 km/ second or 186,000 miles per second), can be significant. Even if all other signalling delays could be eliminated it still takes electromagnetic radio waves about 500 milliseconds, or half a second, to travel from ground level to the satellite and back to the ground, a total of over 71,400 km (44,366 mi) to travel from the source to the destination, and over 143,000 km (88,856 mi) for a round trip (user to ISP, and then back to user, with zero network delays). Factoring in other normal delays from network sources gives a typical one way connection latency of 500–700 ms from the user to the ISP, or about 1,000–1,400 milliseconds latency for the total Round Trip Time (RTT) back to the user. This is far worse than most dialup modem users' experience, at typically only 150–200 ms total latency.

Medium Earth Orbit (MEO) and Low Earth Orbit (LEO) satellites however do not have such great delays. The current LEO constellations of Globalstar and Iridium satellites have delays of less than 40 ms round trip, but their throughput is less than broadband at 64 kbps per channel. The Globalstar constellation orbits 1,420 km above the earth and Iridium orbits at 670 km altitude. The proposed O3b Networks MEO constellation scheduled for deployment in 2010 would orbit at 8,062 km, with RTT latency of approximately 125 ms. The proposed new network is also designed for much higher throughput with links well in excess of 1 Gbps (Giga bits per second).

Most satellite Internet providers also have a FAP (Fair Access Policy). Perhaps one of the largest disadvantages of satellite Internet, these FAPs usually throttle a user's throughput to dial up data rates after a certain "invisible wall" is hit (usually around 200 MB a day). This FAP usually lasts for 24 hours after the wall is hit, and a user's throughput is restored to whatever tier they paid for. This makes bandwidth intensive activities nearly impossible to complete in a reasonable amount of time (examples include P2P and newsgroup binary downloading).

Cellular Broadband

Cellular phone towers are widespread, and as cellular networks move to third generation (3G) networks they can support fast data; using technologies such as EVDO, HSDPA and UMTS.

These can give broadband access to the Internet, with a cell phone, with Cardbus, ExpressCard, or USB cellular modems, or with cellular broadband routers, which allow more than one computer to be connected to the Internet using one cellular connection.

Power-line Internet

This is a new service still in its infancy that may eventually permit broadband Internet data to travel down standard high voltage power lines. However, the system has a number of complex issues, the primary one being that power lines are inherently a very noisy environment. Every time a device turns on or off, it introduces a pop or click into the line. Energy saving devices often introduce noisy harmonics into the line. The system must be designed to deal with these natural signalling disruptions and work around them.

Broadband over power lines (BPL), also known as Power line communication, has developed faster in Europe than in the U.S. due to a historical difference in power system design philosophies. Nearly all large power grids transmit power at high voltages in order to reduce transmission losses, then near the customer use step down transformers to reduce the voltage. Since BPL signals cannot readily pass through transformers, repeaters must be attached to the transformers. In the US, it is common for a small transformer hung from a utility pole to service a single house. In Europe, it is more common for a somewhat larger transformer to service 10 or 100 houses. For delivering power to customers, this difference in design makes little difference, but it means delivering BPL over the power grid of a typical U.S. city will require an order of magnitude more repeaters than would be required in a comparable European city.

The second major issue is signal strength and operating frequency. The system is expected to use frequencies in the 10 to 30 MHz range, which has been used for decades by licensed amateur radio operators, as well as international shortwave broadcasters and a variety of communications systems (military, aeronautical, etc). Power lines are unshielded and will act as transmitters for the signals they carry, and have the potential to completely wipe out the usefulness of the 10 to 30 MHz range for shortwave communications purposes, as well as compromising the security of its users.

Wireless ISP

This typically employs the current low cost 802.11 Wi-Fi radio systems to link remote locations over great distances, but can use other higher power radio communications systems as well.

Traditionally 802.11 was licensed for omnidirectional service spanning only 100-150 metres (300–500 ft). By focussing the signal down to a narrow beam with a Yagi antenna it can instead operate reliably over a distance of many miles, although the technology's line-of-sight requirements hamper connectivity in areas with hilly and heavily foliated terrain. In addition, compared to hard wired connectivity, there are security risks (unless robust security protocols are enabled); speeds are significantly slower (2–50 times slower); and the network can be less stable, due to interference from other wireless devices and networks, weather and line-of-sight problems.

Rural Wireless ISP installations are typically not commercial in nature and are instead a patchwork of systems built up by hobbyists mounting antennas on radio masts and towers, agricultural storage silos, very tall trees, or whatever other tall objects are available. There are currently a number of companies that provide this service. A wireless Internet access provider map for USA is publicly available for WISPS.

WorldSpace

WorldSpace is a digital satellite radio network based in Washington DC. It covers most of Asia and Europe plus all of Africa by satellite. Beside the digital audio, users can receive one way broadband digital data transmission (150 Kilobit/second) from the satellite.

Pricing

Traditionally, U.S. Internet service providers have used an "unlimited time" or flat rate model, with pricing by the maximum bit rate chosen by the customer, rather than an hourly charge. With increased consumer demand for streaming content such as video on demand and peer-to-peer file sharing, the use of high bandwidth applications has increased rapidly.

For ISPs who are bandwidth limited, the flat rate pricing model may become unsustainable as demand for bandwidth increases. Fixed costs represent 80-90% of the cost of providing broadband service, and although most ISPs keep their cost secret, the total cost (January 2008) is estimated to be about $0.10 per gigabyte. Currently some

ISPs estimate that about 5% of users consume about 50% of the total bandwidth.

To provide additional high bandwidth pay services without incurring the additional costs of expanding current broadband infrastructure, Internet Service Providers are exploring new methods to cap current bandwidth usage by customers. This is despite the lagging broadband infrastructure in the United States, according to the Economic Policy Institute: "The United States has also fallen behind other countries in deployment of new broadband technologies."

Some ISPs have begun experimenting with usage based pricing, notably a Time Warner test in Beaumont, Texas. The effort to expand usage based pricing into the Rochester, New York area met with public resistance, however, and was abandoned. Bell Canada has imposed bandwidth caps on customers. An often overlooked analysis when choosing an Internet provider is comparing the different DSL and cable Internet services at the plan level. Doing so will ensure that consumers do not overpay for a bandwidth they will not utilize.

Security of Energy and Power

The Sources of Energy and Power

From: U.S. Energy Information Administration; (lightly edited and formatted)

http://www.eia.doe.gov/emeu/cabs/Canada/Background.html

Canada has considerable natural resources and is one of the world's largest producers and exporters of energy. In 2006, Canada produced 19.3 quadrillion British Thermal Units (Btu) of total energy, the fifth largest amount in the world. Since 1980, Canada's total energy production has increased by 87 percent, while its total energy consumption has increased by only 44 percent. Almost all of Canada's energy exports go to the United States, making it the largest source of U.S. energy imports. Canada is consistently among the top sources for U.S. oil imports, and it is the largest source of U.S. natural gas and electricity imports. Recognizing the importance of the energy trade between the two countries, both participate in the North American Energy Working Group, which seeks to improve energy integration and cooperation between Canada, the U.S., and Mexico.

In 2006, the largest source of energy consumption in Canada was oil (32%), followed by hydroelectricity (25%) and natural gas (24%). Both coal (10%) and nuclear (7%) constitute a smaller share of the country's overall energy mix. From 1986-2006, Canada's overall energy mix has remained relatively stable, though hydroelectricity has decreased from 31% to 25%.

Coal Energy in Canada

From Wikipedia; (lightly edited and formatted):
http://en.wikipedia.org/wiki/Coal_in_Canada

Reserves of coal in Canada rank fourth largest in the world (following the former Soviet Union, the US, China and Australia) at approximately 10 billion tonnes, 4% of the world total. This represents more energy than all of the oil and gas in the country combined. The coal industry generates CDN $5 billion annually. Most of Canada's coal mining occurs in the West of the country. British Columbia has 10 coal mines, Alberta 9, Saskatchewan 3 and New Brunswick one. Nova Scotia operates several small scale mines, Westray having closed following the 1992 disaster there.

In 2005, Canada produced 67.3 million tonnes of coal and its consumption was 60 million tonnes. Of this 56 million tonnes were used for electricity generation. The remaining 4 million tonnes was used in the steel, concrete and other industries. The largest consumers of coal in Canada are Alberta and Ontario. In 1997, Alberta accounted for 47% of Canada's coal consumption at 26.2 million tonnes, and Ontario accounted for 25% at 13.8 million tonnes. Saskatchewan, Manitoba, Nova Scotia and New Brunswick also use coal to generate electricity to varying degrees.

Oil Energy & New Discoveries

From Rense Dow Jones Newswires: (Lightly edited and formatted)
http://www.rense.com/general37/petrol.htm

Canada's Oil Reserves By Campion Walsh, Dow Jones Newswires

Second only To Saudi Arabia

The U.S. government said Thursday Canada holds the world's second largest oil reserves, taking into account Alberta oil sands previously considered too expensive to develop. The Energy Information Administration (EIA), the statistical wing of the U.S. Department of Energy, has included recent private sector estimates that an additional 175 billion barrels of oil could be recovered from resources known to exist in Western Canada since the 19th Century.

At a briefing on this year's the Energy Information Association International Energy Outlook, EIA Administrator Guy Caruso cited a December report in the Oil and Gas Journal that raised Canada's proven oil reserves to 180 billion barrels from 4.9 billion barrels, thanks to inclusion of the tar sands, now considered recoverable with existing technology and market conditions.

"Canada will be producing a lot of oil from the development of these tar sands, but the quality of those reserves differs substantially from the Saudi reserves in terms of cost and ability to bring . . . the productive capacity on in a meaningful way," Caruso said. "There is a difference in the absolute amount versus the ability to turn that into productive capacity," he said.

The latest estimates put Canada ahead of war torn Iraq, which the EIA estimates holds 112.5 billion barrels and is constrained from raising production for entirely different reasons. The U.S. agency estimates Saudi Arabia's recoverable oil reserves at 264 billion barrels. The EIA projects Canadian oil sands could produce 2.2 million barrels a day by 2025 compared with the current level of about 700,000 barrels per day, which already represents more than a fourth of total Canadian output of 3.1 million barrels per day.

The Canadian Association of Petroleum Producers (CAPP) estimates current projects will raise Alberta oil sands production to 1 million barrels per day this year, and continuing development will raise it further to 1.8 million barrels per day by 2010, according to CAPP Vice President Greg Stringham. Current oil sands projects are economically viable at crude oil prices of $18-$20 a barrel, though the quality of oil produced can vary if production comes from "in situ" reserves that require drilling assisted by steam injection pressure or from simple mining, Stringham said.

CAPP's own estimate of Canada's recoverable oil sands is 315 billion barrels, 20% from mining, and the rest from steam assisted drilling. "There's clearly a lot of the stuff in the ground," said David Pursell, oil sector analyst with investment bank Simmons & Co. But the commercial viability of the reserves is sensitive to oil prices, technology and public policy, Pursell said. Among political complications are the additional carbon dioxide emissions from production and processing of the tarry substance. Stringham said despite Canada's ratification of the Kyoto Protocol limiting carbon dioxide emissions, the industry expects the international agreement to add only 25 cents to 30 cents a barrel to development costs through 2012.

Oil sands development, which relies heavily on natural gas, could benefit from development and pipeline transport of large Arctic gas reserves in Alaska's North Slope and Canada's Mackenzie Delta, which under current proposals could be on stream by 2010, the CAPP official said. While cautious about the new reserve estimates, Pursell said oil sands may be "a good contrarian investment" at a time most energy investors are focussed on natural gas. "It's a good potential source of hydrocarbons in this hemisphere," he said.

BG Group (BRGYY.PK)

From BG Group, seekingalpha: (lightly edited and formatted) http://seekingalpha.com/article/82236-the-peak-oil-myth-new-oil-is-plentiful

The 'Peak Oil' Myth: New Oil Is Plentiful

The data are becoming conclusive that peak oil is a myth. High oil prices are doing their job as oil exploration is flush with new finds.

1. An offshore find by Brazilian state oil company Petrobras (PBR) in partnership with BG Group (BRGYY.PK) and Repsol-YPF may be the world's biggest discovery in 30 years, the head of the National Petroleum Agency said. A deep-water exploration area could contain

as much as 33 billion barrels of oil, an amount that would nearly triple Brazil's reserves and make the offshore bloc the world's third-largest known oil reserve. "This would lay to rest some of the peak oil pronouncements that we were out of oil, that we weren't going to find any more and that we have to change our way of life," said Roger Read, an energy analyst and managing director at New York-based investment bank Natixis Bleichroeder Inc.

2. A trio of oil companies led by Chevron Corp. (CVX) has tapped a petroleum pool deep beneath the Gulf of Mexico that could boost U.S. reserves by more than 50 percent. A test well indicates it could be the biggest new domestic oil discovery since Alaska's Prudhoe Bay a generation ago. Chevron estimated the 300 square mile region where its test well sits could hold up to 15 billion barrels of oil and natural gas

3. Kosmos Energy says its oil field at West Cape Three Points is the largest discovery in deep water West Africa and potentially the largest single field discovery in the region.

4. A new oil discovery has been made by Statoil (STO) in the Ragnarrock prospect near the Sleipner area in the North Sea. "It is encouraging that Statoil has made an oil discovery in a little explored exploration model that is close to our North Sea infrastructure," says Frode Fasteland, acting exploration manager for the North Sea.

5. Shell (RDS.A) is currently analyzing and evaluating the well data of their own find in the Gulf of Mexico to determine next steps. This find is rumoured to be capable of producing 100 billion barrels. Operating in ultra deep waters of the Gulf of Mexico, the Perdido spar will float on the surface in nearly 8,000 ft of water and is capable of producing as much as 130,000 barrels of oil equivalent per day.

6. In Iraq, excavators have struck three oil fields with reserves estimated at about 2 billion barrels, the Kurdish region's Oil Minister Ashti Horami said.

7. Iran has discovered an oil field within its southwest Jofeir oilfield that

is expected to boost Jofeir's oil output to 33,000 barrels per day. Iran's new discovery is estimated to have reserves of 750 million barrels, according to Iran's Oil Minister, Gholamhossein Nozari.

8. The United States holds significant oil shale resources underlying a total area of 16,000 square miles. This represents the largest known concentration of oil shale in the world and holds an estimated 1.5 trillion barrels of oil with 800 billion recoverable barrels – enough to meet U.S. demand for oil at current levels for 110 years. More than 70 percent of American oil shale is on Federal land, primarily in Colorado, Utah, and Wyoming. In Utah, a developer says his company already has the technology to produce 4,000 barrels a day using a furnace that can heat up rock using its own fuel. "This is not a science project," said Daniel G. Elcan, managing director of Oil Shale Exploration Corp. "For many years, the high cost of extracting oil from shale exceeded the benefit. But today the calculus is changing," President George Bush said. Sen. Orrin Hatch, R-Utah, said the country has to do everything it can to boost energy production. "We have as much oil in oil shale in Utah, Wyoming and Colorado as the rest of the world combined," he said.

9. In western North Dakota there is a formation known as the Bakken Shale. The formation extends into Montana and Canada. Geologists have estimated the area holds hundreds of billions of barrels of oil. In an interview provided by USGS, scientist Brenda Pierce put the North Dakota oil in context. "Of the current USGS estimates, this is the largest oil accumulation in the lower 48," Pierce says. "It is also the largest continuous type of oil accumulation that we have ever assessed." The USGS study says with today's technology, about 4 billion barrels of oil can be pumped from the Bakken formation. By comparison, the 4 billion barrels in North Dakota represent less than half the oil in the Arctic National Wildlife refuge which has an estimated 10 billion barrels of recoverable oil.

The peak oil theory is a money making scam put out by the speculators looking for high commodity returns in a challenging market environment. Most of the above mentioned finds have occurred in the last two years alone. I didn't even mention the untapped Alaskan oil fields or the recent Danish and Australian finds. In the long term, crude prices will find stability at historic norms because there is no supply problem. How much longer will investors ignore these new oil finds? Probably until they can find other investment alternatives which won't happen in the broad market until financials stop haemorrhaging. Respect the trend but understand that this is a bubble preparing to burst. When oil hit it's high of $139 it represented more than a 600% increase in crude since the bull market began, returns eerily similar to the dot com craze.

There are many theories that sound good but just aren't true. Take Al Gore's global warming crusade. It sounded great, it made perfect sense but there was just one problem, the facts didn't support it. It seems that the masses who were loudly calling for a global warming crisis have shifted their energies to oil. We are bombarded on a daily basis by those who tell us that we should be fearful. They spin good news into bad. The latest absurdity had Goldman Sachs telling investors that China's 18% price increase will actually increase demand! That's a new one. Just like global warming, the rationale for peak oil sounds great, it makes sense, but there is just one small problem, the facts don't support it.

1	33	Billion Barrels	Brazil
2	15	Billion	G / Mexico
3			W. Africa
4			Norway
5	100	Billion	G / Mexico
6	2	Billion	Kurd
7	3/4	Billion	Iran
8	800	Billion	US Shale
9	100's	Billion	Bakken

Giant oil find by BP reopens debate about oil supplies

From Guardian: (lightly edited and formatted)
http://www.guardian.co.uk/business/2009/sep/02/bp-oil-find-gulf-of-mexico

The discovery could be as large as Forties field in North Sea and comes hard on heels of 8.8 billion barrel find by Iran. BP says it has made a giant oil find in the Gulf of Mexico. BP has reopened the debate on when the "peak oil" supply will be reached by announcing a big new discovery in the Gulf of Mexico which some believe could be as large as the Forties, the biggest field ever found in the North Sea. The strike comes days after Iran unveiled an even larger find of 8.8 billion barrels of crude oil, and the moves have encouraged sceptics of theories which say that peak production has been reached, or soon will be, to hail a new golden age of exploration and supply.

BP, already the largest producer of hydrocarbons in the US, said its "giant" Tiber discovery in 4,100 ft (1,250 m) of water was particularly exciting because it promised to open up a whole new area. Shares in BP were up 4% to 539p in afternoon trading, making it the biggest riser in the FTSE 100 despite the company saying much more drilling appraisal work was needed before Tiber's commercial prospects could be guaranteed.

"Tiber represents BP's second material discovery in the emerging lower tertiary play in the Gulf of Mexico, following our earlier Kaskida discovery," said Andy Inglis, chief executive of exploration and production. "These material discoveries, together with our industry leading acreage position, support the continuing growth of our deepwater Gulf of Mexico business into the second half of the next decade."

Analysts agreed that the find appeared to be very significant. "Any time an oil major uses the word 'giant' you have to sit up and take note. Kaskida confirmed the western limits of the lower tertiary play and this extends the limits even further," said Matt Snyder, a Gulf of Mexico specialist at oil consultancy Wood Mackenzie. Fadel Gheit, an equity analyst who follows the oil sector for the Oppenheimer brokerage in New York, said the discovery was a "big feather in BP's cap and reaffirms their leading position in the deep water Gulf of Mexico".

BP itself believes that Tiber is bigger than the prospect on the nearby Kaskida field found in 2006, which has around 3 billion barrels of oil reserves in place, while industry experts said Tiber might be as large as Forties, which has 4 billion barrels. Excitement around Tiber comes amid a welter of new finds both in established oil producing areas such as Iran and in new areas such as Uganda and western Greenland. There has recently been an oil rush in the deep waters off Brazil and talk of large onshore volumes of new gas in Holland, although the UK's North Sea fields have seen a slump in drilling levels.

"Its an amazing turnaround from the gloom of the last 10 years. All these finds will take a long time to bring on stream, but it shows the industry is capable of finding more oil than it uses and shows we have not come to any peak," said Peter Odell, professor emeritus of international energy studies at Erasmus University in Rotterdam.

However, exponents of peak oil theories said the BP find would not fundamentally change the longer term supply and demand picture. "The International Energy Agency said in its 2008 report that the world needed to find six new Saudi Arabias to meet the growing demand for oil in the future," said Jeremy Leggett, chairman of the renewable power company Solarcentury, and a key peak energy specialist. "This (BP) find is welcome but its not going to take concerns away at a time when existing fields are depleting faster than expected and the new discoveries have a very long lead time."

Leggett pointed out that it would take many years for BP to bring any Tiber fields on stream, pointing out that the huge Kashagan find in the Caspian Sea, in which BP has sold its stake, was meant to produce its first oil in 2005 but is now targeting 2013 as a start up date. The oil company will be helped at Tiber by the light nature and high quality of the oil in a development that will cost billions of pounds. The two discoveries, which are about 40 miles apart, make it much easier for BP, which owns 62% of the discovery alongside Petrobras of Brazil and Conoco Phillips of America, to justify building a platform and pipeline to shore. The companies will need to tackle very deep water; the well is one of the deepest ever drilled.

The oil has been found in lower tertiary soils which were created more than 30m years ago. Their commercial prospects will depend on what portion of the reserves at Tiber can be recovered: in the case of Forties it has risen to well over 70%, but can be as low as 30% in other parts of the industry.

Natural Gas Energy in Canada

From Wikipedia: (lightly edited and formatted)
http://en.wikipedia.org/wiki/Natural_gas_in_Canada

At 17.1 billion cubic feet (480,000,000 m3) per day in 2006, Canada is the third largest producer of natural gas in the world. Its proven reserves were 58.2 trillion cubic feet (1,650 km3) at the close of that year. A large portion of Canada's gas is exported to the United States; in 2006, 9.9 billion cubic feet (280,000,000 m3) per day .

From Energy Mines & Resources (EMR):
http://www.emr.gov.yk.ca/oilandgas/faq.html

Pipelines

Canada has nearly 700,000 kilometres of underground pipeline that transport virtually all our country's daily crude oil and natural gas production to consumers in Canada and the United States. Pipelines are the safest, most reliable and cost-effective way of transporting the large amounts of oil and natural gas that must be moved throughout Canada each day. Almost all of Canada's crude oil and natural gas production makes all or part of its journey to market by pipeline. In Canada, natural gas is generally transported only by pipeline.

What are the potential consequences of pipeline construction? If industry chooses the Alaska Highway route for a natural gas pipeline, each river and creek crossing on the proposed route will have to be reviewed and environmental issues addressed as part of the regulatory process. If it's going to be done at all, it's going to be done right.

If a natural gas pipeline is going to be built in the Yukon, almost the entire length will be buried in a trench over a metre deep. The trench is filled in and the topsoil replaced. Then the pipeline right of way is seeded and landscaped with grasses and shrubs that are native to the region.

Hydro Electric Energy in Canada

From Wikipedia;(lightly edited and formatted):
http://en.wikipedia.org/wiki/Hydroelectric_power_in_Canada

Canada is the world's second largest producer of hydroelectricity in the world (after China), and one of few countries to generate the majority of its electricity from hydroelectricity (59% in 2006). In 2007, Canada produced 368 terawatt -hours of electricity using hydroelectric dams, 11% of all the hydroelectricity generated in the world. Some provinces and territories, such as Quebec, Manitoba, Newfoundland & Labrador, and the Yukon, produce over 90% of their electricity in this manner.

Hydro Québec's extensive network of 59 hydroelectric dams have a combined capacity of 34,118 megawatts, accounting for nearly half of the Canadian total. Hydro power accounts for 92% of the supply sold by the Quebec state owned utility. Five of Hydro Québec's hydroelectric facilities are rated above 2,000 MW: the Manic 5, La Grande 4, La Grande 3, La Grande 2A and Robert Bourassa stations: while 7 others have a capacity over 1,000 MW.

Hudson & James Bay Waters

From Industry Canada Canadian Arctic Resources Committee; (lightly edited and formatted):

http://www.carc.org/pubs/v19no3/2.htm

By the Canadian Arctic Resources Committee / Environmental Committee of Sanikiluaq / Rawson Academy of Aquatic Science

Sustainable Development in the Hudson Bay/ James Bay Bio-region

James Bay and Hudson Bay constitute a large, shallow, inland sea connected to the Atlantic Ocean by Hudson Strait and the Labrador Sea, and to the Arctic Ocean by the Foxe Basin, and Fury and Hecla Strait. Currents are strongly affected by influxes of fresh water from rivers and, during the open water season, by wind stress. Cold saline water enters Hudson Bay and James Bay from the northwest. Less saline surface outflows occur along the eastern shores of James Bay and Hudson Bay north to Hudson Strait.

These two "bays" are the largest bodies of water in the world that seasonally freeze over each winter and become ice free each summer. In Hudson Bay, the ice cover starts to form in northern areas by late October and continues to grow until a maximum cover is reached at he end of April. Polynya (open water leads in ice which are known to be important biologically throughout the Arctic) are found predominantly along the north west and east coasts of Hudson Bay, both coasts of James Bay, and in the vicinity of the Belcher Islands. In James Bay, the ice cover begins to decay in May, and the area becomes ice free by the end of July.

The watershed of Hudson Bay and James Bay covers well over one third of Canada, from southern Alberta to central Ontario to Baffin Island, as well as parts of North Dakota and Minnesota in the United States. The rivers flowing into Hudson Bay and James Bay discharge more than twice the flow of either the Mackenzie or St. Lawrence rivers. The seasonal timing of this freshwater discharge is a major factor governing the productivity of the region. Hydro developments that change the timing and rate of flow of fresh water may cause changes in:

- the nature and duration of ice-cover;
- habitats of marine mammals, fish, and migratory birds;
- currents into and out of Hudson Bay/James Bay;
- seasonal and annual loads of sediments and nutrients to marine ecosystems (likely leading to lower biological productivity of estuaries and coastal areas); and
- anadromous fish populations.

Approximately 60 species of fish are known to inhabit the estuarine communities of Hudson Bay and James Bay. Fewer species are found toward the North where arctic species predominate. The importance of fish in the domestic economies of this region cannot be understated. Arctic char, whitefish, arctic cod, and other species contribute directly to the domestic fishery, and indirectly to the food chain of marine and terrestrial mammals and birds.

Ringed seals are found on all coasts of James Bay and Hudson Bay, with populations estimated at 61,000 and 455,000 respectively. Bearded seals are present in Hudson Bay, with a population last estimated at 84,000. Harbour seals occur in small numbers at isolated localities along all coasts, while harp seals are found as far south as the Belcher Islands in the summer, but also in small numbers. In Hudson Bay, the main concentration of walrus is at northeastern Coats Island and southeastern Southampton Island where they are found during all seasons, with an estimated summer population of 2000. In the 1950s and 1960s, the walrus population of Foxe Basin and Hudson Bay together was estimated at 8,500. They are found on both coasts of Hudson Bay and as far south as the Belcher Islands.

Polar bears, which depend on seals as their main food source, are found on the coasts of Hudson Bay and northern James Bay during the summer and fall, and on the islands of northern James Bay. Beluga whales are the main species of whale found in Hudson Bay and James Bay. The most recent report estimates that a population of 8,000 to 9,000 belugas summer in western Hudson Bay, while a small population summers on the east coast of Hudson Bay. Some belugas use the polynya of north west Hudson Bay and James Bay in winter. Estuaries, those affected by existing and proposed hydroelectric developments, are important to belugas as feeding and calving grounds. A population of possibly fewer than 100 bowhead whales inhabits northern Hudson Bay and Hudson Strait, most probably on a year round basis. The species is endangered and has been protected by international protocols.

The Hudson Bay and James Bay coasts provide a major migration pathway and a breeding ground for many species of geese and ducks. Approximately 2.5 million lesser snow geese and 200 000 Canada geese use staging areas on the coastal marshes of the Hudson Bay Lowlands during spring and fall migration. In an average year, 1.5 million lesser snow geese use the James Bay coastal areas. The high fertility and productivity of the coastal zone support a wide range of food types which enable reproduction, growth of juveniles, and fattening of all ages prior to the fall migration. Hydro projects could have negative impacts if breeding waterfowl habitat in Quebec river estuaries were damaged, thereby affecting migratory bird populations wintering in the eastern and southern United States.

A major breeding colony of lesser snow geese is located just west of Cape Henrietta Maria, with smaller breeding areas located on Akimiski Island near Churchill and in the vicinity of Arviat. Approximately 75 per cent of the global population of Atlantic brant geese are concentrated on the eel grass beds of the Quebec coast and parts of the Ontario coast of James Bay, and almost the entire North American population (up to 320,000) of black scoters use southern James Bay as a staging area. Other waterfowl species that utilize inshore, intertidal and brackish coastal habitats in the Hudson Bay/ James Bay bio-region include black duck, pintail, mallard, wigeon, green winged teal, and scaup. Mergansers and loons make extensive use of offshore water for feeding, and a significant number of common eider pass the winter in James Bay and the Belcher Islands.

Important shorebird species include dunlin, blackbellied plover, golden plover, semi-palmated plover, greater and lesser yellowlegs, sanderlings, four species of sandpiper, whimbrel, and marbled godwit. The coasts of both bays are (or were) used by the endangered (or extinct) Eskimo curlew. Finally, the area of northern Hudson Bay and western Hudson Strait supports the third largest seabird community in the Arctic, dominated by the thick billed murre.

Marine mammals and migratory birds inhabiting Hudson Bay and James Bay are especially at risk from changes to marine and freshwater ecosystems. These ecosystems are subject to stress from toxic metals and chemicals such as mercury and organochlorine compounds already present in the water and the food chain. Further large scale developments are likely to compound these stresses when combined with continued loadings of long range transported toxic contaminants and probable regional climatic changes or shifts in sea level caused by global increases in air temperature.

Traditional Use and Occupancy

The Hudson Bay/ James Bay bio-region has been occupied by Cree and Inuit people for thousands of years. The Cree occupy the southern part of the region in Manitoba, Ontario, and northern Quebec as far north as Whapmagoostui. Inuit communities are found along the eastern shores of Hudson Bay in Quebec, north from Kuujjuarapik to Ivujivik and Salluit. In the Northwest Territories, Inuit communities extend from Arviat on the western shore of Hudson Bay to Coral Harbour on Southampton Island. The Inuit community of Sanikiluaq is found on the Belcher Islands in south eastern Hudson Bay, about 100 kilometres from the mouth of the Great Whale River.

As part of their traditional subsistence economy, the Cree hunt migratory birds, particularly in the spring, as well as terrestrial mammals such as moose. The Cree fish the rivers in the region and trap fur bearing mammals such as muskrat and beaver. Traditionally, Inuit have focussed their harvesting efforts on fish and marine mammals such as seals, walrus, and whales. Some communities also depend heavily on caribou.

The Cree and Inuit of northern Quebec signed a comprehensive claims agreement (James Bay and Northern Quebec Agreement) with the federal and Quebec governments in 1975. The Cree in northern Ontario and northern Manitoba signed Treaty 5, with an adhesion in 1929. The Inuit of Nunavut (the eastern and central region of the Northwest Territories, including Hudson Bay communities) signed an agreement-in-principle with the federal government in 1990 for the settlement of the comprehensive claim of Nunavut Inuit. A final agreement remains to be ratified; however, land selection negotiations between the Inuit and federal government have been concluded for the region.

Hydroelectric Projects and Jurisdictional Responsibility

The rivers flowing into Hudson Bay and James Bay carry 30 per cent of the total flow of Canada's river systems, or roughly 30,000 cubic metres per second. In the past, many engineers and politicians have regarded these north flowing rivers as "wasting their way to the sea". It is not surprising, therefore, that a prodigious array of hydroelectric projects are in operation, or are planned, to divert or impound this source of renewable energy.

In the late 1960s and 1970s, large scale hydroelectric projects were announced and constructed in northern Quebec (La Grande Phase I) and northern Manitoba (Churchill- Nelson) with smaller projects in northern Ontario (Moose River basin). In the 1980s and early 1990s, other projects were completed (La Grande Phase 11) and Limestone (northern Manitoba), and new megaprojects were proposed in Manitoba (Conawapa), Quebec (Great Whale, Nottaway - Rupert - Broadback) and Ontario (Moose, Abitibi, Mattagami).

Neither the utilities (all are provincial Crown corporations) nor the provincial governments have addressed the impacts that hydroelectric developments within their jurisdiction may have outside provincial borders. Indeed, the utilities may have no mandate or authority to do so, and certainly provincial governments have little or no authority to apply legislation beyond their borders. The need for new means of co-operation seems obvious.

The waters of Hudson Bay and James Bay fall within exclusive federal jurisdiction and thus are not part of the territory of adjacent provinces or the Northwest territories. All of the islands of Hudson Bay and James Bay are part of the Northwest Territories and are therefore subject to federal jurisdiction as well (in co-operation with the territorial government in Yellowknife and subject to aboriginal claims). There is a federal responsibility to protect the integrity of marine and fresh water ecosystems of the region and to account for the downstream cumulative impacts of provincial projects. Authority to do so exists (e.g. Canada Water Act and the Fisheries Act). The Department of Fisheries and Oceans (DFO) has developed the Arctic Marine Conservation Strategy, although its implementation is in doubt. The federal Department of Environment has recognized the need for a study of cumulative environmental impacts and has consulted with federal departments and provincial and territorial governments. At present the initiative is clouded by uncertainty

Quebec

The James Bay hydroelectric power development in Quebec is one of the largest engineering projects ever undertaken. When all phases are completed, peak power available from the project will be roughly 27,000 megawatts; the equivalent of about 13 Niagara Falls.

Hydro Quebec is a provincially controlled Crown corporation which plays a major role as an economic engine for the Government of Quebec. The four major phases of the project (one of which is complete) would reshape an area the size of France at a 1990 cost of more than $64 billion, resulting in the world's largest complex of dams and dikes. This immense project has faced growing concern based on a combination of economic, environmental, and social impacts. To date, however, an informed public debate about the James Bay projects has been hampered by a number of factors, including the limited availability of information, little assessment of viable alternatives, and uncertainties about the geographic scope and duration of impacts.

Public debate has also been hindered by a lack of organization and focus on the part of non-governmental environmental organizations. This is, in part, a reflection of the fact that most organizations have felt that northern aboriginal groups were best equipped to play the dominant advocacy role. The Grand Council of the Crees, representing the James Bay Cree, and local Inuit communities are opposed to construction of the Great Whale phase of the development, on which some preliminary work has already begun. Makivik Corporation, representing all of the Inuit of northern Quebec, is negotiating with the Quebec government for a measure of control over the Great Whale project (which lies partly within Inuit territory) as well as for self government. Should these negotiations fail, Makivik may oppose the mega- project as well.

Methyl mercury contamination caused by flooding o(the now completed La Grande reservoir is one reason for opposition by the Cree and local Inuit. In 1984, two of every three people in Chisasibi, a community of 2500 at the mouth of the La Grande river, had unacceptably high levels of mercury in their bodies; some elders had 20 times the level deemed acceptable, and some exhibited symptoms of mercury poisoning. According to the Cree, fish and wildlife populations have also been severely affected by La Grande Phase I, with devastating social and economic effects in the community.

An important aspect of the megaprojects proposed for northern Quebec is that Hydro Quebec almost completely dominates the scientific and other research conducted in the region. The Crown corporation has commissioned hundreds of studies assessing impacts related to the megaprojects, but the results of most have not yet been released to the public. Very few of the studies have been subject to peer review; many are available only in the so called "Grey literature" of consultants' reports and industry sponsored papers. Few Quebec biologists or other scientists interested in the North have not, at some point, been hired by Hydro Quebec to carry out project related studies. In this, there is a striking parallel between Hydro Quebec's planning and that which supported a proposed natural gas pipeline in the Mackenzie Valley in the 1970s. Prior to the establishment of the Mackenzie Valley Pipeline Inquiry (the Berger inquiry) in 1974, the industry also cornered much of the information needed for an informed debate, and both the industry and government dealt in private, ignoring most of the concerns raised by aboriginal people, environmentalists, and other concerned Canadians.

It is noteworthy that no public review (such as the Berger inquiry or those conducted more recently under the federal Environmental Assessment and Review Process) has critically examined Hydro Quebec's program in northern Quebec, nor is Hydro Quebec regulated by any regulatory body such as a public utilities board.

However, the federal government announced in July 1991 that it would carry out a panel review of the entire Great Whale project under the Environmental Assessment and Review Process (EARP). The federal and Quebec governments have agreed that their respective environmental assessment procedures will be harmonized. There is much confusion about which process will be employed as a result of a Federal Court of Canada decision in September 1991 which ordered the federal government to apply the environmental assessment rules under the 1975 treaty between the James Bay Cree, the Inuit, and the federal government.

Largely as a result of a lawsuit launched by the Cree, the Canadian Arctic Resources Committee and others, Quebec agreed in October 1991 that the environmental impacts of roads and other infrastructures associated with the Great Whale project will be assessed separately from those of the dams and dikes.

Ontario

Hydroelectric megaprojects are also being proposed by Ontario Hydro for southern James Bay. Of 18 new hydroelectric developments included in Ontario Hydro's Providing the Balance of Power, its demand - supply plan issued in 1990, 12 are in the Hudson Bay/ James Bay bio-region. Six new dams and six redevelopments of existing dams are proposed for the Moose, Abitibi, and Mattagami rivers in northern Ontario. The plan calls for the development of these sites over the period 1990 to 2016. The 12 projects will generate 1890 megawatts of electricity and flood at least 2,299 hectares of land. The published demand supply plan outlines the environmental impacts and indicates that they will be addressed during subsequent project assessments. In October 1991, Ontario Hydro announced that planning and field studies for all Moose River developments (with the exception of the extensions to Mattagami stations) had been suspended.

A large portion of Ontario's hydroelectric potential lies in other rivers flowing into James Bay (the Albany and Attawapiskat) and into Hudson Bay (the Severn and Winisk). While hydroelectric development of these rivers is not proposed in the demand supply plan, the Government of Ontario is considering private sector proposals to produce hydro electric power on these rivers.

Unlike Quebec, Ontario will be holding public hearings on the need and rationale for the developments, including the northern hydroelectric projects proposed in Ontario Hydro's demand supply plan. The hearings may begin as early as late 1991. Cree communities in northern Ontario are participating in the hearings under the aegis of the Moose River/ James Bay Coalition. The coalition is carrying out research on the impacts of Ontario Hydro's proposed developments in the Hudson Bay/lames Bay bio-region. The Rawson Academy of Aquatic Science has been asked to provide independent scientific advice to the coalition. Ontario Hydro is also encouraging the development of the Conawapa Dam on the Nelson River in northern Manitoba by agreeing to purchase electric power to be generated by the project.

Manitoba

The existing Churchill Nelson project has a generating capacity of 2,378 megawatts, and Limestone 1,200 megawatts; Conawapa will produce 1,272 megawatts. The environmental impact assessment for the Churchill Nelson project was initiated after Manitoba Hydro had fixed the configuration, operating regime, and timing of construction for the diversion of the Churchill River into the Nelson River. None the less, serious environmental impacts were experienced.

Severe shoreline erosion, caused by impoundment of Southern Indian Lake as part of the diversion, led to increased turbidity. This resulted in the collapse of the commercial whitefish industry. Whitefish populations in Cross Lake, another large lake in the Churchill Nelson river basin, fell 65 per cent. In addition, walleye and northern pike in all flooded lakes along the diversion route accumulated mercury levels that exceeded Canadian Limits for the protection of human health. Some commercial fisheries were permanently closed, and local residents were encouraged to avoid consumption. The collapse of the commercial fishery placed a severe strain on the social fabric of northern aboriginal communities, forcing them to move and/ or to rely increasingly on compensation payments for income.

The issue of methyl mercury contamination resulting from the northern hydroelectric developments was first understood because of work done in the early 1970s in northern Manitoba, by scientists from the DFO's Freshwater Institute in Winnipeg. While some research remains to be done, we know that on flooded lands the methylation process converts biologically unavailable inorganic mercury info its toxic, biologically available form. This phenomenon was not predicted by Manitoba Hydro, nor was it well understood when Hydro- Quebec began construction of James Bay Phase 1. Yet the effects of incremental loadings of methyl mercury into the aquatic ecosystem are of great importance. It is of particular relevance given the relatively high background levels of mercury in the Hudson Bay/James Bay bio-region. However, methyl mercury contamination is not the only, or necessarily most important, impact to be addressed. Large scale ecological perturbations from within or outside the region also must be understood.

Nuclear Energy in Canada

From Wikipedia: (lightly edited and formatted)
http://en.wikipedia.org/wiki/Nuclear_power_in_Canada

History

Nuclear power in Canada produces about 15% of Canada's electricity. The Nuclear industry (as distinct from the uranium industry) in Canada dates back to 1942 when a joint British-Canadian laboratory was set up in Montreal, Quebec, under the administration of the National Research Council of Canada, to develop a design for a heavy water nuclear reactor. This reactor was called National Research Experimental and would be the most powerful research reactor in the world when completed. In the meantime, in 1944, approval was given to proceed with the construction of the smaller ZEEP (Zero Energy Experimental Pile) test reactor at Chalk River, Ontario and on September 5, 1945 at 3:45 pm, the 10 Watt ZEEP successfully achieved the first self sustained nuclear reaction outside the United States. ZEEP operated for 25 years as a key research facility.

In 1946, Montreal Laboratory was closed, and the work continued at Chalk River Nuclear Laboratories. Building partly on the experimental data obtained from ZEEP, the National Research Experimental (NRX); a natural uranium, heavy water moderated research reactor started up on July 22, 1947. It operated for 43 years, producing radioisotopes, undertaking fuels and materials development work for CANDU reactors, and providing neutrons for physics experiments. It was eventually joined in 1957 by the larger 200 (MW) National Research Universal (NRU) reactor.

In 1952, the Canadian Government formed AECL, a Crown corporation with the mandate to develop peaceful uses of nuclear energy. A partnership was formed between AECL, Ontario Hydro and Canadian General Electric to build Canada's first nuclear power plant, called NPD for Nuclear Power Demonstration. The 20 MW NPD started operation in 1962 and successfully demonstrated the unique concepts of on power refuelling using natural uranium fuel, and heavy water moderator and coolant. These defining features formed the basis of a successful fleet of CANDU power reactors (CANDU is an acronym for CANada Deuterium Uranium) built and operated in Canada and elsewhere.

In the late 1960s (1967-1970), Canada also developed an experimental miniature nuclear reactor named SLOWPOKE (acronym for Safe Low Power Kritical Experiment). The first prototype was built at Chalk River and many SLOWPOKEs were subsequently built, mainly for research. This reactor design is extremely safe and requires almost no maintenance (it is even licensed to operate unattended overnight); it can run for more than 20 years before the nuclear fuel needs replacement. There was an attempt at commercializing the reactor, as it could be used in remote areas or vehicles (research stations, electric diesel submarines). Then China entered the market with its SLOWPOKE like reactor, and thus the project lost its commercial potential. Many SLOWPOKEs are still in use in Canada; there is one running at École Polytechnique de Montréal, for instance.

Nuclear Power Generation

Electricity production in Canada has been dominated by hydroelectricity with nuclear and fossil fuels holding a 15-25% share each over the last two decades. The province of Ontario dominates Canada's nuclear industry, containing most of the country's nuclear power generating capacity. Ontario has 16 operating reactors providing about 50% of the province's electricity, plus two reactors undergoing refurbishment. Quebec and New Brunswick each have one reactor. Overall, nuclear power provides about 15% of Canada's electricity with the majority of Canada's energy as hydro power. The industry employs about 21,000 people directly and 10,000 indirectly. Canada's nuclear energy production peaked in 1994 at 102 TWh, declined to 67 TWh by 1998 as reactors were mothballed, and increased to 85 TWh in 2005 due to improved reactor performance and refurbishment. Recently there has been renewed interest in nuclear energy, spurred by increasing demand (particularly within Ontario), and the desire to comply with Canada's Kyoto Agreement obligations. The Government of Ontario proposed plans in 2004 to build several new nuclear reactors in the province.

Bruce Nuclear Generating Station near Kincardine, Ontario

Natural Resources Canada oversees nuclear power R&D and regulation in Canada, with responsibility for the crown corporations Atomic Energy of Canada Limited (AECL) and the Canadian Nuclear Safety Commission (CNSC). AECL's commercial operations include reactor development, design and construction of CANDU nuclear reactors, and provision of reactor services and technical support to CANDU reactors worldwide. Electricity planning and production are the responsibility of the individual provinces.

Canada's Nuclear Waste Management Organisation (NWMO) was set up in 2002 to investigate and develop an approach to the long term management of used nuclear fuel. After extensive public consultation over a three year period, the study report, released in 2005, recommended "Adaptive Phased Management".

The Province of Ontario has announced plans to build a new nuclear station. The leading candidate is AECL's Advanced CANDU Reactor. Environmental assessments are currently underway for one site next to Bruce Power's Bruce Nuclear Generating Station in Tiverton and another next to Ontario Power Generation's Darlington Nuclear Generating Station. Bruce Power has applied for a license to generate nuclear power at Cardinal Lake.

Nuclear Energy Demand

From the National Post 2009/12/15 by Rebecca W Alberg

Energy Needs Rising

The 21st century is ripe for a nuclear renaissance, many energy analysts say. Reactors are planned in record numbers in China, India and Eastern Europe, and advanced new models will replace existing generators in North America and Western Europe.

Canada is among many countries poised to benefit from a new generation of reactor construction, both domestically and abroad. Base load power demand, the minimum level of energy needed for households and industry, is growing at a rate that Canada's existing generators can't match. "Canada has extensive access to hydro resources," says Jerry Hopwood, vice-president of product development at Atomic Energy of Canada Ltd., "but they're not available everywhere, and are largely tapped out. "Wind and solar power can supplement base load generators, but they're too intermittent to replace them entirely."

Nuclear power generation emits no greenhouse gases, a crucial consideration for new energy infrastructure. It's also much less vulnerable to market volatility than fossil fuels. As the only country in the world with large high grade uranium deposits, Canada stands to gain a high degree of energy independence by relying increasingly upon nuclear generators. While reactors don't pollute, or cause environmental disruption the way large hydro projects do, not everyone sees nuclear as the way of the future. Greenpeace is opposed to new investment in nuclear power in Canada.

Shawn-Patrick Stensil, the NGO's Canadian energy policy analyst, says, "direct and indirect government subsidies have given nuclear power an unfair advantage, and have locked the development of green power in Canada." Harder to quantify is the degree to which the risks of nuclear power, financial and environmental, are borne by the public instead of by the industry itself. Ottawa is currently considering legislation to limit compensation for nuclear accidents, for example, which would effectively exempt this industry from the tort law that applies to virtually all other businesses, including other forms of power generation. In practice, this dramatically lowers the insurance costs reactor operators would otherwise bear," Mr. Stensil says. "Simply put, the nuclear industry can't afford itself - if they had to pay for cost overruns and insurance, nobody would be in that business."

It's a concern shared by Dr. Peter Nemetz, a professor at UBC's Sauder School of Business, and Institute for Resources, Environment and Sustainability, who points out that operating and maintenance costs for Ontario's existing CANDU reactors have run hundreds of millions of dollars over budget. Most of this tab has been settled with public dollars, and such interventions reduce incentives both for reducing consumption and developing alternatives.

"We will likely need to rely on nuclear power to some extent to meet our baseload energy requirements," Dr. Nemetz concedes, "but there is still a lot of room to reduce demand. Setting rates based on peak use times and the marginal cost of generating power has been very successful in the U.S., and we're not yet doing that in Canada."

While financing reactor construction and operations is fraught with economic and political problems, the growth of AECL, which sells CANDU reactors around the world, carries with it many benefits for Canada, in the form of jobs and spin off industries. Dr. Neil Alexander is the president of the Organization of CANDU Industries, a group of 160 small and large companies that provide goods or services necessary for the reactors.

"We represent more than 30,000 jobs throughout the country," Mr. Alexander says, "ranging from manufacturing jobs to research and design. Because of the extremely high standards for quality control, these are jobs that can't be outsourced." As well as representing industries supporting CANDU reactors worldwide, the OCI hopes to make the supply chain better integrated, and thus Canadian reactors more competitive.

On the international stage, the Canadian nuclear industry faces significant challenges from competitors that enjoy more domestic support. The French government owns 92% of nuclear power giant Areva, for example, and backs the company, awarding it contracts even when other corporations, such as Toshiba and General Electric, claim to have submitted lower bids. Areva is also vertically integrated, with uranium extraction and refining, and reactor construction, maintenance and clean up all carried out either in house or by sister companies.

Harrie Vredenberg, Professor of Strategy & Sun cor Energy Chair at the University of Calgary's Haskayne School of Business, believes Canada will ultimately benefit from the international nuclear renaissance if policy makers commit to the industry's success.

"Ottawa should privatize and restructure AECL as soon as possible, which would make it commercially nimble and less subject to government meddling," Dr. Vredenberg says, "as well as favouring Canadian technology and firms domestically, and supporting the training of nuclear workers, a well paid and highly educated group whose employment prospects are stable."

Nuclear Energy Supply in Canada & World

From World Nuclear: (Lightly edited and formatted)
http://www.world-nuclear.org/info/inf75.html

The Supply of Uranium

Uranium is a relatively common metal, found in rocks and seawater. Economic concentrations of it are not uncommon. Its availability to supply world energy needs is great both geologically and because of the technology for its use. Quantities of mineral resources are greater than commonly perceived. The world's known uranium resources increased 15% in two years to 2007 due to increased mineral exploration.

Uranium is ubiquitous on the Earth. It is a metal approximately as common as tin or zinc, and it is a constituent of most rocks and even of the sea. An ore body is, by definition, an occurrence of mineralisation from which the metal is economically recoverable. It is relative to both costs of extraction and market prices. At present neither the oceans nor any granites are ore bodies, but conceivably either could become so if prices were to rise sufficiently.

Measured resources of uranium, the amount known to be economically recoverable from ore bodies, are thus also relative to costs and prices. They are also dependent on the intensity of past exploration effort, and are basically a statement about what is known rather than what is there in the Earth's crust.

Changes in costs or prices, or further exploration, may alter measured resource figures markedly. At ten times the current price, seawater might become a potential source of vast amounts of uranium. Thus, any predictions of the future availability of any mineral, including uranium, which are based on current cost and price data and current geological knowledge are likely to be extremely conservative.

From time to time concerns are raised that the known resources might be insufficient when judged as a multiple of present rate of use. But this is the Limits to Growth fallacy, a major intellectual blunder recycled from the 1970s, which takes no account of the very limited nature of the knowledge we have at any time of what is actually in the Earth's crust. Our knowledge of geology is such that we can be confident that identified resources of metal minerals are a small fraction of what is there.

The Availability of Uranium

With those major qualifications the following gives some idea of our present knowledge of uranium resources. The countries of the world having major deposits of low cost uranium are: Australia (23%),

Kazakhstan (15%), Russia (10%), South Africa (8%), Canada (8%), and the USA (6%), and Brazil (5%).

Uranium Resources

Current usage is about 65,000 tonnes Uranium per year. Thus the world's present measured resources of uranium, in the cost category somewhat below present spot prices and used only in conventional reactors, are enough to last for over 80 years. This represents a higher level of assured resources than is normal for most minerals. Further exploration and higher prices will certainly yield further resources as present resources are used up.

An initial uranium exploration cycle was military driven, over 1945 to 1958. The second cycle was about 1974 to 1983, driven by civil nuclear power. There was relatively little uranium exploration between 1985 and 2003, so the significant increase in exploration effort that we are now seeing could readily double the known economic resources. In the two years 2005-06 the world's known uranium resources tabulated above and graphed below increased by 15% (17% in the cost category to $80/kgU). World uranium exploration expenditure in 2006 was US$ 774 million, and the 2007 level was much the same. In the third uranium exploration cycle from 2003 to the end of 2009 about US$ 3.4 billion will have been spent on uranium exploration and deposit delineation on over 600 projects. In this period over 400 new junior companies were formed or changed their orientation to raise over US$ 2 billion for uranium exploration. About 60% of this was spent on previously known deposits. All this was in response to increased uranium price in the market.

The price of a mineral commodity also directly determines the amount of known resources which are economically extractable. On the basis of analogies with other metal minerals, a doubling of price from present levels could be expected to create about a tenfold increase in measured economic resources, over time, due to both the increased exploration and the reclassification of resources regarding what is economically recoverable.

This is in fact suggested in the IAEA-NEA figures if those covering estimates of all conventional resources are considered - 10.5 million tonnes (beyond the 5.5 million tonnes known economic resources), which takes us to over 200 years' supply at today's rate of consumption. This still ignores the technological factor mentioned below. It also omits unconventional resources such as phosphate/ phosphorite deposits (22 Mt U recoverable as by product) and seawater (up to 4000 Mt), which would be uneconomic to extract in the foreseeable future.

Uranium Resources and Exploration Expenditure

It is clear from this Figure that known uranium resources have increased threefold since 1975, in line with expenditure on uranium exploration. (The decrease in the decade 1983-93 is due to some countries tightening their criteria for reporting. If this were carried back two decades, the lines would fit even more closely.) Increased exploration expenditure in the future is likely to result in a corresponding increase in known resources.

About 20% of U.S. uranium came from central Florida's phosphate deposits to the mid 1990s, as a by product, but it then became uneconomic. With higher uranium prices today that resource is being examined again, as is another lower grade one in Morocco. Plans for Florida extend only to 400 tU/yr at this stage.

Coal ash is another easily accessible though minor uranium resource in many parts of the world. In central Yunnan province in China the coal uranium content varies up to 315 ppm and averages about 65 ppm. The ash averages about 210 ppm U (0.021%U) - above the cut off level for some uranium mines. The Xiaolongtang power station ash heap contains over 1000 tU, with annual arisings of 190 tU. Recovery of this by acid leaching is about 70%.

Widespread use of the fast breeder reactor could increase the utilisation of uranium 50 fold or more. This type of reactor can be started up on plutonium derived from conventional reactors and operated in closed circuit with its reprocessing plant. Such a reactor, supplied with natural or depleted uranium for its "fertile blanket", can be operated so that each tonne of ore yields 60 times more energy than in a conventional reactor.

Nuclear Reactor Fuel Requirements

The world's power reactors, with combined capacity of some 370 GWe, require about 65,000 tonnes of uranium from mines or elsewhere each year. While this capacity is being run more productively, with higher capacity factors and reactor power levels, the uranium fuel requirement is increasing, but not necessarily at the same rate. The factors increasing fuel demand are offset by a trend for higher burn up of fuel and other efficiencies, so demand is steady. (Over the years 1980 to 2008 the electricity generated by nuclear power increased 3.6 fold while uranium used increased by a factor of only 2.5.)

Reducing the tails assay in enrichment reduces the amount of natural uranium required for a given amount of fuel. Reprocessing of spent fuel from conventional light water reactors also utilises present resources more efficiently, by a factor of about 1.3 overall. Today's reactor fuel requirements are met from primary supply (direct mine output) and secondary sources: commercial stockpiles, nuclear weapons stockpiles, recycled plutonium and uranium from reprocessing used fuel, and re-enrichment of depleted uranium tails (left over from original enrichment). These various secondary sources make uranium unique among energy minerals.

Nuclear Weapons as a Source of Fuel

An important source of nuclear fuel is the world's nuclear weapons stockpiles. Since 1987 the United States and countries of the former USSR have signed a series of disarmament treaties to reduce the nuclear arsenals of the signatory countries by approximately 80 percent. The weapons contain a great deal of uranium enriched to over 90 percent U-235 (ie up to 25 times the proportion in reactor fuel). Some weapons have plutonium-239, which can be used in mixed oxide (MOX) fuel for civil reactors. From 2000 the dilution of 30 tonnes of military high enriched uranium has been displacing about 10,600 tonnes of uranium oxide per year from mines, which represents about 13% of the world's reactor requirements. Details of the utilisation of military stockpiles are in the paper Military warheads as a source of nuclear fuel.

Other Secondary Sources of Uranium

The most obvious source is civil stockpiles held by utilities and governments. The amount held here is difficult to quantify, due to commercial confidentiality. As at January 2007 some 55,000 tU was known on the basis of partial data (Red Book) and 120,000 tU estimated just for utilities (WNA Market Report). These reserves are expected not to be drawn down, but to increase steadily to provide energy security for utilities and governments. Recycled uranium and plutonium is another source, and currently saves 1500-2000 tU per year of primary supply, depending on whether just the plutonium or also the uranium is considered. In fact, plutonium is quickly recycled as MOX fuel, whereas the reprocessed uranium (RepU) is mostly stockpiled.

Re-enrichment of depleted uranium (DU) is another secondary source. There are about 1.5 million tonnes of depleted uranium available, from both military and civil enrichment activity since the 1940s, most at tails assay of 0.25 - 0.35% U-235. Non-nuclear uses of DU are very minor relative to annual arisings of over 35,000 tU per year. This leaves most DU available for mixing with recycled plutonium on MOX fuel or as a future fuel resource for fast neutron reactors. However, some that has relatively high assay can be fed through under utilised enrichment plants to produce natural uranium equivalent, or even enriched uranium ready for fuel fabrication. Russian enrichment plants have treated 10-15,000 tonnes per year of DU assaying over 0.3% U-235, stripping it down to 0.1% and producing a few thousand tonnes per year of natural uranium equivalent. This Russian program is due to wind down, however, but a new U.S. one is expected to start, treating about 140,000 tonnes of old DU.

Thorium as a Nuclear Fuel

Today uranium is the only fuel supplied for nuclear reactors. However, thorium can also be utilised as a fuel for CANDU reactors or in reactors specially designed for this purpose. Neutron efficient reactors, such as CANDU, are capable of operating on a thorium fuel cycle, once they are started using a fissile material such as U-235 or Pu-239. Then the thorium (Th-232) atom captures a neutron in the reactor to become fissile uranium (U-233), which continues the reaction. Some advanced reactor designs are likely to be able to make use of thorium on a substantial scale. The thorium fuel cycle has some attractive features, though it is not yet in commercial use. Thorium is reported to be about three times as abundant in the earth's crust as uranium. The 2007 IAEA-NEA "Red Book" gives a figure of 4.4 million tonnes of known and estimated resources, but points out that this excludes data from much of the world.

Uranium & Investment Canada

From Investment Canada: (Lightly edited and formatted)
http://www.ic.gc.ca/eic/site/ica-lic.nsf/eng/h_lk00007.html

The purpose of the Investment Canada Act (the Act) is "to provide for the review of significant investments in Canada by non-Canadians in order to ensure such benefit to Canada" (s. 2). The legislation describing the "review function" and associated rules are complex and because of that complexity, this document is intended to serve both as an introduction to and a description of the key features of the Act. It will hopefully help investors and others who are interested in the application of the legislation understand how non-Canadian investors are to respond to the requirements of the Act.

It should be noted, however, that this is only a general guide for the reader. It does not include all the details found in the Act and is not intended to express a legal opinion of the Government of Canada as to the interpretation of the Act nor is it bound by its content. For the application of the Act to a particular situation, the reader is advised to consult the specific provisions of the Act and obtain appropriate legal counsel.

With respect to all investments except those that fall within a prescribed type of business activity as set out in Schedule IV of the Regulations, the Department responsible for the administration of the Act is Industry Canada. With respect to investments which fall within a Schedule IV prescribed business activity, the Department responsible for the administration of the Act is the Department of Canadian Heritage.

If you are a non-Canadian then you must file a notification each and every time you commence a new business activity in Canada and each time you acquire control of an existing Canadian business where the establishment or acquisition of control is not a reviewable transaction. A Notification must be filed no later than thirty days after the implementation of the investment.

Wind Energy in Canada

From Wikipedia: (lightly edited and formatted)
http://en.wikipedia.org/wiki/Wind_power_in_Canada

As a means of pumping water and generating electricity in remote locations, wind power has a history in Canada dating back many decades, particularly on prairie farms. The amount of electricity generated by wind in Canada remains, however, small compared to other sources such as hydro dams and coal, although it is the fastest growing source. As of December 2008, wind power supplies approximately 1 percent of Canada's electricity demand, with 85 wind farms representing approximately 2,246 MW of generating capacity. The Canadian Wind Energy Association has outlined a future strategy for wind energy that would reach a capacity of 55,000 MW by 2025, meeting 20% of the country's energy needs.

Overview

Canadian installed wind power capacity by year

Year	MW installed
2000	137
2001	198
2002	236
2003	322
2004	444
2005	684
2006	1460
2007	1770
2008	2369
2009	3150

Installed wind power capacity, province or territory (2009)

Year	MW installed
ON	1161
QC	659
AB	590
SK	171
PEI	151
MB	104
BC	102
NB	96
NS	59
NL	54
YK	0.81

Early development of wind energy in Canada was located primarily in Ontario, Quebec, and Alberta. Throughout the late 1990s and early years of the 21st Century, every Canadian province has pursued wind energy to supplement their provincial energy grids. As of August 2007, British Columbia is the only province without an operating commercial wind farm, but BC Hydro has currently issued Electricity Purchase

Agreements for over 300 MW of wind powered electricity. A 102 MW wind farm at Bear Mountain, Dawson Creek, is currently being built and another at Skokie Ridge, Hudson Hope is about to come online. With increasing population growth, Canada has seen wind power as a way to diversify energy supplies away from traditional reliance on fossil fuel burning thermal plants, and heavy reliance on hydroelectricity in some provinces.

In provinces like Nova Scotia, where only 12% of electricity comes from renewable sources, the development of wind energy projects will provide a measure of electricity security that some jurisdictions are lacking. In the case of British Columbia, wind energy will help close the electricity deficit that the province is facing into the 2010s and help reduce the reliance on importing power from other jurisdictions. An additional 2,004 megawatts of wind power is to come on stream in Quebec between 2011 and 2015. The new energy will cost 10.5 cents per kilowatt-hour, a price the utility described as "highly competitive".

Wind Hybrid Projects

Of potential use in smaller isolated communities not connected to the main power grid are Wind-Diesel and Wind-Hydrogen. One Canadian example is the community of Rama, Newfoundland and Labrador that initially used a Wind-Diesel system and is now being converted to Wind-Hydrogen technology.

Wind Tower Manufacture

Canadian industry has started to supply major components for Wind Tower projects, Hitachi Canadian Industries being one example.

Public Opinion

In a survey conducted by Angus Reid Strategies in October 2007, 89 per cent of respondents said that using renewable energy sources like wind or solar power was positive for Canada, because these sources were better for the environment. Only 4 per cent considered using renewable sources as negative since they can be unreliable and expensive.

According to a Saint Consulting survey in April 2007, wind power was the alternative energy source most likely to gain public support for future development in Canada, with only 16% opposed to this type of energy. By contrast, 3 out of 4 Canadians opposed nuclear power developments.

Despite this general support for the concept of wind power in the public at large, local opposition often exists, primarily from residents concerned about a perceived "eyesore", noise or reduced property values. This has delayed or aborted a number of projects. This opposition has been described as a case of NIMBYism. Several wind farms in Canada have become tourist attractions, to the surprise of the owners.

Proposed Future Strategies

Wind Farms on Crown Land

Some rural communities want Alberta to grant companies the right to develop wind farms on leased Crown land.

Wind Vision 2025

In 2008, the Canadian Wind Energy Association (CanWEA), a non-profit trade association, outlined a future strategy for wind energy that would reach a capacity of 55,000 MW by 2025, fulfilling 20% of the country's energy needs. The plan, Wind Vision 2025, could create over 50,000 jobs and represent around CDN$165 million annual revenue. If achieved, CanWEA's target would make the country a major player in the wind power sector and would create around CDN$79 billion of investment. It would also save an estimated 17 megatonnes of greenhouse gas emissions annually.

Manitoba

Manitoba is planning to build the largest wind mill farm in Canada in the southern part of the province near the cities of Brandon and Portage la Prairie.

Solar Energy in Canada

From Wikipedia: (lightly edited and formatted)
http://en.wikipedia.org/wiki/Solar_power_in_Canada

Canada has plentiful solar energy resources, with the most extensive resources being found in southern Ontario, Quebec and the Prairies. The territories have a smaller potential, and less direct sunlight, because of their higher latitude.

The main applications of solar energy technologies in Canada have been for non-electric active solar system applications for space heating, water heating and drying crops and lumber. In 2001, there were more than 12,000 residential solar water heating systems and 300 commercial or industrial solar hot water systems in use. These systems presently comprise a small fraction of Canada's energy use, but some government studies suggest they could make up as much as five per cent of the country's energy needs by the year 2025.

Canada has many regions that are sparsely populated and difficult to access. Photovoltaic (PV) cells are increasingly used as standalone units, mostly as off grid distributed electricity generation to power remote homes, telecommunications equipment, oil and pipeline monitoring stations and navigational devices. The Canadian PV market has grown quickly and Canadian companies make solar modules, controls, specialized water pumps, high efficiency refrigerators and solar lighting systems.

One of the most important uses for PV cells is in northern communities, many of which depend on high cost diesel fuel to generate electricity.

Since the 1970s, the federal government and industry has encouraged the development of solar technologies for these communities. Some of these efforts have focussed on the use of hybrid systems that provide power 24 hours a day, using solar power when sunlight is available, in combination with another energy source. About 50 MW of photovoltaic solar farms will be on line by the end of 2009, with more to follow. Development is being driven by an extremely high feed in tariff of $CAD 0.42/KWh.

Space Based Solar Power

From the Globe and Mail 2010/04/05 by Neil Reynolds
(Lightly edited and formatted) reynolds.globe@gmail.com

Space Based Solar Power (SBSP)

Anyone can do their part for the planet, as millions of people did for an hour last month by turning off the lights. The trick is to do it without resorting to darkness.

For the moment, Japan leads the way with its ambitious program to collect solar energy in space, convert it into electro- magnetic microwaves and deliver it wirelessly to precise locations on Earth. This transmission technology will do to terrestrial power lines what cell phones did to telephone poles. Funded in part by a consortium of 16 corporations (led Mitsubishi Electric), Japan expects its prototype spaced power station to provide electricity to 300,000 Tokyo homes by 2030.

In the end, though, the United States won't be far behind, and for competitive reasons, probably will surpass Japan in pursuit of space-based solar power. Ostensibly at least, Tokyo lacks the military motive of Washington, although as a resources bereft country, Japan must ensure its energy supply from some where else simply to survive.

For its part, the U.S. Defence Department's National Security Space Office (NSSO) adopted space based energy as a strategic priority in

2007. President Barack Obama's 2010 budget, which essentially cut lunar adventures to fund economy class spaceships, may be interpreted as a prerequisite investment in space based energy. A power station in space, 36,000 kilometres or more above Earth, will require 120 launches (of maintenance crews) a year.

With its unclassified assessment of space based solar power, the NSSO remains an accessible source of information on the relevant science and technology. For a bureaucratic organization in a military hierarchy, the NSSO compiled its report in a uniquely collaborative way . . . at no cost. The agency simply created an access controlled website and invited the world's leading scientists to participate, and 170 did. The NSSO report reflects the scientific consensus.

The strategic prize, the NSSO concludes, is obvious: Space based satellites can economically tap an inexhaustible strategic reservoir of clean, renewable energy by 2050 or earlier.

The military importance, it notes: is also obvious: "For the Department of Defence specifically, beamed energy from space . . . has the potential to be a disruptive game changer on the battlefield." With wireless technology, space based solar power could deliver electricity across an entire theatre of war, right down to the individual soldier. It could dramatically reduce the chance of international conflict arising from energy shortages, and it could provide demand on energy for humanitarian purposes in disaster zones. In short, the NSSO says, it could enable the U.S. military "to remain relevant" for the 21st century.

"The basic idea is very straightforward," the NSSO says. "Place very large solar arrays into an intensely sunlit Earth orbit. Collect gigawatts of electrical energy and electro- magnetically beam them to Earth." The electricity could be delivered to either conventional electrical grids or directly to consumers. It could also be used to manufacture synthetic hydrocarbons.

Spread an array of solar collectors over a single square kilometre, the NSSO says, and you can collect a supply of energy every year, equal to the energy contained in all of the known recoverable conventional oil reserves on Earth today. This amount of energy indicates that there is enormous energy potential for nations who construct and possess a SBSP capability. The NSSO says that Canada is one of the countries that has expressed its interest in acquiring such a capability.

Although complicated, the delivery of spaced based energy would not be much more heroic than the construction of a large modern aircraft carrier, a skyscraper or a large hydro electric dam. A single solar power satellite would be 15 times the size of the International Space Station (344 metric tonnes). In comparison, the Great Pyramid at Giza has a mass of 5.9 million tonnes.

Although the space beam would require a sizable target on Earth, this receiver would be based in a desert, perhaps in South Dakota or sub-Saharan Africa. With its abundant supply of energy, though, these desert zones would be transformed into lush agricultural land. The NSSO compares the intensity of the space beam to the heat thrown off by a campfire. The NSSO expresses considerable curiosity why environmentalists appear obsessed with much more difficult terrestrial energy sources that can't be as efficiently or cleanly produced as space based power, which on a "life cycle" basis would produce 1/60th of the carbon emitted by fossil fuels.

You would think that environmentalists would be thrilled to join forces with the Pentagon. As Thomas Edison put it in 1931: "I'd put my money on the sun and solar energy."

Geothermal Energy in Canada

From The Pembina Institute: (lightly edited and formatted)
http://re.pembina.org/sources/geothermal

Geothermal energy is produced from naturally occurring steam and hot water trapped in reservoirs under the surface of the earth (about 500 to 2,000 metres below the surface). The energy from this heat can be used directly to heat home or indirectly to generate electricity. Geothermal energy has been used for a century. It is cost effective and reliable but not that easy to find at high temperatures, unless one happens to live in a volcanic region.

Capturing and Using Geothermal

The most common current way of capturing the geothermal energy is to tap into naturally occurring hydrothermal convection systems containing pressurized hot water or steam. These are forced to the surface and used to drive steam turbine generators, or used to heat hot water or air for space or water heating.

Benefits

- Geothermal power plants do not have to use an intermediate technology to produce steam to power the turbine generators.
- The land needed for geothermal power plants is smaller per megawatt than for almost any other type of power plant.
- Geothermal plants can run 24/7 and are flexible; additional units can be installed as necessary.

Challenges

- Geothermal energy can only be used in areas where the earth's crust is thin and the steam or hot water sources are close to the surface.
- Sometimes the hot water that is pumped to the surface contains pollutants such as sulphur, which must be removed before using in a power plant.

Global Status and Potential

Geothermal energy is used widely in Iceland, the Philippines, Italy, Indonesia, Mexico, New Zealand, Japan and China. Iceland relies on geysers as its primary source of heat. The United States is the world's largest producer of geothermal electricity with 2,800 MW in service.

More than 75 countries have geothermal heating capacity; more than 20 have geothermal electricity capacity. More than 1 GW of geothermal power was added to the global renewable energy equation between 2000 and 2004.

Canadian Status and Potential

Meager Mountain, a volcanic complex in British Columbia, is the only Canadian site where geothermal energy is being actively pursued. Western GeoPower Corp is developing its geothermal power generating facility and sees a potential of 100—250 MW of electricity.

Power, Parliament & the BNA

From the Freedom Party of Canada: (lightly edited and formatted)
http://www.freedomparty.ca/htm/en/constitution1867.htm

Section 91(2) gives Parliament the power to make law related to the "regulation of trade and commerce." In comparison with the U.S. Constitution's approach to trade and commerce, the power given to Parliament is more broadly worded than that given to the U.S. government, but in Canada since Citizen's Insurance Co. v. Parsons in the 1880s it has nevertheless been typically read more narrowly, as some judges have felt that it overlaps with the provincial authority over property and civil rights. Parliament's authority over trade and commerce is said to include its "general" aspects, although this was an ambiguous definition until the 1980s when in General Motors of Canada Ltd. v. City National Leasing it was ruled Parliament could regulate trade and commerce if its object was to achieve something a provincial government alone could not achieve. The following quote is from the decision of the Supreme Court that the provinces alone were incapable of regulating competition;

> 'It is evident from this discussion that competition cannot be effectively regulated unless it is regulated nationally. As I have said, in my view combines legislation fulfills the three

> *indicia* of national scope as described in *Canadian National Transportation*: it is legislation "aimed at the economy as a single integrated national unit rather than as a collection of separate local enterprises", it is legislation "that the provinces jointly or severally would be constitutionally incapable of passing" and "failure to include one or more provinces or localities would jeopardize successful operation" of the legislation "in other parts of the country"'.

Power Generation & the BNA

From the Freedom Party of Canada: (lightly edited and formatted)
http://www.freedomparty.ca/htm/en/constitution1867.htm

Exclusive Powers of Provincial Legislatures

Section 92. Subjects of exclusive Provincial Legislation.

> In each Province the Legislature may exclusively make Laws in relation to Matters coming within the Classes of Subject next hereinafter enumerated; that is to say,--

Non-Renewable Natural Resources, Forestry Resources and Electrical Energy

Section 92 A.

(1) Laws respecting non-renewable natural resources, forestry resources and electrical energy. In each province, the legislature may exclusively make laws in relation to
  (a) exploration for non-renewable natural resources in the province;
  (b) development, conservation and management of non-renewable resources natural resources and forestry resources in the province, including laws in relation to the rate of primary production therefrom; and

(c) development, conservation and management of sites and facilities in the province for the generation and production of electrical energy.

(2) In each province, the legislature may make laws in relation to the export from the province to another part of Canada of the primary production from non-renewable natural resources and forestry resources in the province and the production from facilities in the province for the generation of electrical energy, but such laws may not authorize or provide for discrimination in prices or in supplies exported to another part of Canada.

(3) Nothing in subsection (2) derogates from the authority of Parliament to enact laws in relation to the matters referred to in that subsection and, where such a law of Parliament and a law of a province conflict, the law of Parliament prevails to the extent of the conflict.

(4) In each province, the legislature may make laws in relation to the raising of money by any mode or system of taxation in respect of

(a) non-renewable natural resources and forestry resources in the province and the primary production therefrom, and
(b) sites and facilities in the province for the generation of electrical energy and the production therefrom,

whether or not such production is exported in whole or in part from the province, but such laws may not authorize or provide for taxation that differentiates between production exported to another part of Canada and production not exported from the province.

(5) The expression "primary production" has the meaning assigned by the Sixth Schedule.

(6) Nothing in subsections (1) to (5) derogates from any power or rights that a legislature or government of a province had immediately before the coming into force of this section.

The Sixth Schedule

Primary Production from Non-Renewable Natural Resources and Forestry Resources

1. For the purposes of Section 92A of this Act,

   (a) production from a non-renewable natural resource is primary production therefrom if

      (i) it is in the form in which it exists upon its recovery or severance from its natural state, or

      (ii) it is a product resulting from processing or refining the resource, and is not a manufactured product or a product resulting from refining crude oil, refining upgraded heavy crude oil, refining gases or liquids derived from coal, or refining synthetic equivalent of crude oil; and

   (b) production from a forestry resource is primary production therefrom if it consists of saw logs, poles, lumber, wood chips, sawdust or other primary wood product or wood pulp, and is not a product manufactured from wood.

Power Transmission & the BNA

From Wikipedia: (lightly edited and formatted)
http://en.wikipedia.org/wiki/Canadian_federalism

The Division of Legislative Powers in the Constitution Act, 1867

The federal- provincial distribution of legislative powers (also known as the division of powers) defines the scope of the power of the federal parliament of Canada and the powers of each individual provincial legislature or assembly. These are contained in sections 91, 92, 92A, 93, 94, 94A and 95 of the Constitution Act, 1867. Much of the distribution, however, has been ambiguous, leading to disputes that have been decided by the Judicial Committee of the Privy Council and, after 1949, the Supreme Court of Canada. Doctrines of judicial interpretation of federalism include pith and substance, double aspect, paramountcy and inter-jurisdictional immunity.

Unlike the United States Constitution (which reserves un-enumerated powers to the states), the Canadian constitution has created an overarching federal jurisdiction based upon the power known as peace, order and good government (section 91). However, the Canadian constitution also recognizes certain powers that are exclusive to the provinces and outside federal jurisdiction (section 92). The preamble of section 91 makes this clear: "It shall be lawful for the Queen, (...) to make laws for the Peace, Order, and good Government of Canada, in relation to all Matters not coming within the Classes of Subjects by this Act assigned exclusively to the Legislatures of the Provinces;" Thus, the federal government of Canada is partly limited by the powers assigned exclusively to the provincial legislatures. For example, the Canadian constitution created a very broad provincial jurisdiction over direct taxation, property, and civil rights. Many disputes between the two levels of government revolve around conflicting interpretations of the meaning of these two powers.

A quick perusal of these powers shows that while the federal government has exclusive jurisdiction over criminal law (defined in the Margarine Reference) and procedure (section 91(27)) the provinces have jurisdiction over the administration of justice, including criminal matters (section 92(14)) and penal matters (section 92(15)) regarding any laws made within provincial jurisdiction. Thus Canada has a single Criminal Code but many provincial laws that can result in incarceration or penalty. The courts have recognized that the provinces and the federal government have the right to create corporations; only the federal government has the right to incorporate banks, though provinces may incorporate credit unions which offer similar services as the federally chartered banks.

In relation to marriage and divorce, the federal government's exclusive authority over these subjects (section 91(26)) has given Canada uniform legislation on them, yet the provinces can pass laws regulating the solemnization of marriage (section 92(12)) and wide variety of subjects pertaining to civil and political rights (section 92(13)) and have created institutions such as common-law marriage and civil union.

Nowhere in the division of powers of the Constitution Act, 1867 is there a mention of a treaty power, reserved to the British Empire. Power for external relations was granted to Canada only after the passage of the Statute of Westminster in 1931. The domestic implementation of treaties, however, remains divided between the two levels of government.

Trade and commerce

Section 91(2) gives Parliament the power to make law related to the "regulation of trade and commerce." In comparison with the U.S. Constitution's approach to trade and commerce, the power given to Parliament is more broadly worded than that given to the U.S. government, but in Canada since Citizen's Insurance Co. v. Parsons in the 1880s it has nevertheless been typically read more narrowly, as some judges have felt that it overlaps with the provincial authority over property and civil rights. Parliament's authority over trade and commerce is said to include its "general" aspects, although this was an ambiguous definition until the 1980s when in General Motors of Canada Ltd. v. City National Leasing it was ruled Parliament could regulate trade and commerce if its object was to achieve something a provincial government alone could not achieve.

Property and civil rights

Section 92(13) gives the provinces the exclusive power to make law related to "property and civil rights in the province". In practice, this power has been read broadly giving the provinces authority over numerous matters such as professional trades, labour relations, family law and consumer protection. Property and civil rights is a term that predates the Constitution Act, 1867, and does not mean what it means today. It primarily refers to interactions between private persons. This would include the great majority of what any government would regulate, which means Parliament would be powerless if it were not for its enumerated powers in section 91 and for peace, order, and good government.

Transportation and communication

Like many other powers, transportation and communication have overlapping powers between the two jurisdictions. Section 92(10) gives the provinces power over "local work and undertakings". However, the section also excludes the provinces from undertakings related to "ships, railways, canals, telegraphs, and other works and undertakings connecting the province with any other or others of the provinces", as well as ship lines, and such works "declared by the Parliament of Canada to be for the general advantage of Canada or for the advantage of two or more provinces."

Federalism and the Charter

In 1982 the Canadian Charter of Rights and Freedoms was brought into effect. This was not meant to affect the workings of federalism, though some content was moved from section 91 to section 4 of the Charter. Mainly, the Charter is meant to decrease powers of both levels of government by ensuring both federal and provincial laws respect Charter rights, under section 32. The relationship between federalism and the Charter is directly dealt with in section 31, in which it is made clear neither the federal nor provincial governments gain powers under the Charter.

In R. v. Big M Drug Mart Ltd. (1985) it was found that if laws violate Charter rights, they cannot be justified under section 1 of the Charter if their purpose was inconsistent with the proper division of powers.

History

The relationship between Canada and the provinces has changed throughout time, with an increasing amount of decentralization taking place as years passed. Throughout the Macdonald era (1867-1873, 1878-1891), the Confederation was such that it has been described by political scientist K. C. Where as "Quasi-Federalism". This meant that the political and judicial elites of the 19th century read the Constitution of Canada in a way that gave the federal Parliament extensive powers that essentially made the provinces "subordinate to Ottawa." The

Macdonald government's use of disallowance and reservation also reinforced the supremacy of the federal government at that time.

With the election of Sir Wilfrid Laurier came a new phase of Confederation that Dyck refers to as "Classical Federalism". This was marked by a more equal relationship between the federal government and the provinces, as the Judicial Committee of the Privy Council settled several disputes in favour of the latter. The federal government also allowed its disallowance and reservation powers to fall into disuse. This style of governance continued throughout the early years of the leadership of Prime Minister William Lyon Mackenzie King (although legislation from Alberta was disallowed in the 1930s).

During the two world wars, Ottawa expanded its powers greatly. This was done through the War Measures Act and constitutionally justified by the peace, order and good government clause. During the First World War, Parliament increased its taxation powers by establishing income taxes. Finally, during the Second World War, the federal government convinced the provinces to transfer jurisdiction over unemployment insurance to Ottawa.

Canada emerged from the Second World War with more association or cooperation between federal and provincial levels of government. This owed to the rise of the welfare state and the health care system (as the Canadian government acted to ensure that Canadians as a people had some common quality of service), to the fact that many of the jurisdictions of the two levels of government were closely related, and to the fact that this allowed the federal government to retain a great deal of control that they had enjoyed during World War II. Keynesian economics were also introduced by the federal government through this system. The period was also marked by a number of First Ministers meetings (ie., meetings between the prime minister and the provincial premiers).

After 1960 and Quebec's Quiet Revolution, Canada moved toward a greater degree of administrative decentralization, with Quebec often opting out of important federal initiatives, such as the Canada Pension Plan (Quebec created its own pension plan). As the federal government became more centralist in ideology. Under the leadership of Prime Minister Pierre Trudeau, Canada entered a stage of "conflictual federalism" that could be said to have lasted from 1970 to 1984. The National Energy Program sparked a great deal of bitterness against the federal government in Alberta; indeed, the federal government was also involved in disputes over oil with Newfoundland and Saskatchewan at this time. (These culminated in the addition of section 92A to the Constitution Act, 1867, by the Constitution Act, 1982; the new section gave the provinces more power with regard to these resources).(7)

The Progressive Conservative Party of Canada under Joe Clark and Brian Mulroney favoured devolution of powers to the provinces, culminating in the failed Meech Lake and Charlottetown accords. After a merger with the heavily devolutionist Canadian Alliance, the new Conservative Party of Canada under Stephen Harper has continued the same stance.

After the 1995 Quebec referendum on Quebec sovereignty, one of several actions by then Prime Minister Jean Chrétien was to put some limits on the ability of the federal government to spend money in areas of provincial jurisdiction. Thus, in 1999, the federal government and all provincial governments except Quebec's agreed to the Social Union Framework Agreement, which promoted common standards for social programs across Canada.(8) Former Prime Minister Paul Martin has used the term asymmetrical federalism to describe this arrangement.

Electrical Power Transmission in Canada

From Centre for Energy: (lightly edited and formatted)
http://www.centreforenergy.com

The Canadian Centre for Energy Information

Canada's bulk transmission network consists of more than 160,000 kilometres of high voltage lines. This is enough to cross the entire country roughly 27 times. These lines carry electricity at voltages above

50 kilovolts to move electricity in bulk over long distances. Because of Canada's vast geographic size, its electricity systems require different types of high voltage lines (typically at 115 kilovolt, 230 kilovolt and 500 kilovolt levels) to deliver electricity safely, reliably and economically to customers.

Electrical Transmission Grids

Most of Canada's provinces and territories are part of interconnected electricity "grids," networks of power plants and transmission lines that cross international, provincial and territorial borders. These networks provide electric utilities with alternative power paths in emergencies, to buy and sell power from each other and from other power suppliers.

Canada has three power grids: the Western grid, the Eastern grid, and the Quebec grid, which includes Atlantic Canada. The border between the Eastern and Western grids is the Alberta Saskatchewan border. Canadian grids are also tied into the U.S. grids (the Western Interconnection, the Eastern Interconnection and the Texas Interconnection). For example, the electricity grid in Alberta and British Columbia is part of the Western Interconnection in the United States.

North - South Pattern

There is a predominantly north- south pattern to Canada's transmission high voltage lines. This has emerged over time as utilities develop generation sites in northern areas of the country to produce and transmit electricity to urban markets in the south. Hydro-Québec's system, for example, extends more than 1,100 kilometres from Churchill Falls in Labrador to Montreal, and from James Bay to southern load centres, which include U.S. markets. In Manitoba, a large 500 kilovolt DC system brings hydro power from the Nelson River to customers in the Winnipeg area. In Ontario and British Columbia, major 500 kilovolt systems bring electric power from northern generating sites to markets in the south.

Restructuring the Grids

Transmission lines in a given area may be owned by a single company or by a number of different companies. Similarly, the generation and the distribution facilities the transmission lines connect can be owned by the same company, or by different companies.

In most provinces and territories, vertically integrated, government owned utilities look after the planning, building and operation of transmission as part of their bundled services. Some provinces are undergoing fundamental changes that have restructured their markets and unbundled generation, transmission and distribution services. The pace of change is occurring at different rates across the country. The extent of restructuring varies because regulation of the electricity industry is generally the responsibility of the provinces and territories.

In provinces such as Ontario and Alberta, vertically integrated utilities have been divided into separate generation, transmission and distribution companies. In 1999, Ontario Hydro was split into a number of successor organizations, including Ontario Power Generation and Hydro One. The former manages generation plants, and the latter owns and operates the province's transmission system. This change is most advanced in Alberta, where restructuring started in the mid-1990s, unbundling vertically integrated utilities, opening up transmission access and creating a competitive wholesale electricity market. Today Alberta's transmission facilities have become the properties of separate companies or continue to be owned by the utilities and operated by an independent system operator (ISO). Transmission facilities continue to be regulated by a commission or board in most jurisdictions.

Because of industry restructuring, "open access" has emerged as a way to ensure that owners of transmission lines allow non-discriminatory access to their lines. This is essential to enabling buyers to purchase electricity from the most competitive generation sources. Alberta, Ontario, British Columbia, Saskatchewan, Manitoba and Quebec all offer open access to transmission.

Electricity Trade

Canada, the world's second largest exporter of electricity, is an active participant in North American electricity trade. Most provinces are connected with their nearest U.S. neighbours. This cross-border trade allows generators to operate more efficiently, as they can continue to generate electricity, even when local demand is low. With open markets and shared transmission lines, power can be sold across hundreds of kilometres.

Canada typically exports between six and 10 per cent of its production to the United States. In 2002, Canada exported 36 terawatt-hours of electricity (worth $1.8 billion) to the United States. Exports are sold primarily to the New England states, New York State, the Midwest, and the Pacific Northwest and California.

Hydro power systems, which can store water during off peak systems and then release the water for power production during peak periods, are well suited for the export of electricity. As a result, provinces with large hydro systems, such as Quebec, Manitoba and British Columbia, have been the largest exporters of electricity to the United States. In 2002, Canada imported about 17 terawatt-hours of electricity from U.S. suppliers.

North American Transmission Grid

In the United States, the Federal Energy Regulatory Commission (FERC) has mandated that regional transmission organizations (RTOs) oversee the administration of transmission systems in competitive electricity markets. Given the international nature of the transmission grid, FERC has encouraged Canadian participation and, in some cases, has directed the RTOs to indicate how Canadian transmission entities would be represented.

All provinces are interconnected with neighbouring provinces, allowing them to import and export power. East-west transmission is less common than north-south transmission. To date, most of the inter-provincial exchange of power has occurred in Eastern Canada, with the largest transfers between Quebec and Labrador. Canadian utilities and government leaders are exploring ways to increase east-west electricity flow, especially between Ontario and Manitoba and Ontario and Quebec. The territories are neither interconnected, nor do they have connections with the provinces or the United States.

Churchill Falls Hydro Electricity

From the National Post 2009/12/01 by Lynn Moore

Newfoundland & Labrador seeks new deal from Hydro Quebec . . . Gross Inequity

MONTREAL: Newfoundland and Labrador has formally requested a new deal with Hydro Quebec to replace the controversial 1969 Churchill Falls power contract. Newfoundland is using provisions of Quebec's unique Civil Code to buttress its long held argument that Quebec has short changed the economically stressed province on the power agreement and wants to continue to do so.

"The gross inequity of this agreement cannot be denied", Premier Danny Williams said in a statement yesterday to the province's House of Assembly. "For example, last year we have estimated that Hydro Quebec reaped profits from the Upper Churchill Falls contract of approximately $1.7 billion, while Newfoundland and Labrador received a mere $63 million." Mr. Williams said. "Power which is bought from our province for a quarter of a cent per kilowatt hour is then resold by Hydro Quebec for up to 36 times the price they pay for it."

We have a very legitimate and compelling legal argument.

Yesterday, Ed Martin, president of Churchill Falls (Labrador) Corp. and of utility Nalcor Energy, said he had sent a letter to Hydro-Quebec CEO Thierry Vandal requesting that his company renegotiate the pricing terms for the remainder of the 1969 contract "to establish a fair and equitable return to both CF(L)Co and Hydro Quebec for the future."

The present purchase price under the contract is one quarter of one cent per kw/h and the renewal contract fixes the purchase price at one-fifth of one cent for the 25 year period beginning in 2016, he said. This will mean that, for the remaining 32 years of the power contract, Upper Churchill power will be sold to Hydro Quebec for less than 5% of its recent commercial value. This permits virtually no return to Churchill Falls (Labrador) and its shareholders for the next 32 years, Mr. Martin's statement said.

Mr. Williams told the provincial legislature that "a very legitimate and compelling legal argument" has been discovered that will require Quebec to renegotiate the deal. "Under Quebec's own civil code, there is an obligation imposed by law for parties to act in good faith in all legal relationships, including the negotiation and ongoing performance of contracts." he told the house.

"It is a very important and fundamental underpinning of the Quebec civil code, and one we feel is very relevant to the 1969 Upper Churchill contract. After many, many months of research and having received firm legal opinions from some of the most eminent and brilliant legal minds in Quebec, our Department of Justice informed CF(L)Co of our legal opinion." Hydro Quebec has been asked to reply to Newfoundland and Labrador's request to commence negotiations by 15 Jan 2010.

Proposed Sale of New Brunswick Power Corp

From the National Post 2010/02/27 by Shawn McCarthy, Ottawa

Voters need to be sold on NB Power sale

The New Brunswick government will take another crack rt selling sceptical voters on he benefits of the $3.2 billion sale of its power system to Hydro-Quebec, delaying the signing of the deal until it has held televised hearings on it.

New Brunswick Energy Minister Jack Keir said the government is still on track to complete a final agreement with Quebec by the end of March, and will then submit it to the legislature for scrutiny. While he insisted there is growing support for the deal, Mr. Keir acknowledged that many voters want more information, and said the hearings could provide valuable input for regulatory policies that remain in provincial hands. I think it's a mixed bag - a lot of folks favour the deal but some don't understand the benefits and why we're doing what we're doing," he said in an interview.

After proposing to sell all of New Brunswick Power to Hydro-Quebec last fall, Premier Shawn Graham scaled back the ambition, announcing a deal last month that would sell virtually all of the utility's generating assets but keep its transmission and distribution operations.

Donald Savoie, a political scientist at University of Moncton, said the government has fumbled the political selling of the New Brunswick Power deal from the outset, and will have a tough time bringing voters on side. Mr. Savoie said the Graham government never communicated the seriousness of New Brunswick Power's financial problems before it dramatically unveiled the highly controversial proposed sale aimed at solving them. "It was negotiated in the dark of night and the next minute they were telling people, 'We have a problem and we have a solution,' " Mr. Savoie said. "But in New Brunswick - and elsewhere in North America - people are in no mood to be told by elites that they know what is best for you."

The Progressive Conservative opposition is demanding the government shelve the Hydro Quebec deal until Mr. Graham faces the voters in a general election in September. The hearing in the legislature "is no more than a public relations exercise," Conservative Leader David Alward said. "They've failed miserably in trying to persuade New Brunswickers that this is a good deal because New Brunswickers know better."

Security of the People

Wahabbi Muslim Culture & Beliefs

From the New World Encyclopaedia, (lightly edited and formatted) http://www.newworldencyclopedia.org/entry/Wahhabism

Wahhabism is a branch of Sunni Islam practised by those who follow the teachings of Muhammad ibn Abd-al-Wahhab, after whom the movement is named. Wahhabism is the dominant form of Sunni Islam found in Saudi Arabia, Kuwait, and Qatar, as well as some pockets of Somalia, Algeria, Palestine, and Mauritania.

The term "Wahhabi" is considered derogatory and rarely used by the people it is said to describe, who prefer to call themselves followers of Salafism ("Monotheism"). For them, Wahhabism / Salafism is not a school of thought within Islam, but rather is Islam itself. Thus, Wahhabis see themselves as adherents of the true, authentic Islam, the so called original Islam that existed in the time of the Prophet. According to some scholars, Wahhabism is properly seen as a reform movement within Islam, rather than a sect.

Wahhabis argue that the rest of the Muslim community should emulate their "proper" view of Islam. Consequently, Wahhabism holds in contempt any deviations in belief and practice found in other Muslim communities and the movement spurns Bid'ah, which refers to any innovation separate from the doctrines and practices set out by the Qur'an. Wahhabis are particularly vehement towards the Islamic mystics, the Sufis, for their attempts to experience Allah personally rather than through strict adherence to Islamic law.

Wahabbi History

Muhammad ibn Abd-al-Wahhab (1703–1792 CE) was born in the central Arabian region of NAD that would eventually become known as Saudi Arabia. Little is known about his early life other than that he was clearly influenced by the works of Ibn Taymiyyah, the fourteenth century Hanbali theologian. Ibn Taymiyya endorsed the Hanbali school of Sharia (Islamic law), one of four great schools in Sunni Islam. This school was named after Ibn Hanbal (780–855 CE), who espoused a literal interpretation of Sharia.

Ibn Taymiyyah also put great emphasis on the societal values of solidarity and justice. He condemned Islamic mystics, Sufis, for straying away from the path of doctrines and rituals set out in the Qur'an. The message of Ibn Taymiyyah would become much more radicalized in the teachings of Ibn Abd al-Wahhab who was also devoted literal and critical interpretations of the Qur'an.

Following extensive travels through the Middle East in his early adulthood, Ibn Abd al-Wahhab returned to NAD to announce that Muslims everywhere should surrender to his vision of the authentic Islam as practised during Prophet Muhammad's time. His preaching can be summarized into three points:

- firstly, ritual action is more important than intentions;
- secondly, Muslims should not revere the dead; and
- finally, Muslims should not make intercessory prayers to God through the Prophet or saints, and should oppose any thought or action that mars the oneness of God.

As a result, Ibn Abd al-Wahhab condemned honouring anyone other than Allah as idolatry, including the Prophet Muhammad. He abhorred the practice of reciting blessings on the Prophet during congregational prayers. Ibn Abd al-Wahhab fought all forms of worship to the Prophet, the pilgrims' practice of making hajj to visit the Prophet's tomb, the celebration of the Prophet's birthday, and the inscription of the Prophet's name in mosques.

Wahhabis explain their opposition to the traditional praise of the Prophet by saying this praise renders a human to God like status. They compare Muslims' praise of the Prophet to the Christian worship of Jesus, which is rejected by Muslims who see it as adding "partners" to God and destroying monotheistic belief in God's unity. However, anti-Wahhabi scholars point out that one cannot be a Muslim without honouring the Prophet, as the Muslim profession of faith and the call to prayer include two parts: "I affirm there is no God but Allah; and I affirm Muhammad is the Prophet of God."

Ibn Abd al-Wahhab proceeded to take shocking actions to reform the faith. He ordered that graves of Muslim saints be dug up and scattered or even turned into latrines. He ordered the burning of books, saying the Qur'an offered more than enough reading material. He also condemned music, claiming that it led people to forget God and give themselves to sin. In contrast, the mystical Sufis used music as a way of giving themselves to the consciousness of God.

While some Muslims see Ibn Abd al-Wahhab as one of many Muslim reformers at the time led by a sense of duty to preach and correct what he saw as immoral and incorrect practices, the majority of Islamic scholars did not support him and argued that his behaviour went against the Qur'an and the four schools of Islam. Moreover, his brother complained that he was trying to add another pillar to the five pillars of Islam; the infallibility of Ibn Abd al-Wahhab.

Ibn Abd al-Wahhab responded by denouncing his detractors as idolater and apostates, and urged people to abandon the four traditional schools to follow him. He openly stated his belief that all Muslims had fallen into disbelief, and that if they did not follow the path of redemption he had laid out, they should be killed, their women kin beaten, and their possessions taken from them. He further believed the Shias, Sufis, and other supposedly unorthodox Muslims should be extinguished, and that all other faiths should be humiliated and destroyed. It has been suggested that Wahhabi doctrine set the stage for the rise of Islamic fundamentalism.

In 1744, Ibn Abd al-Wahhab sought refuge in the village of Dariyah. This district was ruled by the rebel Muhammad ibn Sa'ud and his family, Al Sa'ud, which was responsible for organized banditry within NAD. The family ruled Dariyah according to its own whims and the village was a place of lawlessness when Ibn Abd al-Wahhab settled there. In 1747, he made a power sharing agreement with the family; he would become Dariyah's religious authority, while the Al Sa'ud family would be responsible for the village's political leadership.

The Al Sa'ud family also benefited from the pact, as the Wahhabi movement and its extreme religious fervour helped to legitimize their rule. The fusion of religious and political control would come to represent the modern Saudi Arabia, as well as mark the break between the Islam of the past, in which traditional Muslim scholars focussed on inward contemplation as opposed to focussing on gaining global and political power. With this new power arrangement in place, Ibn Abd al-Wahhab and his followers urged a "jihad," or the struggle to promote the faith, against other Muslims, and thus, the Wahhabis began a blood soaked campaign for expansion and domination. Ibn Abdul-Wahhab's views were opposed to the mainstream Muslim scholars of Mecca and Medina of that time. For example, he called intermediation of Muhammad an act of polytheism. Ibn Abdul-Wahhab went so far as to declare jihad against Muslims who practised so-called acts of polytheism. By 1788, the Wahhab / Sa'ud alliance controlled most of the Arabian peninsula.

In 1801, the Wahhabis began a campaign to gain control over the two holy cities of Islam. They raided Mecca and Medina and stole holy books, works of art, and other gifts the city had accumulated over the last thousand years. While they controlled the Two Holy Places, they imposed Wahhabism upon the populace, destroyed shrines and cemeteries, closed off entrance to the holy city to Ottoman pilgrims, barred pilgrims from performing the hajj, and murdered respected citizens in both holy cities.

Through the 1820s to the 1860s, the Wahhabis launched attacks upon the Ottoman empire, urged on by Great Britain, which was eager to see the collapse of the Turkish empire and the distribution of its overseas possessions.

The Wahhabis' power grew and shrank by turns throughout the century, until 1901, when the latest representative of the Al Sa'ud and Wahhabi alliance decided to try and re-seize control over the two holy cities, Mecca and Medina. Abdul-Aziz Ibn Abdur-Rahman Ibn Muhammad Al Sa'ud journeyed to Riyadh, where he murdered the city's ruler and took over control of the country. Over the next twenty-five years, he went on to unify the Arabian peninsula through force. Wahhabism was the only official faith sanctioned in the state that would come to be formed there. To this day, no other religious establishment is allowed in Saudi Arabia.

Wahabbi Beliefs

Wahhabi theology treats the Qur'an and Hadith as the supreme texts, interpreted according to the first three generations of Islam and further explained by the commentaries of Muhammad ibn Abd-al-Wahhab. His book called Kitab al-Tawhid (Book of Monotheism), and the works of the earlier scholar Ibn Taymiyya (1263–1328) are fundamental to Wahabism.

Wahhabis see their role as restoring Islam from what they perceive to be polytheism and innovations, superstitions, deviations, heresies and idolatries. There are many practices that they believe are contrary to Islam, such as:

- Listening to music in praise of Muhammad
- Praying to God while visiting tombs (praying near Muhammad's tomb is also considered polytheism by the Wahhabis)
- Blindly following any madhhabs (schools of thought) of Islamic jurisprudence in their legal expertise, "except for one who is under necessity and can not reach the Sunnah".
- Using non-literal explanations of God's attributes exclusively in preference to literal.
- Celebrating the Mawlid (birthday of Muhammad)

- Supposed or actual innovations (bid'ah) in matters of religion (for example, new supplementary methods of worship or laws not sanctioned by the Qur'an or Sunnah)

Wahhabism also denounces "the practice of unthinking adherence to the interpretations of scholars and the blind acceptance of practices that were passed on within the family or tribe. Muhammad ibn Abd-al-Wahhab believed in the responsibility of the individual Muslim to learn and obey the divine commands as they were revealed in the Quran and in the hadith."

Wahhabism in the 20th century and beyond

In 1924, the al-Saud dynasty (who were influenced by the teachings of Abdul Wahhab) conquered Mecca and Medina, the Muslim holy cities. This gave them control of the Hajj, the annual pilgrimage, and the opportunity to preach their version of Islam to the assembled pilgrims. However, Wahhabism was a minor current within Islam until the discovery of oil in Arabia, in 1938. Vast oil revenues gave an immense impetus to the spread of conservative Islamic theology.

Wahhabi ideas began to spread to other countries through pilgrims who came to the Hajj and returned to their countries of origin. This theology spread into Oman during the eighteenth century where it played a role in the internal disputes and succession struggles of the country. However, many of the traditional mullahs are not quietly accepting the Wahhabi foray into their countries; they are fiercely defending the tribal Islam rooted in their communities. Deference for elders is of utmost importance in tribal communities and traditional mullahs point out that Wahhabis are guilty of the utmost disrespect because they do not follow the commentaries of the faith's learned scholars. These mullahs paint the Wahhabis as foreigners who sacrificed the true vision of Islam for money.

These mullahs and other Muslim preachers urge their followers to accept the path of the "Greater Jihad." Wahhabi clerics preach the lesser jihad of war, death and blood, citing the Qur'an's description of war against unbelievers to justify the killing of less observant Muslims and to an even greater extent, non-Muslims. However, this path of jihad has long been abandoned by the majority of Muslims in favour of the "Greater Jihad," the struggle to come closer to Allah through piety and devotion.

While all of Islam accepts the unity of God and monotheism, not all of Islam recognizes the need for the religion to become one monolithic, static force, preserving the same beliefs and practices throughout its history. Muslim preachers and followers across the world, from Saudi Arabia to Iran to Afghanistan to America, accept in their religion a diversity of interpretations and expression of faith; this diversity should continue to hold in the face of opposition, murder and terror in the cloak of orthodoxy.

Wahhabi doctrine continues to be firmly rooted within the kingdom of Saudi Arabia today. All students are taught religion from the beginning of primary school, with the curriculum based only on Wahhabism, and libraries consist exclusively of Wahhabi texts. The Wahhabi clerics issue strict guidelines for sex, prohibit keeping pet dogs, prohibit women's attendance at funerals, and insist that women veil themselves.

Influence on Other Groups

The formation of the Egyptian Muslim Brotherhood was likely influenced by the Wahhabis, since they also claimed to be purifying and restoring Islam. Indeed, when the Muslim Brotherhood was banned in various Middle Eastern countries, Saudi Arabia gave refuge to Brotherhood exiles. However, Salafis in Saudi Arabia reject the Muslim Brotherhood and other ideas they believe contravene Salafist theology.

There are also those who argue that Saudi promotion of Wahhabism as part of a Sunni-Shi'a rivalry contributed to the development of the religious ideology of al-Qaeda. Islamist groups such as the Taliban and al-Qaeda have been heavily influenced by Wahhabi though. However, Mattson points out that Saudi scholars of Wahhabism have denounced terrorism. Ultimately, however, its influence lessened over time despite early success. Its alliance with the House of Saud became strained after the September 11, 2001 attacks and suicide bombings in Riyadh in May, 2003.

Immigration Guidebook & Farzana Hassan

News Agencies 2009/11/13

From Euro-Islam.info (lightly edited and formatted)
http://www.euro-islam.info/2009/11/13/new-guide-for-canadian-immigrants-denounces-%E2%80%9Chonor-killings%E2%80%9D-and-calls-for-gender-equity/

New guide for Canadian immigrants denounces "honour killings" and calls for gender equity

The new document, which will be the citizenship study guide for the 250,000 immigrants who arrive in Canada each year, thus instantly becomes one of the country's most widely read and potentially influential pieces of writing.

Canada's revamped citizenship guide warns newcomers that "barbaric cultural practices" such as honour killings will not be tolerated, marking a stronger tone against importing beliefs that clash with Canadian values. "In Canada, men and women are equal under the law," the document says. "Canada's openness and generosity do not extend to barbaric cultural practices that tolerate spousal abuse, 'honour killings,' female genital mutilation or other gender based violence. Those guilty of these crimes are severely punished under Canada's criminal laws." No longer will new Canadians be told that Canada is strictly a nation of peacekeepers, for example. The new guide places a much greater emphasis on Canada's military history, from the Great War to the present day. It also tackles other issues of historical significance, from Confederation to Quebec's separatist movement.

The guide, released yesterday and called "Discover Canada: The Rights and Responsibilities of Canadian Citizenship", is the first of its kind to explicitly denounce violence in the name of family honour, a crime in the headlines just this week after an Ottawa man was sentenced to a year in jail for threatening violence against his daughter. While honour killings remain relatively rare in Canada, several high profile cases have drawn attention to the issue. Even the use of the term "honour killings" has stirred debate, as critics of the wording say it implies the practice is accepted by certain religions when, in fact, it is not.

The inclusion of honour killings and spousal abuse in the guide reminded some onlookers of the tension over reasonable accommodation, a concept that came to a boiling point in Herouxville, Quebec. Farzana Hassan, spokeswoman for the Muslim Canadian Congress, said there is nothing controversial about the statement in the new guide, adding that it is a long overdue step toward tackling a cultural practice that does not jibe with Canadian values. Antonia Maioni, director of the McGill Institute for the Study of Canada, said the new guide fits with a Conservative strategy to redefine itself with regard to immigration, an issue that historically has been closely linked with the Liberal Party.

Honour Killings in Canada 2009

Canwest News Service 2009/07/23 By Shannon Proudfoot,

'Honour killings' of females on rise in Canada: Expert

As many as 5,000 women and girls lose their lives, most at the hands of family members in "honour killings", around the world each year according to the United Nations.

Up to a dozen have died for the same reason in Canada in the last decade, and it's happening more often, says Amin Muhammad, a psychiatrist who studies honour killings at Memorial University in Newfoundland.

"There are a number of organizations which don't accept the idea of honour killing; they say it's a Western propagated myth by the media. But that's not true," he says. "Honour killings are there, and we should acknowledge it, and Canada should take it seriously."

Kingston, Ontario, police are now investigating that as a motive in the deaths of three teenage sisters and an older female relative who were found in a car submerged in the Rideau Canal in Kingston on June 30. The girls' mother, father and brother were arrested on Wednesday and charged with first degree murder.

"In our Canadian society, we value the cultural values of everyone that makes up this great country, and some of us have different core beliefs, different family values, different sets of rules," Kingston Police Chief Stephen Tanner said at a news conference on Thursday. "Certainly, these individuals, in particular the three teenagers, were Canadian teenagers who had all the freedom and rights of expression of all Canadians."

He added that he'd received an email from an extended family member of the girls, suggesting honour killing was to blame for their deaths.

Honour killings can be sparked by a woman talking to a man, having a boyfriend, wearing makeup or revealing clothing, or even seeking a divorce, says Diana Nammi, founder of the London based International Campaign Against Honour Killings. Nammi, originally from Iran, says children of immigrants who grow up in western nations take those freedoms for granted, which can throw them into conflict with their parents' rigid standards.

"When people are moving to another country, they leave everything they have, all their possessions, behind. But what they can bring with them is what they believe, their culture, their traditions, their religion," she says. "Unfortunately, they are choosing to show the worst part of that, and the worst and criminal part of that is controlling women."

One of the earliest honour killings involving a Canadian occurred in

2000, when Maple Ridge, BC, resident Jaswinder Sidhu was murdered in India in what police called a contract killing, after she married a man she met while travelling.

In 2003, Amandeep Atwal, 17, died after her father stabbed her 17 times. The Kitimat, BC, teen had been secretly seeing a boyfriend.

Sixteen year old Aqsa Parvez's father and brother are currently awaiting trial for her strangulation death in 2007, and friends said the Brampton, Ontario teen had been clashing with her family over her refusal to wear the hijab.

In May, an Ottawa man was sentenced to life in prison for killing his sister, Khatera Sadiqi, 20, and her fiancé.

"We cannot say there's a huge number of cases, but now the cases are increasing, and very soon we'll have a problem in Canada," says Muhammad. Men occasionally die in honour killings, he says, but young women are almost always the victims in western countries.

Honour killing is most prevalent in nations with large Muslim populations, but Aysan Sev'er, a professor of sociology at University of Toronto, Scarborough and author of an upcoming book on the subject, says there's nothing in Islam that sanctions the practice. Some perpetrators use religion as a "cloak" she says, but honour killing is about patriarchy, not religion.

"A few women are sacrificed to terrorize all women, to push them into submission, where they are not in the position to defend themselves or even their daughters or sisters," Sev'er says. It's wrong-headed to blame particular cultures or further stereotype the Middle East, she emphasizes, but Canada cannot overlook the motivation for these "heinous crimes." "In Canada, we have been extremely culturally sensitive, and that's a good thing," she says. "But in this particular case, we may have pushed the pendulum a little to the other side, in the sense that there are cultural components in these types of crimes which we cannot ignore."

Honour Killings & Domestic Abuse

From The Phyllis Chesler Organization: lightly edited and formatted http://www.phyllis-chesler.com/201/honor-killings-the-islamic-connection

Honour Killings: The Islamic Connection by Phyllis Chesler
November 13, 2008

She told her friends that her father was going to kill her. She ran away, stayed at a shelter, stayed with friends. She was lured back home by honeyed sentences. Her family could not sleep without her. Late last year, on December 10th, in Toronto, sixteen year-old Aqsa Parvez's father. Mohammed, and her brother, Waqas, collaborated in her murder. Aqsa's crime? She refused to wear hijab, she was becoming too assimilated. Mohammed and Waqas Parvez are currently in jail awaiting trial.

Known honour killings first arrived in North America in 1989 when Palestina Isa was murdered. Her father, a Palestinian terrorist, and her mother both slaughtered their hard working and much abused 16 year old daughter Palestina. Her crime? She was becoming too "American", too independent, too academically ambitious, and she had a boy friend, who was African American. Her mother held her down and her father butchered her with tremendous animal ferocity.

On January 1st of this year, Yasser Said shot his daughters Sarah and Amina to death in Dallas and probably escaped back to Egypt. Like Palestina, they were teenagers (aged 17 and 18). Their mother collaborated in their murder by luring them back home to their deaths. The FBI has been hunting for Said and recently featured him on their Ten Most Wanted List. They described Said as having committed an "honour killing."

For reasons that remain unclear, within a week, the FBI removed that description. Some say that the Bureau caved into Islamist pressure.

Others, myself included, suggest that it would not necessarily help them capture Said if he were seen as a "Muslim hero," who was being persecuted because he is a Muslim. After Parvez was honour killed, Mohammed Elmasry, of the Canadian Islamic Congress, was quoted as saying: "I don't want the public to think that this is an Islamic issue or an immigrant issue. It is a teenager issue."

Islamists insist that honour killings have nothing to do with Islam. They say that it is a "cultural" but not an "Islamic" crime. They are wrong. Islamists also say that honour murders are the same as domestic violence. All men, all religions engage in it. Wrong. Most honour killings are committed by Muslims who believe that what they are doing is a sacred, religious act. They may misunderstand the Qu'ran but as yet, no mullah or imam has stood up in the global, public square to condemn such murders as dishonourable and anti-Islamic. No fatwa has ever been issued against a Muslim honour killer.

In terms of domestic violence, western style domestic batterers rarely kill their daughters. That is a characteristic of an honour killing. And, western style domestic batterers act alone when they kill their adult partners. An honour killing is a collaborative act between several or many members of the same family. It is unfortunate, even shameful, but not surprising that Islamists seek to cover up this sin against Muslim girls and women by attacking those who would dare expose it as "Islamophobes." We cannot afford to fall for this deception. A crime is a crime. The shame resides in the criminal, not in his victim. The shame will become ours if we justify the brutal sacrifice of Muslim girls and women in order to remain multi-culturally and politically correct.

Canada's Immigration Guide & Honour Killings

From the National Post 2009/11/17 by Barbara Kay

Last week the Post published excerpts from the new guidebook issued by Citizenship and Immigration Canada, *"Discover Canada: The Rights and Responsibilities of Citizenship"*.

I was asked by a radio talk show host what difference the guidebook would make in terms of my own writing on issues the new text raised, especially the section on gender relations, one of my niche topics. I replied that I would still be saying exactly what I have always said, but now that the government's official position is the same as mine, I won't have to feel defensive anymore. I was thinking specifically of the passage in the section "The Equality of Women and Men" (note the word order) where the guidebook says: "Canada's openness and generosity do not extend to barbaric cultural practices that tolerate spousal abuse, 'honour killings', or other gender based violence."

Barbaric? Barbaric? That's a negative judgment of other people's cultural practices. We may have arrived at a watershed moment in the history of multiculturalism. Indeed, this may be our official policy of multiculturalism's "tear down this wall" moment. It may soon be possible to say that multiculturalism has failed as a national policy without being labelled a racist.

Good on Jason Kenney for pointing out this particular naked emperor. For too long violence in the West directed against girls and women from honour/shame societies by their male relatives, often with the complicity of their female relatives, has been reflexively lumped in with all domestic violence (DV). The refusal to distinguish between the two types of violence is championed by gender ideologues who can't bear the idea that some forms of violence against women are a culturally imposed pathology and not, as they would prefer, a tragic but predictable example of the inherently misogynistic and controlling instincts of all men. Ideologues are abetted in this wilful sabotage of common sense by ethnic associations who at best ignore the abuse and at worst deflect criticism from their cultural "values" by insisting such abuse is normative.

When 16-year-old Aqsa Parvez was allegedly murdered by her father in Mississauga, Ont., reportedly in part for not wearing a hijab, Mohamed Elmasry of the Canadian Islamic Congress brushed off the tragedy with a stunningly cynical dumbing down of its horror: "I don't want the public to think that this is an Islamic issue or an immigrant issue. It is a teenager issue."

Many honour killings are passed off to authorities as suicides or accidents

But Elmasry is right about one thing: Honour killing is largely (about 90%), but not solely, a practice of Muslim societies. Amandeep Atwal, 17, of British Columbia, was stabbed 11 times by her father, Rajinder Singh Atwal, for refusing to end a relationship with a non-Sikh boyfriend. Hindus and even Christians coming from South Asian cultures kill girls and women for reasons of family or community "honour." It's difficult to ascertain numbers: many honour killings are passed off by the victims' families to authorities as suicide or accidents.

While honour killings are a minority of all domestic killings, they are also a distinct phenomenon. Lenore Walker, author of The Battered Woman Syndrome (2000), notes the difference between the victim-perpetrator in honour killings and those in Western society. "In ordinary domestic violence involving Westerners, it is rare for brothers to kill sisters or for male cousins to kill female cousins. And while child abuse occurs in which fathers may kill infants and children, it is very rare for Western fathers to kill teenage daughters."

In the West it is far more typical for fathers who disapprove of their daughters' lifestyle or behaviour to shun them or disassociate from them. There are a whole slew of differences besides these between honour killing and normative domestic violence.

- Honour killings target mostly daughters; normal domestic violence is bilateral between intimate adult partners.
- Honour killings are carefully planned; domestic violence is spontaneous.
- Honour killings involve complicity with family members; domestic violence is a private affair.
- Honour killing is motivated by perceived family humiliation; domestic violence is not about honour: Domestic violence springs from personal psychological problems.

- Honour killings are perpetrated with extreme ferocity (rape, burning, stoning, hacking, even burying alive); domestic violence is hastily executed - by gun, knife or blunt object.
- Most important: Honour killings elicit approval in their communities; domestic violence elicits disgust.

Perhaps now that the government has exposed the obvious fact that systemic, socially approved male violence against women is not a genetic but a cultural pathology, we can begin to address it seriously and help the thousands of immigrant women who are kept in ignorance of their rights and the thousands of immigrant men who are oblivious of their culpability. But we must do more than educate them. Because even when these brainwashed women become aware they have rights, they are usually too frightened of retribution for their perceived rebelliousness, and justifiably so, to challenge the collective dogmas of their kinship groups.

This guidebook is a great first step. The next step should be to extend meaningful outreach and protection to women inside these communities. I would hope that feminists would applaud Jason Kenney's courage in admitting an unpleasant truth, and support him loudly and clearly. If they don't, they can hardly call themselves feminists.

Muslims Raping Daughters-in-law

From Faithfreedom.org: (lightly edited and formatted)
http://www.faithfreedom.org/islam/raping-daughters-law-following-holy-tradition-prophet

Following Holy Tradition of the Prophet
by Dr Radhasyam Brahmachari 2009/12/17

A Recent Incident

On December 9, 2009, a leading Bengali daily in Kolkata reported that Mukhtar Sheikh of the village of Dangrail in the district of

Murshidabad, West Bengal, raped his newly married daughter-in-law Amina (name changed) on November 24, while his son Salam Sheikh was away. Salam, a mason, has to stay away occasionally from home according to demand of his job. On the fateful day, he went to his construction site at Asansol and Mukhtar utilized the opportunity and raped Salam's wife. When Salam returned home, he advised his wife to hush up the matter. He also locked her in a room so that she might not go outdoors and tell the story to outsiders.

After a few days, when Salam set Amina free, she immediately informed the incident to her father Latifur Sheikh of the nearby village. Latifur took her to the nearest police station and submitted a written complaint against Mukhtar, Mukhtar's wife, and Salam. Mukhtar and Salam were arrested immediately while Amiron Bibi was found absconding. On December 8, the culprits were produced in the Jangipur Sub-divisional Court and were remanded in police custody for 14 days.

The report also said the marriage of Salam and Amina took place only six months ago. So far, Latifur was happy with the marriage of his daughter to Salam, but the rape incident upset him. The investigating police officer told reporters that, in 2005, when the entire nation was tumultuous with the raping of Imrana by her father-in-law in the Charthwala village in Uttar Pradesh (see below), a similar incident happened in the village of Belgharia in the Sagardighi area of Murshidabad district. In 2006, a similar incident took place in the Baliarghati village of the Suti area of Murshidabad. In the Baliarghati incident, the matter was settled by a kangaroo court of local clerics, while the incident in the Beigharia is still to be decided in the court of law. These incidents make it quite clear that the raping of daughters-in-law by their fathers-in-law is a regular occurrence in Muslim society and that most of these cases are either hushed up or settled by the local clerics. Cases that appear in the media are only the tip of the iceberg. A few such incidents that surfaced in public are narrated below.

A few other incidents

On December 9, 2007, police arrested Mortaza Ali—a resident of the Dakshinberia village, near Baduria in the North 24 Pargana district of West Bengal and a local leader of the Communist Party of India, Marxist (CPIM)—on charges of raping his 21 year old daughter in law Fatima Bibi (name changed), wife of his son Joirul Islam. He was remanded in judicial custody for two weeks, after being produced before the Basirhat sub-divisional magistrate's court on December 10. The victim Fatima Bibi had reported the rape to police on 15 November, which occurred on 8 November when she was alone at her residence. According to police, culprit had allegedly threatened the victim of dire consequences if she dared to disclose the incident to anyone. But Fatima Bibi confided the incident to her husband Joirul Islam and urged him to accompany her to the police station. But Joirul advised her to keep mum and not to inform police. But Fatima Bibi somehow managed to go to her parents' house in the Jhunjhunia village near Habra, North 24 Parganas district and with her father's assistance, finally succeeded to lodge a complaint with the police on 15 November.

In the same year, on 10 December, Rojina Bibi (name changed), a housewife of the Kirdoli village in the Sikar district of Rajasthan alleged that Nizamu Khan, her father in law, raped her and killed her newborn baby. A case was subsequently registered with the police. Rojina Bibi, 22, had moved to her husband's house in Kirdoli village after her marriage five years earlier. Some 16 months before the rape, her husband left for Dubai with a job. Rojina Bibi also alleged that Nizamu had threatened her to keep mum or face dire consequence.

According to another press report in the Bengali daily Ananda Bazar Patrika, on 1 October, 2007, Abu Hossein Ghazi, resident of the Najahari village under the Bishnupur police station, South 24 Parganas district, West Bengal, was arrested for molesting his daughter in law. The victim, in her written complaint, alleged that her husband was residing in some other place to attend his job, when her father in law molested and raped her.

The story of a lone fighter: Aleya Bibi

The Ananda Bazar Patrika on 4 October, 2007, reported another case, in which a rapist, named Gedu Shaikh of the district of Maldah, West Bengal, was sentenced to 10 years rigorous imprisonment for raping his daughter in law Aleya Bibi. The rapist and the victim fought a legal battle against the will of her relatives and local clerics. The local kangaroo court, presided over by clerics, offered her 2 bighas of land and 50 thousand rupees, as compensation, and she withdraw the case against her father in law. But Aleya refused. Her husband Shamirul Shaikh also sided with his father and threatened her with a divorce. But all these odds failed to dampen the spirit of Aleya Bibi.

Aleya Bibi told reporters that she fought the legal battle not only for herself but also for all housewives who are falling victim to lust of their fathers in law. She asserted that the judgment would certainly scare offenders, who would think twice before raping their daughters in law. She also said: "It is better to leave a husband who sides with the rapist of his wife."

She told the reporters that her husband was living in a neighbouring state to attend his job and she was living with other relatives of the family. On April 2, 2006, all the members of the family went to attend a marriage party in a nearby village, leaving her under the care of her father in law, providing him an opportunity to rape and molest her.

Rape and cruel murder of Rihana Bibi

The most gruesome incident of raping daughters in laws by Muslims was raping and killing of Rihana Bibi (25), wife of Abdur Rahman Mandal, by her father in law Abdur Rezzak Mandal, a resident of Panigobra village under the Basirhat police station in the North 24-Parganas district of West Bengal. The news of rape and murder of Rihana appeared in leading dailies of Kolkata on Friday, 1 August, 2007. On July 30 night, Rihana was murdered by Abdur Rezak and Abdur Rahman before the eyes of 7 year old Ranuara Khatun and 5 year old Omar, daughter and son of Rihana. According to neighbours,

Abdur Rezzak had raped Rihana Bibi for quite a long time, under the threat of life. A few years earlier, Abdur Rezzak had confessed his guilt before a kangaroo court of village elders and clerics. Whenever Rihana complained to her husband Abdur Rahman, he held her responsible.

Ranuara and Omar told police that on the night of the murder incident, when Abdur Rezzak was committing sexual assault on Rihana, Abdur Rahman appeared on the scene. Then Abdur Rahman started stabbing her indiscriminately with a sharp weapon, while Abdur Rezzak held Rihana by her hands and neck. As the murder incident occurred, Ranuara and Omar rushed out and tried to arouse sleeping neighbours, but no one responded. When returned home, they found Rihana lying in a pool of blood, while their father, grandfather and grandmother had fled.

Rihana Khatun was married to Abdur Rahman Mandal, a day labourer for about 9 years. Liaqat Biswas, uncle of Rihana, told investigating officers: "We were aware of the fact that Rihana's father in law used to rape her regularly. But after the court of arbitration, the recurrence of the crime came down considerably. But this time, they have killed the unfortunate girl by stabbing her with a dagger, mutilated one of her breasts and introduced an iron rod into her private part."

Muslim Populations in Europe

From The Brookings Institution: (lightly edited and formatted)
http://www.brookings.edu/opinions/2003/03middleeast_taspinar.aspx

The Brookings Institution, 2010/02/28
Mer. Taspinar, Nonresident Fellow, Foreign Policy

Islam may still be a faraway religion for millions of Americans. But for the Europeans it is local politics. The 15 million Muslims of the European Union (EU), up to three times as many as live in the United States, are becoming a more powerful political force than the fabled

Arab street. Europe's Muslims hail from different countries and display diverse religious tendencies, but the common denominator that links them to the Muslim world is their sympathy for Palestine and Palestinians. And unlike most of their Arab brethren, growing numbers of Europe's Muslims can vote in elections that count.

This political ascendance threatens to exacerbate existing strains within the trans-Atlantic relationship. The presence of nearly 10 million Muslims versus only 700,000 Jews in France and Germany alone helps explain why continental Europe might look at the Middle East from a different angle than does the United States. Indeed, French and German concerns about a unilateral U.S. attack on Iraq or Washington's blind support for Israel are at least partly related to nervousness about the Muslim street at home.

Whether Brussels, Berlin, Paris, or Washington like it or not, Europe's Muslim constituencies are likely to become an even more vocal foreign policy lobby. Two trends are empowering Europe's Muslim street: demographics and opportunities for full citizenship.

It's worth remembering that Europe's Muslim population is an unintended consequence of actions taken nearly a half century ago. During the postwar labour shortage in the 1950s and 1960s, Turks, Algerians, Moroccans, Tunisians, and Pakistanis were called to help spur Europe's economic recovery. No host country expected these 'guest workers,' *(Gastarbeiter)* as the Germans called them with characteristic frankness, to overstay their welcome. Like all good guests, they were supposed to leave, preferably when the recession hit and the party was over in the 1970s. They didn't. Instead, their families joined them, and new generations of European Turks, Algerians, Moroccans, Tunisians, and Pakistanis were born.

More are on the way. Today, the Muslim birth rate in Europe is three times higher than the non-Muslim one. If current trends continue, the Muslim population of Europe will nearly double by 2015, while the non-Muslim population will shrink by 3.5 percent.

A parallel process of Muslim enfranchisement is accompanying this population surge. Nearly half of the 5 million to 7 million Muslims in France are already French citizens. The situation is similar for most of the 2 million Muslims in Great Britain, where they have established 1,600 mosques (Switzerland has four mosques, and has banned minarets). Most recently, in 2000, Germany joined the countries where citizenship is granted according to birthplace instead of ancestry. The new German citizenship laws added already a half million voters to the rolls and have opened the road to citizenship to all other Muslims in Germany. With currently 160,000 new Muslim citizens a year, the number of voters might total 3 million in the next decade.

In Germany and elsewhere in Europe, a Muslim swing vote is already having a critical impact. Consider the electoral push that newly enfranchised German Turks gave to Germany's incumbent Social Democrat (SPD) Green coalition in last September's down to the wire election. These Muslim Germans punished the anti-immigrant Christian Democrats, who oppose Turkey's membership to the EU. And they expressed their gratitude for efforts by the SPD Green coalition to change the archaic laws of German citizenship. The bad news for the German Christian Democrats is that in the next general elections in 2006, roughly 1 million German Turks will be eager to cast their votes.

A big boost to the organizational capacity of Muslims in Europe came recently from France, home to Europe's largest Muslim community. The country's diverse Muslim community is now represented by a unified French Council of the Islamic Faith, a potential boon to its lobbying clout. French Muslims have also gained higher political visibility with the inclusion in Prime Minister Jean-Pierre Raffarin's government of two cabinet members of North African origin.

Armed with the power of the vote and quickly learning the mechanics of lobbying, the Muslim street in Europe is on its way to having more political weight than the Arab street of Egypt or Saudi Arabia. But the attacks of September 11 have cast the growing influence of European Muslims in a more ominous light. Although the overwhelming majority of Muslims living in Europe (or, for that matter, the United States) are peaceful and law abiding, many European governments worry under their breath about the role of some European Muslims in past and future terrorist attacks, a concern stoked by the discovery of al Qaeda cells in Germany, France, Italy, and Britain. Given these suspicions and prejudices, one casualty of a major Islamic terrorist attack on European soil would likely be Europe's budding multiculturalism.

Another major concern is the relationship between Europe's Muslims and what is perceived in some quarters as Europe's growing anti-Semitism. True, continental Europeans are much more critical of Israel and generally more supportive of the Palestinian cause. Overall, Europeans have a difficult time understanding how a small country like Israel can have so much influence over the sole superpower. But only a few in the United States notice that the communities most resentful of Israel in Europe are Muslim. The perpetrators of anti-Semitic incidents in France are not right wing extremists protecting the 'French race' from Jewish contamination: The 400 or so anti-Semitic incidents documented in the country during 2001 have mostly been attributed to Muslim youth of North African origin. Such incidents tend to spike upwards during times of Israeli Palestinian trouble, further proof of the Muslim role. Economic problems such as unemployment and a lack of upward mobility also contribute to the frustration of Muslims in Europe, who often feel discriminated against.

On the positive side, demographic growth and enfranchisement are already integrating European Muslims into the political mainstream and have the potential to produce a moderate type of Euro-Islam. Yet the implications of a more vocal Muslim lobby in Europe's Middle East policy offer no good news for the United States. Home to a minuscule Jewish minority and growing Muslim masses, Europe will only get better at confronting the United States at the game of ethnic lobby influence, a small price to pay, perhaps, for the emergence of a truly multicultural Europe.

Europe's War Against Islam

From Maclean's 2010/01/18 (Lightly edited) BY Michael Petrou

Attacks on religious freedoms are going mainstream

Perhaps it is fitting that it was French President Nicolas Sarkozy who came to the defence of the Swiss, who voted in November to ban the construction of new minarets in their country. Sarkozy's father was an immigrant to France, and his mother's ancestors included Ottoman Sephardic Jews from Thessalonica. Sarkozy's father abandoned his family and refused to help them financially. Sarkozy grew up poorer than his peers and resented it. "What made me who I am now is the sum of all the humiliations suffered during childhood."

He was, in other words, something of an outsider. It wouldn't be a stretch to imagine that he might be predisposed to sympathy toward the millions of other outsiders now trying to find their place in Europe; the continent's growing Muslim population. Yet Sarkozy reacted to the Swiss vote by urging that it be respected. "Instead of condemning the Swiss out of hand, we should try to understand what they meant to express and what so many people in Europe feel, including people in France," he wrote in the French newspaper Le Monde. "Nothing would be worse than denial." He urged French Muslims, who make up four per cent of France's population and are more numerous than in any other country in Europe, not to challenge France's Christian heritage and republican values.

Sarkozy, a populist politician, was simply reflecting widespread popular discomfort about Islam in Europe. **A 2008 survey funded by the Germany Marshall Fund of the United States found that more than 50 per cent of respondents in Germany, Italy, Holland, and France believe that "Western and Muslim ways of life are irreconcilable."** Another study, by the Pew Research Center, revealed an increase in negative views toward Muslims and Jews in Europe from 2004 to 2008. (Attitudes towards Muslims and Jews in the United States improved during the same time period.)

Some sort of symbolic demonstration was likely inevitable. But the Swiss never looked like obvious candidates to launch what is arguably the most illiberal and bigoted legislation Europe has seen in years. Switzerland hasn't suffered an Islamist terror attack. And Swiss Muslims, who make up about five per cent of the population, are more integrated and upwardly mobile than Muslims elsewhere in Europe. Most Swiss Muslims come from Turkey, Albania, and the former Yugoslavia. Few are radical or even all that conservative. Women who hide their faces behind Islamic niqabs are a common sight in east London, but not in Berne.

Islam's presence isn't that visible in Swiss architecture, either. In the entire country, there are a grand total of four minarets, the steeple like spires that often adorn mosques where Muslims pray. But that was four too many for the Swiss. More than 57 per cent of participating voters approved the proposed ban, with majorities in 22 out of 26 cantons supporting the constitutional amendment.

The conservative Swiss People's Party spearheaded the referendum campaign. Their anti- immigrant public relations campaigns in the past have included posters depicting three white sheep kicking a black sheep off a Swiss flag. This time around, their posters featured a sinister woman in a black burka standing before a Swiss flag riddled with missile like minarets.

Those supporting a minaret ban pointed to a poem Turkish Prime Minister Recep Tayyip Erdogan recited more than 10 years ago that compares minarets to bayonets. But the vote wasn't really about minarets, or architectural harmony, or even, as some have suggested, the Swiss thumbing their noses at political and media elites who assured them that the responsible thing to do would be to reject the proposed ban. There are only four minarets left in Switzerland; and the Swiss People's Party printed posters featuring missile like minarets. "The minarets are an excuse," says Stefano Allievi, a sociologist at the University of Padua, "The issue is Islam."

According to Clive Church, an emeritus professor at the University of Kent, many Swiss are slow to accept foreigners. Citizenship can be denied to third generation Swiss residents, whose grandparents immigrated decades ago. There is also anger in Switzerland over the arrest in Libya of two Swiss businessmen who were detained in 2008, shortly after Geneva police arrested Libyan dictator Moammar Gadhafi's son and wife on suspicion that they beat their domestic staff. Gadhafi's son and daughter in law were quickly freed, while the Swiss businessmen were jailed for more than year before they were released on bail in November. They have since been convicted of immigration offences and sentenced to 16 month jail terms. Some Swiss anger over this affair was channelled into the movement to ban minarets.

Still, it would be wrong to portray the minaret vote as some sort of freak storm that will soon dissipate. The vote tapped into a deep well of unease. Already there are moves to build on it. Christophe Darbellay, head of Switzerland's Christian Democratic People's Party, wants a ban on separate Muslim and Jewish cemeteries. And the Swiss People's Party is planning further measures to reverse what one of its MPs describes as the Islamicization of the country. "Voters gave a strong signal to stop the claim to power by political Islam at the expense of our laws and values" Adrian Amstutz told a news agency. "Forced marriages, female circumcision, special dispensation from swimming lessons, and the burka are top of the list."

Elsewhere on the continent, the Swiss vote has intensified a debate as Europeans grapple with the fact that the demographic makeup of their countries is changing rapidly, and likely forever. Many want to halt this transformation, or at least erase its most visible manifestations.

One in four Swedes is in favour of banning the construction of more minarets. In Italy, a member of the Northern League, which is a junior partner in Prime Minister Silvio Berlusconi's coalition government, called for a vote to ban minarets modelled after the Swiss referendum.

Interior Minister Roberto Maroni, of the Northern League, says he would have "no objections." A nationwide vote may not be necessary. Allievi, the Italian sociologist, says mosques in northern Italy frequently have electricity and water cut off. The official explanation is that they have transgressed fire or zoning bylaws. "The real reason is they detest Islam," he says.

Protesters in 2006 left a severed pig's head outside a mosque being built in Tuscany. The following year, those opposed to the construction of a mosque in Padua paraded a pig around the site to "desecrate" the soil for Muslims. Roberto Calderoli, a Northern League senator, has called for a "Pig Day" to protest the construction of a mosque in Bologna.

Opposition to visible signs of Islam in Germany is rarely so explicit. Anti-mosque rallies draw more police than activists. One last year brought out a handful of anti-Islam protesters, and some 40,000 supporters. But, says, Josef Joffe, editor of the German news weekly Die Zeit, "We do this more subtly." People are unlikely to complain about the mosque itself, but rather the resulting noise or lack of parking.

In France, where a law already prevents French students from wearing" conspicuous" religious symbols at state schools, a parliamentary panel is exploring possible laws that would forbid women from wearing burqas. Sarkozy has voiced his support for such a ban. "The burka," he said, "is not a sign of religion. It is a sign of subservience. It will not be welcome on the territory of the French republic." Last month, the country's justice minister, Michele Alliot- Marie, said that men who force their wives to wear Burqas should not be granted French citizenship. "There are a certain number of basics on which we must stand firm," she said. "For instance, someone whose wife wears the full veil is someone who would not appear to be sharing the values of our country."

France's former prime minister, Jean-Pierre Raffarin, has accused the government of starting a "barroom discussion" about identity. This is probably a good thing, at least until the discussion moves from the bar to the gutter outside, where several political parties have set up camp and are seeking to exploit tensions regarding Islam's growth in Europe.

The far right National Front in France has predictably called for a referendum, but one that would extend beyond the simple issue of minarets to include immigration and the impact of religious and ethnic minorities on French society. In Holland, Geert Wilders, the platinum haired leader of the Party for Freedom, has seen his popularity soar on the strength of an unequivocal stand against Islam. Never mind minarets. He wants to ban the Quran.

The British National Party, a far right organization that is only now moving toward allowing non-white members (because Britain's Human Rights Commission threatened legal action), today focuses its vitriol almost exclusively against Muslims. "To go anywhere near inciting racial hatred is grotesquely unfair because no one can change how they are born," BNP chairman Nick Griffin has said. "On the other hand, to criticize a religion in much stronger terms, even if it does cross the line imposed by law, I think is entirely justifiable, because everybody has the choice to change a religion if it's bad."

Griffin describes Islam as "a wicked, vicious faith" and "a cancer eating away at our freedoms and our democracy and rights for our women." This June, the BNP won two seats in the European Parliament. The party is poised to accept its first non-white member, Rajinder Singh, a septuagenarian Sikh who hates Muslims. "He is perhaps the kind of immigrant you want, if you are going to have them," a BNP spokesman says.

At issue is a question of national identity, what it means to be Dutch, or French, or German, or Italian. "The big problem in Europe is that the way we create identities is unlike how it is done in classic immigration nations like the United States, Canada, and Australia," says Jan Techau, director of the Europe program at the German Council on Foreign Relations. "We have not developed any kind of mechanism that allows people from all over the place to enter our societies, play by a certain set of rules, and become one of us."

Indeed, many of the Muslims in continental European countries are the descendants of migrants who arrived a generation or two ago as "guest workers" (*Gastarbeiter*). They were never meant to stay, and therefore little effort was made to integrate them. But they did stay. And they had children who are now considered foreigners despite their native birth. Often without citizenship, they have little stake in the political process, and withdraw into isolated Muslim enclaves that are common in dozens of European cities.

It would be wrong, however, to blame this segregation solely on the host societies. Integration is not always sought by European Muslims, either. Many mosques and Muslim organizations in Britain have ties to South Asian Islamist groups that discourage friendly interaction with non-believers. In some European Muslim communities, brides are imported from poor and backward villages in North Africa. They arrive too late to attend school and have little opportunity to learn the language, get a job, or become part of the larger society.

"It takes two to tango" says Joffe. "The indigenous have to be more generous about accepting 'the Other' and his unfamiliar ways. The newcomers have to adapt to local mores: don't drop out of school, learn a trade, become a bit like us, try exogamy, don't build mosques that are higher than the church steeple next door, don't live in 'parallel universes: as a classic shibboleth has it. This is going to be a long bargaining process-painful for both sides, but absolutely necessary". For several years, Usama Hasan, a part time imam at the al-Tawhid mosque in east London and a professor of artificial intelligence at Middlesex University, has been trying to encourage the growth of a "Western, British Islam" that is both modern and moderate, and rejects the cultural and political baggage of South Asia and the Middle East.

Last year, he helped launch the Quilliam Foundation, which dubs itself the "world's first counter extremism think tank," and whose founders are ex-Islamists who now reject the ideology they once followed. "It's worrying, this kind of development," Hasan said of the Swiss referendum in an interview with Maclean's. "It underlines the need for more dialogue, more interaction, more balanced and sane voices to speak up. That's the only way forward after this."

Tariq Ramadan, a Swiss author and academic, blamed the minaret ban partly on his compatriots' fear of Islam. "While European countries are going through a real and deep identity crisis, the new visibility of Muslims is problematic, and it's scary," he wrote in the wake of the vote. But Ramadan also blamed his fellow Swiss Muslims for their passive role in the debate, for not engaging with their countrymen. "I have been repeating for years to Muslim people that they have to be positively visible, active and proactive within their respective Western societies," he said. Integration won't be easy. And there are many European Muslims and non-Muslims who don't appear to want it. But it's difficult to imagine a stable and harmonious continent unless this occurs. Those who want to ban minarets might not want to acknowledge it, but Islam is now a European religion.

Islamization of Catholic Europe

From the National Post 2009/01/07 (lightly edited) by Simon Caldwell

Continent lacks "firm spiritual foundations"

Cardinal Miroslav Vlk, Archbishop of Prague

LONDON· Europeans are allowing Islam to "conquer" the continent, according to a leading Roman Catholic cardinal. Miloslav Vlk, the Archbishop of Prague, said Muslims were well placed to fill the spiritual void "created as Europeans systematically empty the Christian content of their lives . . . Europe will pay dearly for having left its spiritual foundations".

This was the last chance to do something about it and the opportunity would not last for decades, he says in comments posted on his web site. "Today our continent does not have firm spiritual and moral foundations," said Archbishop Vlk, 77.

"The Muslims definitely have many reasons to be heading here. They also have a religious one, to bring the spiritual values of faith in God to the pagan environment of Europe, to its atheistic style of life. "Unless the Christians wake up, life may be Islamized and Christianity will not have the strength to imprint its character on the life of people, not to say society." His remarks were made in an interview to mark his retirement after 19 years as leader of the Czech church.

The Cardinal does not blame Muslims for the crisis, saying Europeans have brought it on themselves by exchanging their Christian culture for an aggressive secularism that embraced atheism. "Europe has denied its Christian roots from which it has risen and which could give it the strength to fend off the danger that it will be conquered by Muslims, which is actually happening gradually", he said.

"At the end of the Middle Ages and in the early modern age, Islam failed to conquer Europe with arms. The Christians beat them then. Today, when the fighting is done with spiritual weapons, which Europe lacks while Muslims are perfectly armed, the fall of Europe is looming."

Archbishop Vlk believes Czechs can help reinforce Christianity because of their experience with the transition from Communist totality to freedom. "Neither the free market nor freedom without responsibility are strong enough to form the basis of society. Not even democracy alone is a panacea unless it is embedded in God," he said, adding people cannot live for ever without fundamental spiritual values. He also called on Christians to respond by living their faith more observantly.

Sharia Courts & Laws in Britain

Posted in London Times 20100110 (Lightly Edited and formatted)

by Douglas Murray

http://tinyurl.com/yk36p5a

Sharia Courts a threat to Britain's future as 'tolerant' society

In February 2008 the 104th Archbishop of Canterbury, Dr. Rowan Williams delivered a lecture at the Royal Courts of Justice titled 'Civil and Religious Law in England: a Religious Perspective.' The

Archbishop talked about Islamic sharia law and compared sharia courts in the UK to the Jewish 'Beth Din' courts. This quotation, combined with the Archbishop's assertion that 'the application of Sharia in certain circumstances' in the UK was 'unavoidable' caused extensive press comment.

The issue died down until July when the retiring Lord Chief Justice of England and Wales, Lord Phillips, gave a talk on 'Equality before the law'. He described sharia as suffering from 'widespread misunderstanding.' Whilst admitting that stoning, the chopping off of hands and flogging would be unacceptable, he backed sharia principles being applied to marriage arrangements in the UK and was supportive of the sharia finance initiatives which the Treasury had observed since 2002. Lord Phillips said: 'There is no reason why sharia principles, or any other religious code, should not be the basis for mediation or other forms of alternative dispute resolution (with the understanding) . . . that any sanctions for a failure to comply with the agreed terms of mediation would be drawn from the Laws of England and Wales.'

And so the most senior judge in England followed the most senior member of the national church in backing the integration of elements of sharia law into British life. However low level the sharia they were advocating might have been, they propelled the issue to the forefront of the nation's consciousness. And there it has stayed.

The European Court of Human Rights (ECHR) is just one of the institutions worldwide which has deemed sharia to be actively 'incompatible' with human rights. As a signatory to the ECHR and the Universal Declaration of Human Rights (UDHR), Britain has acknowledged the incompatibility of sharia with its own legal system.

Thus both sides have acknowledged that sharia and the liberal democratic norms and rights of Western democracies are not compatible. The stumbling blocks are not in mere details. They go to the centre of what liberal democratic societies have fought for centuries to develop and sustain. There is serious omission at the heart of sharia and Islam itself on core issues, the rights of half of the species.

Islamic scriptures routinely accord women half the rights accorded to their male kin. Verse after verse in the Koran discriminates against them. Many Muslims may disagree, but in Islam's core texts, women are repeatedly deemed to possess half the worth of men. Partly because Muslims believe their holy book to have been dictated direct by god, rather than merely inspired by god, Islam has a unique doctrinal issue at the heart of the faith.

Finally, there is the fundamental incompatibility at the heart of sharia of punishment known as 'hudud'. Sharia punishments range from lashings, to the amputation of limbs (including the amputation of an arm and a leg on alternate sides of the body) whilst death sentences include death by stoning, beheading and crucifixion. Last December Hamas government in the Gaza reintroduced hudud punishments, including crucifixion, in the territory.

The leaders of all major political parties united to condemn the comments and so did a complete sweep of the British press. The country seemed to have awakened to the suggestion that sharia would inevitably become part of British life and the nation appeared to respond with a single resounding 'no.'

The issue died down until July when the retiring Lord Chief Justice of England and Wales, Lord Phillips, gave a talk on 'Equality before the law'. He described sharia as suffering from 'widespread misunderstanding. ' While admitting that stoning, the chopping-off of hands and flogging would be unacceptable, he backed sharia principles applied to marriage arrangements in the UK and was supportive of the sharia finance initiatives which the Treasury had observed since 2002.

Yet the whole concept of sharia finance is a contradiction in terms. In 7th century Arabia, where Mohammed received his revelations, there was no organised banking system. There were no bonds, no pensions and no mortgages. There was nothing in existence akin to anything which people in contemporary Britain know as finance. Yet 'Islamic finance' or 'sharia finance' have become commonly heard terms in recent years.

Western commentators and leaders appear to be under the impression that sharia finance is intrinsic to Islam - an ancient and unalterable position. In fact, as the scholar Timur Kuran has shown in his book 'Islam and Mammon', it is an entirely 'invented tradition'. It is not a millennia old necessity of faith for Muslims. It was made up in 1940s India.

Despite the obscure origin of the concept of sharia finance, despite the fact that the first generation of Muslim immigrants into post war Britain would have had no idea what such a thing was, and despite its more recent Islamist connotations, the British government has in recent years chosen to accept it without criticism or even question.

This is why the encouragement given to the growth of sharia by the Prime Minister, the Archbishop of Canterbury, and the former Lord Chief Justice, is so divisive and so dangerous. The attitude of British Muslims towards sharia law is changing. The majority favour British law but a consistently large minority appear to desire sharia, and the desire appears to be greatest among the young. A 2006 social research poll for Channel 4 asked 1,000 British Muslims: 'Would you prefer to live under Sharia law?' 30% of respondents said that, yes, they wanted to live under Sharia law, 15 % were undecided, and 54% wanted to live under British law. But Muslim respondents aged between 18 and 44 were twelve per cent more likely than their elders to prefer living under sharia. Other polls have shown similar results.

In my research two names in particular recurred as examples of the type of people who may well have more and more influence in sharia courts in Britain if such courts were allowed to thrive. They are Sheikh Suhaib Hasan and Anjem Choudary, who is a solicitor.

Sheikh Suhaib Hasan is Secretary General of the Islamic Sharia Council. His vision of a future sharia Britain does not stop at overseeing marital disputes. In speeches on Islamic websites he calls for 'the chopping of the hands of the thieves, the flogging of the adulterers and flogging of the drunkards.' This, he says will allow the launch of a jihad: 'Then jihad against the non-Muslims, against those people who are the oppressors.'

Asked whether he approves of the stoning of adulterers he confirmed that he does because he 'never saw any adultery' when he was in Saudi Arabia. In an interview last December he said: 'Even though cutting off the hands and feet, or flogging the drunkard and fornicator, seem to be very abhorrent, once they are implemented they become a deterrent for the whole society. This is why in Saudi Arabia, the crime rate is very, very, low.'

Today the sharia snow ball is gathering speed. The UK government is now preparing legislation that would allow the institution of what they are calling 'sharia pensions.' There is also the new initiative, advertised by the Guardian last October, of' sharia car-insurance'.

Consider the case of Gina Khan. She is a Muslim women's rights campaigner based in Birmingham. Several years ago she attempted to get a sharia divorce. Many Muslims have portrayed the granting of extra rights to sharia courts as part of a drive to improve the rights of women. Khan believes that this concern is a fake. I asked her what she thought of the authorities, the Archbishops and Lord Chief Justices who were speaking as authorities while admitting their own ignorance of the system they were propelling which was a society by which her daughter's generation might soon be expected to live. "I really do wish that these men wouldn't make these statements without having any indication of the consequences for Muslim women. To whom is he listening? Have they come into the communities? Start asking the women and finding some real people. This is Britain, and there should be one law."

The sentiments could hardly be a more appropriate aspiration to the fundamental rights which the European courts and the UDHR are meant to grant us all. But the rights which Muslim women might have expected when they immigrated into Britain two generations ago are not the rights which Britain appears to expect of them today. Sharia is based on the writings and declarations of a seventh century tradesman. Individuals should be free to choose whether or his words constitute sacred, divinely dictated, texts and whether to base their consciences and behaviour on its strictures.

But the British state and British law dare not accept deference to these texts. They cannot be the basis for law. This country and Western society has fought for many centuries to base law on reason. The greatness of the British system is that totalitarian laws or governance will not ultimately prevail because they will dissolve under the light of reason. We have inherited this right through the Judaeo Christian tradition which believes in the interpretation of its texts and from enlightenment. From Montesquieu and Mill, our societies have fought against the totalitarian grip of scriptures which men and women were once born into accepting, and which they either volunteered to accept or struggled to throw off.

In 2009 most people born in Britain do not have to go through the process of shrugging off laws or re-capturing rights not granted to people in their community. But the piecemeal adoption of Sharia law presents us with an issue which we have so long taken to be settled that we have forgotten how we attained it. The problem is what to do about those who would base laws on textual literalism.

It presents us with a new challenge, which previous struggles against literalism did not have to tackle. We are allowing different laws to be applied to people of different ethnic origins. This is the truly shocking thing about the sharia debate. Like the doctrine of multiculturalism which has allowed this debate to flourish, the encouragement of sharia law in British life is based not on equality or respect for other cultures, but on unfairness and separation. The encouragement of sharia is based on the notion that there are laws which would not be good for us but which are good for Muslims, not good enough for the British people in the country but good for immigrant Muslims from other lands. It enforces differences and makes double standards acceptable. If the future of sharia in Britain is indeed 'inevitable' then Britain's future as a tolerant and pluralistic society will not survive.

From Mail Online 29th June 2009 By Steve Doughty http://www.dailymail.co.uk/news/article-1196165/Britain-85-sharia-courts-The-astonishing-spread-Islamic-justice-closed-doors.html

Britain has 85 sharia courts:

The astonishing spread of the Islamic justice behind closed doors. At least 85 Islamic sharia courts are operating in Britain, a study claimed yesterday. The astonishing figure is 17 times higher than previously accepted. The tribunals, working mainly from mosques, settle financial and family disputes according to religious principles. They lay down judgments which can be given full legal status if approved in national law courts. sharia law meeting

Disputes: Islamic leaders rule on disagreements

However, they operate behind doors that are closed to independent observers and their decisions are likely to be unfair to women and backed by intimidation, a report by independent think tank Civitas said. Commentators on the influence of sharia law often count only the five courts in London, Manchester, Bradford, Birmingham and Nuneaton that are run by the Muslim Arbitration Tribunal, a body whose rulings are enforced through the state courts under the 1996 Arbitration Act.

But the study by academic and Islamic specialist Denis MacEoin estimates there are at least 85 working tribunals. The spread of sharia law has become increasingly controversial since its role was backed last year by Archbishop of Canterbury Dr Rowan Williams and Lord Phillips, the Lord Chief Justice who stepped down last October. Dr Williams said a recognised role for sharia law seemed 'unavoidable' and Lord Phillips said there was no reason why decisions made on sharia principles should not be recognised by the national courts.

But the Civitas report said the principles on which sharia courts work are indicated by the fatwas - religious decrees - set out on websites run by British mosques. Mr MacEoin said: 'Among the rulings we find some that advise illegal actions and others that transgress human rights standards as applied by British courts.' Examples set out in his study include a ruling that no Muslim woman may marry a non-Muslim man unless he converts to Islam and that any children of a woman who does should be taken from her until she marries a Muslim. Further rulings, according to the report, approve polygamous marriage and enforce a woman's duty to have sex with her husband on his demand.

The report added: 'The fact that so many sharia rulings in Britain relate to cases concerning divorce and custody of children is of particular concern, as women are not equal in sharia law, and sharia contains no specific commitment to the best interests of the child that is fundamental to family law in the UK. 'Under sharia, a male child belongs to the father after the age of seven, regardless of circumstances.'

It said: 'Sharia courts operating in Britain may be handing down rulings that are inappropriate to this country because they are linked to elements in Islamic law that are seriously out of step with trends in Western legislation.' The study pointed out that the House of Lords ruled in a child custody case last year that the sharia rules on the matter were 'arbitrary and discriminatory'.

And a 2003 judgment of the European Court of Human Rights in Strasbourg said it was 'difficult to declare one's respect for democracy and human rights while at the same time supporting a regime based on sharia, which clearly diverges from Convention values.'

However last year Justice Minister Bridget Prentice told MPs that 'if, in a family dispute ...the parties to a judgment in a sharia council wish to have this recognised by English authorities, they are at liberty to draft a consent order embodying the terms of the agreement and submit it to an English court. 'This allows judges to scrutinise it to ensure it complies with English legal tenets.' Decisions from sharia tribunals can be presented to a family court judge for approval with no more detail than is necessary to complete a two page form. The sharia courts in the Muslim Arbitration Tribunal are recognised as courts under the Arbitration Act. This law, which covers Jewish Beth Din courts, gives legal powers to a tribunal if all parties involved accept its authority.

Theocracy Trumps Democracy in Ontario

From the National Post 2010/01/13 by Megan O'Toole

Fatwa Cleared Way for Attack, Court Hears

Toronto 18 Case - Decree made plot Islamically sound, "Witness testifies".

BRAMPTON, ONTARIO: Weeks before police rounded up the "Toronto 18," Shareef Abdelhaleem obtained a fatwa from his father confirming that a terrorist attack on Canadian soil would be justifiable, a Brampton Superior Court judge heard yesterday. "He told me his father told him there is nothing wrong with it; in other words, it's acceptable," witness and police agent Shaher Elsohemy testified during the trial of Mr. Abdelhaleem, who stands accused of playing a key role in the foiled 2006 plot to attack targets in Ottawa and Toronto.

The fatwa, or religious ruling, from Mr. Abdelhaleem's father would have held significance because the elder Mr. Abdelhaleem ran an Islamic education school in Mississauga, the court heard. For Shareef Abdelhaleem, who had been somewhat sceptical, the fatwa affirmed that the plot to detonate truck bombs in southern Ontario was Islamically sound, Mr. Elsohemy testified. He said Mr. Abdelhaleem would later interpret the fatwa to mean simply, "nothing to them," in reference to Canadian citizens. "He informed me that by obtaining this fatwa, things are clear for him now. He has no doubts about (the plot's) Islamic correctness," Mr. Elsohemy told the judge.

The court heard hours of testimony yesterday about meetings between Mr. Abdelhaleem and Mr. Elsohemy at restaurants and coffee shops in the Toronto area in the months leading to the 2006 arrests. On more than one occasion, Mr. Abdelhaleem referred to himself as a "co-ordinator" or "planner" of the terrorism plot, Mr. Elsohemy alleged.

Much of their time was spent discussing the logistics of obtaining various chemicals, including two tonnes of ammonium nitrate, that could be used to manufacture bombs, Mr. Elsohemy testified.

Mr. Elsohemy, who masqueraded as a co-conspirator while covertly working as an informant for the RCMP and the Canadian Security Intelligence Service, became the "go-to" guy for the chemicals after indicating his uncle could procure them. At one point, Mr. Abdelhaleem produced an envelope stuffed with $960 in cash as a "down payment" on the chemicals, Mr. Elsohemy testified. Mr. Elsohemy is the Crown's star witness at Mr. Abdelhaleem's trial on charges that he participated in a terrorist group and took action toward causing an explosion likely to harm people or property. Mr. Abdelhaleem has pleaded not guilty on both counts.

During their meetings, Mr. Abdelhaleem confided his goal as a member of the terrorist group was not mass casualties, Mr. Elsohemy told the court because if it was, he would have picked different targets.

Bombing the Square One Mall in Mississsauga or a local football game, or poisoning a food factory, would have made more sense if the objective were to kill the most people, Mr. Abdelhaleem allegedly told Mr. Elsohemy. The men's discussion about methods of terrorism was spurred, Mr. Elsohemy said, by a suggestion from another member of the Toronto 18 to include "metal chips" in the bombs the group planned to manufacture. Those bombs were supposed to target the Toronto Stock Exchange, a CSIS site and a military base.

Mr. Abdelhaleem was against the idea of adding metal fragments to the explosive devices, Mr. Elsohemy testified, because "that would increase the number of people who would die," Mr. Abdelhaleem also advocated setting the bombs off at 6 a.m. - when most workers would still be at home - rather than 9 a.m., the time allegedly suggested by one of the plot leaders, the court heard. Rather than causing needless death, Mr. Abdelhaleem wanted to make a political point, Mr. Elsohemy said, particularly through bombing the TSE.

"The country would lose half-a-trillion dollars as a result of the closure," the witness testified, noting Mr. Abdelhaleem hoped to profit from the shakeup and stash the windfall in a Barbados bank account. The trial continues.

Muslim Confiscation of Schools in Ontario

From the National Post 2009/11/30 by Barbara Kay

My attention has been drawn to the disturbing phenomenon of overt Jew hatred in high schools, especially those with high populations of students from countries where Jew hatred is officially sanctioned in the law of their countries of origin. As a case in point I offer one particularly disturbing story, because I believe it points to wider issues of concern for the educational system and for our society. It involves a Jewish teacher in an Ontario French high school whose name I cannot reveal because she fears physical retaliation.

"Miriam" had taught in French language schools in the 1970s and 1980s in schools with large Lebanese Christian populations without incurring any anti-Semitism. In her current career she works with Muslims. A child of Holocaust survivors, Miriam is demonstrably neither racist nor anti-Muslim.

In 2001 Miriam started teaching at a school largely populated by children of refugees, mainly from Djibouti and Eritrea, countries where there are no Jews but where hatred of Jews is deeply entrenched in the culture. During the academic year of 2002-2003 Miriam started to encounter anti-Semitic taunts from students, such as "Does someone see a Jew here, someone smell a Jew? It stinks here". When she reported this and similar insults to the principal, the principal did not follow up. Indeed, the principal seemed more concerned about the students' sensibilities than hers. The principal instructed teachers not to offend their Muslim students; they were not to look students in the eye, they were not to gesture with the forefinger to bid them approach and they were not to interfere with male students who were physically aggressive to male teachers.

During the invasion of Iraq, moments of silence were held in the classroom. Cultural presentations involved only Muslim culture and no Canadian content. Students were allowed to leave assembly during the playing of the national anthem. The crisis of this story occurred when Miriam admonished a student for wearing a Walkman in class. The student screamed at her: "I don't have to listen to you; you are not a person, you are nothing, you do not exist as a person." When Miriam demanded he accompany her to the principal's office, the student followed her down the hall yelling, "Don't speak to me, don't look at me, you are not human, you are a Jew".

Although the student was ultimately suspended for 10 days, his parents expressed puzzlement about the punishment since they patiently explained the teacher was Jewish. They complained about the severity of the punishment to the school board. There were no sensitivity courses laid on for the students or the parents. When, over her objections, the offending student and another guilty of the same offence were returned to Miriam's class, she decided she could no longer work under such circumstances. She contacted the Hate Crime Unit of the local police and reported everything.

The School board treated Miriam as the source of the problem and asked her to retire. A top litigator told Miriam she had an excellent case for a lawsuit but fearing for her family's safety under the glare of publicity, she decided not to sue. Lest you assume Miriam was paranoid, or Islamophobic, or that this was an isolated case of a few bad apples: In 2004 the year Miriam left, a full 60 out of 75 francophone teachers asked for a transfer, not because of anti-Semitism but because of anti-Westernism, a growing discomfort in other areas for which anti-Semitism is the proverbial canary in the mine. French Canadian children had already stopped enrolling and as I understand it, the school is now virtually all Muslim, including the teachers and principal.

There are many immigrants entering Canada from countries where overt hatred of Jews is endemic to the culture and even officially sanctioned in law. When they arrive here, it is somehow assumed they will absorb Canadian values . . . but they don't, and their toxic attitudes persist. Instead of confronting their bigotry, this principal and the school board chose not to apply long standing normative codes of behaviour and human rights law. An instinctive political correctness set in. Out of fear of being labelled racist or Islamophobic, those in charge stifled their commitment to professional ethics and behaviour codes reflecting Canadian standards of pluralism and respect.

Imagine a reverse situation. Imagine if the aggressors and bigots were heritage Canadians harassing a Muslim teacher with these hateful words. It would have been a *'cause célèbre'* and the media would have called for an investigative inquiry into the origins of the serious social problem represented by these racialized students and their families.

If preventative measures are not taken, if it is not made clear in no uncertain terms through education and persuasive push back in this school and all schools where there are critical masses of students arriving from countries drenched in anti-Semitism, hatred of Jews will metastasize in those cultural communities that consider it a norm, increasing exponentially. There are many such schools in Britain and Europe where the atmosphere is so strained and hostile to anyone but Islamic kinship groups that they are simply no-go fiefdoms . . . Islamic mini-societies within the larger culture. We mustn't think that can't happen here, because it can. It is happening already.

Recruiting Jihadis in North America

From the National Post 2009/11/25 by Daveed Gartenstein- Ross

On Monday, the United States unsealed terrorism charges against eight defendants for supporting a Somali Islamist group called al-Shabab.

While few lay people in Canada or the United States have heard of al-Shabab, the al-Qaeda connected extremist organization, which controls a significant amount of territory in Somalia, has recently become a particular concern for analysts examining possible homegrown terrorist flashpoints in North America.

Beginning in late 2007, dozens of young men of Somali descent started disappearing from diaspora communities in the West. It turned out they were returning to Somalia to train in Shabab camps or to take up arms against Shabab's enemies within the country. Islamists of non-Somali descent were also travelling there to join Shabab.

This phenomenon has been repeating itself in a number of countries. Canadian government sources claim that 20 to 30 Canadians have joined Shabab, a development that public safety minister Peter Van Loan has said "alarmed" him. In the US, the disappearances have primarily clustered around Minneapolis - St. Paul, but there are credible reports of disappearances in other US. cities with large Somali populations as well.

The Times of London reports that British security services believe "dozens of Islamic extremists have returned to Britain from terror training camps in Somalia." SAPO, Sweden's security service, believes that about 20 people have left that country to join Shabab. And Australian authorities think as many as 40 Somali refugees may have gone from Australia to Somalia to liaise with Shabab.

Many factors cause young men in the West to join Somali Islamist movements. For one, the Somali diaspora is less integrated than other immigrant communities; this can lead to disaffection and the development of a mythologized sense of homeland, leaving newcomers especially vulnerable to recruitment.

There is also a political dimension to support for Shabab. In March 2009 U.S. Senate testimony, Professor Ken Menkhaus noted that Shabab thrives on the "complex cocktail of nationalist, Islamist, anti-Ethiopian, anti-Western, anti-foreigner sentiments" that resulted from Ethiopia's December 2006 invasion of Somalia.

Of course, there's a religious aspect too. American convert Daniel Maldonado, who pleaded guilty in April 2007 to receiving training from a foreign terrorist organization, told U.S. authorities that when he decided to travel to Somalia, it was to fight jihad - something he described in religious terms as "raising the word of Allah uppermost by speaking and fighting against all those who are against the Islamic State".

Shabab recruiting is a security concern for both Somalia and the rest of the world Within Somalia, Shabab's implementation of a strict version of shariah in areas it controls raises human rlghts worries. For example, according to Amnesty International, Shabab jurists sentenced a 13 year old rape victim in Kismayo to be stoned to death last year for alleged adultery.

Internationally, the problem is Shabab's links to global jihadist groups like al-Qaeda. One important document explaining Shabab's outlook, entitled A Message to the Mujaahideen in Particular and Muslims in General, and written by the American mujahid Omar Hammami (aka Abu Mansoor al-Amriki) made its way around the jihadist web in early 2008. In it, Hammami contrasted Shabab with previous Somali Islamist movements, such as the Islamic Courts Union. Ahmed, whose nephew was killed in Mogadishu, says families of men who disappeared 'have been threatened for just speaking out'

In making this distinction, Hammami put Shabab into the same ideological category as al-Qaeda. He said that while the Islamic Courts' objectives were limited by national boundaries, "the Shabab had a global goal including the establishment" of an Islamic caliphate. He also wrote that Shabab's religious methodology was the same as that expressed by such recognizable jihadist icons as Osama bin Laden, Ayman al-Zawahiri and Abu Musab alZarqawi.

In August 2008, Shabab spokesman Sheikh Mukhtar Robow said that Shabab was "negotiating how we can unite into one" with al-Qaeda. In the same month, Saleh Ali Saleh Nabhan, Shabab's chief military strategist (who was killed by U.S. commandos in September 2009), reached out to al-Qaeda's senior leadership in a 24minute video entitled March Forth.

On Nov. 19, 2008, Zawahiri responded to Nabhan's video with one in which he called Shabab "my brothers, the lions of Islam in Somalia". He urged them not to lay down their weapons "before the mujahid state of Islam" has been established in Somalia.

But authorities' biggest concern is not what people pulled into Somalia do while they're there, but what happens when they return to the countries from which they came. There are fears that these men could end up involved in a terrorist plot - fears bolstered by the fact that Shabab's training is both military and ideological, with the camps fostering what Nairobi-based journalist Fredrick Nzwili described as a fundamentalist ideology."

A clear picture of Shabab's recruiting networks in the West still has not emerged, although a significant thread running through a number of cases is the presence of recruiters. This could be seen, for example, following 25 year old Abdifatah Yusuf Isse's guilty plea in Minnesota to providing material support to terrorists based on his travel to Somalia. Omar Jamal, director of Minneapolis's Somali Justice Advocacy Center, told the media that recruiters had approached Isse at the Abubakar as-Saddique mosque, the Twin Cities' largest Somali mosque. This account was corroborated by Isse's attorney.

Similarly, when 26 year old Salah Osman Abmed pled guilty to the same charges, he spoke elliptically of recruiters who helped draw him to Somalia, mentioning "secret meetings" beginning in October 2007 with people he would only describe as "guys".

In other U.S. based terrorism cases where recruiters played a prominent role, the recruiters enjoyed little support from the mosques they frequented; in the Lackawanna Six case, for example, leaders of the Islamic Center in Lackawanna, N.Y., chastised Juma al-Dosari when he lectured about the need for jihad. But in the Shabab recruitment cases, there have been allegations of mosque complicity.

Many of these allegations have focussed on the Abubakar as-Saddique mosque where Isse was allegedly recruited. Osman Ahmed, whose nephew was killed in Mogadishu in June 2009 after disappearing from the Minneapolis area, pointed his finger at that mosque in testimony before the U.S. Senate, claiming that family members of men who disappeared "have been threatened for just speaking out".

The investigation into al-Shabab recruitment in the West must continue. Only by better understanding these recruiting networks will authorities be able to stem the flow of young men to Shabab's destructive camps.

National Post I Daveed Gartenstein- Ross is the director of the Center for Terrorism Research (CTR) at the Foundation for Defense of Democracies, and a PhD candidate in world politics at the Catholic University of America. The Nov. 4 issue of the Centre's regular publication, CTR Vantage, is devoted to al-Shabab's recruiting efforts in the West.

A Fatwa against Terrorism & Al Qaeda

From BBC News: (Lightly edited and formatted) By Dominic Casciani
http://news.bbc.co.uk/2/hi/uk_news/8544531.stm

Islamic scholar Tahir ul-Qadri issues anti-terrorism fatwa

Dr. Tahir ul-Qadri, an influential Muslim scholar, has issued a 600 page global ruling against terrorism and suicide bombing. Dr. Tahir ul-Qadri, from Pakistan, says his 600 page judgement known as a fatwa, completely dismantles al-Qaeda's violent ideology. The scholar describes al-Qaeda as an "old evil with a new name" that has not been sufficiently challenged.

The scholar's movement is growing in the UK and has attracted the interest of policymakers and security chiefs. In his religious ruling, delivered in London, Dr. Qadri says that Islam forbids the massacre of innocent citizens and suicide bombings. Although many scholars have made similar rulings in the past, Dr. Qadri argued that his massive document goes much further by omitting "ifs and buts" added by other thinkers. He said that it set out a point by point theological rebuttal of every argument used by al-Qaeda inspired recruiters. The populist scholar developed his document last year as a response to the increase in bombings across Pakistan by militants.

The basic text has been extended to 600 pages to cover global issues, in an attempt to get its theological arguments taken up by Muslims in Western nations. It will be promoted in the UK by Dr.Qadri's organisation, Minhaj ul-Quran International. Dr.Qadri spoke for more than hour to an audience of Muslims, clergy, MPs, police officers and other security officials.

"They (terrorists) can't claim that their suicide bombings are martyrdom operations and that they become the heroes of the Muslim Umma (global brotherhood). No, they become heroes of hellfire, and they are leading towards hellfire," he said. "There is no place for any martyrdom and their act is never, ever to be considered jihad."

Acts of vengeance

The document is not the first to condemn terrorism and suicide bombing to be launched in the UK. Scholars from across the UK came together in the wake of the 7 July London attacks to denounce the bombers and urge communities to root out extremists. But some scholarly rulings in the Middle East have argued that the conflict between Israel and the Palestinians is an exceptional situation where "martyrdom" attacks can be justified.

Dr.Qadri said he rejected that view saying there were no situations under which acts of vengeance, such as attacks on market places or commuter trains, could ever be considered a justifiable act of war. Although Dr. Qadri has many followers in Pakistan, Minhaj ul-Quran International remained largely unknown in the UK until relatively recently.

It now has 10 mosques in cities with significant Muslim communities and says it is targeting younger generations it believes have been let down by traditional leaders. The organisation is attracting the attention of policymakers and security chiefs who are continuing to look for allies in the fight against extremists. The Department for Communities, which runs most of the government's Preventing Violent Extremism strategy, has tried building bridges with a variety of liberal groups, but found that they have limited actual influence at the grassroots.

Muslim Populations in Canada - Census 2001

From Madinat Al-Muslimeen; (Lightly edited and formatted)
http://jannah.org/madina/index.php?topic=2593.0

Muslim Population in Canada to Double by 2017
« on: Mar 10, 2009 11:34 AM »

Once considered a predominantly Christian country, Canada is in for a dramatic shift in the religious composition of its population when it reaches its 150th birthday. Statistics Canadaforecasts major changes to the religious landscape of the country by 2017. Projections of the size of religious groups suggest potentially important challenges for the future as governments across the country examine issues associated with the place of religion in schools and in public institutions.

Of the scenarios issued by Statistics Canada, it is scenario B that is considered to most likely. As observed below it foresees an increase of approximately 160% in the numbers of Muslims in Canada, 35% in the number of Buddhists, 65% in the number of Sikhs and 10% in the number of Jews. Moreover, if the proportion of youth from these groups is any indication-as indicated in Table 1a then the composition of schools in many parts of Canada will change fundamentally with considerably higher rates of non-Christians than is actually the case. As other tables reveal much of the concentration of these groups is in Canada's largest cities. In the greater Toronto area, approximately one out of six residents will be either Muslim or Hindu and the two groups combined will pass the one million mark. In the nation's capital, much like in Montreal the Muslim population will be greater than all other religious groups combined as it will near the 100,000 mark.

Year	Muslim Population	(% of Total Canadian)
2001	579,700	(1.89%)
2006	783,700	(2.49%)
2011	1,101,800	(3.32%)
2017	1,421,400	(4.11%)

Source: Statistics Canada, Projections 2001-2017

Muslim Population (by City Total)

Montreal
2001 = 96,200 (out of 3.4 Million)
2017 = 227,400 (out of 3.8 Million)

Toronto
2001 = 258,500 (out of 4.8 Million)
2017 = 657,000 (out of 6.3 Million)

Ottawa-Gatineau
2001 = 39,000 (out of 0.82 Million)
2017 = 96,000 (out of 1.13 Million)

European Court of Human Rights

From Wikipedia: (lightly edited and formatted)
http://en.wikipedia.org/wiki/European_Court_of_Human_Rights

European Court of Human Rights (ECHR)

The European Court of Human Rights (French: Cour européenne des droits de l'homme) in Strasbourg is an international judicial body established under the European Convention on Human Rights of 1950 to monitor respect of human rights by states. The European Convention on Human Rights, or formally named Convention for the Protection of Human Rights and Fundamental Freedoms, is a convention adopted by the Council of Europe. All 47 member states of the Council of Europe are parties to the Convention. Applications against Contracting Parties for human rights violations can be brought before the Court by other states, other parties or individuals.

Relationship to the European Court of Justice (ECJ)

The Court of Justice of the European Union (ECJ) is not related to the European Court of Human Rights. However, since all EU states are members of the Council of Europe and have signed the Convention on Human Rights, there are concerns about consistency in case law between the two courts. Therefore, the ECJ refers to the case law of the Court of Human Rights and treats the Convention on Human Rights as though it was part of the EU's legal system. Even though its members have joined, the European Union itself has not, as it did not have competence to do so under previous treaties. However, EU institutions are bound under article 6 of the EU treaty of Nice to respect human rights under the Convention. Furthermore, since the Treaty of Lisbon has taken effect on 1 December 2009, the EU is expected to sign the Convention. This would make the Court of Justice bound by the judicial precedents of the Court of Human Rights and thus be subject to its human rights law, resolving this way the issue of conflicting case law.

Some notable cases - Refah Partisi v Turkey (2003)

In upholding the Turkish Constitutional Court's dissolution of The Welfare Party (Refah Partisi) for violating Turkey's principle of secularism (by calling for the re-introduction of religious law) the court held "**that sharia is incompatible with the fundamental principles of democracy.**"

The Court justified the breach of the appellants' rights by reasoning that a legal regime based on sharia would diverge from the Convention's values, "particularly with regard to its criminal law and criminal procedure, its rules on the status of women and the way it intervenes in all spheres of private and public life in accordance with religious precepts."

Canada's Limits to Tolerance

From The Ottawa Citizen, 2010/03/21 (Lightly edited and formatted)
by Janice Kennedy

The real issues behind the veil.

Canada has long boasted an international reputation for tolerance, and rightly so. We tend to welcome newcomers respectfully and with reasonably open arms. And tor the most part, we celebrate the diversity that has come increasingly to define, and enrich, us. (I mean, of course, the Canadian collectivity. Individually, we do not always do ourselves quite as proud.)

As the nation of immigrants we have always been - a kind of metaphor for hope and faith in the future - we have learned how to appreciate each new thread added to the fabric of our identity. Most Canadians, it is fair to say, do try to be culturally sensitive. But there are limits. We Canadians may be people who say "Sorry" when somebody steps on our toes, but we're also people who can be downright aggressive in the defence of rights and freedoms. Think of our history at home and abroad. Historically, culturally, legally, we do not, as a nation, countenance abuse, intolerance, persecution or anything else that abrogates human rights.

So the face covering question is troubling indeed. Whether it wears the name niqab (as it has in recent news stories out of Quebec), or burqa (as it routinely does in stories from Afghanistan), the material that covers a woman's face in the name of Islamic observance challenges all of us who are seeing it more and more across the Canadian landscape.

In Quebec, with its significant population of Muslim newcomers, the issue has risen noisily to the surface in recent days after an Egyptian immigrant refused to remove her niqab for government sponsored French language lessons. The instructor had requested it because the woman's pronunciation behind the veil was unclear, but she refused, twice. The woman, who hopes to work as a pharmacist, is charging religious discrimination in a complaint to Quebec's human rights commission.

And in a separate development just last week, that same commission ruled that a woman must uncover her face to prove her identity when applying for medicare. Canadian observers of different persuasions, including liberals, who have traditionally and rightly been squeamish about cultural insensitivity, have condemned Quebec's position. It's proof of bigotry, they say. Intolerance. "Minority phobia," according to one Calgary columnist.

But is it? Maybe it's a case of public security. In our culture, where the masked face has always been a totem of outlawry, is it far fetched to suggest that a veiled woman represents the potential for fraud? Is that masked student taking the test, or the pharmacist mixing your meds, really the person she's supposed to be?

And maybe the Quebec position is also a tough (and courageous) denunciation of a symbol that announces blatant gender discrimination, intended or not. What is religious expression in Egypt can look like the public debasement of women on Canadian soil.

It's more than simply a "when in Rome," question *(Do as the Romans do).* The Canadian version of "when in Rome" involves a vastness of multicultural potential. When in Canada, you could happily wear a turban, a yarmulke, a head scarf, a tam 0' shanter, a tuque, even a nun's wimple in public, and you'd fit right in. Nobody cares what clothing you adopt here, or whether or not it reflects a particular religion or ethnic heritage. And no one thinks you should be told what you can or cannot wear.

But that's not what the public face covering debate is about. While non-

Muslims must leave the religious aspects of the discussion to Muslims (because there is apparently a sharp diversity of opinion on this within Muslim communities), other elements of the debate should be clear to everyone.

There are many things we do not do in Canada, things we will never do. We do not make it a crime to convert to another religion, as they do in Saudi Arabia, where abandoning Islam for Christianity can get you thrown in jail, or worse. In fact, we don't take a position at all on an individual's religion or lack thereof, a subject that is none of the state's business. We do not insist legally that women wear particular clothing (as is the case in many parts of Saudi Arabia), or dictate that not only must a woman's face and form be fully hidden, but that she must avoid bright colours and other "provocations." We do not condone female genital mutilation, an act of butchery still practised routinely throughout Africa and into the Middle East, which we have designated a criminal offence. We do not execute people for their sexual orientation. We object strenuously to cultural conventions, for example, bride burning and female infanticide, that while hardly legal, are sickeningly commonplace on the Indian subcontinent and in Asia.

We do not accept any of these things, and we rightly condemn them. Many newcomers to Canada might have come from cultures where such laws and practices exist, and we can certainly be sensitive to that reality. But we will not adapt our basic understanding of morality or modify our sense of human rights to accommodate their former reality here.

Simply put, these things are wrong, by any standard of evolved civilization. And we have no difficulty saying so. Why, then, are we so diffident about public face coverings? Community security issues matter. So do fundamental perceptions of discrimination. The banned niqab should be a simple matter of black and white. Without apology.

Canadians Against Terrorism

From the Ottawa Citizen, 2010/04/24 Editorial

A Canadian Member of Parliament has done something courageous, and now he needs, and deserves, the support of all Canadians.

Ujjal Dosanjh, the Liberal MP for Vancouver South, issued some public statements in favour of moderation, peace, order and the rule of law - which ought not to be controversial for a politician or anyone else to make, but in this case could be very dangerous for Dosanjh. He was speaking about the rise of extremism in his own religious community, Canadian Sikhs.

Opposing Sikh militancy has caused grief for Dosanjh before. In 1985, he was savagely beaten with a metal bar for expressing his views on the debate over Khalistan, the homeland some Sikhs want to establish in India. Eleven years later, someone threw a Molotov cocktail into his office.

Now he faces more threats. First, organizers of a major Sikh parade in Surrey had told Dosanjh and another B.C. Sikh politician, MLA Dave Rayer, that they weren't welcome at the event. The men should bring bodyguards if they showed up, organizers warned.

The parade featured prominent photos of Sikh "martyrs" - terrorists - but when Dosanjh spoke out publicly against this, and against extremism generally, death threats against him appeared on Facebook. The parade organizers have tried to suggest that these weren't threats, but simply warnings that Dosanjh would find useful, but Dosanjh himself knows a threat when he sees one.

In a parallel event last week, an American group calling itself Muslim Revolution issued death threats of its own against the creators of the

TV show South Park, who portrayed a cartoon version of the prophet Muhammad in a bear suit. This militant group also deniedthat it was threatening murder, but rather simply passing on useful information for the South Park crew to consider (specifically, urging them to remember that a Dutch filmmaker was murdered for a film that Muslims considered insulting).

Canadians used to hear this sort of cynical, extortionist rhetoric - albeit on a lesser scale - from Jean Claude Parrot when he was head of the Canadian Union of Postal Workers during fractious times. During labour disputes, Parrot would say with great flourish that of course he didn't condone violence from his members . . . though of course he and other union leaders would understand how those members might lose control, what with the great provocations they have had to endure from management.

Parrot was making a threat, as are Sikh extremists who tell Hayer and Dosanjh that they had better bring bodyguards if they attend public events. The Sikh case occurs against a backdrop of violence not limited to the Air India bombing of 1985, or the fatal shootings by Kuldip Singh Samra in a Toronto courtroom in 1982. There have been serious injuries this spring at two Toronto area Sikh temples where members fought with knives, machetes and hammers.

Officials from India have noted Sikhs in Canada are often more extreme that those in India, which raises the uncomfortable possibility that Canada may be an incubator for people who immigrate here and nurse hatred for political opponents in their native countries. Dosanjh and Rayer should be applauded for standing up to goons who, one hopes, represent a small fringe of Canadian Sikhs yet have the ability to damage the whole community.

A Salute to Denmark

Family Security Matters July 23 2007 (lightly edited and formatted)
By Susan MacAllen
http://europenews.dk/en/node/6517

Salute the Danish Flag - it's a Symbol of Western Freedom

Some will pretend this article is racist, but it should be seen as the reality our politicians refuse to acknowledge. This could very well happen here on our Continent. In Denmark, once liberal immigration policies have forced huge governmental change and zero tolerance for Muslim immigrants intent on turning Denmark into an Islamic welfare haven. FSM Contributing Editor Susan MacAllen reveals a shocking reaction there and lessons America must learn.

In 1978-79, I was living and studying in Denmark. An elderly woman to whom I was close said something to me one day that puzzled me for many years after. I forget what the context of our conversation was, but she commented that I, as a young American in Denmark, should not let any Dane scold me about the way America had treated its black population, because the Danes in her view treated their immigrants at least as badly. I wasn't sure which immigrants she meant, so I asked her. She answered that she meant those from the Mid East.

In 1978 even in Copenhagen, one didn't see Muslim immigrants. The Danish population embraced visitors, celebrated the exotic, went out of its way to protect each of its citizens. It was proud of its new brand of socialist liberalism, one in development since the conservatives had lost power in 1929, a system where no worker had to struggle to survive, where one ultimately could count upon the state as in perhaps no other western nation at the time.

The rest of Europe saw the Scandinavians as free thinking, progressive and infinitely generous in their welfare policies. Denmark boasted low crime rates, devotion to the environment, a superior educational system, and a history of humanitarianism.

Denmark was also most generous in its immigration policies - it offered the best welcome in Europe to the new immigrant: generous welfare payments from first arrival, plus additional perks in transportation, housing and education. It was determined to set a world example for inclusiveness and multiculturalism. How could it have predicted that one day in 2005 a series of political cartoons in a newspaper would spark violence that would leave dozens dead in the streets, all because its commitment to multiculturalism would come back to bite?

By the 1990's the growing urban Muslim population was obvious - and its unwillingness to integrate into Danish society was obvious. For years the immigrants had settled into Muslim exclusive enclaves. As the Muslim leadership became more vocal about what they considered the decadence of Denmark's liberal way of life, the Danes - once so welcoming - began to feel slighted. Many Danes had begun to see Islam as incompatible with their long standing values: a belief in personal liberty and free speech, equality for women, tolerance for other ethnic groups, and a deep pride in Danish heritage and history.

An article by Daniel Pipes and Lars Hedegaard, in which they forecasted accurately that the growing immigrant problem in Denmark would explode. In the article they reported:

- 'Muslim immigrants constitute 5 percent of the population, but consume upwards of 40 percent of the welfare spending.'

- 'Muslims constitute only 4 percent of Denmark's 5.4 million people, but make up a majority of the country's convicted rapists, an especially combustible issue since practically all the female victims are non-Muslim. Similar, if lesser disproportions are found in other crimes.'

- 'Over time as Muslim immigrants increase in numbers, they wish less to mix with the indigenous population. A recent survey finds that only 5 percent of young Muslim immigrants would readily marry a Dane.'

- 'Forced marriages, promising a daughter born in Denmark to a male cousin in the home country, then compelling her to marry him, sometimes on pain of death, are one problem'
- 'Muslim leaders openly declare their goal of introducing Islamic law once Denmark's Muslim population grows enough; not a remote prospect. If present trends persist, one sociologist estimates in 40 years a third of Denmark's inhabitants will be Muslim.'

It is easy to understand why a growing number of Danes would feel that Muslim immigrants show little respect for Danish values and laws. An example is the phenomenon common to other European countries and Canada: some Muslims in Denmark who opted to leave the Muslim faith have been murdered in the name of Islam, while others hide in fear for their lives. Jews are also threatened and harassed openly by Muslim leaders in Denmark, a country where once Christian citizens worked to smuggle out nearly all of their 7,000 Jews by night to Sweden - before the Nazis could invade. I think of my Danish friend Elsa who, as a teenager, had dreaded crossing the street to the bakery every morning under the eyes of occupying Nazi soldiers - and I wonder what she would say today.

In 2001, Denmark elected the most conservative government in some 70 years - one that had some decidedly non-generous ideas about unfettered, liberal immigration. Today, Denmark has the strictest immigration policies in Europe. Its effort to protect itself has been met with accusations of 'racism' by liberal media across Europe - even as other governments struggle to right the social problems wrought by years of too lax immigration.

If you wish to become Danish, you must attend three years of language classes. You must pass a test on Denmark's history, culture, and a Danish language test. You must live in Denmark for 7 years before applying for citizenship. You must demonstrate an intent to work, and have a job waiting. If you wish to bring a spouse into Denmark, you must both be over 24 years of age, and you won't find it so easy anymore to move your friends and family to Denmark with you.

You will not be allowed to build a mosque in Copenhagen. Although your children have a choice of some 30 Arabic culture and language schools in Denmark, they will be strongly encouraged to assimilate to Danish society in ways that past immigrants weren't.

In 2006, the Danish minister for employment, Claus Hjort Frederiksen, spoke publicly of the burden of Muslim immigrants on the Danish welfare system, and it was horrifying: the government's welfare committee had calculated that if immigration from Third World countries were blocked, 75 percent of the cuts needed to sustain the huge welfare system in coming decades would be unnecessary. In other words, the welfare system, as it existed, was being exploited by immigrants to the point of eventually bankrupting the government. 'We are simply forced to adopt a new policy on immigration'.

'The calculations of the welfare committee are terrifying and show how unsuccessful the integration of immigrants has been up to now,' he said.

A large thorn in the side of Denmark's imams is the Minister of Immigration and Integration, Rikke Hvilshoj. She makes no bones about the new policy toward immigration. 'The number of foreigners coming to the country makes a difference,' Hvilshoj says. 'There is an inverse correlation between how many come here and how well we can receive the foreigners that come.' And on Muslim immigrants needing to demonstrate a willingness to blend in, 'In my view Denmark should be a country with room for different cultures and religions. Some values, however, are more important than others. We refuse to question democracy, equal rights, and freedom of speech.'

Hvilshoj has paid a price for her show of backbone. Perhaps to test her resolve, the leading radical imam in Denmark, Ahmed Abdel Rahman

Abu Laban, demanded that the government pay blood money to the family of a Muslim who was murdered in a suburb of Copenhagen, stating that the family's thirst for revenge could be thwarted for money. When Hvilshoj dismissed his demand, he argued that in Muslim culture the payment of retribution money was common, to which Hvilshoj replied that what is done in a Muslim country is not necessarily what is done in Denmark.

The Muslim reply came soon after - her house was torched while she, her husband and children slept. All managed to escape unharmed, but she and her family were moved to a secret location, and she and other ministers were assigned bodyguards for the first time - in a country where such murderous violence was once so scarce.

Her government has moved to the right, and her borders have tightened. Many believe that what happens in the next decade will determine whether Denmark survives as a bastion of good living, humane thinking and social responsibility, or whether it becomes a nation at civil war with supporters of Sharia law.

And meanwhile, Canadians clamour for stricter immigration policies, and demand an end to state welfare programs that allow many immigrants to live on the public dole. As we in Canada look at the enclaves of Muslims amongst us, and see those who enter our shores too easily, and dare to live on our taxes, yet refuse to embrace our culture, respect our traditions, participate in our legal system, obey our laws, speak our language, appreciate our history, we would do well to look to Denmark, and say a prayer for her future and for our own future.

If you agree with this article, please pass it on . . . Islam is no different than CANCER, it is working its way into every culture like a disease, and if we don't do something NOW (as described above) then all other cultures will be in serious trouble. WW3 will be Islam against the rest of the world.